D1098962

Developing U

Eastern African Studies

Developing Uganda

EDITED BY
HOLGER BERNT HANSEN
& MICHAEL TWADDLE

JAMES CURREY
Oxford

FOUNTAIN PUBLISHERS
Kampala

OHIO UNIVERSITY PRESS
Athens

E.A.E.P.
Nairobi

James Currey Ltd
73 Botley Road
Oxford OX2 0BS

Fountain Publishers
P.O. Box 488
Kampala

Ohio University Press
Scott Quadrangle
Athens, Ohio 45701, USA

East African Educational Publishers
Kijabe Street, P.O. Box 45314
Nairobi, Kenya

1 2 3 4 5 01 02 00 99 98

British Library Cataloguing in Publication Data
Developing Uganda. – (Eastern African studies)
1. Uganda – History –1979 – 2. Uganda – Politics and government – 1979
– 3. Uganda – Economic conditions – 1979 – I. Hansen, Holger Bernt
II. Twaddle, Michael
967. 6′1′04

ISBN 0-85255-395-1 Paper (James Currey)
ISBN 0-85255-396-X Cloth (James Currey)
ISBN 9970 02 141 9 Paper (Fountain Publishers)
ISBN 0-8214-1209-4 Paper (Ohio)
ISBN 0-8214-1208-6 Cloth (Ohio)

Library of Congress Cataloging-in-Publication Data
Developing Uganda/edited by Holger Bernt Hansen & Michael Twaddle.
p. cm. — (Eastern African studies)
Includes bibliographical references and index.
ISBN 0-8214-1208-6 (hardcover: alk. paper). — ISBN 0-8214-1209-4
(pbk.: alk. paper)
1. Uganda—Economic conditions—1979- 2. Uganda—Economic policy.
3. Uganda—Politics and government—1979- I. Hansen, Holger Bernt. II. Twaddle
Michael. III. Series.
HC870.D48 1998   88-23026
338.96761–dc21   CIP

Typeset in 9½/10½pt Baskerville
by Saxon Graphics Ltd
Printed in Great Britain
by Villiers Publications, London N3

CONTENTS

v

Contents
PART FOUR

Policy imperatives

PART FIVE

Development at the grassroots

CONTRIBUTORS

Philip Amis is a specialist on East Africa at the School of Public Policy, University of Birmingham.

Heike Behrend is Professor of Anthropology at the University of Cologne.

Paul Collier is Professor of Economics and Director of the Centre for the Study of African Economies, University of Oxford.

Susan Dicklich teaches in the Department of Government and International Studies at the University of South Carolina.

Holger Bernt Hansen is Professor at the University of Copenhagen and Director of its Centre of African Studies.

Goran Hyden is Professor of Political Science at the University of Florida at Gainesville and Co-Director of its Center for African Studies.

Vali Jamal is Rural Sector Specialist at ILO, Geneva.

Edward Kirumira is Head of the Department of Sociology at Makerere University.

Ian Livingstone is Professor of Development Studies at the University of East Anglia.

Maryinez Lyons is a researcher attached to the Makerere Institute of Social Research, and the Institute of Commonwealth Studies, University of London.

Mark A. Marquardt was a researcher at the Land Tenure Center, University of Wisconsin, and headed its Land Access Project at Makerere 1991–96.

Daniel G. Maxwell was formerly a researcher with the Land Tenure Center of the University of Wisconsin, and he is currently working in Ghana.

Rose Mbowa is Head of the Department of Music, Dance and Drama at Makerere.

Mary Mugyenyi teaches in the Department of Women's Studies at Makerere University.

Christine Obbo is a social anthropologist currently attached to the Centre of African Studies at the School of Oriental and African Studies, University of London.

Sanjay Pradhan is a researcher at the Centre for the Study of African Economies, University of Oxford.

Anthony J. Regan is a constitutional lawyer currently teaching at the Australian National University at Canberra. Formerly he worked for the Uganda Constitutional Commission.

Abby Sebina-Zziwa is a research fellow at the Makerere Institute of Social Research currently studying for her Ph.D. at the Department of Anthropology, University of Copenhagen.

Aidan Southall was Professor of Anthropology successively at Makerere University and the University of Wisconsin at Madison.

Aili Mari Tripp teaches in the Department of Political Science, University of Wisconsin at Madison.

Geoffrey B. Tukahebwa teaches in the Department of Political Science and Public Administration at Makerere University.

Michael Twaddle is Reader at the Institute of Commonwealth Studies, University of London, teaching history and politics.

Michael A. Whyte teaches in the Institute of Anthropology at Copenhagen.

Susan Reynolds Whyte is a medical anthropologist, at Copenhagen University.

LIST OF MAPS

ACKNOWLEDGEMENTS

Holger Bernt Hansen and Michael Twaddle wish to thank colleagues in the Universities of Copenhagen and London for logistical support for the fifth conference at Lyngby Landbrugsskole, at which earlier version of papers published in this book were presented.

We are grateful to everybody who attended the conference for their comments; to President Yoweri Kaguta Museveni for taking time out of a busy tour of Europe to open its proceedings; to staff at Lyngby Landbrugsskole and the Danish National Museum for their hospitality; to the Danish Council for Development Research and DANIDA for financial support; and to staff at the Centre of African Studies at the University of Copenhagen for their help in facilitating the appearance of this book. Our warm thanks, too, to staff at James Currey Publishers (now transferred from London to Oxford) for their diligent assistance in its production, and to Margaret Cornell for her characteristically efficient copy-editing and for compiling the Index.

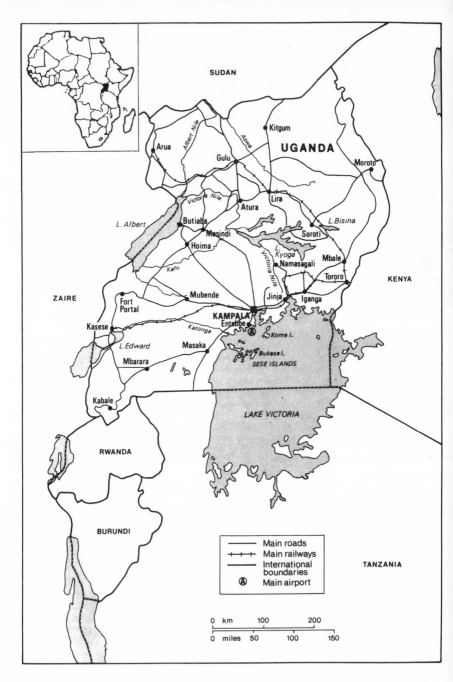

Map 1 *Uganda*

PART ONE
INTRODUCTION

ONE
The changing state of Uganda

Michael Twaddle & Holger Bernt Hansen

Uganda straddles the equator, surrounded by Sudan, Congo, Rwanda, Tanzania and Kenya. It is a landlocked country dependent on its neighbours for access to the sea. Turbulence in neighbouring countries inevitably affects its fortunes. Nonetheless, shortly before Yoweri Kaguta Museveni became its president in January 1986, Uganda itself was one of the greatest single sources of political instability, social dislocation and economic disruption in the Great Lakes region of sub-Saharan Africa.

This was because of the militarization of Uganda which had intensified in 1966–7 with the dismantling of the country's kingdoms and the inauguration of an executive presidency by Milton Obote. Obote had been prime minister of Uganda in 1962, when it achieved independence from Britain following a democratic multi-party general election. His government ruled the country with Mutesa II, king of Buganda, as its president; the last British Governor, Sir Walter Coutts, was governor-general for only a very short period just before this. The political alliance between the Buganda monarchy and Obote's first republic also lasted for only a short time. In 1966–7 a military force under the command of Obote's army ally, Idi Amin, stormed the Ganda king's palace in the capital and Obote was installed as president with greatly increased powers. These powers continued until 1971 when, following his deposition from power by Idi Amin, even more arbitrary government ensued.

To start with, Amin was hailed by many Ugandans and foreign observers as an improvement on Obote. Politicians imprisoned by him were freed and a number became cabinet ministers. So too did certain former top civil servants. In Moscow as much as in London and Washington at this time, soldiers in newly independent states were considered to come from a wider spectrum of society than politicians, and to be more efficient, patriotic and developmentally-minded as a result. Amin's Uganda soon undermined this view. Killings of opponents quickly commenced. Foreign advisers were changed, Israelis were replaced by Libyan, Palestinian and Saudi supporters. South Asian traders, bank clerks, teachers and artisans, many of whose families had been residents of Uganda since before the First World War, were

1

expelled in 1972 en masse, citizens and non-citizens alike. Bankers unwilling to print unlimited banknotes were replaced by ones who would. Inflation rocketed as a result. Quarrels over borders with neighbouring states became increasingly bitter. Kenya refused to return territory to the west of Naivasha included before 1902 within the colonial borders of Uganda. Tanzania was invaded in 1978 in the Kagera triangle, a disputed area of land since colonial times. This particular quarrel proved especially unwise as it prompted armed retaliation by Tanzanian footsoldiers and Amin's replacement as supreme ruler of Uganda in 1979 by the Uganda National Liberation Front.[1]

A rapid succession of short-lived governments followed. Then, in December 1980, as the result of a controversial multi-party election, Milton Obote returned to power as president for a second time.

It was a difficult time for him to return as Uganda's head of state. In southern areas of the country, the election which had restored him to power was regarded as fraudulent. After Amin's years as president, the country's export economy was in poor shape. Foreign exchange was extremely scarce. Marketing facilities were very poor. Inflation was higher than ever. Western governments insisted on liberalizing (or 'floating') the Ugandan shilling and a considerable reduction in state expenditure as the price of financial assistance. It was a brutal bargain. It also proved a corrupt one. As the foreign aid packages put together by international civil servants at this time were some of the very first experiments in 'structural adjustment' programmes for Third World countries, and the officials putting them together were economists more notable for mathematical skills than for local knowledge, the resultant SAPs were not as appropriate for Uganda's developmental needs as they might have been. Corruption among Obote's ministers and officials increased considerably when foreign currency was made available to the Ugandan government through one 'window' on preferential terms for essential imports and auctioned to the highest bidder through another 'window' for imports not considered essential for the country's needs. Corruption associated with the first externally-imposed structural adjustment programmes in the country did much to discredit Obote's credibility and to increase support for the National Resistance Movement's guerrilla campaigns against his government during the early 1980s. These campaigns received further support as the atrocities committed by Obote's troops, particularly against the peoples of southern and western Uganda, multiplied and were publicized by Amnesty International and other human rights organizations.[2]

It was against this background that our first volume of studies of the country's developmental needs, *Uganda Now: Between Decay and Development* (1988) took shape. Our own earlier researches had touched upon the growth of state power in the late nineteenth and early twentieth centuries as well as other matters (see Hansen, 1989; Twaddle, 1993). Now questions were being raised increasingly by other social scientists and contemporary historians as well as ourselves about the mis-

use of the Ugandan state under Milton Obote.
more numerous under Obote 2 than during the A
the atrocities of the early 1980s the consequences
lapse occurring during Amin's period of office rathe
which happened during either of Obote's presidenc
were IMF/World Bank policies of 'structural adjustme
this situation? Was it wise to dismiss the post-colonial st
World more generally as 'over-developed',[3] and to   ...out
demur suggestions increasingly made in the early 1980 ͻy the international financial institutions of the capitalist world that state expenditures in poor countries like Uganda should be reduced still further? see
Mosley et al., 1995 for further discussion). Our first 'call for papers' in
December 1984 stated that:

> At present, scholarly discussion of Ugandan affairs is deeply fragmented
> between fierce defenders of the Obote government and fierce opponents,
> and there is little theoretical tie-in between discussions of human rights and
> refugees, economic reconstruction, and state collapse as a result of the Amin
> regime. Our workshop [would provide an] opportunity to 'pool resources'
> and discuss the interrelationships between these currently quite separate
> areas of discussion, amongst scholars in the international community who
> have done some research in Uganda [recently] but not yet had adequate
> opportunity to compare their findings.

Our suggestion was therefore for

> a workshop of between 25 and 30 experts from Africa as well as Europe and
> America to convene for three days to present and discuss papers on a vari-
> ety of aspects of political, economic and social crisis in Uganda that should
> lead to at least one scholarly publication (most probably in symposium form)
> on the problems of the country since independence which might well be of
> interest to planners and aid and refugee personnel as well as to scholars. The
> workshop will therefore essentially be an academic and research enterprise
> rather than any propagandist attempt to vilify the present Ugandan gov-
> ernment – or uncritically defend it.

In fact, our 'call for papers' on Uganda has led to not one but four symposia considering the country's affairs; or five, if a further conference
and volume considering Uganda's politico-religious divisions within
the wider Eastern African context is also included.[4]

The present volume is the last of this quartet, or quintet, of publications. Like all such studies, it reflects the differing interests of its
authors and their respective expertises. Nonetheless, we hope that the
further pooling of information and analysis represented in it will not
only fill gaps in earlier volumes but also contribute to greater debate
about, and concern with, Uganda's developmental problems.

ARMY AND SOCIETY

One problem concerns the country's army. Six years ago, a newly
arrived research student from Uganda went for an initial exploratory

...d Copenhagen and suddenly asked: 'Where are all the sol-
...-ier question was prompted by the absence of the army vehicles
... soldiers carrying guns then still common in Kampala as in many
other African capitals today. The Danish royal guard could not match
that scene in 1992. Nor can Kampala six years later.

During these years, two processes among others have been at work.
The first was called for explicitly by the late Dan Mudoola in our collection of essays on *Changing Uganda* in 1991: the domestication of the
National Resistance Army. Essentially, Mudoola argued that the NRA
should change from being a guerrilla force into one serving the civilian
government and society at large in a more orderly, long-term and integrated manner (Mudoola, 1991). Major steps in this direction were in
fact taken when Museveni's army was represented on the Commission
charged with the task of preparing a new constitution for the country
at the end of the 1980s, and in the Constituent Assembly deciding upon
a final draft in 1994–5. When the articles of the new constitution were
finally agreed upon, the NRA was renamed the Uganda Peoples'
Defence Forces. Along with youth, women, trade unionists and the disabled, the military retained special representatives in the national parliament together with the obligation 'to engage in productive activities
for the development of Uganda' under article 134. As E.A.Brett argues
in our earlier volume *From Chaos to Order; The Politics of Constitution-
Making in Uganda* (1994), the remarkable achievement has been the
neutralization of the military as an autonomous political force (Brett,
1994: 79).

A second process at work in recent years has been a major reduction
in the size of the Ugandan armed forces. In 1993 an exercise commenced to demobilize roughly 35,000 soldiers over a 3-year period and
to reintegrate them into private life in their rural homelands.
Effectively, this meant a demobilization of the country's army by 30 per
cent within an extremely short period. That this second process succeeded even partially – in view of the regional turbulence associated
with the Rwandan genocide of 1994 and the disintegration of Mobutu's
Zaire and its violent displacement in 1996–7 by Kabila's Rwandan-sup-
ported government – must be attributed to the encouragement accorded to it both by the leading international aid agencies operating in
Uganda and by Museveni's own government.

To be sure, it was in the Museveni government's own interest to
transform the NRA from a large guerrilla force into a smaller modern
army backing a democratically elected administration. It needed to
bring the remaining unruly areas in the north of the country under its
control so that a balanced programme of development could be
applied to the whole of Uganda. Otherwise the north-south divide, to
which Aidan Southall draws attention so pertinently in Chapter 19 of
this volume, would persist and grow sharper. In addition, a better
trained and more generously paid army was needed in order to avoid
the violations of human rights committed earlier against rebels in the

4

north of the country. Many of these atrocities had been committed by opposition groups incorporated into the Ugandan armed forces at the start of Museveni's government essentially for reasons of reconciliation and consensus-building. In retrospect, it may have been a mistake to have stationed so many of these earlier opponents as far as possible from Entebbe-Kampala (presumably for reasons of initial security) because that made it much more difficult to prevent them from committing atrocities. A policy of partial demobilization in the 1990s therefore fulfilled several objectives simultaneously. It reduced the likelihood of future infringements of human rights by cleansing the army of known undesirables. It reduced the large numbers of westerners and Baganda still clustering in the rank and file of the NRA (because of the largely western Ugandan and Buganda-based nature of the guerrilla war against Obote 2 and the tyranny of the Okellos which controlled the country in the second half of 1985) without antagonizing these rank and file unduly on explicitly ethnic grounds. Finally, partial demobilization was likely to provide Uganda ultimately with a less costly army as well as one better balanced regionally.

Until early 1996, the policy of demobilization appeared to be working successfully. But then complications arose.

Some complications were connected with the presidential and parliamentary elections held later in 1996. Despite the technically 'no party' ground rules under which both sets of elections were held, there were basically only two competitors of importance in these elections – Yoweri Kaguta Museveni and the National Resistance Movement on one side, and Paulo Semogerere with the combined support of the Democratic Party and the Uganda Peoples' Congress on the other. In retrospect, it might seem that Museveni's side was bound to win both contests. Besides the benefits of incumbency, Museveni clearly profited from the electorate's fears of a resurgence of the earlier instability in the country. Only in the Nilotic-speaking areas of northern Uganda did anti-Museveni forces gain substantial majorities of votes. It was also in those areas that the Lord's Resistance Army renewed its insurgency in the months immediately preceding both elections.

The LRA's insurgency was now supported by the government of Sudan, presumably acting on the principle that my enemy's enemy is my enemy – in response to the Museveni government's earlier support for southern Sudanese rebels. In her discussions of 'Is Alice Lakwena a witch? The Holy Spirit Movement and its fight against evil' in *Changing Uganda* (pp. 162–77) and of 'The Holy Spirit Movement and the forces of nature in the north of Uganda 1985–1987' in *Religion and Politics in East Africa* (pp. 59–71), Heike Behrend analyzed the cultural background to the most recent insurgency in Acholiland. In Chapter 18 of the present volume, she outlines further this millenarian movement's ideas of 'development'. These ideas are difficult to reconcile with the development policies nowadays espoused by the Museveni government and its principal advisers in the International Monetary Fund and the

World Bank. Nonetheless, they resonate sufficiently coherently with present members of the Lord's Resistance Army which grew out of the Holy Spirit Movement, and with the wider population of Acholiland, for it to have been extremely difficult for the UPDF to obtain co-operation locally in resisting the LRA's attacks. Another reason for the failure of Nilotic-speaking Ugandans to provide accurate intelligence about the LRA's whereabouts appears to be a feeling in Acholiland that Museveni's government has failed to keep its very first promise to create peace and stability in the area against attacks by Karamojong rustlers from the east[5] and by Obote's former soldiers exiled in Sudan from the north. Museveni's soldiers recruited initially from opposition groups appear to have been a further part of the problem.

Nevertheless, whatever the explanation for the support enjoyed by the Lord's Resistance Army in northern Uganda recently, one of its consequences has been a reversal in the demobilization of soldiers throughout the country, and a corresponding increase in the size of the national defence budget. Veterans were recalled to active duty in order to fight in the north in both 1996 and 1997. The worsening military situation along the western border, associated with continuing insecurity in Rwanda, the toppling of Mobutu's regime by Laurent Kabila's forces in Congo, and counter-attacks by Muslim dissidents, *interahamwe* fighters from Rwanda's previous government, and secessionists from the Ruwenzori mountains, led to further former NRA personnel returning to active service.

International donors may grumble at these developments but currently they seem to accept them as inevitable consequences of Uganda's strategic position in the Great Lakes region of sub-Saharan Africa. US policy-makers go furthest nowadays in supporting Museveni's soldiers on active service. Together with Senegal, Uganda is one of the first black African countries to receive US military advisers to train their troops as part of an Africa-wide peacekeeping force. As a better behaved army than either of its predecessors under Amin or Obote, and as a presumed bulwark against the spread of Islamist sentiment into the region from Sudan (because of the predominantly Christian character of the Ugandan populations from which it was initially recruited), the UPDF has in recent years been supported in its war against the Lord's Resistance Army both financially and through the supply of weapons by the United States.

Economically and regionally, the effects on the development of Uganda of this reversal of demobilization policy may turn out to be negative. But, strategically, they should prove positive for the prestige of the country's armed forces, provided they are not defeated in the field by the Lord's Resistance Army in the near future.

DONORS AND DEVELOPMENT

Immediately after seizing power in January 1986, the Museveni government embarked on an economic policy seemingly totally opposed to that of Milton Obote. Instead of liberalizing the Ugandan shilling, Museveni's first finance minister attempted to freeze its value in foreign currency and then actually to raise it (see Twaddle, 1988, for an account of some of the early results of this policy). Besides responding warily to the advice of Western governments regarding other areas of the economy, barter deals were set up with communist countries like Cuba and Yugoslavia whereby tropical products would be exchanged for additional supplies of sugar and assistance with road building and repairs. This was an approach which could not survive in substantive form the political and economic collapse of the Soviet Union and the disintegration of Yugoslavia from the end of the 1980s onwards. The attempt to revalue the Ugandan shilling upwards also failed within a few months. Effectively, there were then only two realistic economic options open to Uganda at governmental level: accepting the advice offered by the International Monetary Fund, the World Bank, and the Paris Club quickly, or accepting it less quickly.

In *Changing Uganda*, published in 1991, Joshua Mugyenyi describes the difficulties the government encountered in dealing with advanced capitalist countries' institutions like the Paris Club and the IMF during President Museveni's early years in power. It was a very unequal relationship, with the handful of representatives of the poor African country sitting on one side of the table, and a multiplicity of envoys of the advanced capitalist countries, each advised by its own experts, on the other. It was doubtless partly the inequality of this relationship which prompted Museveni to change position – from being the most severe critic of the World Bank and the IMF in the early and mid-1980s to becoming one of their most eloquent supporters ten years later. In the 1990s the Soviet Union no longer existed as a powerful alternative model and facilitator of centrally-controlled development in sub-Saharan Africa; Yugoslavia had imploded; and Cuba was not only a long way away geographically but much less influential without the Soviet Union's assistance.

But there was probably also another reason. Pressures by the more advanced capitalist countries for political changes as well as for economic reforms in the Third World multiplied in the years immediately following the end of the Cold War. Politically, Museveni was unwilling to yield to demands by any outsiders for multi-party democracy to be re-established quickly in Uganda. Basically, this was because it had been the multi-party democracy espoused by Milton Obote's government against which his followers had fought so doggedly throughout the course of their bush war. That guerrilla campaign, in turn, had led to its own sort of democracy in the form of resistance councils. On seizing supreme power in January 1986, the National Resistance Movement transformed these resistance councils into the base of a pyramid of higher councils, each of which elected members of the council immediately above it from among its own personnel. At the apex of the pyramid was the National Resistance Council. This pyramid was extended to cover the whole of Uganda after the bitterly contested civil war with Obote's second presidency and the Okellos' tyranny which replaced it during the last months of 1985. Yoweri Museveni and his associates were clearly unwilling to abolish it before a better system of political representation was ready. This took the Odoki Commission four years to consider, and the Constituent Assembly a further year and more to accept. When Museveni became president of Uganda in January 1986 at the head of the National Resistance Movement, its politics were not negotiable. Economics was quite another matter, or very quickly became so once the NRM's initial economic policies went seriously awry.

The first economic dance in the 1980s between Uganda under Obote's second administration and the international institutions of the capitalist world had taken place to a monetarist tune not heard so insistently since the era of free trade and William Gladstone in the late nineteenth century (Gladstone was the last British prime minister not to want Britain to establish a Uganda Protectorate during that century). Keith Edmonds, a contributor to *Uganda Now: Between Decay and Development* (1988), the first volume in our quintet of symposia, stressed the comparative success of Obote's second government in attempting to dance to this rediscovered tune of economic liberalism and state retreat – 'the substantial reduction in the inflation rate that took place between 1980 and 1984, the achievement of the supply side, the increases in exports of cash crops, and the stemming of the widespread retreat by many small Ugandan farmers into subsistence agriculture'. Admittedly, there had been 'a precarious balance' between the implementation of 'domestic policies, donors' commitments of funds, and a restoration of growth in the officially recorded sector of the country's economy at the expense of the parallel economy or black market'.But what caused everything to go awry, in Edmonds's view, was an excessive pay award to civil servants in 1984. 'This single act itself fuelled further inflation,and thus helped to bring the national economy of Uganda still closer to collapse. Deteriorating security during 1984–5 clearly made an already dire economic situation still worse. In this, the end of Obote's second government came to mirror very closely the immediately post-Amin crisis of 1979–80' (Edmonds, 1988).

After the immediate problems confronting Museveni's first administration had been dealt with, other visiting economists still sang of the benefits to Uganda's long-term economic health of floating its shilling freely on global money markets. But increasingly it was a monetarist song with a difference. In *Changing Uganda: The Dilemmas of Structural Adjustment and Revolutionary Change* (1991), K. Sarwar Lateef stressed the importance of continuing with the economic recovery programme launched in May 1987. This was aimed at restoring economic stability, establishing more realistic prices for primary products, and rehabilitating the country's productive and social infrastructure. But Lateef and others now stressed that it was important not to neglect the poorest people who benefitted least in the short term from the new policies. A distinctive feature of the policy proposed was also 'its heavy reliance on NGOs and community-based rural organizations (the resistance councils) which are well placed to supplement the government's capacity to implement projects directed at the poor'. This was because governmental capability in Uganda was so limited. For this reason it would be necessary to rely increasingly on private support for projects concerned with the wider population as well:

> ... the state will need to withdraw gradually from areas where it is least competent at present: i.e., production, marketing and distribution responsibilities and from the extensive regulation of the private sector, while concentrating its energies on creating an enabling environment, political stability, human rights, a sound policy framework aimed at strengthening the working of markets, and rehabilitation of the economic and social infrastructure needed for development. (Lateef, 1991: 40)

The song was still one of state retreat, but not of complete retreat from the economic sphere. Also the needs of the poorest people, who were least benefitted by structural adjustment policies in the short term, were now recognized.

These needs have been recognized even more strongly by donors in the most recent structural adjustment policies applied to Uganda. As soldiers were demobilized and the civil service reduced in size (and individual civil servants given salaries closer to a living wage) donors like Danida and the World Bank have made the redirection of funds to the social sector a further condition of assistance. In 1995 this was underlined at the Social Summit in Copenhagen, where the 20:20 principle was introduced whereby donors would allocate 20 per cent of all their aid to health and education in return for the recipient government itself allocating 20 per cent of its budget to the same social sectors. Inevitably, two questions are raised. To what extent is this additional conditionality donor-driven? To what extent is it also consistent with the other objective of making the recipient government revenue-generating rather than revenue-consuming?

Undoubtedly the Ugandan government will continue to find it difficult to allocate funds to the social sector at a time when its room for manoeuvre is restricted by the need to link the national budget to the annual growth rate. Following earlier advice offered by the international financial institutions, Museveni's government has increased its revenue substantially through improved collection of taxes and duties and by introducing value added tax. But the increased revenues do not yet match the demands of donors for increased expenditure even on the reform of the civil service, which in turn is so important for the government's ability to push through other reforms. Admittedly, by an agreement dating from the first half of 1997, international donors have nominated Uganda to be the first African beneficiary of a new debt relief scheme. But its benefits are likely to be long-term. In the short term the debt relief currently envisaged is unlikely to enable the government to meet the full costs of new expenditures such as the free primary education for the first four members of each Ugandan family promised by President Museveni during his electioneering in 1996. There is therefore a serious gap between donors' demands for increased social expenditure and reduction of poverty in Uganda, and the government's ability to meet these additional demands.

To what extent are these demands principally the demands of donors rather than of Ugandans? It is difficult to answer this question straightforwardly for several reasons. One reason is that, after the failure of most of the initial barter schemes and of the upward revaluation of the Ugandan shilling, the government's financial policies and donors' demands have become so closely intertwined that it is difficult for those not privy to government-donor discussions to decide which are the more important. Another consideration is that, in the eyes of many donors, Uganda in recent years represents a developmental success story necessary for the donors' own self-confidence at a time when the volume of aid to sub-Saharan Africa is low and when disasters afflicting African countries are numerous. Thirdly, Ugandans are not all of one class, tribe or mentality, and their ideas of development differ as much among themselves as from those of foreign donors.

LOCAL IDEAS OF DEVELOPMENT

Uganda has been a state for only just over a hundred years. The British created this entity in 1894 as a result of competition among the European powers for colonial dependencies in Africa, but they were so concerned to limit the extent of their obligations to the new state that for the first two-thirds of its chronological life Uganda remained a 'protectorate' rather than a 'colony' like neighbouring Kenya (see Morris and Read, 1966). Qualified as it was, this claim still had to be paid for. Local peoples therefore had to pay taxes to the imperial treasury. Where tax was refused, the local peoples were persuaded to pay it by fair means or foul (see Twaddle, 1988b).

By the time power was handed over to an African successor government in 1962, Uganda had become a patchwork of district administrations subdivided into counties and consolidated into provinces. The entity as a whole was administered, as it had been from the start of the British protectorate, from a capital situated on the northern shore of Lake Victoria at Entebbe or by departments with headquarters situated twenty miles further inland at Kampala.

Both Entebbe and Kampala lie at the heart of the ancient kingdom of Buganda. As the result of a treaty with the British protectorate authorities in 1900, Buganda retained its monarch together with a modified version of its government and a distinctive form of quasi-freehold land tenure (see below Chapter 12). This *mailo* land quickly became a vital element in a colonial economy of cashcropping smallholder farmers assisted by immigrant traders and exporters from British India and by British-controlled marketing boards set up to cover the whole of the Uganda

Protectorate. Because of its special privileges, Buganda became the envy of other African peoples both inside and outside Uganda. As independence approached, British officials agonized over Buganda's privileges under Uganda's constitution.[6] Shortly after independence, it was the position of Buganda under this constitution which in part prompted the militarization of Uganda, initially and mildly under Milton Obote's first presidency, then manically and uncontrollably under Idi Amin. It took several years before the Constituent Assembly under Museveni's government came up with a compromise recommending that Buganda's special position within Uganda should be recognized by the right of its constituent districts to combine for cultural co-operation and development under the guidance of their monarch, should majorities within these districts so decide. Needless to say, similar rights were extended to all other districts in the country; but it was clearly Buganda which most concerned the CADs (Constituent Assembly Delegates) and the authors of the Odoki Commission Report (see Hansen and Twaddle, 1994: 1–17).

The Alur, considered by Aidan Southall in Chapter 19 of this volume, were attracted to Buganda early in the twentieth century to work for farmers cultivating cotton and coffee for export. During the British colonial period, migrant Alur formed a significant section of the Buganda kingdom's underclass. Nowadays their general feeling that independence has dealt them a harsh hand also seems considerable. Southall stresses their geographical and structural position on the periphery of modern Uganda. He also stresses the importance for the unity and equity of the country of not treating them as permanent developmental outcasts (see Southall, 1956).

The Alur, like the Acholi described by Heike Behrend in Chapter 18, were administered within Uganda's Northern Province for most of the British colonial period. Like the Acholi, the Alur speak a Nilotic language. Other peoples administered alongside them speak languages classified by linguists as Sudanic.[7] Most peoples grouped in the Uganda Protectorate's other Provinces – Western, Buganda or Eastern – were Bantu-speakers (see Mukama, 1991; Ladefoged, 1971 for further data), with comparatively small numbers of Nilotic or Paranilotic speakers also occupying pockets of land in eastern Uganda, such as the Jopadhola and the Iteso who live nowadays in Tororo District, and who occupy immediately adjacent counties to the Banyole considered by Michael and Susan Whyte in Chapter 17.

The Whytes suggest that Banyole ideas of development may be divided into three types – aspirations for personal development and attempts at kinsfolk advancement common to many societies, and desire for the common good. Behind the universal values lies a local model of 'developing' or 'growing' (*ohuhula*, 'to grow' in Lunyole) very similar to the Baganda popular aspiration for 'growing' (*okukula*, 'to grow' in Luganda) introduced into the area at the start of the twentieth century by agents employed by the protectorate government or by missionaries – principally Protestant Anglicans and

11

Roman Catholics but also including Muslims excluded from Buganda by the political triumph of European Christianity there at the close of the nineteenth century (see Kasozi, 1986: 56ff.). South Asian traders of a variety of religious confessions were also attracted into the East African interior by the construction of colonial railways from the Indian Ocean littoral, and these traders further strengthened local aspirations for modernization by providing consumer goods and credit more widely (Ramchandani, 1976 is the best account of this period).

Within fifty years of the establishment of the British Protectorate, most Ugandan societies were criss-crossed by cashcropping farmers, principally growing cotton and coffee for export or migrating to work on farms outside their home areas in order to pay taxes, purchase education for their children at Christian schools, and buy land, property and consumer goods with any surplus. After World War II, an anti-colonial movement built up on the resentments which developed among farmers and farmworkers on the score that prices paid for their cash crops were too low. For a time it seemed that educated Ugandans might lead a powerful and united movement of protest against British rule. But then the British authorities deported the king of Buganda and 'our things' (*ebintu ebyange*) became a slogan splitting the leaders of the independence struggle into pro-Baganda and anti-Baganda factions (See Apter, 1961/1997; Low, 1971).

These conflicting models of development continue to influence Museveni's Uganda. According to the Whytes (Chapter 17), many Banyole have escape routes into individual or family employment at times of tension or disruption nationally; geographical proximity to Kenya is especially convenient at such times. The Alur do not have the same opportunities in Congo or Sudan nowadays, nor do they share as intensely as the Acholi the millenarian enthusiasms of either the Holy Spirit Movement or the Lord's Resistance Army which developed out of it. Aidan Southall speaks for Ugandan peoples who consider themselves to be falling behind in social development because of their geographical and cultural isolation (Chapter 19), and he notes how strongly Alur continue to articulate their fears in religious language. So do many Acholi, according to Heike Behrend:

> One of the paradoxes of development is that, despite the attempts to impose Western rationality in Africa, we nowadays find a proliferation of various religious discourses, centring round spirits, spirit possession and witchcraft. It seems that in contemporary Africa, political issues are increasingly expressed in religious discourses. To gain or conquer the central power, i.e. the state, religious discourses are invented ... Especially in countries devastated by war, like Uganda, the reconstruction that takes place at the local level will not be understood without taking into account religious discourses and practices that try to heal individuals and society (Chapter 18, pp. 245–6).

12

MUSEVENI'S UGANDA
This is something which Museveni's government cannot ignore, not least because as a result of a century and a quarter of European Christian endeavour large folk churches of Protestant Anglicans and also Roman Catholics have been established in Uganda. The three political parties which led the country into independence from Britain in the early 1960s were attached respectively to the Roman Catholic Church (through the Democratic Party) and to the Anglican Church of Uganda (through the Uganda Peoples' Congress and the Kabaka Yekka movement).[8] But, since the earliest days of its bush war against Milton Obote's government in the early 1980s, the National Resistance Movement has been a self-consciously secular association, campaigning with virulence against the 'sectarianism' associated, in its eyes, with the UPC at least in part because of that party's links with Ugandan Anglicanism (see further Twaddle, 1988c: 238).

This anti-clericalism creates additional problems for programmes dealing with the current AIDS epidemic and HIV infection. In contrast to the Museveni government's admonition to 'Love carefully', both of Uganda's largest Christian churches advise their members to 'Love faithfully'. A report by George Bond and Joan Vincent underlined the catastrophic situation caused by sexually transmitted diseases during Yoweri Museveni's first years in power in their account of 'Living on the edge: changing social structures in the context of AIDS' in Hansen and Twaddle, 1991.

In the present volume, Maryinez Lyons and Christine Obbo (Chapters 14 and 15) provide additional documentation. However, in his contribution on 'Developing a population policy for Uganda' (Chapter 13), Edward Kirumira points out that the Museveni government has not been the only one to clash with the churches over AIDS. 'Successive governments have been keen not to antagonize religious groups, especially the Roman Catholic church in this respect. They have also lacked sufficient grassroots political support to risk encouraging far-reaching policies on family planning issues' (p.190). Kirumira argues that a 'prerequisite for success will be the expansion of government national development planning beyond the short term, or even medium-term periods, and the depoliticization of the population question' (p. 193). Clearly, for this to happen, the government needs to develop not only more cordial relations with the churches but also more effective state structures both administratively and economically throughout the country.

Are these wholly unattainable objectives in present circumstances? Paul Collier and Sanjay Pradhan think not. Indeed, in analyzing economic aspects of Uganda's remarkable recovery from twenty years of civil war (Chapter 2), they argue that a period of transition to more peaceful conditions is the most suitable time for radical policy initiatives to be undertaken. It is in this context that Uganda's structural adjustment programme (or SAP) should be judged. Measured by the recent growth in the country's GNP to 7–8 per cent per year – exceeding the rate of population growth of 2.5 per cent outlined by Kirumira for the same period – the figures are impressive. Sadly, the same figures seem less impressive if we look at the economic sector affecting the majority of the population: agriculture. Agricultural growth rates in Uganda currently barely exceed the rate of population increase.

A further reservation must be entered: the remarkable economic recovery which has occurred during the Museveni government's years in office has taken place at the expense of social expenditure, and in disregard of the poverty suffered by the poorest 20 per cent of Ugandans. The first SAP to be imposed on the country paid far too little attention to either the poverty dimension or to social expenditure, because of its predominantly macroeconomic character. However, we have to agree with Collier and Pradhan that the first SAPs do not appear to have made the situation worse as regards either the poverty of the poorest Ugandans or the state of the country's health and educational sectors; both were in a pretty parlous condition at the close of years of civil war. For the future, it is important to ensure that economic policy does not ignore social expenditure or the poverty dimension.

What else needs to be done? President Museveni himself has repeatedly stressed the importance of attracting more private investment to Uganda in order to replace the foreign aid which can only be regarded as temporary. Other sectors needing attention are industrialization and privatization. Industrialization is discussed by Ian Livingstone. In Chapter 3 he stresses the necessity of re-examining this sector critically. As a landlocked country, Uganda needs to look to markets among its immediate neighbours; one opportunity might be the new government of Rwanda, another Laurent Kabila's new (and we trust) Democratic Republic of Congo. Livingstone suggests that Uganda's new strategy should include developing more linkages between agriculture and industry. It also needs to respond to people's basic needs. And it needs to be small-scale. Only thus can industrialization contribute to economic welfare and sustainable development in Uganda.

Privatization also needs to be reconsidered, in the opinion of Geoffrey Tukahebwa. Privatization has contributed to the country's record rate of economic growth of 7–8 per cent, but so far it has not increased employment opportunities at all significantly. Nor has it enlarged the number of Ugandan entrepreneurs. Poverty, too, has not been reduced so far by privatization.

How do poor Ugandans cope? In Chapter 6, Dan Maxwell provides yet more evidence of the courage and endurance displayed by the Ugandan poor in his analysis of urban agriculture. He describes the most creative responses imaginable to the realities of daily life in Kampala nowadays, first and foremost by women, who cope with urban crisis by engaging in various informal trades. The analysis of poverty in Museveni's Uganda is taken further in Vali Jamal's careful survey (Chapter 5). On the World Bank's figures, between 50 and 60 per cent of Ugandans must be considered poor. Jamal distinguishes between poverty in towns and in the countryside. In rural areas, the least favoured members of the population have suffered most. Growing food crops for subsistence may have kept hunger and starvation at bay for most Ugandans since Museveni's coming to power in 1986, but only just. Jamal is sceptical about the positive distributive effects of present rural-urban terms of trade. He advocates a developmental strategy involving all sections of the population. Poverty, in his view, should be tackled through broad-based strategies.

Coping at national level under the impact of the first structural adjustment programmes meant relying much more on non-governmental organizations for delivery of services. As Susan Dicklich points out (Chapter 10), NGOs have become significant providers of services in Uganda to the detriment of their democratic activities and wider political impact. Apart from the educational sector, where Parent-Teacher Associations have shouldered the burden of running primary schools, NGOs carrying the greatest burdens in service provision have been those operating within the areas of AIDS and HIV infection, as outlined by Maryinez Lyons in Chapter 14. Philip Amis (Chapter 16) also has much to say about stress in service provision in his account of Jinja Municipal Council and the National Water and Sewerage Corporation.

There is some evidence that this situation may change in the near future. There are a number of reasons for this. If, as envisaged under structural adjustment packages assembled since the Copenhagen Social Summit of 1995, the Ugandan state again becomes directly involved in the social sector and in poverty alleviation programmes, NGOs active in these areas will necessarily become more political – because they will have to deal with a more socially involved state. NGOs will also become more active members of Uganda's civil society. Secondly, and as Anthony Regan points out in Chapter 11, civil society in general will need to be strengthened in order to monitor the state's action. Goran Hyden (Chapter 7) also attaches considerable importance to strengthening institutions outside government in Uganda, capable of keeping an eye on it.

Clearly, Ugandan women have an important role to play in this process. Both Aili Mari Tripp (Chapter 8) and Mary Mugyenyi (Chapter 9) note the significant empowerment of women which has taken place in Museveni's Uganda. Tripp outlines the variety of strategies which women's associations have pursued in dealings with state authorities throughout the country. Incidentally, she provides a corrective to uncritical praise for Resistance Councils, particularly those operating at lower levels, by drawing attention to their comparative lack of accountability and their dominance by men. Mugyenyi stresses the need for Ugandan women to be protected more effectively by the central government from attacks at district and sub-district level for departing excessively from 'tradition'.

These are not the only areas in which there have recently been strong calls for greater state intervention in Uganda, politically as well as economically. One such area concerns land reform, to which Chapter 12 is devoted. Population policy is another (Chapter 13). Environmental concerns, from the continuing disappearance of trees throughout the countryside to the sudden spread of the water hyacinth on Lake Victoria, also invite state action. What these various demands for more state action underline is the desire for a better state, a more effective state, a state capable of responding significantly to the needs of its citizens. In Chapter 11, Anthony Regan argues that the current crisis in Africa is to a very considerable extent a crisis of the state. He suggests that it has been the intention of the National Resistance Movement from the start to 'transform the state into a less dominant and more accountable institution'. One way of making this possible is to encourage 'the emergence of a wide range of political and economic forces which can help to control future state action'. Decentralization is to be a key instrument in this transformation.

Until recently this approach has been anathema to most Western donor countries. In general, these donors have considered market forces and the state to be polar opposites. They have called for reductions, not increases, in state activity. Geoffrey Tukahebwa (Chapter 4) argues that the Museveni government's policy on privatization has been influenced by these assumptions to a very considerable extent in recent years – and that they need to change. Tukahebwa calls for the Ugandan state to act on its own behalf in the face of market forces. It is this acceptance of the state as a partner in national development, rather than as a hindrance or an irrelevance, which the World Bank advocates in its *World Development Report 1997: The State in a Changing World*.

This summarizes a discussion which has been going on for some time among donor countries and within the World Bank itself. Its basic new assumptions are that an effective state and a properly functioning political system are both essential for economic stability and growth. Policy does matter. Two things are required. First, governments should not attempt to do too much with too little: instead they should concentrate on the core tasks which markets and voluntary agencies do not cover. One core task of government is investing in basic social services such as education and health. Another is providing a safety net for the most vulnerable members of society – the poor. Secondly, public institutions need to be reinvigorated. An efficient civil service is needed in particular to collect taxes whereby core governmental activities can be financed. Through these means corruption can be combated more effectively. Currently, corruption is possibly the most serious single issue poisoning relations between donors and recipients in poor countries.

In the Ugandan context this new thinking, or rather rethinking, does not appear especially radical nowadays. Nonetheless, it has had an undoubtedly legitimizing effect upon the constitutional reforms from which the National Resistance Movement already appears to be benefiting. At the centre of current political change in Uganda are the wider processes of democratization which Goran Hyden discusses in Chapter 7, and the reshaping of the state which Anthony Regan analyzes in Chapter 11. Hyden considers that the constitutional reform already undertaken in Museveni's Uganda gives it 'a democratic surplus' as far as international donors are concerned. This 'surplus' does much to compensate for the 'democratic deficit' caused in their view by repeated prolongations of earlier mandates to rule Uganda without the benefit of multi-party national elections, Regan is more concerned with state structures and the prospects for the planned decentralization of powers from Entebbe and Kampala to the local districts.

Development, remarks Rose Mbowa in her concluding chapter, is a matter of both public and private concerns.'One is a matter of figures and infrastructures, gross national product, the growth of industries and suchlike.' Another concerns 'the attitudes and potential of the great mass of Uganda's people, who remain to a very considerable extent illiterate and poor'. Her personal concern with Theatre for Development in Museveni's Uganda has been with empowering Ugandans 'to transform their condition' so that they might 'become the makers, the subjects and the objects of their own lives and history' (p. 261). This is a highly desirable objective. But it cannot be achieved without close attention to figures and infrastructures. It is therefore to these aspects of development that we turn next.

Notes

---

1. Accounts of these years are provided by, among others, Donald Rothchild and Michael Rogin, 'Uganda', in Gwendolen M. Carter, (ed.), *National Unity and Regionalism in Eight African States* (Ithaca, NY: Cornell University Press, 1966); Grace Ibingira, *African Upheavals since Independence* (Boulder, CO: Westview, 1980), esp. pp. 65 and following; James M. Mittelmann, *Ideology and Politics in Uganda: From Obote to Amin* (Ithaca, NY and London: Cornell University Press, 1975); Holger Bernt Hansen, *Ethnicity and Military Rule in Uganda* (Uppsala: Scandinavian Institute of African Studies, 1977); A.G.G. Gingyera-Pinycwa, *Apolo Milton Obote and His Times* (New York: NOK, 1978); J.J.Jorgensen, *Uganda, a Modern History* (London: Croom Helm, 1981), pp. 213 and following; Amii Omara-Otunnu, *Politics and the Military in Uganda* (London: Macmillan, 1987); and Kenneth Ingham, *Obote: a Political Biography* (London: Routledge, 1994).
2. Accounts of Obote 2 are less numerous than of Obote 1 but they include: Kenneth Ingham's biography op. cit., Twaddle, 1983 and Mutibwa, 1992; 148ff.
3. For the debate on the 'over-developed state', see especially Mamdani,' 1975; Saul, 1975; Leys, 1975.
4. In addition to the present volume on *Developing Uganda* [1998], these publications are *Uganda Now: Between Decay and Development* [1988]; *Changing Uganda: the Dilemmas of Structural Adjustment and Revolutionary Change* [1991]; *From Chaos to Order: the Politics of*

Constitution-making in Uganda [1994]; and *Religion and Politics in East Africa: the Period since Independence* [1995].

5. These attacks have been aggravated by environmental crises affecting dry-farming areas in northern Uganda in general and Karamoja in particular. For further documentation, see Mamdani, 1982; Gartrell, 1988; and a whole section on Karamoja in Dodge and Wiebe, 1985: 127–89.
6. See for example, the *Report on Ugandan Relationships* chaired by Lord Munster (Entebbe: Government Printer, 1961); and Christopher Wrigley, 'Four Steps Towards Disaster', in Hansen and Twaddle, 1988.
7. One example is the Kakwa people, of whom the former dictator Idi Amin is a member.
8. F.B. Welbourn, *Religion and Politics in Uganda 1952–62* (Nairobi: EAPH, 1965) is still useful, but for fuller discussion see the accounts in Hansen and Twaddle, 1995 by Ronald Kassimir, John Waliggo and Kevin Ward at pp. 120–148, 106–119 and 72–105 respectively. See also the late Dan Mudoola's book, *Religion, Ethnicity and Politics* (Kampala, 1993).

TWO
Economic aspects of the transition from civil war

Paul Collier & Sanjay Pradhan

INTRODUCTION:
THE ECONOMIC MEANING OF 'CIVIL WAR'

This chapter attempts to construct an analytical account of the economic recovery of Uganda from the prolonged civil disorder which preceded the Museveni government. Section 2 considers the impact of civil war and its aftermath on the macroeconomy. The next two sections look at private responses: inter-sectoral and inter-temporal substitutions brought about by civil war which gradually become unwound in the post-war period. The following two sections consider government revenue and expenditure responses. We begin, however, with a discussion of the economic meaning of civil war in the Ugandan context.

A civil war is often very different from an international war. International wars usually seem to strengthen the state. Indeed, Herbst (1990) has argued that it is the absence of a history of international wars in Africa which at least in part accounts for the weakness of state structures. By contrast, civil wars usually weaken the state. Civil war increases insecurity in two senses, both of which have economic consequences. It increases *micro-insecurity*, by which we mean the danger of violence against the person and against property. It also increases *macro-insecurity*, by which we mean the danger that those state-level institutions which provide the framework for economic activity, such as non-arbitrary taxation, the rule of law, and sanctity of contract, are destroyed. Obviously, a civil war is not the only circumstance in which these insecurities can arise, but they are probably intrinsic to civil war and, we shall argue, are in economic terms its defining feature.

Whereas international wars can invariably be dated precisely, civil wars often build up and wind down gradually. We shall date the start of the Ugandan civil war to 1972. In military terms this cannot be justified since organized violent opposition to the state did not develop until later. However, this was the time of the declaration by the Amin government of 'Economic War' on its Asian community and the resulting expulsion of that community. The use of the state for sustained extra-legal punitive action against a major social group is a key economic characteristic of civil war, and from 1972 the Asian community suffered extreme *macro-insecurity* and both this and micro-

19

insecurity spread fairly rapidly to other sections of the population. During the Amin era (1972–9) up to 500,000 Ugandans died as a result of the regime. Exiles in Tanzania mounted two invasion attempts, the 1979 one being successful. Whereas the 1979 campaign was short and decisive, the first part of the 1980s was a period of extreme military instability as successive governments gradually lost control of territory to insurgent forces. By 1985 some 7 per cent of the population was displaced or refugees. Once a government declares 'economic war' on a part of its population, it abandons the central economic functions of government: the provision of impartial arbitration, protection and contract enforcement. While some of these functions can in principle be provided privately, in Uganda, as in most societies, the state had reserved to itself the monopoly of supply and so the sudden cessation of state provision could not be met from alternative sources. Hence, a defining economic feature of the Ugandan civil war was that public officials, military personnel and private agents were to a considerable extent able to behave outside the due process of law. This extended beyond the expropriations suffered by Asian entrepreneurs. Many of the Asian businesses were acquired in a rather confused and *ad hoc* manner by soldiers, ministers and other members of the political elite. There was generally *de facto* control but not the acquisition of good title, giving rise to insecurity of tenure and non-marketability of the enterprises. In these circumstances there was a tendency for those who currently controlled the enterprise to strip it of its assets.

In January 1986 the National Resistance Army gained control of Kampala and secured more complete territorial control the following year, this marking the start of the return to peace. Just as the Asian community was the first to be embroiled in the war, it has been among the last to be incorporated in the peace. The return of confiscated assets is still in process, and to date only a small proportion of the community (and those assets which it expatriated) has returned despite strenuous efforts on the part of the NRM government. In addition to the slow process of Asian repatriation, Northern Uganda has not yet been entirely integrated into the present civil society.

The economic consequences of the civil war in Uganda are not primarily related to military expenditure and material destruction, they are about the removal of legitimate authority. It is this which makes the economic consequences of civil war quite different from those of a conventional international war: civil war removes legitimate authority. Consequently, the restoration of 'economic peace' is not the automatic corollary of military victory, it is the reconstruction of systems of legitimacy.

The longer a society stays in a state of civil war, the more the conventions of legitimate conduct decay. In this sense, the period 1972–86 was a fairly continuous descent from civil society, while the post-1986 period is better conceptualized not as post-war material reconstruction but as the gradual re-emergence of the institutions and conventions of civil society. 1971 marks the last full year of peace, and 1986 onwards marks the period of a gradual and partial return to economic peace.

AGGREGATE CONSEQUENCES OF WAR AND PEACE: PRODUCTION AND EXPENDITURE

We begin by describing the salient changes in the level of production and expenditure during and after the war. Production, as measured by constant price GDP, declined by 13 per cent between 1971 and 1986. Since human births far exceeded deaths, this is an amazing scale of contraction. For example, a normal slow-growing African economy would have expanded by around 3.5 per cent per annum during this period. Had the Ugandan economy grown at this rate it would have been double its actual 1986 size. To a small extent the decline in output relative to this counterfactual is due to endogenous losses of the labour force through emigration. Although only a small proportion of the labour force left Uganda, this was disproportionately the most productive part of it. The expelled Asian community was highly skilled, and the Amin regime systematically targeted the educated Africans. Hence, not only did these groups have the best earning opportunities abroad, they also had pressing reasons to leave. However, a decline on this scale must predominantly be explained by a reduction in the productivity of a given stock of labour. This was partly a matter of reduced productivity in all sectors, and partly reallocation between sectors to those with initially lower returns. With the return to peace post-1986, this output loss has been reversed. Between 1986 and 1992 GDP has grown by 37 per cent. Although this is above the growth rate for the region as a whole, the economy is still far short of the 1971 level of per capita production.

The concept for expenditure analogous to GDP as a measure of production is constant price Gross Domestic Expenditure (GDE). The decline in per capita GDE during the war exceeded that in GDP. This was for both exogenous and endogenous reasons. Exogenously, the terms of trade deteriorated, though with major fluctuations. Endogenously, the disproportionate decline in the export sector (discussed below) reduced the real income of the economy, being equivalent in terms of income loss to the introduction of severe trade restrictions. A second endogenous income loss was the decline in aid. Neither the Amin regime nor its successors were very attractive to donors and had little appeal to commercial banks. Hence, relative to need, Uganda was considerably underborrowed by 1986. Indeed, during the first half of the 1980s the balance of official merchandise trade was approximately zero. Further, as argued below in our analysis of private response, there is likely to have been a private capital outflow.

There were thus three endogenous reasons why expenditure relative to GDP was lower than in the counterfactual. Post-1986 there was a more rapid reversion in aggregate expenditure than in aggregate production. First, the shift of resources back into the tradable sector produced a trade-liberalization effect, enhancing real income for a given level of production. Secondly, there was a resumption of aid flows on a large and conceivably unsustainable scale. This seems to be a common pattern in war-peace transitions; for example in the first three post-war years Zimbabwe was able to run a payments deficit approaching 10 per cent of GDP. Thirdly, there was some repatriation of private capital. In 1992 private capital inflows totalled $200m. Offsetting these endogenous gains there was an exogenous loss due to the collapse in the world coffee price. The resulting collapse in export earnings proved temporary in that the coffee price has subsequently recovered from its historic low, and the Ugandan economy will gradually diversify its exports away from the extraordinary dependence upon coffee which was a by-product of the war. However, during the post-1986 period until 1994 the endogenous gain was approximately offset by the exogenous loss.

PRIVATE RESPONSES: CHANGES IN THE COMPOSITION OF PRODUCTION

Social disorder has distinct economic consequences for different sectors because it jeopardizes transactions and assets. That war jeopardizes transactions follows closely from North's analysis of transactions costs and economic development (North, 1990). His argument is that an environment in which transactions can be conducted cheaply requires considerable social capital. The range of social capital required is rather wide. In the early twentieth century informal agricultural marketing was greatly eased by the introduction of standardized weights and measures (which of course requires a continuous process of public checks) (Ensminger, 1992). The provision of a legal system enables the parties to a contract to enforce it relatively cheaply. The provision of a communications system reduces the costs of information, and a transport system reduces the costs of movement. Many aspects of a transaction cannot be specified in a contract because not all contingencies can be anticipated. An environment of co-operation, achieved either by the internalization of activities within an organization (the integrated firm) or by a high expectation of repeat transactions, is necessary to reduce the incidence of opportunistic behaviour. All these dimensions of social capital gradually decayed in Uganda. The disruption and consequent shortening of horizons encouraged the growth of opportunism in economic behaviour, and this persisted into the present. For example, a recent study of the credit market found that there was insufficient trust between agents even for informal savings and credit arrangements which are normally quite standard.

Activities vary considerably in their transactions intensity. The least transactions-intensive activity is subsistence production. However, it should be noted that, although subsistence production does not, by definition, involve the marketing of output, it will still usually involve the purchase of some inputs. Hence, it is not immune from a rise in the cost of transactions. An intermediate stage in the hierarchy of transactions intensity comprises activities which depend upon the market for the sale of output, but are not very dependent upon it for inputs. Marketed agricultural produce has this characteristic. The most vulnerable activities are those which depend upon the market for both inputs and outputs. Formal sector manufacturing is the main instance of such an activity.

That war jeopardizes assets follows as a special, but important, instance of the more general decay of social capital. Assets depend upon enforceable rights. Not only did Asians lose property, but the new owners held their claims only in a most insecure form. Not only might they expect that at some stage the property might be restored to its Asian owners but, of more immediate concern, they lacked clear title and so could neither sell not borrow against the asset, and risked having it reassigned to some other 'owner' through the same arbitrary process by which they themselves had acquired it. The illegitimate possession of an asset creates powerful incentives to strip it. Since possession is likely only to be temporary it is safest to transform it into an invisible form: invisibility is the best substitute for legitimacy, other than the possession of overwhelming force. This transformation is worthwhile even if in the process a substantial part of the value of the asset is forfeit. Invisible assets take various forms. The least visible is an asset held abroad. Cash may also be easy to conceal. Finally, crops which can be kept underground (tubers) are safer than those which must be stored above ground (grains). In addition to invisibility, immobility is desirable in an asset. Immobility will not constitute a defence against large-scale predation such as the arbitrary power of a ruler, but it is a defence against the micro-insecurity of casual theft. An immobile asset is only forfeit if another agent is able to secure the space on a long-term basis. Obvious immobile assets are land and buildings. There are no assets which are both immobile and invisible, but there are some which are both mobile and visible, such as vehicles and consumer durables.

Just as activities vary in their transactions intensity, so they vary in their intensity in visible and mobile assets. Manufacturing is again highly vulnerable since both its inputs and its outputs must be stored at the site of production and are by their nature mobile. Subsistence is in one respect more asset-vulnerable than production for the market, in that the latter can be sold as it is harvested, whereas the former cannot usually be eaten as it is harvested (except for some tubers) and so must be stored on site. Livestock is a disastrously asset-vulnerable activity, in that it is capital-intensive and the entire capital is fairly visible and highly mobile. The service sector is relatively invulnerable in that its inputs are largely people and buildings.

So far we have considered how sectors differ according to whether they use visible or mobile assets, and whether their production process is intensive in transactions. A particularly vulnerable sector on these criteria suffers a large cost-shock. However, in addition, some sectors produce either assets or transactions. These sectors suffer a demand collapse because war operates like a tax on their output. In Uganda the asset-producing sectors are construction and livestock; transactions production covers transport, trade, and the financial services sector.

To summarize, we have distinguished activities according to whether they are transactions-intensive, vulnerable asset-intensive, transaction-providing, or asset-providing. To give an illustrative parody of the above analysis, the worst possible activity in which to be engaged might be the manufacture of cash-registers. The production process is vulnerable because manufacturing uses mobile assets and has a high ratio of transactions to value-added. The demand for output collapses because it is a mobile capital good and one used only for processing transactions. At the other end of the spectrum would be growing cassava for own consumption. We now show how this is consistent with the remarkable changes in the composition of GDP both during and after the period of war.

A measure of the relative performance of a sector is how the quantity of its value-added changed relative to GDP, this being shown in Table 2.1. On this measure between 1971 and 1986 three sectors stand out as disasters and two as successes. The sector which contracted most severely, more than halving relative to GDP (which itself halved relative to a reasonable counterfactual), was manufacturing. This is consistent with the above analysis since manufacturing is intensive both in transactions and in visible and mobile assets. Manufacturing was also the most successful sector post-1986. By 1992 it had recovered half of the ground which it had lost relative to GDP as a whole. The next most contracting sector was the asset-providing sector, construction. Again, this was the second most successful sector post-1986.

The other important component of the asset-providing sector, livestock, is not adequately captured in National Accounts data. However, a detailed micro-level study of the response of dairy farmers to a weakened state is provided by Kasfir (1993). Kasfir's theme is the resourcefulness of Ugandan dairy farmers in the face of the extreme difficulties which they faced as state services and security collapsed. However, despite their resourcefulness, many farmers suffered egregious losses and Kasfir's paper reveals a detailed catalogue of both increased asset-vulnerability as, for example, Amin's soldiers steal cattle, and transactions vulnerability, as essential veterinary inputs become unobtainable. The other sector which suffered severely during the war period was a transactions-providing sector, commerce. Again this grew more rapidly than GDP post-war, but remained much smaller relative to GDP than its pre-war level.

The two sectors which did relatively well out of the war were subsistence agriculture and government services. Subsistence grew relative to GDP during the war and contracted relatively thereafter. However, it is noteworthy that even subsistence output was stagnant between 1971 and 1986: its performance is only good in relative terms. In effect, the

24

substitution of resources into subsistence as they became less productive in other sectors, was offset by the negative effects of the war through the disruption of inputs, and government services are measured by the quantity of their inputs, which are largely labour. They follow qualitatively the same path as subsistence, though the changes relative to GDP are more marked.

**Table 2.1 The composition of Ugandan GDP by war-vulnerability
(% share of GDP at 1991 constant prices)**

	1993/94	1971	1986
Transaction and asset intensity:			
high: manufacturing	8.8	4.4	6.0
medium: marketed agriculture	22.6	24.5	22.7
low: subsistence	20.5	36.0	32.1
Transaction-providing:transport			
and commerce	17.2	21.2	16.1
Asset-providing: construction	12.5	3.5	5.5
Unassigned activities	14.4	15.5	16.5

Note: The National Accounts provide data at 1966 prices for 1963–85 and at 1991 prices for 1982–93/94. 1982 was selected as the year to be used for conversion from 1966 to 1991 prices. Since output changes 1971–92 are only measured at 1966 relative prices, the conversion of 1971 output to 1991 prices is only approximate. Sector i in 1971 at 1991 prices is approximated as: [(sector i in 1971 at 1966 prices)/(sector i in 1982 at 1966 prices)].[sector i in 1982 at 1991 prices]. This has the advantage that, since 1982–91 GDP was calculated on a consistent set of definitions of sectors, changes in definitions between the 1966 series and the 1991 series only lead to a mis-estimate to the extent that they alter the growth rate of the sector between 1971 and 1982. Total GDP in 1971 at 1991 prices was then calculated as the sum of the sectoral outputs so revalued. Note that this will differ from a direct adjustment of total GDP in 1971 by the factor [(total GDP in 1982 at 1991 prices)/(total GDP in 1982 at 1966 prices)]. Sector shares in 1971 at 1991 prices are then sector output/GDP.

PRIVATE RESPONSES: ASSETS AND RISK

The increase in the cost of transactions during the period of social disorder will have widened the margins of traders and so enabled profits to be sustained and conceivably even increased. Collier and Gunning (1995) argue that this is a common feature of civil wars, and that because investment opportunities are severely curtailed, entrepreneurs build up large holdings of financial assets. In Uganda these assets took the form of dollars because domestic currency was manifestly not a viable way of maintaining the value of assets. Parallel with this exodus of financial capital there was an exodus of human capital as the educated saw their earnings in Uganda collapse, reflecting the disproportionate decline in

25

those sectors which used skilled labour. Potentially, these two external resources represent a 'peace dividend' for the economy. However, the realization of this dividend is neither automatic nor swift, since it depends upon the choices of many private agents to repatriate either themselves or their assets.

We begin with an implication of the accumulated high liquidity in foreign assets for domestic financial markets and then discuss the switch back into domestic real assets. Because of the large accumulated holdings of foreign exchange, the capital account is *de facto* open even prior to *de jure* liberalization. Hence, once the domestic financial market is liberalized, the domestic interest rate becomes set by the conventional open capital account condition that it should equal the interest rate on dollars plus the expected depreciation of the shilling against the dollar. In turn, the expected exchange rate reflected the credibility of the government's macroeconomic strategy. A transition government has had little opportunity to acquire reputation and the economy is subject to external aid shocks. Hence, private agents attach some probability to a high-inflation scenario. Interviews with the business community in March 1993 established that the consensus expectation of the exchange rate for the end of 1993 was 1500 shillings per dollar, as against 1200 at the time of the interviews. The differential between domestic and foreign interest rates prevailing at the time was consistent with those expectations of depreciation. However, in the event, the government's tight macroeconomic policy was sustained so that by late November 1993 the actual exchange rate had appreciated to 1150. The result was that real interest rates for borrowing denominated in domestic currency were around 30 per cent, whereas the real interest rate for those who were financing investment in foreign currency was around zero. This created considerable tension, since the entrepreneurs with foreign assets were disproportionately Asian, whereas newly entering African businessmen needed to borrow locally and were thus at a heavy disadvantage. This configuration of incredible disinflation leading to high real interest rates for a part of the business community is not unique to war-peace transition, but it may be a common feature given the conjunction of dollarization of financial assets and the likelihood of bouts of high inflation during the transition period as the budget is subject to shocks and the demand for money function shifts in an unpredictable manner. For example, no matter what a post-war Angolan government were to do, it would be unable initially to generate a credible expectation of sustained single figure inflation.

The domestic financial sector is doubly damaged by civil war and its aftermath. First, using the classification of the previous section it is transactions-providing, and so contracts sharply during the war. In addition, it is intensive in a government-provided service, namely a numeraire, and this is undermined both during and after the war. In those sophisticated economies where the government has a history of high and variable inflation, such as much of Latin America, the government nevertheless provides a numeraire through the publication of a reliable Consumer Price Index, permitting indexation of contracts. In Uganda the government is not trusted to produce a price index. In fact the government has invested in an accurate and rapid consumer price index, but in interviews it was evident that its use for purposes of indexation of contracts was not practicable, given private scepticism. Indeed, an article in *Uganda Confidential* had claimed (inaccurately) that the CPI was manipulated by the government. Hence, the domestic financial sector lacks a numeraire which can be trusted to maintain its value. The government therefore faces the dilemma that it either grants the private sector the inflation which it expects, achieving low real interest rates but high inflation, or maintains low inflation, yielding high real interest rates until private expectations adjust. The latter option continually wrong-foots the private sector. For example, during 1992–3 the government disinflated from an annualized inflation rate of 230 per cent to zero. Although this was unexpected, so that real interest rates became very high, the disruption cost was remarkably low. The economy grew at 7.2 per cent during the year. The reason for the low cost of disinflation was that there were few long-term contracts denominated in domestic currency and in particular few credit transactions. Thus, the legacy of the civil war was an inability of the domestic financial sector to function, and this in turn made disinflation an unusually cheap option. An implication is that the early post-transition years, during which the domestic financial sector is inevitably truncated, are a good time for the government to invest in a once-and-for-all disinflation. However, the price of this will be that the credit market will divide into a predominantly low real interest rate foreign currency-denominated market, and a minor but politically sensitive high real interest rate domestic currency market.

We now turn to the switch from foreign financial assets to domestic real assets. Although private investment recovered a little from the very low levels of the civil war period, even by 1993 it was only around 7 per cent of GDP according to World Bank estimates. This suggests that up to that date there had been little if any net repatriation into real assets. A household survey conducted in 1990 (Bigsten and Kayizzi-Mugerwa, 1994) asked some long-recall questions on asset transactions and migration, and so provides some basis for comparing the immediate post-war situation with that four years after recovery. One marked change was the increase in land transactions. Bigsten and Kayizzi-Mugerwa argue that this reflected the pent-up need for asset transactions and that, while peace enabled fairly small-scale land transactions to take place, transactions in other assets remained very difficult. In effect, social conventions related to land transactions were sufficiently strong for the restoration of basic social order to be enough to permit them without recourse to the more complex legal framework needed for other asset transactions. A second marked change was the reduction in urban-to-rural migration. This is again consistent with the reversal of the retreat to the rural economy induced by the war.

Private investment tended to be concentrated in three types of capital: housing, transport equipment and machinery for manufacturing. The housing boom is reflected in the National Accounts, where the construction sector expands substantially more rapidly than GDP, and in the Bigsten and Kayizzi-Mugerwa survey, which found a high incidence of house construction. The concentration on vehicles and machinery is found from the breakdown of investment in data supplied by the Uganda Investment Authority. As discussed in Collier and Gunning (1995), if private investors are worried about a reversion to 'war' this may be the expected pattern. An advantage of transport equipment is that it can be removed from the country if conditions deteriorate, and since it does not last long, the investor does not have to take a favourable view of the long-term future. Housing has neither of these features: it depreciates only slowly and it cannot be removed from the country. However, it is relatively immune to war since the flow of its services is not transactions-intensive and it is not highly lootable.

The housing boom has taken two forms, dwellings for owner-occupation and dwellings for rental to expatriates ('dollar houses'). The former are part of the subsistence economy. In effect, were agents to view peace as only temporary, they would use the opportunity of the temporary reduction in transactions costs to undertake the transaction-intensive business of investment, but locate the investment in the subsistence part of the economy. The dollar house is superficially precisely the sort of investment which might appear most difficult to attract: irreversible investment in the export sector of the economy. However, once the investment has been made, the activity is again transactions-extensive. The services provided by the house are not very dependent upon a production process and so are not transactions-intensive. When they are sold to expatriates, the latter can pay rent direct from one foreign bank account into another, so that the main transaction in this export activity is relatively immune from government control. Finally, in the worst case scenario (in which expatriates leave), the house can be occupied by the owner. Although not internationally mobile, the capital can thus be switched from the export sector into the subsistence sector. Collier and Gunning argue that the social return on irreversible investments in transactions-intensive sectors is higher than the private return, because the latter must allow for the risks of 'war'. Non-tradable investments are irreversible (whereas imported capital can often be exported if necessary). The private sector will therefore underinvest in non-tradable capital in the tradable sector (the latter being transactions-intensive). The evidence for this is that, of the investments reported to the Uganda Investment Authority (all large-scale investment in the economy), currently only around 3 per cent is going into agriculture, which is the sector most intensive in non-tradable capital. Tea estates, for example, could be rehabilitated at a far faster rate. Hence, there is a case for public inducement of private investment of non-tradable capital in the tradable sector. Collier and Gunning argue that during the 'war' private investment collapsed by more than private savings so that there was a substantial acquisition of foreign financial assets. Hence, private investment is not severely financially constrained so much as being deterred by high war-related transactions costs and perceived risks of a reversion to 'war'. The policy problem with respect to private investment is thus to encourage repatriation into the purchase of irreversible capital goods for the export sector. One way of achieving this is to offer substantial tax relief on such investments.

The retreat into a subsistence economy reduces average income sharply, and also leaves some private agents more exposed to risk: the representative urban household becomes more diversified, whereas the representative rural household becomes less diversified. The urban response is because of the collapse of incomes in the formal sector. As Bigsten and Kayizzi-Mugerwa show, by 1990 the typical urban household with a base in the formal sector nevertheless drew a substantial part of its income from informal activities, including agriculture. By contrast, the representative rural household loses remittances from urban households (there is evidence of a sharp decline in remittances), loses the chance to work in the rural labour market as the latter contracts disproportionately, withdraws from the non-coffee export crops almost completely, and reduces its earnings from coffee. Finally, as discussed below, whatever domestic financial assets it is holding evaporate due to inflation. Although there are large foreign asset holdings in the economy, these are clearly not held by the poorest households. Hence, exposure to risk increases in the rural economy just as the mechanisms for coping with risk are reduced. These features are altered only gradually by the restoration of peace.

To some extent, risk reduction in the rural economy is an externality provided by other agents. For example, opportunities in the labour market reduce risk even for those who choose not to enter the market and so enable more risky but higher-yielding production decisions to be taken. Hence, there is a social premium upon the reconstruction of markets because of the externality of risk-reduction. There is therefore a case for public subsidy of transactions. Although it might seem that such a subsidy would be difficult, in fact the government has a readily usable instrument at its disposal. One private transactions cost is the inflation tax on money. Agents need to hold money for transactions purposes and so loss of value of money implied by inflation is a cost which is borne not by economic activity in general but by transactions. If the recovery of the transactions part of the economy is socially too slow because the risk-reducing effect is an externality, then there is a case for subsidizing transactions. It is very difficult for the government directly to subsidize transactions, however; indirectly it is taxing them through inflation. Since the government is short of revenue (see below) there would be a case for setting the inflation tax at the revenue-maximizing level which may be around 10 per cent (see Adam, 1992 and Adam et al., 1993).

However, the case for subsidizing transactions tends to offset this case for an implicit tax. Logically, it is possible to subsidize transactions by means of a falling price level. However, a falling price level gives rise to side-effects to the extent that there are nominal rigidities such as wage rates. It might therefore be better to aim for price stability: the government forgoes implicit taxation of transactions in the interest of compensating for the externalities which transactions generate for risk-reduction.

GOVERNMENT RESPONSES: REVENUE

The war had undermined government revenue and thereby gradually reduced expenditure. However, whereas the share of government expenditure in GDP was radically reduced between 1971 and 1986, in terms of employment the government actually expanded. During the war the country acquired a very large and very low-price government sector. Post-war the share of government expenditure in GDP has reverted to its 1971 level, but the quantity of government has expanded less rapidly than GDP. Hence, the increase in expenditure has reflected an increase in the unit price of government. Comparing 1992 with 1971, the government was much larger relative to GDP in quantity terms though as a share of expenditure it was similar. The unit cost of government was much lower and the quantity of government was correspondingly higher. If the 1971 structure is viewed as normal, and so in some sense the target to be aimed at, the most striking feature is the failure to contract the quantity of government post-1986.

During the war the government had not been in a good position to borrow either abroad or domestically, and so it had resorted to the inflation tax. Adam (1992) estimates that the long-term revenue-maximizing inflation tax rate in Kenya has been around 10 per cent. Were it to apply approximately to Uganda, it would suggest that the actual rate of inflation had grossly exceeded the revenue-maximizing rate: the government had snatched a short-term gain in exceeding it, but this gradually reduced the real demand for money and so reduced the sustainable yield. By 1986 the government had few tax handles. The economy had shifted towards subsistence and transactions-extensive activities. The civil service had decayed to the extent that revenue collection was arbitrary and ineffective. Because of the exodus of the professional classes, enterprises were operated on an informal basis with poor book-keeping, and tax officials were not proficient in applying normal accountancy rules. The conjunction of these features made the taxation of enterprises a process of coercion countered by bluff. Although there are always elements of this in a tax system, the extreme form reached in Uganda implied that until the restoration of a well-functioning civil society, most notably in this instance a trustworthy audit profession, extra tax revenue from enterprises would to an extent be at the price of a higher incidence of coercion and arbitrariness: in other words, extra revenue from this source would be at the price of regression in the move to 'peace' in its wider meaning.

The government had relied heavily on coffee taxation. The fall in the world coffee price induced the government to repeal this tax, but it attempted to collect import duties more vigorously. This switch from export to import taxes is analytically immaterial. According to the Lerner equivalence theorem, the two have common effects, with two exceptions. First, that portion of imports which is not financed by exports now pays the tax, whereas under export taxation it would not. However, most of these imports are financed by government sales of foreign aid. Since private agents pay the market-clearing price for imports, if the government taxes them, then private agents will simply offer correspondingly less for the aid dollars. The government is therefore paying its own import duty by selling the foreign exchange more cheaply than it otherwise would. Secondly, that component of exports which is not coffee was untaxed during the phase of the export tax on coffee, but is implicitly taxed when trade taxes are levied on imports. In 1986 non-coffee exports were negligible and so this was not a significant consideration. Further, since it is very much in the economy's interest that exports re-diversify out of coffee, it is not clear that the government should want to tax them in the short term. Thus, if the case for dropping taxation of coffee was a good one, and it probably was, then there is little to be said for replacing it with taxes on imports. In response to the 1994 coffee boom the government re-imposed export taxes on coffee without reducing taxes on imports. This restored a very high tax burden on the coffee sector. Taking into account the shifting of import taxes onto the export sector, the tax rate on coffee exports was in excess of 50 per cent.

So far we have suggested that the government's major revenue options of extra taxation of enterprises and extra taxation of imports should not be exercised in the short term. Further, the risk externality argument set out above implies that the government should forgo the revenue-maximizing inflation tax. This implies that the government should not place much emphasis upon revenue recovery in the early phase of transition.

There is a final argument for low taxation during the transition phase. As discussed below, aid is endogenously very high during the early stages of peace. Since aid is channelled to the government, this enables public expenditure to recover more swiftly than private expenditure. As we have seen, public expenditure doubled as a share of GDP in the first five years of peace, fully regaining its previous level. It is arguable that this pace of recovery is too fast relative to the private sector. The most slowly adjusting component of the economy is a wide variety of private activities, including private consumption. Some private recovery is indeed dependent upon public recovery, and so to this extent it is justifiable for the public sector to recover at a more rapid rate. However, public recovery financed by higher taxation is directly at the cost of private recovery, and so the indirect effects need to be substantial for the net effect to be beneficial. As sug-

31

gested above, some of the indirect effects, such as the arbitrary coercion by the tax authorities, are negative. There is therefore a case for part of the aid (which is there to finance recovery in both the public and private sectors) being passed on indirectly to the private sector by reduced tax effort (relative to the no-aid counterfactual). In other words, even though the economy was generating very little government revenue, increasing that would not be a high priority. Donor conditionality of revenue recovery, by gearing up aid with tax revenue, forces a rapid recovery in the public sector which may be at variance with private sector needs.

During the war the Ugandan government was predatory and this is still how government is perceived by the population. During the early stages of peace this predation needs to be downplayed: what is most scarce during 'war' is not the material services of government, but coherent and restrained authority. Services can be expanded massively by the infusion of aid and any change through revenue is peripheral. In Uganda, public expenditure has more than doubled as a share of GDP, increasing by 11 percentage points of GDP. Revenue has also nearly doubled, but its increase of 3.6 percentage points is evidently a minor part of financing. The question is thus whether, given that public expenditure has increased by around 150 per cent, the marginal 18 per cent has been worth incurring the 100 per cent increase in predation which it cost. Might it not be more appropriate for there to be a temporary decrease in predation? If the objective is to re-establish the private activity conditioned on peacetime authority patterns, the critical path might be first to remove the wartime authority patterns rather than attempt to get public expenditure up to its peacetime share, regardless of the authority patterns which that effort must entail if it is to succeed. These considerations apply with particular force with respect to the taxation of the coffee boom windfall. Since this is a known temporary income gain (due to a frost in Brazil), the private sector can be expected to have a high savings and investment rate out of it, as did Kenyans during the previous coffee boom (see Bevan et al., 1992). High taxation of this windfall therefore transfers resources away from private investment, most especially investments by peasant farmers, to enhanced government revenue, a transfer which is unlikely to be growth-enhancing.

GOVERNMENT RESPONSES: EXPENDITURES

At the end of international wars it is usually possible to achieve a large and swift 'peace dividend' from reductions in military expenditure. In Uganda, far from there being a fiscal 'peace dividend', government military expenditure increased substantially in real terms for the first post-war years, not falling significantly until 1992/93 with a large demobilization of troops. Prior to this, military expenditure was seen as necessary to maintain macro-security, and there was also a fear that demobilization would give rise to micro-insecurity as unskilled ex-soldiers

32

turned to banditry. It is too early to assess whether the fears of macro-insecurity were well-founded, although post-demobilization there has been an upsurge in resistance fighting in the North of Uganda and part of the demobilized army probably joined the RPF army which success-fully invaded Rwanda in the early 1990s. The effect of the demobiliza-tion on micro-security was analysed in Collier (1994) by quantifying the impact of the different incidence of demobilization between districts on crime levels. The results showed that in the first three months after the demobilization it had had two statistically significant effects on crime. Those soldiers who, prior to demobilization, had described themselves as lacking access to land were around one hundred times more likely than the average Ugandan to commit crime. However, more than off-setting this, the large majority (88 per cent) of demobilized soldiers who had claimed to have access to land actually reduced crime. Local leaders confirmed that the presence of demobilized soldiers tended to discourage the existing criminals. Overall, in the first months after the demobilization crime fell by 7 per cent. Over the next year both of these effects disappeared: the demobilized, landless or not, became indistinguishable from the rest of the population as far as criminal activity was concerned. This suggests that the fears of micro-insecurity which had contributed to the delay in demobilization were probably exaggerated.

A second distinctive aspect of government expenditure which reflect-ed the legacy of the civil war was the prioritization of particular com-ponents of expenditure, notably the rehabilitation of transport infra-structure. We discuss first the evidence from project evaluations and then the perceptions of private households. The war had inflicted very substantial damage on transport infrastructure. In the first few years of recovery all major trunk roads were rehabilitated. Since all of these projects were largely donor-financed, they were subject to estimates of the social rate of return. While such estimates are necessarily fragile, they at least deploy a common methodology internationally. The post-war road rehabilitation projects are estimated to have had an average annual real rate of return of 39 per cent, considerably higher than both other Ugandan projects and transport projects in other developing countries. Further evidence is provided by private prioritizations of public services found in a survey of rural households conducted in 1990 (Bigsten and Kayizzi-Mugerwa, 1994). Respondents were asked to name the single biggest improvement in their area brought about by the government since 1985. For 34 per cent the biggest improvement was peace, and for 48 per cent it was the road network. These respons-es can be compared with those to identical questions asked in surveys conducted in Kenya in 1982 and Tanzania in 1983 (Bevan et al., 1989). In Kenya (in Central and Nyanza provinces) the most valued public expenditure over the preceding seven years was also roads, chosen by 43 per cent and 55 per cent of respondents respectively. Hence, the Kenyan average was virtually the same as the Ugandan. In Tanzania, by contrast, road expenditure was chosen by less than 10 per cent of respondents, the most valued service being primary schooling. Rural Tanzania in 1983 was in one important respect analogous to rural Uganda in 1986, namely, there had been a retreat from the market (though for somewhat different reasons). The low valuation placed upon road expenditure 1975–83 in rural Tanzania was not that the government had not made such expenditures, but that they were irrelevent to a peasant society which during this period was in retreat from the market. By contrast, the Kenyan peasantry in 1982 had over the previous seven years experienced the coffee boom and was deeply integrated into the market. Road improvements were consequently very important. The high valuation of road improvements in rural Uganda 1986–90 must therefore indicate not merely that peasants recognized that this was the main focus of the public expenditure commitment, but that the expenditure was actually found useful. Thus, there must have been a desire to reintegrate into the market.

The Bigsten and Kayizzi-Mugerwa survey also investigated what people now most wanted the government to provide. Further expenditure on roads was fairly low on the list of priorities. The most desired improvement was for health facilities (40 per cent) and the next most wanted improvement (27 per cent) was the streamlining of the functions of the local administration (the Resistance Councils). These responses can again be compared to the priorities given in rural Kenya in 1982 and rural Tanzania in 1983. As in Uganda, what people most wanted in the future was different from what they had most appreciated in the past. In both Kenyan provinces studied the most desired expenditure was on water supply, and in Tanzania it was on health services. Thus, in Kenya, although the reduction in transactions costs implied by road expenditure was most appreciated, 'the new demand was in effect for more labour time, since piped water replaced a very labour-intensive activity. The Kenyan prioritizations can be interpreted as the move from market integration to its consequence, an increased value of labour time. The Tanzanian valuations, a switch from primary schooling to health, can be interpreted as the response of a peasantry which saw less value in market integration and consequently had a lower opportunity cost of labour. The provision of free primary education in villages had largely satisfied the demand for this social service, leaving health care as the next social service demand. The Ugandan prioritization is distinctive, but it is closer to the Tanzanian than to the Kenyan. It is distinctive in that the high priority placed on the reform of local government institutions has no parallel. It is akin to Tanzania in that social services rather than output-enhancing services are demanded. However, within social service provision the ranking is somewhat different. In Tanzania, although health care was now the top priority, this was because of the satisfaction of the previous priority of primary schooling. In Uganda, primary schooling featured neither as a past priority nor as the future one. Hence, the prioritization responses are atypical for the region in that the design of local government is seen as an important issue, and greater weight was placed upon distress-related social services than either education or production-enhancing services.

It might seem surprising that the second most popular request should be something to do with local administration reform. However, this takes us back to the wider notion of how civil war has affected the economy. Our argument has been that the predominant route is not through the physical damage or risk of violence inherent in war, but rather in the more generalized breakdown in the institutions of civil society. While the former type of cost very largely ceased (except for a high incidence of crime discussed below), the rebuilding of civil society after a civil war is a slow process. Four years after the end of it, the second most important perceived need in rural Uganda was that the power of public officials should be contained and clearly demarcated. That this is ranked above everything except health care suggests that it is regarded as really important.

The relatively high demand for health facilities partly reflects their chronic deterioration during the war. The World Bank (1993a) estimates that by 1985 government real expenditure on health services had declined by 91 per cent from its 1972 level. In addition, the legacy of warfare and vagrancy was an unusually high level of sickness and debility.

However, the high ranking of health is also partly due to the relatively low demand for public expenditure on education. This is consistent with evidence on the private returns to education in rural areas. Bigsten and Kayizzi-Mugerwa construct agricultural production functions and find that formal schooling does not contribute to agricultural productivity in Uganda. Previous studies have found different results for Kenya, but the contrast is consistent with the Schultz hypothesis that while peasants are confined to traditional activities they are efficient, so that education is only useful in modernizing environments. War produces a 'traditionalizing' environment. A recent comparative study of the rate of return to agricultural technology transfer in various parts of Africa (Oehmke and Crawford, 1993) finds that Uganda during the period 1986–91 is a very rare exception to a general pattern of quite high returns. In Uganda the return was negative (Laker-Ojok, 1992). The negative return was attributed to the effects of the war, in part the costs involved in the reconstruction of buildings and staffing, and in part the lack of an adequate distribution system for seed and an adequate market for output. In such a context investment in innovation, whether public (i.e. technology transfer programmes) or private (i.e. education), does not pay. Bigsten and Kayizzi-Mugerwa also investigate the entry decision into non-farm enterprises using logit analysis and find similarly that in the small-scale business sector education plays no role in the entry decision. This again is likely to be the case only while the range of business activities is highly conservative. Essentially, until the economy has surpassed its previous frontier, there is no need for innovation and so the private returns to education are likely to be low. This showed up in the Bigsten and Kayizi-Mugerwa analysis of rural income distribution. The high income group was landed rather than educated.

The evidence from prioritization of past and future public expenditures therefore points to the Ugandan peasantry re-entering the market (and so valuing roads unlike their counterparts in Tanzania in 1983) but not yet to the extent that the valuation of labour time has risen much (so water supply is not demanded as it is in Kenya, but rather social services as in Tanzania). Within social services, both private priorities and objective evidence from earnings functions and the return on agricultural technology transfer point to the low return to education. The take-up of school places is correspondingly low in rural Uganda and we now consider whether this is a socially optimal response, given the circumstances which have produced a low rate of return, or whether there is a case for public intervention.

The decline in private investment in education need not be socially sub-optimal. While the private economy has retreated into subsistence and non-tradable activities, the social return to education has fallen and so the case for public investment in education is correspondingly reduced. However, the low current returns to education are likely to be temporary. Once the economy returns to the production frontier, the returns to education will then rise. Since the gestation period on primary education is extremely long, the returns now are a poor guide to the returns on new investments in education. There is a case for social intervention in that the present signals generating private decisions are a temporary reflection of the effects of war and so are predictably lower than the returns which will apply to children educated now. Private decisions reflect current returns, social decisions can legitimately anticipate what the returns will be once the economy has recovered to the old frontier.

CONCLUSION: COMMITMENT AND
ADJUSTMENT IN A FRIGHTENED SOCIETY

Dornbusch has recently suggested that the adjustment costs of policy reform are higher in societies which are polarized. The two key adjustments which he has in mind are disinflation and trade liberalization. The underlying argument is that polarized societies are particularly sensitive to redistribution and are organized so as to block it. Uganda does not accord well with the Dornbusch hypothesis. Whatever is meant by a 'polarized' society, it would be hard to maintain a definition on which, in the aftermath of a civil war, polarization is other than extreme: on to the disputes which provoked the war are added the legacy of atrocities committed during the war. Yet in Uganda, during 1989–91 there was a comprehensive trade liberalization, and during 1992 there was a spectacular disinflation from 230 per cent to -1 per cent. The ease of reform is perhaps explicable in terms of three features.

Economic aspects of the transition from civil war

First, few people benefit from a wartime regime. Government expenditure is so heavily skewed towards the military that, other than the political problem of demobilization, there is unlikely to be a major group which suffers from recomposition of public expenditure. In Uganda non-military public expenditure was such a small fraction of GDP that no group needed to be squeezed. The same is broadly true of trade policy. In Uganda the borders were sufficiently porous during the war for the underlying trade regime to be free trade other than for a certain level of export confiscation. In particular, it was not possible for industries to gain protection from imports by quantitative restrictions. Further, as discussed above, the transactions-intensive activities such as import-substitute manufacturing were particularly vulnerable to 'war' and so contracted. It was therefore a weak lobby and a lobby much more concerned with the ending of predation than the removal of trade restrictions which were in any case notional. With the gradual reduction in predation, the import-substitute manufacturing sector has been able to double between 1987 and 1993 despite trade liberalization.

Secondly, people have become used to flux and so have avoided the irreversible specific commitments which are the source of many of the redistributive effects of policy reform. The Ugandan disinflation is a remarkable instance. In most societies such a rapid disinflation would have produced enormous intra-private transfers. In Uganda the credit market was so limited that such transfers were small.

Thirdly, in Olsen's hypothesis, defeat in international war breaks up the domestic coalitions which normally block policy change. By extension, if civil war is resolved by defeat of the government as in Uganda (and Ethiopia), the vested interests which must be challenged are predominantly those of the enemy, and the fact that the regime has just been defeated means that the new regime has the power to impose change.

Hence, the period of transition to peace is a particularly suitable time for radical policy reform despite the high degree of polarization. The policy inheritance makes reform necessary, and the uncertainty surrounding prospective reform will reinforce the reluctance to make irreversible decisions until reforms have been implemented. Far from increasing uncertainty, speedy reform will reduce it. This is important not only because the reforms are desirable in themselves, but because it is the reluctance of the private sector to make irreversible decisions which is perhaps the major impediment to rapid recovery. After a civil war private agents are frightened. They are frightened of each other, and most of all they are frightened of the government in its various forms. The transition to peace is partly the reconstruction of damaged infrastructure, but primarily it is the transition from fear and the defensive responses which have become ingrained.

37

THREE

Developing industry in Uganda in the 1990s

Ian Livingstone

THE BACKGROUND OF POLITICAL AND ECONOMIC CHANGE

Current economic prospects in Uganda need to be seen against a legacy left by political turmoil and civil war extending through the 1970s and much of the 1980s, prior to the advent of the present NRM government in 1986. During the war of liberation which ended the Amin regime in April 1979, there was widespread destruction of infrastructure and of industrial plant, much of which was looted. During the period 1971–8 the economy declined constantly, GDP falling at an average annual rate of 1.6 per cent, implying, with a population growth rate of 2.8 per cent, a rate of fall of GDP per capita of 4.4 per cent. By 1980, real GDP per capita was only 62 per cent of that in 1971.

Within manufacturing, out of 930 enterprises registered in 1971, only 300 remained in operation in the early 1980s, with an estimated average capacity utilization in 1980 of just 5 per cent. In 1970 as many as 50 factories were functioning in the medium and large-scale sector: by 1981, 15 of these were non-operational, while capacity utilization in the remainder was about 25 per cent (UNIDO, 1990). In the small-scale sector, of 870 establishments operating in 1971 only 418 could be identified in 1981, of which 162 had closed and 256 were operating intermittently whenever input supplies and other conditions permitted.

Obote took up the Presidency again in 1980, after some short-term governments following Amin. Political divisions remained, however, with a further military coup in July 1985, and, after some improvement in the early 1980s, the economy declined again in 1984, when GDP at constant prices fell by 8.5 per cent and GDP per capita by 11 per cent. Negative per capita growth was recorded again in 1985 and 1986. During this period, with heavy military spending, the overall budget deficit expanded from UShs 22.2 bn in 1983/84 to Shs 63.1 bn in 1984/85 and Shs 164 bn in 1985/86. Funded by government borrowing at the Central Bank, this left an inherited situation of hyperinflation. During this inflation civil service and other formal sector wages were raised very little in money terms, reducing their real value to nominal levels and creating a serious problem of morale and efficiency within the public service.

This situation was inherited when, following a guerrilla war, the NRM came to power in 1986. This has been followed by a period of political stability and greatly improved security. In these conditions economic activity has begun to thrive, notwithstanding the obvious difficulties, and a GDP increase at constant prices of 21 per cent was achieved in the first three years to 1989, with annual growth rates of 6 or 7 per cent, and a particular improvement in manufactured goods production.

Table 3.1 contrasts what might be called the 'Amin decade', 1970–80, with the overall post-Amin decade, 1981–9. This brings out the damage done to the economy over the first decade, especially in respect of manufacturing and MVA (manufacturing value added) per capita, the latter declining at an average annual rate of over 11 per cent.

**Table 3.1 Comparative average annual rates of growth by economic sector
(at constant 1980 prices)**

Sectors	Period	Uganda	Africa	Developing Countries Total	Developed Market Economies
Agriculture	1970–1980	–0.6	0.2	2.3	0.9
	1981–1989	1.9	2.8	2.8	1.6
	1970–1989	0.3	1.2	2.5	1.4
Total Industrial	1970–1980	–10.0	2.7	4.7	2.9
Activity (incl. MVA)	1981–1989	4.5	2.1	3.1	3.4
	1970–1989	–5.1	1.4	2.5	2.7
Manufacturing	1970–1980	–9.1	5.0	6.6	3.1
	1981–1989	4.6	4.2	4.8	3.7
	1970–1989	–4.6	5.1	5.1	2.8
Construction	1970–1980	–8.5	8.1	8.6	0.7
	1981–1989	5.7	–0.9	–0.6	2.0
	1970–1989	–5.4	3.6	3.9	0.5
Wholesale & retail	1970–1980	–5.0	3.8	5.5	3.4
trade, hotels etc.	1981–1989	2.2	2.2	2.5	3.5
	1970–1989	–2.4	3.0	4.1	3.1
Transport, storage	1970–1980	–7.5	6.7	8.4	3.9
and communications	1981–1989	7.7	2.9	3.7	3.5
	1970–1989	–1.0	5.0	6.0	3.2
Other services	1970–1980	2.6	6.5	6.7	3.7
	1981–1989	2.0	3.3	3.4	3.5
		2.0	5.4	5.1	3.4
GOP per capita	1970–1980	–4.3	1.7	3.1	2.2
		–2.7	–1.2	0.2	2.6
	1970–1989	–3.3	–0.0	1.3	2.0
MVA per capita	1970–1980	–11.5	2.1	4.1	2.2
	1981–1989	0.9	1.1	2.3	3.1
	1970–1989	–7.6	2.1	2.6	2.0

Source: Industrial Statistics and Sectoral Surveys Branch, UNIDO. Based on data supplied by the UN Statistical Office, with estimates by the UNIDO Secretariat. UNIDO (1992) Table 1.2.

Growing out of poverty

Despite the progress made by the NRM government in re-establishing normal civil and economic life in Uganda, a further exogenous shock hit the economy with the collapse of the International Coffee Organization quota system in July 1989, producing a 40 per cent fall in one year in the price of coffee, almost Uganda's sole export at the time. In April 1990, the price of robusta of 57 cents/lb was actually less than half the 1985 price. There has been an accompanying decline in the volume of coffee exports, from an average of 151,000 tonnes in 1982–9 to 114,000 tonnes in 1993, this 25 per cent fall contributing to a fall in value of 67 per cent.

PROGRESS IN MANUFACTURING

The index of industrial production (Table 3.2) shows that there was no increase over the period 1982–4, followed by a substantial decline in 1984–6. From 1986 onwards, right up to 1993, there was a substantial annual increase in industrial output every year of between 7 and 24 per cent, producing an increase of nearly 150 per cent over seven years. Over half the increase in production after 1987 is accounted for by Food Processing and Chemicals, Paint and Soap and over two-thirds if Drinks and Tobacco is also included. This reflects the restoration of the domestic market and of the basic industries directed towards it. The substantial expansion in the Bricks and Cement sector reflects the reconstruction which has been going on.

What is noticeable is the failure of two specific industries to bounce back, Textiles and Clothing, standing at less than half the 1982 level, and Leather and Footwear, at below 40 per cent of the 1984 peak. Quantitatively, Textiles is much the more important of these.

Data for the production of principal manufactured commodities (Table 3.3) show the re-establishment of high levels of production after 1987 of beer, soft drinks and cigarettes (the last of these from 1985), while the production of cement, having fallen to just under 15,000 tonnes in 1988, was 3.5 times bigger in 1993.

The failure of textile production to revive, however, is again revealed, production here having declined since 1987 to just over 70 per cent of the 1987 quantity and only 40 per cent of that in 1982. To put the revival of the other commodities into perspective, however, a comparison with 1970 figures (Table 3.4) shows that in 1990 only in a few cases was production up towards the level of twenty years earlier: beer, waragi, cigarettes and animal feeds, with in only one case, soap, production substantially in excess of the earlier figure. In 9 out of 16 cases output was 16 per cent or less of the 1970 level.

The weak state of Ugandan manufacturing is further indicated by pervasive and serious excess capacity affecting most activities, as shown in Table 3.5. As can be seen, this condition has persisted over a long period, although there has been a distinct improvement compared with 1984, the number of activities in which capacity utilization is at least 20 per cent having increased from 10 out of 51 to 20 out of 54 in

Table 3.2 Index of industrial production 1982–93 (Base 1987 = 100)

Period	Food Pro-cessing	Drinks and Tobacco	Textiles and Clothing	Leather and Footwear	Timber Paper etc	Chemicals Paint & Soap	Bricks and Cement	Steel & Steel Products	Miscell-aneous	ALL ITEMS	% increase on pre-ceding year
NO. OF ESTABS	54	12	13	8	23	23	14	19	21	187	
WEIGHT	20.7	26.1	16.3	2.3	9.0	12.3	4.3	5.3	3.7	100.0	
Annual											
1982	106.7	48.6	196.7	77.9	68.2	64.6	163.7	81.6	87.6	97.3	–
1983	103.7	59.8	177.6	152.8	79.6	68.8	177.4	118.5	124.3	103.7	6.6
1984	99.8	79.4	136.9	175.5	88.7	61.2	156.5	110.7	139.5	101.0	-2.6
1985	93.9	84.8	98.9	86.9	76.8	58.6	122.7	133.1	139.1	91.3	-9.6
1986	85.3	82.2	92.9	90.0	72.0	58.8	120.6	105.9	141.0	86.1	-5.7
1987	100.0	100.0	100.0	100.0	100.0	100.0	100.0	100.0	100.0	100.0	16.1
1988	128.0	139.6	121.8	62.0	135.1	111.2	94.5	87.2	134.0	123.7	23.7
1989	153.7	143.7	132.7	62.9	169.4	162.9	109.0	98.9	204.2	145.2	17.4
1990	174.9	155.2	116.3	75.3	83.6	183.5	154.2	107.7	181.3	155.5	7.1
1991	227.4	176.1	110.9	60.1	198.2	192.9	162.6	149.3	251.2	178.2	14.6
1992	245.6	155.2	111.9	79.5	220.5	252.0	203.1	190.7	272.3	191.2	7.3
1993	246.3	170.9	93.5	68.4	237.8	339.2	263.7	258.5	371.1	214.3	12.1
Share of Increase 1987–93 (%)	26.5	16.2	-0.9	-0.6	10.9	25.7	6.2	7.8	8.8	100	

41

Table 3.3 Production of principal manufactured commodities

Period	Sugar	Beer (excl chibuku)	Soft Drinks	Cigarettes	Textiles	Cement	Electri-city	Laundry Soap
Unit	Tonnes	000 Ltr	000 Ltr	Million	000 Sq M	Tonnes	000 Kwh	Tonnes
Annual								
1982	3.289	9.787	1.795	745.0	18.557	18.471	559.800	n.a.
1983	3.133	14.206	3.953	645.0	16.607	30.780	515.500	n.a.
1984	2.943	14.817	5.784	965.8	11.475	24.921	614.400	n.a.
1985	808	8.184	5.002	1.416.4	10.418	11.749	626.500	n.a.
1986	0	6.603	5.049	1.420.1	9.733	16.376	637.200	2.902
1987	0	16.484	5.875	1.434.8	10.465	15.904	618.087	15.508
1988	7.534	21.139	13.431	1.637.6	11.067	14.960	565.900	17.929
1989	15.859	19.516	16.178	1.686.9	11.586	17.378	669.971	26.872
1990	28.915	19.420	24.275	1.289.7	8.172	26.920	736.500	30.816
1991	42.456	19.529	25.982	1.688.2	8.901	27.138	782.518	33.283
1992	53.539	18.718	21.769	1.575.0	9.650	37.881	986.278	38.660
1993	49.264	23.881	26.899	1.412.5	7.481	51.985	974.677	47.588

Source: Statistics Dept, MFEP, *Key Economic Indicators*, April 1994

1991, and the number with at least 50 per cent utilization from 2 to 10 (in order of utilization, soap, cigarettes, number plates, steel doors and windows, animal feeds, plastic jerry cans, cardboard boxes, motor batteries, plastic tableware, school chalk – all for the domestic market, it may be noted).

Table 3.4 Production of selected manufactured goods, 1970–90

	1970 –	1975 1984	1978 1985	1978 1986	1980 1987	1981 1988	1982 1989	1983 1990	1990 as % of 1970
Beer	27.8	38.8	22.5	9.8	12.2	7.3	10.0	14.2	–
(mn. litres)		15.1	8.4	6.9	16.9	21.5	19.3	19.4	70
Uganda Waragi	563	859	420	124	33	20	35	28	–
('000 litres)	–	32	153	116	159	157	364	376	67
Cigarettes	1536	1754	1303	598	629	205	746	345	–
(mn. sticks)	–	966	1416	1420	1435	1638	1586	1290	84
Cotton &									
rayon fabrics	49.6	33.5	28.4	15.1	208.7	19.4	20.0	17.0	–
(mn. sq. m.)	–	11.5	10.4	9.7	10.2	11.5	11.8	8.2	16
Blankets	1164	309	174	76	93	133	129	120	–
('000 pieces)		82	25	41	147	49	87	69	6
Soap	12925	3574	795	34	–	165	249	–	–
(tonnes)	–	1019	773	3291	15772	18452	27110	30552	236
Matches –									
small size	49.3	25.1	4.5	4.4	3.3	2.0	1.9	1.0	–
('000 cartons)	–	–	0.1	0.2	0.04	0.07	0.4	0.04	0.1
Matches –									
large size	–	6.3	2.5	2.5	1.6	0.4	1.6	1.5	–
('000 cartons)	–	–	–	–	0.4	0.4	0.2	0.06	0.9
(% = of 1975)									
Steel ingots	17.6	6.3	6.5	4.0	0.4	1.8	1.4	2.3	–
('000 tonnes)	–	1.4	2.5	0.9	0.9	1.1	–	–	0
Corrugated									
iron sheets	11.9	1.4	2.0	0.4	0.6	0.4	2.5	3.0	–
('000 tonnes)	–	2.0	2.4	1.1	0.6	0.7	1.4	1.3	11
Cement	191.0	98.0	44.0	2.0	10.0	8.0	16.5	30.8	–
('000 tonnes)	–	24.9	11.7	16.4	15.9	15.0	17.4	26.9	14
Paint	1.6	0.9	0.8	0.2	0.3	35	523	426	–
('000 litres)		396	436	298	170	176	315	148	28
(% = of 1982)									
Animal feeds	18.1	10.0	–	–	5.8	3.5	2.3	5.2	–
('000 tonnes)	–	3.1	4.2	6.5	12.2	11.0	16.0	15.0	83
Footwear	–	1586	1268	678	942	463	476	916	–
('000 pairs)	–	1136	582	547	664	363	359	319	20
(% = of 1975)									
Fishnets	489	299	141	47	36	12	38	75	–
('000 pieces)	–	59	28	33	47	52	55	62	13
Cycle tyres									
& tubes	–	503	746	353	85	20	–	136	–
('000 pieces)	–	150	126	100	37	110	2	18	4
(% = of 1975)									

Source: Statistics Department, Ministry of Planning and Economic Development.

Table 3.5 **Percentage capacity utilization in Ugandan manufacturing, selected establishments, 1984 and 1991**

Percentage capacity utilization	No. of manufactured products	
	1984	1991
0.0	7	4
0.1–	28	21
10.0–	6	9
20.0–	5	4
30.0–	2	4
40.0–	1	2
50.0–	2	4
60.0–	–	1
70.0–	–	1
80.0–	–	3
90.0–100	–	1
Total	51	54

Source: Statistics Dept., MFEP

Note: Establishments covered are those included in the Index of Industrial Production and do not necessarily reflect total production of manufactured commodities in Uganda.

These data are based on submissions made by the relevant firms. A direct survey of 20 establishments made in 1992 suggested that such estimates actually overstated capacity utilization, on average, in the sample, by about 8 per cent (Tumwebaze, 1992).

The most important causes of excess capacity mentioned by firms in the latter survey were, in order of importance, lack of working capital, lack of market demand, and shortage of the required inputs. Variation in utilization levels between activities, as well as the generally low level, appears to reflect demand as one important factor, and shows the problems which Uganda would face in pursuing a conventional import-substituting industrialization policy with a small domestic market and patterns of consumption constrained by domestic purchasing power and low incomes per head.

THE NEW CONTEXT FOR INDUSTRIAL DEVELOPMENT

Uganda may be said to have experienced its first industrial development strategy in the 1950s, when it was still under colonial jurisdiction. The Owen Falls Dam had been completed in 1950 and it was thought the cheap electricity forthcoming would give the country a significant advantage over its neighbours and provide the basis for industrial development. Its offsetting disadvantage in developing industry, its landlockedness, was not given any weight or much mention.

In part because of its advantage of cheap power, it entered into negotiations, subsequently, for economic integration with its two East African neighbours, and in the establishment in 1967 of the East African Community, with no sense of inferiority stemming from the other handicap. With its relatively good level of agricultural incomes, of course, it could offer a useful market, as part of the East African market, as a further selling point. There had been the Kampala Agreement of 1964 which attempted (unsuccessfully, as it turned out) to share out industries among the three East African countries, and then there was the Treaty for East African Co-operation itself, which included measures, such as the transfer tax system and the East African Development Bank, aimed at distributing industry within East Africa. It is reasonable to suggest that any strategy for industrial development during this period was based on a view of East African industrial development rather than one which identified the specific circumstances of Uganda. The East African strategy throughout the 1960s and 1970s was the standard one for the period, that of import substitution, though Uganda had to apply this with particular reference to its own market, while negotiating for some share of the larger East African market.

Further evidence of Uganda's ambitiousness in the area of industrial development, and a further reason for being ambitious, was that it had established a very effective vehicle for the accelerated development of industry in the form of the Ugandan Development Corporation (UDC), which had been set up as early as 1952. This was seen as a means not of nationalization but of generating new investment and activity, which was to be carried out through a combination of 'injector' and 'catalytic' roles (Nyhart, 1959). In the former case, where local or foreign private investment was less readily forthcoming, the UDC could take the initiative by directly establishing a subsidiary company in which it would have a majority holding. In the latter case, enterprises would consist of joint ventures in which the UDC had a minority holding. In practice a wide variety of arrangements for joint participation with private capital and enterprise were entered into. The spread of UDC interests was impressive and already in 1970 involved gross resources of nearly UShs 340 million (£17 m). More than half of these resources were in manufacturing and processing. The UDC by this time had established an international reputation as an exceptional and positive initiative in a developing country.

This strong platform for industrial development has been one casualty of the Amin period and subsequent disturbances, though how it would have progressed otherwise is difficult to say. But with the expulsion in 1972 of the Asian business community a large number of establishments were transferred to public sector management. At the end of 1989, there were 116 public companies, of which about 60 were industrial. The UDC in 1991 controlled just 35 companies, including tea estates, of which 28 were in operation. Only 4 of these were associated companies with a minority UDC holding, and the fact that 31 out of the

35 were subsidiaries reflected both the inherited more interventionist policy of public ownership and the limited recent interest of local and foreign private entrepreneurs. Separately from the UDC, many enterprises were owned directly by government ministries, in particular the Ministry of Industry and Technology, which was responsible for 45 parastatals. The Ministry of Agriculture owned a sugar mill and the Ministry of the Environment Protection several sawmills. A number of other enterprises were being run by the Custodian Board.

As indicated earlier, the condition of most of these state-owned enterprises has been poor. As a result the present government decided to adopt a policy of divestiture. However, it has made only slow progress, and other measures, particularly through the newly established Investment Authority, aimed at giving maximum encouragement to private local and foreign investment, are being encouraged.

In the new situation a very different, much reduced role is envisaged for the UDC compared with its hey-day. UDC shares are to be transferred to the Ministry of Finance, in the name of the Secretary of the Treasury, while supervision of the UDC will be the responsibility of the Ministry of Industry and Technology. The UDC will disengage from management and ownership functions, beyond a transitional stage, in respect of subsidiary and associated enterprises; these are to enjoy parity of treatment with non-UDC public enterprises, which will be autonomous, subject to certain monitoring and evaluation mechanisms. The UDC will thus abandon its 'injector' role and concentrate on a narrow 'catalytic' role, helping to initiate projects by serving as an industrial promotion agency, but divesting itself of shares after an implementation phase.

This much reduced role for the UDC, however inevitable in present circumstances, constitutes a significant change in the situation as compared with the 1960s. While the emphasis is now on active soliciting of new foreign investment, such investment must of necessity take into consideration the limitations of Uganda's small domestic market and its geographical handicaps within the regional market.

A third major change in circumstances stems from the wholesale expulsion of Asian businessmen in 1972. The Asian community had to a large extent monopolized the wholesale and retail trade, but also had major investments in manufacturing and plantations. The consequences have not been wholly negative, since the vacuum created has stimulated the growth of an African business class, while it is evident that the economy has now been effectively Ugandanized in terms of managers, technicians and skilled workers, whatever problems exist in respect of acquired skills and experience at all levels (many of the departing Asians were, of course, Ugandan citizens). Nevertheless, a gap has undoubtedly been left in terms of entrepreneurship, technical background and experience of industry, international market connections and access to capital, and it is likely that new African entrepreneurs will for these reasons involve themselves in smaller-scale indus-

46

trial activities, as well as trade and services. While former Asian entrepreneurs are being encouraged to return they may not do so in anything like the previous numbers and, as indicated above, may be much
more selective in their interests.

CHANGES IN THE TRADE SITUATION

The change which must be most emphasized here is that in respect of
Uganda's economic relations with its neighbours. While Uganda continues to pursue regional interests through the African Preferential
Trade Area (PTA), it does not at present have the same market advantages for manufactured goods as were offered to it previously through
the East African Community. The transport handicap associated with
landlockedness is, of course, even more serious in relation to PTA
trade, where overland distances and loading/unloading costs, which
constitute the most important transport costs, may well be doubled.
However, even within East Africa, the position has further altered since
the 1960s in that during Uganda's period of dislocation productive
capacity in neighbouring countries, particularly Kenya, capable of supplying their own domestic and the East African market, has also
expanded. This is particularly true of textiles, where a number of
plants have been set up over the years in both Kenya and Tanzania.

The difficulties facing the development of manufacturing for export
in Uganda can be seen by examining what was happening to interstate
trade in manufactures within the East African Community up to 1973,
before the major disruptions of the economy (Table 3.6). Comparing

**Table 3.6 Interstate trade in manufactures between the three East African
Countries, 1967–73 (Sh.m.)**

	1960	1967	1973
Total interstate trade in manufactures	–	690	855
Interstate manufactures exports			
from Kenya:	–	439	670
from Tanzania:	–	52	115
from Uganda:	–	199	70
Balance of trade in manufactures			
Kenya:	–	+238	+503
Tanzania:	–	-179	-191
Uganda:	–	-59	-312
Manufactured exports to other partner states as % of imports from other partner states:			
Tanzania:	11	22	38
Uganda:	93	77	18

Source: Hazlewood (1975)

Table 3.7 Exports (including re-exports) by commodity group, 1982–92

SITC Code	Group	1982 (US$000)	1992 (US$000)	1992 %	Increase 1982–92 (US$000)
0	Food & Live Animals	350710	117205	68.4	-233505
	(Coffee)	(349400)	(95140)	(55.5)	(-254260)
1	Beverages & Tobacco	9	4730	2.8	4721
2	Crude Materials excl. fuels	6349	40953	23.9	34604
	(Oilseeds & Nuts)	(0)	(22305)	(13.0)	(22305)
3	Mineral Fuels, etc.	9082	5149	3.0	3933
4	Animal & Veg. Oils & Fats	0	1	–	1
5	Chemicals	415	309	0.2	-106
6	Basic Manufactures	221	689	0.4	468
7	Machinery & Transport Equip.	4585	1512	0.9	-3073
8	Misc. Manufactured Goods	196	757	0.4	561
9	Goods not Classified by Kind	129	49	–	-80
	Total Exports and Re-Exports	371696	171353	100	-200343

Source: Statistics Dept, MFEP, *Statistical Bulletin* No. EXT/1, *Imports & Exports, Uganda, 1981–1992*, December 1993.

1967 and 1973, while Tanzania's trade balance in manufactures showed roughly the same deficit, a small deficit for Uganda had become a substantial new one. The momentum of industry in Kenya had expanded its own manufactured exports within East Africa considerably between 1967 and 1973, but Tanzania's exports had also shown an encouraging increase in value, whereas Uganda's had declined by 65 per cent. While Uganda's position in 1973 might already have been aggravated by political events after 1971, the trend in its manufactured exports to other partner states as a percentage of imports from them was already clearly downward from the impressive 93 per cent figure in 1960, indicating that Uganda had already been losing the advantages obtained by the bright start prior to 1960. It seems likely that transport costs and other locational disadvantages were already having their effects.

Table 3.7 shows the composition of exports in 1992, dominated by coffee, with oilseeds and nuts an important additional component. The two commodity groups containing these items (Food and Live Animals and Crude Materials, excluding Fuels) together accounted for 92 per cent of exports, while manufactured goods exports (and re-exports) in Categories 5–8 together accounted for only 2 per cent.

Table 3.8 shows that, while exports in the latter categories have remained negligible, imports in the same categories have expanded since 1981 by 87 per cent, and the negative balance of trade in them by about the same percentage. Looking specifically at Uganda's trade with

Table 3.8 Uganda: Imports and exports of major manufacturing categories, 1981–92

Code		1981	1982	1983	1984	1985	1986	1987	1988	1989	1990	1991	1992
						STC							
						Imports (US$ 000)							
5	Chemicals	26300	35019	31698	29092	27556	36858	48728	30113	38425	38806	37655	43770
6	Basic Mfrs	53661	45502	46575	61768	56573	71245	102529	92047	111075	86552	110631	114680
7	Machinery & Transport Equipment	98779	104327	97095	87923	96526	127312	239027	214207	211310	217913	198898	168994
8	Misc. Mfd. Goods	22433	32937	18832	23193	33249	37327	47303	42989	47291	51970	46396	49109
5–8		201173	217785	194200	201976	213904	272742	437587	379356	408101	395241	393580	376553
						Exports (US$ 000)							
5–8		2592	5417	2079	1640	3272	2184	2519	6204	3917	2459	2495	3267
					Balance of Trade (Imports–Exports) (US$ 000)								
5–8		198581	212368	192121	200335	210632	270558	435068	373152	404184	392782	391085	373286
					Balance of Trade (Imports–Exports) (1981 = 100)								
5–8		100	107	97	101	106	136	219	188	204	198	197	188

Source: *Ibid.*

49

Table 3.9 Uganda's balance of trade with PTA countries, 1981–92

(US$ 000)

Countries		1981	1982	1983	1984	1985	1986	1987	1988	1989	1990	1991	1992
Kenya	X	1339	1925	2496	3339	1423	3088	1804	1590	3374	6241	12354	16035
	M	126341	109495	112171	102826	89080	97575	92323	102807	92987	71133	82751	118357
	X–M	-125002	-107570	-109675	-99487	-87657	-94487	-90519	-101217	-89613	-64892	-70397	-102322
Tanzania	M	10707	931	2418	3448	1972	2130	3290	4583	6927	9541	13162	16959
Zimbabwe	M	55	0	22	154	578	1167	986	775	1794	6228	1486	1351
Sudan	X	108	13	27	37	61	180	0	243	587	1946	2839	3001
PTA, excl. Kenya	X	208	104	49	37	108	214	43	289	792	7249	5100	6396
	M	11061	1306	2455	4237	3667	7664	4813	6318	9423	16471	18284	22019
	X–M	-10853	-1202	-2406	-4200	-3559	-7450	-4770	-6029	-8631	-9222	-13184	-15623
Total PTA	X	1547	2029	2545	3376	1531	3302	1847	1879	4166	13490	21135	22431
	M	137402	110801	114626	107063	92747	105239	97136	109125	102410	87604	101035	140376
	X–M	-135855	-108772	-112081	-103687	-91216	-101936	-95289	-107246	-98244	-74114	-79900	-117945

Source: *Ibid.*
Note: X = Exports and Re-Exports, M = Imports

PTA countries in all commodities, it can be seen (Table 3.9) that Uganda has had a large deficit with Kenya throughout the 1980s. Its deficit with all other PTA countries taken together has fluctuated, though always negative, and has increased quite rapidly, more than three-fold, since 1987, due particularly to imports from Tanzania.

CURRENT LEVELS OF EMPLOYMENT IN MANUFACTURING

Both the long-term trends referred to and the major periodic disturbances have affected the structure of employment in Uganda. A recent World Bank report (World Bank, 1993) estimated the level and composition of urban employment in mid-1992, as shown in Table 3.10. If we guesstimate the share of manufacturing in informal sector employment as 20 per cent, this would indicate some 66,000 persons engaged in informal sector manufacturing in urban areas, to which one would need to add corresponding employment in rural areas.

Using the proportions shown by the 1989/90 Household Budget Survey for the distribution of population by primary activity, it is possible to estimate this distribution for mid-1992 as in Table 3.11. Industries are defined here to include both modern and informal sector manufacturing and construction, electricity, gas and water, but still account for only just over 3 per cent of workers, although they are 13 per cent of urban employment and 20 per cent of urban male employment. Thus manufacturing proper, as compared with Industry, is particularly small in Uganda, even by developing country standards. Formal sector manufacturing enterprises, defined as those employing 5 or more persons, employed only 53,500 workers in 1988, according to the National Manpower Survey, or only 0.8 per cent of the labour force. This indicates quite forcefully the problems of standard import substitution in a landlocked situation with a small domestic market.

Table 3.10 The distribution of urban employment in Uganda, mid-1992

Sector	No. (000)	%
Public sector	314.7	43.4
o/w Traditional civil service	97.9	13.5
Other govt/parastatals	216.8	29.9
Formal private (& misc) sector	80.4	11.1
Informal sector	330.7	45.6
Total urban employment	725.8	100

Source: World Bank, 1993a, Table 6.3

51

Table 3.11 Distribution of Ugandan population by primary activity, mid-1992

	Urban			Rural			Total	Uganda
	Male (%)	Female (%)	Total (000)	Male (%)	Female (%)	Total (000)	(000)	%
Agriculture	12.9	24.4	129.4	81.3	94.0	5103.1	5232.5	79.6
Industries	20.1	4.3	96.7	3.2	0.7	116.3	213.0	3.2
Services	63.6	66.5	470.9	15.2	5.1	613.0	1083.9	16.5
Unemployed	3.4	4.7	28.8	0.3	0.2	16.0	44.8	0.7
Total	100	100	725.8	100	100	5848.4	6574.2	100

Source: *Ibid*, Table 6.2
Note: Proportions assumed to be as indicated in the Household Budget Survey for 1989–90, for distribution of population by primary activity.

APPROPRIATE DIRECTIONS FOR NEW INDUSTRIAL DEVELOPMENT

The age and run-down condition of much industrial plant in Uganda, and the very low current levels of capacity utilization in most cases, have certain implications for the country's industrial development strategy in the 1990s. On the one hand, previous production levels point the way to what has been attainable in the past in the different manufacturing activities, and which might therefore be possible again. On the other hand, with the new circumstances referred to above and a situation approaching a *tabula rasa* in respect of manufacturing, rather than attempting automatic re-establishment of the original structure, which was criticized as representing the outcome of an entirely orthodox import-substituting policy, the opportunity should be taken of adopting a more careful and selective approach, based on a completely fresh look at possibilities and potential.

This should take account especially of the transport cost factor, affecting the capacity to export and types of export, and the small size of the domestic market, affecting the scope for production directed towards that market. The small domestic market suggests a bias towards small-scale industries and the avoidance of many products for which production exhibits economies of scale. Since an import-substituting strategy biased towards the consumer goods bought by the higher income groups is unlikely to be viable, any import-substituting response should be directed towards consumers with low or average incomes, including what have been referred to as 'appropriate products', i.e. those which satisfy the same basic requirements as more expensive versions but which can be produced much more cheaply.

Such products, simple furniture, for example, are often the products of small industry or the informal manufacturing sector, and use local materials. Such industry is capable of producing a wide range of the basic goods consumed by the population where incomes are relatively low.

Also relevant to industrialization policy and affecting the scope for conventional import substitution is the comparatively low degree of urbanization in Uganda. There was, between 1980 and 1991, an increase in the number of small towns, the number of towns of 20,000 people or more going up from 8 to 16. During this period also, Kampala grew at an average annual rate of 5.0 per cent, compared with an overall population growth rate of 2.8 per cent. At the same time, however, the proportion of people in towns of 20,000 or more grew from below 5 per cent to just below 8 per cent, very low even by African levels of urbanization. Uganda continues to have, therefore, a largely rural economy.

Not much study has been made of the implications of landlockedness for the industrial development strategy. One study (Livingstone, 1986) has shown that the relatively high cost of overland transport compared with sea transport means that landlocked countries suffer a major disadvantage relative to their coastal neighbours and that, because capital is mobile, transport costs will always favour the location of industry in coastal countries, other things remaining the same. In particular, any advantage in labour-intensive manufactures may be more than wiped out by the freight factor, cheap labour being equally available in coastal and transit countries.

High freight factors point to the need to concentrate on high value-to-bulk products for export, and also, with respect to the domestic market, on low value-to-bulk products, which enjoy a degree of natural protection. In respect of the domestic market there should also be maximization of local content: import content, not just in the form of materials and components but also in the form of capital equipment, increases the freight factor considerably. Local content also means an emphasis on resource-based industry and, with a substantial rural population, points specifically to dispersed rural industry.

The 1989 Census of Business Establishments in Uganda revealed a wide-ranging degree of import dependency among manufacturers, imports accounting for about 30 per cent of all purchases made by the manufacturing sector. There were, however, wide variations between industries: those which made 90 per cent or more of their purchases from abroad included chemicals, steel, plastics, paper and printed products and fabricated metal products, while beverages and dairy product purchases from abroad were about 66 per cent.

Manufacturing in the form of processing which reduces bulk may in effect carry negative external transport costs, so that resource-based industry is favoured in respect of the export as well as the domestic market. There may also be scope for resource-based manufacturing by landlocked countries for export to other countries still further inland, in this case Rwanda and Sudan.

Resource-based industry means in particular agriculture-based industry, agriculture being capable of generating strong backward or forward linkages, through processing and other vertically integrated industry, into manufacturing. The importance of forward linkages through agricultural processing is indicated in the recent Census for

53

Growing out of poverty

Business Establishments (Manufacturing Sector) which shows (Table 3.12) that coffee processing, grain milling, tea processing, sugar and jaggery, and cotton ginning provided 37 per cent of both value added and persons engaged. Two further natural resource-based activities, sawmilling, wood and straw products and mineral products, nec (brickmaking, etc), provided a further 4 per cent of value added and 9 per cent of persons engaged.

The textile industry was an important second-stage resource-based industry in Uganda, the products of which satisfy the high value-to-bulk criterion for an export industry, and still has potential, therefore, if cotton growing can continue its revival. A 1990 study (APC, 1990) projected a substantial expansion of production over the following 5 years to 155,400 bales. This would also offer opportunities for expanding the oil milling industry, which had in the past depended heavily on cotton seeds, and now has available a certain amount of sunflower seed and soya bean also.

A third major area is sugar production. With domestic demand for sugar expanding rapidly with population, the low level of domestic production during the 1980s led to the substantial importation of sugar. Revival of production during 1990–3 reduced imports by 60 per cent, but there remained scope for useful import substitution.

Apart from direct forward linkages into processing, however, demand linkages stemming from agriculture are important for the development

Table 3.12 **Composition of Ugandan manufacturing in 1989**

Activity	Employment		Value Added	
	No.	%	Sh.m.	%
Coffee processing	11097	20.6	7794	21.1
Textile goods	4378	8.1	2503	6.8
Furniture	3579	6.6	1393	3.8
Motor vehicle repair	3339	6.2	965	2.6
Sugar & jaggery	3266	6.1	3290	8.9
Grain milling	2870	5.3	1765	4.8
Non-metallic mineral prodn	2715	5.0	870	2.4
Spinning & weaving	2108	3.9	179	0.5
Beverages	2080	3.9	4103	11.1
Sawmilling	1970	3.9	657	≥1.8
Tea processing	1744	3.2	367	≤1.0
Fabricated metal products	1650	3.1	1529	4.1
Chemical products	1255	2.3	2107	5.7
Cotton ginning	1137	2.1	582	≤1.6
Tobacco products	719	1.3	3089	8.4
Total	53902	100	36994	100

Source: Census of Business Establishments, Manufacturing Sector (Establishments with 5 persons or more)

of rural small-scale enterprise. Hence future industrial development strategy must go hand-in-hand with agricultural development.

THE DEVELOPMENT OF SMALL INDUSTRY AND THE INFORMAL SECTOR

Small industry has performed an important and increased role in Uganda since the difficult period of the 1970s and 1980s when the large-scale sector was in retrogression. With the demise of substantial sections of the latter, small-scale and informal sector industries are more firmly established in the economy than they used to be, and are relatively more important. The return of general security has produced an impressive expansion of the sector, because of its close association with the level of agricultural incomes, though a geographically uneven one. The 'boom' in brickmaking and rural and urban house construction, carrying with it linkages in metal fabrication and woodworking, is particularly noticeable across the south and east of the country. By ensuring security, the government may be said to be playing an important enabling role in creating an environment in which small-scale enterprises (SSEs) can prosper. The need to provide such an environment, as well as the potential of the small-scale sector for labour absorption, is recognized in the 1989 manpower survey report (MPED, 1989), which states that:

> The potential of the informal sector to continue to absorb large numbers of yearly additions to the labour force will depend largely on the extent to which the various constraints facing it are removed and official encouragement is given.

The expansion and current importance of the sector were indicated in Table 3.10, which estimated employment in the informal sector as accounting for 45 per cent of total urban employment, four times as much as the formal private sector. Table 3.11 showed 20 per cent of the urban male workforce as being in manufacturing, much of this informal.

Despite this quantitative importance very little is known about the productivity and potential of the sector or rather different components of the sector (since it is known that it is a very heterogeneous one), and systematic research into informal sector manufacturing is clearly needed. An interesting study (Twinomujuni, 1992) showed that quite a wide range of 'capital goods' was produced in informal sector engineering workshops in Kampala and Jinja. These included equipment used in agro-based industries (maize and rice mills, coffee hullers, oil presses, crop shellers, jaggery mills, crop threshers), agro-oriented industries (ploughs, feed mixers for poultry and dairy animal feed, grass choppers/cutters), the transport sector (parts for motor vehicles, motorcycles and bicycles, tractor trailers), the energy sector (biogas burner frames, welding sets, battery chargers, water pumps) and construction (brick, block and tile-making machines, various types of saw, planing machines). While these products were not as professionally finished as their imported counterparts, they were produced in several illustrative cases at a fraction of the cost (excluding duties) of the imported version.

Worth noting also are estimates made in the 1989 Manpower Survey that SSE entrepreneurs (not just in manufacturing) were earning an average of UShs 84,000 per month and employees UShs 3,200 (excluding allowances, particularly housing), and employees in the private and parastatal large-scale sector UShs 11,300 p.m. More reliable estimates of the distribution of earnings and productivity across the sector are needed, however.

The Census of Business Establishments (Manufacturing Sector), referred to earlier, covers establishments of 5 persons and above only. Most microenterprises in developing countries are in the size range 1–4 persons (often 1–2). Of 640 microenterprises in Uganda none employed more than 3: about 3 out of 5 establishments covered estimated the capital required to start an equivalent enterprise as less than US$ 800 (MPEP, 1992, 1.1). Reference may also be made to a series of District diagnostic surveys carried out by the Ministry of Industry and Technology: out of 5 districts, including Kampala District, the proportion of manufacturing enterprises employing 1–5 persons varied from 53 per cent to 71 per cent, and the proportion employing 10 persons or fewer from 73 per cent to 87 per cent. The most important activities were, in Kampala, structural and fabricated metal products, followed by furniture, bakeries and grain mills, and in two of the rural districts (Mbarara and Kabarole) structural clay products, i.e. bricks etc., furniture, grain mills and bakeries.

Data were collected from these surveys in eight districts, including Kampala, regarding the problems with which entrepreneurs felt they were confronted. The most evident problem was that of capital shortage in the forms of working capital and finance, machinery, equipment and tools, and premises, including poor buildings, lack of workshops or sheds, stores or simply space in which to work (Table 3.13). While questionnaire responses in respect of stated capital needs are notoriously unreliable, casual visits to a few establishments readily support the view that a major handicap exists in respect of physical facilities, in very many cases, and in working capital and materials.

While not necessarily perceived as such by the entrepreneurs themselves, technical experience and skills are a constraint if the small-scale sector is to play a much more prominent and dynamic role in future, and produce a wider and more advanced range of goods. The potential is indicated by the fact that a few of the small enterprises have successfully innovated with new products, entirely without help from extension agents of any kind, while the majority continue to produce a limited identical range of items.

As indicated earlier, the broad return of security has been of major importance in providing an enabling environment in which SSE could flourish. One policy weakness, however, affecting SSEs negatively, and commented upon in a report (ApT Design and Development, 1992,

56

Table 3.13 Problems cited by small-scale manufacturing establishments in eight selected survey districts

Problem	Proportion of times cited (%)		
	Kampala	Other Districts*	Total
Capital, finance	19.3	22.8	21.2
Machinery, equipt., tools	12.4	13.3	12.9
Premises, space	11.3	8.7	9.9
Power availability and reliability	8.6	8.1	8.3
Transport	5.4	10.1	8.0
Price of materials	13.1	5.4	8.8
Scarcity, seasonality, unreliability of materials supply	0.0	9.9	5.5
Spare parts	3.6	6.0	4.9
Skills, training assistance	3.6	4.9	4.3
Markets, marketing	2.8	3.7	3.3
Taxes	5.1	1.5	3.1
Others	14.8	5.7	9.7
Total	100	100	100
(No. of establishments covered)	(3904)	(4834)	(8738)

Source: Derived from MOIT District Diagnostic Surveys
   * Including Jinja, Masaka, Mbarara, Mukono, Kabarole, Rukungiri and Lira

Ch. 6), is the level and unequal incidence of taxes imposed on the SSE sector. The tax with the heaviest impact on SSEs is the income tax, levied on SSEs through a deposit system, which has a number of separate effects. Further questions of relative burden arise in relation to tariff policy. Large-scale manufacturers continue to be protected by zero tariffs on the importation of machinery and equipment, with, in addition, high tariffs against competing imports. In contrast, small-scale industrial enterprises, as users of large-scale enterprise products, are often made to pay higher than international prices. They do not have the same exemptions and have to pay substantial tariff charges on materials, including alloy steel sheets and plates (20%), sewing machines (30%), tailor's scissors (30%), calculating machines (30%), weighing machines (20%), nails (40%), ball bearings (20%), butcher's saws (30%), woven fabrics (30%), man-made fibres (30%), sheep's or lamb's wool for blankets (30%), compressed fibre building board (30%), water-thinned paint (30%) and glazier's putty (30%) (quoted in ApT, 1992). These are likely to have significant effects on SSEs in metal working, including small-scale machine-making, woodworking, tailoring and garment-making, construction and housing, as well as many service activities.

CONCLUDING REMARKS

Industrial development in Uganda has been set back by the best part of two decades, and its large-scale industrial sector, largely inherited from the past, was in a state of substantial disrepair and excess capacity in 1986. In considering the position now, Uganda needs to examine its industrial development strategy *de novo*, recognizing that a number of the initial conditions have changed. It no longer has the early impetus of the UDC as a particularly effective vehicle for industrial promotion. The composition and experience of its entrepreneurial class have changed. Most important, its position within the East African market region is no longer the same, and the most direct factors affecting its economic situation, as regards industrial development, are that it is landlocked, with a substantial transport cost disadvantage, and that its own market is small. These factors suggest a strategy emphasizing resource-based industrial development, maximizing agriculture-industry linkages, small-scale industry, and 'informal' urban and rural manufacturing responding to the basic needs of the mass of the population. This need not preclude substantial development and contribution to economic welfare, in a dynamic context, by Ugandan industry.

Privatization as a development policy

Geoffrey B. Tukahebwa

The post-independence era (1960s and 1970s) witnessed the mush-rooming of Public Enterprises (PEs) in the former colonies of Africa. The PEs were created for various reasons in different countries. Basically, they were created for ideological and pragmatic reasons, the ideological reasons deriving from the socialist model of development, while the pragmatic ones include economic nationalism and lack of indigenous entrepreneurial skills and domestic capital. Nonetheless, the boundary between the two was blurred.

In Uganda, PEs were created in the post-independence era to provide goods and services, to take control of the 'commanding heights' of the economy and to spearhead industrial development which the indigenous private sector was incapable of undertaking because of lack of capital (Suruma, 1993). Some PEs, notably some marketing boards in the agricultural sector, especially the lint (for cotton) and coffee boards, were created before independence to facilitate the colonial government's monopoly in purchasing and marketing these crops, in order to restrict competition from other powers, particularly the United States and Japan.

In 1972, when the then President Idi Amin declared an 'economic war' and expropriated foreign-owned businesses and industries, especially those of Asians, there was a glut of PEs. The Amin regime's nationalization policy and expulsion of foreigners were purportedly driven by economic nationalism and the need to indigenize the economy. There was resentment against foreigners dominating the economy, as had been the case before independence. A survey shortly before the nationalizations revealed that 4,000 non-Africans controlled 70 per cent of the distributive trade, while 16,000 Africans were responsible for only 30 per cent of it (Udoji, 1975).

In Uganda, ideological reasons for creating PEs are not easy to isolate. Although many PEs originated during the period when the contest between capitalist and communist ideologies was at its peak, Uganda followed the model of a mixed economy (Suruma, 1993). The only time it showed strong inclinations towards the socialist model as such was in 1969 when the then President Obote issued a series of policy documents and statements collectively known as the 'move to the

59

left' (Tukahebwa, 1992; Low, 1991). His regime, however, did not live to implement these policies. Nonetheless, PEs continued to multiply and a survey carried out in 1992 revealed that there were 156 PEs in Uganda (PERDS, 1993).

This survey also revealed that, of the 156 PEs, 133 were commercially oriented and 20 were dormant. Many operated at a loss, with low capacity utilization, low productivity and decreasing liquidity. PEs are revenue-generating entities which are supposed to finance their operations and generate income for the national treasury. The reality, however, is that PEs in developing countries, including Uganda, have performed poorly (Abeywickrama, 1993; Ndongko, 1991; Nellis and Kikeri, 1989). Instead of generating revenue, they have become a drain on the treasury which finances their loss-making activities. For example, at the turn of 1993, of the 156 PEs in Uganda, only one, the New Vision Printing and Publishing Corporation, was making a profit (Tukahebwa, 1993). As policy instruments, PEs in Uganda have failed to achieve the objectives for which they were created, namely, to spearhead development through industrialization and commercial activities. The National Resistance Movement (NRM) government, which came to power in 1986, therefore decided to privatize them (*ibid.*).

Privatization of PEs is a world-wide economic reform policy that has attained prominence since the 1980s in both developed and developing countries. In industrialized economies, including the ex-communist countries of Eastern Europe and the former Soviet Union, as well as in most developing countries, private sector development is a policy priority, and privatization is now seen as one way to achieve this objective (UNIDO, 1993).

Whereas privatization is being carried out in many countries, the objectives, reasons, methods and results vary from country to country. In industrialized countries, the primary objectives are to achieve greater efficiency and competitiveness in the already established framework of an efficient capital market and a strong response from the private sector. In the ex-communist countries, privatization is part of a more comprehensive shift to a market economy. In the developing countries, the objectives are a mix of these two approaches and vary from country to country (UNIDO, 1993). In Uganda, however, there is currently still no framework of an efficient capital market and a strong private sector response.

In developing countries, though privatization can be seen as the corollary to the poor performance of PEs and the financial burdens of these countries, it can also be viewed as one of a gamut of structural adjustment policies imposed by external donors and creditors (Bienen and Waterbury, 1989). Uganda is one of these countries. At present, it is pertinent to note that the original objectives of the PEs have not been achieved. Thus one issue is whether the development which Uganda set out to achieve originally through PEs, and has not yet managed to achieve after more than two decades, will be accomplished through the present privatization policy, or whether it will turn out to be part of yet another vicious cycle.

This chapter will adopt Dudley Seers's definition of 'development'. He saw development as the creation of the conditions necessary for the realization of human personality, and contended that any evaluation of 'development' must take into account whether there had been a reduction in poverty, unemployment and inequality (Seers, 1984). He further argues that Gross National Product can grow rapidly without any improvement on these criteria, and that, in such a case, proper development has not taken place. He maintains that development must be measured on how it has affected the quality of life. To Seers, use of a single aggregative indicator of development such as per capita income which can rise without any reduction in poverty, unemployment and inequality, avoids the real problems of development. Thus the question to ask about a country's development is what has been happening to poverty, inequality and unemployment. If the three have become less severe, then we can talk of development. But, if one or the other has grown worse, and especially if all three have grown worse, Seers's view is that it would be strange to call the result 'development' even if per capita income had soared.

Seers says that this applies to the future as well as the past. He postulates that a 'plan' which includes no targets for the reduction of poverty, unemployment and inequality can hardly be considered a proper 'development plan', and that a government can hardly claim to be 'developing' a country just because its education system is expanding or political order is being established, if hunger, unemployment and inequality are significant and growing or even if they are merely static (Seers, 1984:24). I have quoted Seers at length because his thinking about development, though not contradictory to the commonly cited indicators such as national income, GDP, GNP, and per capita income commonly used by politicians, demonstrates that these indicators are not enough by themselves. Development must be seen, not just in figures or statistics, which are in most cases historical, but in people's present capacity to buy physical necessities and gainfully harness the environment around them.

Development is multi-dimensional and involves changes in structure, capacity and output (Baster, 1984). It has political, social and economic dimensions, however these may be defined. There is a tendency today to view development only in economic terms. Baster notes that it is dangerous to use the economic dimension alone as an indicator of development. To evaluate development, political as well as social indicators are also important. To assess whether a public policy like privatization will positively or negatively affect development requires looking at how it affects people. Development strategies which bypass large numbers of people are not effective for developing countries to raise their long-run growth rates (Meir, 1989). It is against these measures of development that privatization policy now in the implementation stage in Uganda will be assessed.

61

METHODS OF PRIVATIZATION

Privatization can be defined as 'a transfer of ownership or control from the public to the private sector with particular reference to asset sales' (van de Walle, 1989: 643). Privatization can take the form of outright sale or divestiture, equity sales, or management or leasing arrangements between government and private entrepreneurs. Privatization can be partial or whole. With whole privatization, the government divests itself completely from a PE and the private investor takes over ownership of the enterprise. Partial privatization takes the form of joint ventures, lease agreements or management contracts.

In the case of leasing out, the government retains full ownership of the PE but leases out operations to a private entrepreneur in return for a fee. In this case, lease agreements are normally signed. In the case of management contracts, the government transfers management of the PE to the private entrepreneur but retains full ownership. It pays the contractor a fee and the contract may or may not specify a performance guarantee. Another type of partial privatization is a joint venture, in which the government sells some shares to private entrepreneurs and retains a majority or minority share in the enterprise.

Choice of the method of privatization is normally related to certain objectives. For example, if the objective is to get fiscal relief, any of the above methods may be used. If the objective is to broaden ownership, the government may sell shares with limitations on the number of shares an individual entrepreneur is allowed to purchase. If the objective is to improve performance of the PE, privatization may take the form of a management contract or lease agreement. In Uganda, except for the sale of shares and broadening of ownership, the other methods have been preferred.

PRIVATIZATION IN THE UGANDAN CONTEXT

Privatization policy in Uganda is an integral part of the Structural Adjustment Programme (SAP) currently being implemented in the country. While SAPs vary in detail from country to country, the standard menu includes currency devaluations, raising interest rates to fight inflation, promotion of savings and allocation of capital to the highest bidders, strict control of the money supply and credit expansion, cuts in government spending, deregulation of prices of goods and services, export promotion, and privatization of public sector enterprises (Ecumenical Coalition for Economic Justice, 1990; Efange and Balogun, 1989). The intended benefits of SAPs are increased exports, increased investment, economic growth and, eventually, economic development.

The current SAP in Uganda has four main elements: liberalization of the economy, the return of expropriated properties,[1] reduction and control of government spending, and privatization of PEs. These policies are in the process of implementation. The focus here is on the privatization of PEs within the wider context of structural adjustment.

Privatization as a development policy

The Ugandan government's policy for public enterprise reform and divestiture (PERD) was first published in Gazette No.48 of 1 November 1991, but did not have legal force until 15 September 1993, when the law was enacted (Statute No.9, 1993). The stipulated objectives of privatization in Uganda are:

- to relieve the national treasury of the burden of the PEs' financial losses and capital expenditure
- to generate revenue for the treasury
- to promote and develop an efficient private sector, and
- to improve the performance of PEs retained by the government with partial or whole ownership.

The overall objective is to revitalize the private sector, increase economic efficiency and thereby generate economic growth and consequently development. The government's hope is that when the private sector is revitalized and production increased, it will raise income through increased tax revenue. This is a long-term objective whose achievement will depend not only on whether privatization is successfully completed or not, but also on how well the privatized PEs and the private sector in general perform. It will depend on whether the private sector is revitalized through new investment and on the type of investment which is attracted to Uganda.

For the purposes of privatization, the Uganda government has categorized PEs into five classes as shown in Table 4.1. This classification is not rigid. Statute No. 9, 1993 provides that the Minister responsible for finance may amend it or transfer a PE from one class to another by statutory instrument. For example, Uganda Posts and Telecommunications and the Uganda Electricity Board, which were originally in class I, are going to be privatized.

Table 4.1 Classification of PEs

Class	Share holding	No. of PEs	Action
I	100%	10	Retain
II	> 50%	17	Majority shares
III	< 50%	20	Minority shares
IV	Nil	43	Fully divest
V	Nil	17	Liquidate
Total		107	

Source: PERD Statute, No. 9, 1st Schedule, 1993

Institutional framework and implementation

The Uganda privatization law established a body known as the Divestiture and Reform Implementation Committee (DRIC) to carry out the reform and privatization of PEs. The committee consists of the

Minister responsible for finance as its chairman, the Attorney General, the Minister responsible for the PE to be privatized, the Chairman of the Economic Committee of the legislature, the Chairman of the Committee on parastatal bodies, the Chairman of the Uganda Investment Authority, and three eminent Ugandans (none of whom is a minister) appointed by the prime minister on the advice of the Cabinet. Although the DRIC is by law the body responsible for the implementation of privatization policy, it is not a technical committee. The institution that initially handled the 'nuts' and 'bolts' of privatization in Uganda was the Public Enterprises Reform and Divestiture Secretariat (PERDS).

PERDS, which has now been abolished, had two main adjacent departments, namely, the Divestiture and Reform Secretariats. PERDS was headed by a Co-ordinator who was also Secretary to the DRIC and responsible to the Minister of Finance. It was initially run by a large number of expatriate staff and was set up with the help of a loan from the International Development Association, an affiliate of the World Bank. PERDS's activities in privatizing and restructuring PEs were stated to cost Uganda US$ 65.6 million in loans and US$ 25.641 mn to be raised locally (Rutaagi, 1993). The privatization policy is currently being implemented at a cost of US$ 91.24mn, much of it borrowed. PERDS was more or less a technical organization to implement privatization, but it was scrapped by a presidential pronouncement early in 1995 after barely two years of existence. Privatization has now been put directly under the Ministry of Finance and the Minister of State has taken direct responsibility for implementing the policy.

However, the controversies that rocked PERDS have not been solved by the creation of a new unit. The issues of the valuation of the PEs and how to involve indigenous entrepreneurs remain as controversial as when PERDs existed. Two cases may suffice to illustrate this; Agricultural Enterprises Limited (AEL) and Uganda Fisheries Enterprises Limited (UFEL), the former privatized by PERDS, the latter by the newly established unit.

In the case of AEL, PERDS in agreement with a foreign firm put its value at US $ 7.5 million. This valuation was disputed by AEL's management, who valued it at US $ 36 mn. The PE was eventually sold for US$ 12.7 mn (Rugasira, 1995). These discrepancies in the PE's value, let alone the sale price, vividly demonstrate how imprecisely privatization is being implemented in Uganda. UFEL was commissioned in 1989 having cost US$ 14 mn received as a grant from the Italian government. Barely five years later the factory was privatized for US $ 1.1 mn (*New Vision*, 1 June 1995). This sum raised concern, not only among ordinary citizens but among some government officials who viewed it as a giveaway price.

Privatization policy was not popular with Ugandans from the start. To begin with, PERDS was instituted and began privatization activities before the necessary legislation was put in place. Secondly, citizens were not sensitized or educated about the policy and its benefits. Lack of a proper communication strategy and citizen participation in the privatization policy led to the National Resistance Council (NRC) or Parliament suspending the sale of PEs and PERDS' activities in March 1993 (*New Vision*, 5 March 1993). It took a closed session of the NRC eventually to pass the bill. This shows how contentious privatization has been in Uganda. Now, somewhat belatedly, the government has embarked on a propaganda campaign through advertisements in the newspapers, radio and a drama group to persuade the public that privatization is a good idea. In this campaign the government suggests there will be better jobs, education and health after privatization.

Moreover, since privatization has been legalized, there has been opposition to it. Opposition comes from the peasants in the countryside. At issue are the concessions or lease agreements to foreign companies to run hotel and tourist services in the National Parks, which the peasants have interpreted as selling their land to foreigners. Although the government has not conceded ownership of the National Parks as such, and is only privatizing hotel and tourist services, Ugandans are not aware of this and the benefits it may bring to the country. There is need for transparency and better communication of policy to Ugandan citizens. In the case of concessions in the National Parks, local government structures could be used to inform and educate the public. This would help to clear away the misconception held by most Ugandans that 'privatization is a deliberate policy decision taken by government to sell PEs to foreigners' (Onyach-Olaa, 1992: 14).

The PERDS statute provides for the following methods of privatization: outright sale of government holdings, or of the portions the government wishes to dispose of; negotiated repossession by previous owners; transfer of equity in exchange for the acceptance of existing long-term debt (debt-equity swaps); dilution of holdings through an increase of share capital to be taken up by new investors; joint ventures; management contracts; employee stock ownership plans; leasing; and BOT, i.e. build operate and transfer (Statute No.9, 1993). The statute provides that any of these methods can be used when deemed appropriate. Thus there is flexibility about which method to use, depending on the objectives and circumstances of the PEs to be privatized.

In Uganda, there is lack of domestic capital to facilitate the privatization policy. In a study of the role the Ugandan private sector might play in divestiture policy, it was found that, though Ugandan entrepreneurs were willing to purchase PEs, they were constrained by lack of resources (World Bank, 1991a). The World Bank noted that, while effective demand for divested enterprises rests mainly with foreign companies, the government would prefer to sell to domestic entrepreneurs. However, no policy has been put in place with regard to this. Although the PERDS statute stipulates that it is government policy to broaden the basis of ownership among Ugandans, this has not been the case. Broadening ownership can be achieved through the public offering of shares in the stock market. But no steps have been taken to create a stock market in Uganda or to help the fledgling Kampala Stock Exchange (KSE) to get going. It has been observed that there is no noticeable evidence of viable capital mechanisms to assist in the process of divestiture (Divestiture Secretariat, 1994). Thus the method being relied on is simply sale to the highest bidder.

The idea of floating shares has only recently been mooted by the government. The public securities bill was delayed in the NRC sectoral committee and was not enacted for two years (*National Analyst*, 7 September–5 October 1995). Even after such a long delay, the idea still seems a long way from becoming policy. Serious consideration of public flotation by the government was sparked off by the opposition to the sale of the Uganda Commercial Bank (UCB). The NRC insisted that indigenous entrepreneurs should be involved in its purchase, but such conditions cannot be enforced when the highest bidder method is used. The UCB is the only bank in Uganda that has provided substantial credit to rural farmers, and is also the only bank with branches in remote areas of the country. Opponents to its sale contended that, even if a PE made no profit but rendered a vital service which the private sector could not provide, it should still be maintained under government ownership.

With regard to the objective of spreading ownership of privatized PEs, the Zambian and Nigerian examples could provide lessons to Uganda. In Zambia, as in Uganda, there is limited availability of domestic capital. The Zambian privatization law, unlike that of Uganda, emphasizes distribution of ownership among a broad segment of the population. Aware of the capital constraint, the Zambian law, adopted in 1992, provided for the establishment of a Privatization Trust Fund (UNIDO, 1993), which is supposed to hold shares on behalf of Zambian investors until they are able to purchase them. In addition, credit is to be offered to certain classes of investors who will be allowed to repay in instalments. If such procedures existed in Uganda, local entrepreneurs would be able to participate in the privatization process. The Zambian law also limits foreign participation. It states that foreign participation is to be encouraged when it is necessary to develop the export market, or where the nature of the business requires global linkages and international exposure, or where foreign investment or technology is required to expand the capacity of operations (*ibid.*, 1993). In Uganda, there are no such restrictions. The PE to be privatized is taken by the highest bidder, regardless of whether the bidder is indigenous or foreign. This puts local entrepreneurs with limited capital at a disadvantage. The likely consequence is that the privatized PEs will be taken over by transnational corporations and will thus deepen Uganda's external dependence still further.

In Nigeria there is a restriction on how much equity in a PE being privatized an individual or individual group may purchase. Nigeria has implemented its privatization through the stock market. Its procedures provide that no individual or individual group can acquire more than 1 per cent of the PE being privatized, the only exception being when the PE is taken over by the management (UNIDO, 1993). The implication is that the government's policy is to broaden ownership of the privatized PEs among its citizens and to avoid majority holdings by foreigners. Even in joint ventures, the government sells its shares through the stock market rather than allowing its foreign partner to acquire the enterprise. For example, the Nigerian government did not permit the local Volkswagen enterprise to increase its shares beyond its holding of 40 per cent, when it decided to remove itself from this particular joint venture.

Uganda's privatization policy is an open one. It is designed to attract foreign investment, which is a cornerstone of NRM government economic policy, expected to be achieved through privatization together with the accompanying liberalization and deregulation policies. With regard to privatization, however, the expected foreign investment seems not to be forthcoming very quickly. In a review of the divestiture programme, it was noted that the momentum of investor interest was weakening and responses to bid invitations had dwindled (Divestiture Secretariat, 1994).

As the trend stands now, privatization in Uganda, if there is no change in policy, will be dominated by foreigners. Signs of this have already emerged. For example, of a total of 17 lease agreements signed between Uganda National Parks (UNP) and private companies to run tourist and hotel services formerly run by UNP, only 5 were leased to Ugandan companies while the remaining 12 have gone to foreign companies. Concession agreements provide that the lessee pays an annual fee of US $2,000, with no specific period for review. These are indeed concessional terms, yet the agreements are to last for 30 years. The agreements also give the lessee an exclusive zone of 40 sq. km where the company operates as a monopoly. This provision does not tally with the principles of liberalization and the spirit of competition. It is more or less creating islands of monopoly in the national parks. Also, the agreements do not provide for protection of the environment. National Parks are national heritages which should be protected. These agreements should set standards to ensure protection of the environment.

In a related sector, the Game Reserves Department, one game reserve (Kyambura Game Reserve) has been leased to the Zwilling group, a transnational corporation. This lease has attracted criticism for two main reasons. First, the deal is uneconomic; the lessee pays the modest fee of US $10,000 per annum to the government. Secondly, it has affected the local community adversely. When Zwilling took over, it prevented the local people from hunting and fishing in the reserve (*New Vision*, 10 November 1994). The local people have thus lost an important source of food (game meat and fish). On the other hand, the lessee has reportedly been shooting more animals than the number specified in the agreement. Thus there is the issue of post-privatization monitoring and regulation. The problem of regulation after privatization applies not only to this case but to other sectors as well. The question is whether Uganda has the capacity to successfully regulate the activities of powerful transnational corporations taking over PEs. The answer may well be in the negative because of the country's weak regulatory system and the widespread corruption among officials enforcing the regulations. Despite these problems, however, the NRM government is committed to privatization.

The most outstanding PE so far privatized through a management contract is the former Kampala International Hotel. In this particular case the government has handed over the management of the hotel to the Sheraton Management Corporation but retained ownership of it. This management service agreement was signed in 1987, and was to last for ten years with the provision to extend it for another ten years. Management of the hotel was privatized after it had been rehabilitated at a cost of US$21 million. The government pays Sheraton the cost of the basic incentive licence and reservation fees which total up to 18 per cent of the turnover. According to the contract, even if the hotel fails to make a profit, Sheraton will still be paid its basic and incentive fees. No performance guarantee is specified within the contract.

The government is determined to divest itself from the hotel business. Uganda Hotels Ltd, a PE holding, had hotels all over the country. Most of them have been privatized. These sales have been opposed especially by the management and board directors. In the case of the White Horse Inn and Hotel Margherita, a challenge to their sale was lodged in the courts. At issue was not only what the opponents regarded as illegal sales, but that they were sold for less than their full value.

PRIVATIZATION AND DEVELOPMENT

It has been pointed out that in Africa policy-makers created PEs because, among other reasons, they thought they were panaceas which would lead to industrialization and ensure fair distribution of income (Ndongko, 1991). This has not been realized. The reasons commonly advanced for the failure of PEs to perform satisfactorily in earlier times include political interference, lack of clearly defined objectives, lack of managerial skills and corruption (Abeywickrama, 1993). However, PEs have played an important role in the economy. For example, in the early 1980s PEs in Africa contributed 17 per cent of GDP, and in the mid-1980s 54 per cent of non-agricultural employees in African countries were employed by the public sector (UNIDO, 1993).

In Uganda, the public sector is the biggest formal employer (excluding peasants). Information on unemployment in developing countries is poor and there is no decent study of how privatization affects unemployment (Bienen and Waterbury, 1989). In Uganda, however, privatization is bound to lead to unemployment in the short run, partly because the PEs have been overstaffed, and partly because companies taking over PEs want to reduce wage bills. Some of the privatized PEs

Privatization as a development policy

have already started retrenching workers. For example, since October 1993, the government has paid out about US$3.7 million as retrenchment settlements to former employees of 9 PEs which have been privatized (*New Vision*, 4 September 1995). Moreover, retrenchment in the PEs has been concurrent with retrenchment in the civil service and demobilization in the army. Thus the natural pool of the unemployed has actually swollen in recent years. Privatization may therefore be discounted as a development policy according to Seers's definition of development. It is, however, important to note that in Uganda there are no accurate employment statistics and the actual rate of unemployment is therefore not known. In its annual budgets the government always keeps quiet about it.

With regard to inequality, SAPs in general and privatization of PEs in particular have failed to address this issue. The methods of privatization so far used in Uganda have ignored the distribution of these assets to a wider population. In Eastern Europe, notably Hungary, as well as in Russia, the question was tackled by issuing cheap share certificates to citizens. In Zambia, allowing private entrepreneurs to purchase on credit and repay in instalments permitted people without cash to participate in the privatization process. This in a way addresses inequality at one level. In Nigeria the provision that no individual can acquire more than 1 per cent of any PE is a deliberate policy to avoid concentration of ownership. Inequality of incomes is caused by many factors and cannot be attributed to any single policy such as privatization. Seers contended that it was associated with other inequalities, especially in education and political power, which reinforced it (Seers, 1984). Nonetheless, there is no reason why a public policy that is developmentally oriented should not attempt to address this matter.

As regards poverty, the reality is that in Uganda living standards, especially in the countryside, are not improving (Mamdani, 1995). The worsening standard of living, however, cannot be attributed to the single policy of privatization but to the overall economic policy of the government as embodied in the SAPs. 'Cost-sharing' in health and education started in 1990 (Uganda Government, 1990), and this only compounded poverty in the country. The school drop-out rate, largely due to a lack of money for fees, has been a vivid testimony to the depth of poverty in Uganda. Only 70 per cent of children of school age enter primary one, and of these only 18 per cent complete primary education. The proceeds from the sale of PEs are not earmarked for poverty alleviation programmes as such in Uganda. Mamdani contends that the reality of privatization is that it has introduced a new and more vicious round of corruption from which foreign nationals and state officials are the sole beneficiaries. He further argues that, rather than hurting government officials, privatization has proved to be a bonanza for them. Opportunities for corruption unleashed by the privatization programme have coincided with a lack of accountability in higher-level Resistance Councils to aggravate the situation still further.

The proceeds from the divestiture of PEs are to be deposited in the divestiture account in commercial and development banks and the money will be used to promote industrial development by Ugandan entrepreneurs (Statute No. 9, 1993). The statute further stipulates that employees who become redundant as a result of restructuring or liquidation of a PE are to be compensated from a redundancy account to be opened in a commercial bank. The redundancy account acts as some sort of safety net. However, the statute does not mention where the money is to come from. If it is to come from the proceeds of divestiture, no specific percentage has been earmarked. Although the divestiture account is supposed to provide investment capital for Ugandan entrepreneurs, no specific industrialization programme has been put in place to link up with it. A specific programme is needed showing the priority industries and the requirements for entrepreneurs to acquire this investment capital. It is doubtful, however, whether the amount to be realized from divestiture is substantial enough to foster meaningful industrial development. For example, information from the Divestiture Secretariat reveals that as of 30 June 1995, a total of US $ 86.72 million had been realized from 47 PEs divested. From this amount, US $ 3.7 mn had been paid out in retrenchment settlements, while US $ 4 mn had been used to capitalize Kinyara Sugar Works, a PE currently operating under a management contract. Other payments from the divestiture account amount to US$ 3.807 mn, made up of creditor settlements, salaries and wages arrears, taxes, and audit and legal fees. Out of the US$86.72 mn realized from the sales only US $21.81 mn is in cash (*New Vision*, 4 September 1995). From the above data, it can be seen that the proceeds from privatization may well not be sufficient to provide a basis for indigenous private sector industrial development in Uganda.

While the private sector development emphasized through privatization and the enhancement of market mechanisms can result in economic efficiency and effective performance, it also has its own imperfections. In privatizing PEs, the possibility of 'market failures' needs to be considered. Failure of public ownership should not be taken as automatic proof that private entrepreneurs will do better, especially in the Third World where economic environments are often distorted and difficult (Nellis and Kikeri 1989). In Uganda where there is no stock market, very limited capital, a weak internal market due to low incomes, and a demonstration effect in consumption patterns, the private sector may well find it difficult to take root.

CONCLUSION

There is no doubt that PEs have performed poorly and have been a drain on the national treasury in Uganda, either through the treasury financing their losses or the government underwriting loans for them. The PEs failed to achieve the objective of industrialization and development, let alone fair distribution of wealth within the country. They have done little or nothing to alleviate the poverty in which the majority of Ugandans live. One of the major reasons why they failed to perform earlier at least at a profit on a corporation level, was political interference. It was the politicians who decided to create the PEs, and they are the ones who have decided to privatize them. In Uganda, the principle of privatization extends beyond PEs to include education and health. Including education and health among privatization candidates in future is likely to aggravate further inequality and poverty in the country.

Privatization may increase production efficiency but it does not in itself increase industrial capital in Uganda. Moreover, the proceeds from privatization which are earmarked to promote industrial development are in fact very meagre, and so far there is no information on private entrepreneurs who have acquired investment capital from them. The scale of modern industrialization is beyond the capacity of most Ugandans, and it may be premature for the government to withdraw from the industrialization sphere.

Privatization in Uganda has so far not achieved its stipulated goal of developing private entrepreneurship. Unless there is a change in the way the policy is implemented, this goal will not be achieved at an early date. Middle-level entrepreneurs who lack large amounts of capital will remain on the sidelines, as transnational corporations take over the remaining PEs. Privatization policy in Uganda has ignored the broadening of ownership which is one way to promote local private entrepreneurship.

Political interference which affected the performance of PEs in earlier decades is not absent from the privatization of the same PEs today. In Uganda, the decision on which PE to privatize and when, is a political decision rather than a technical one. Before its dissolution, the Divestiture Secretariat had complained about political interference and how it distorted its work plan (Divestiture Secretariat, 1994). Moreover, PERDS has been dissolved and the new unit has been set up by presidential pronouncement. Experts should be left to do their job, once the politicians have decided which PEs to privatize.

Privatization may not be the only option. Both PEs and market solutions may fail. One alternative might be to devote more emphasis to ways of monitoring PEs rather than focusing on the ownership structure or privatization alone (Bardhan, 1993). More emphasis might be placed on creating high powered incentives within the company, and on decentralizing the PEs to local and regional governments. This solution may not work in Uganda, however. The problems that affected PEs under the central government also affect them under local governments. Privatization policy may be well intentioned, but its implementation leaves a lot to be desired. A strategy which excludes many people and has no explicit targets to reduce unemployment and poverty, as is the case with privatization policy in Uganda, is not developmental in Dudley Seers's sense of the word. Privatization may lead to an increase of GDP, which stands at about 6 per cent in Uganda today, but this alone does not constitute true development.

71

Notes

1. These are properties that were nationalized in 1972 when the then president Idi Amin declared an 'Economic War' which basically meant chasing away foreigners (who were mainly Asians) and confiscating their properties. Repossession of these properties is actually reprivatization. The repossession exercise has now been completed and the government is currently in the process of selling unclaimed properties to the highest bidder.

FIVE
Changes in poverty patterns in Uganda

Vali Jamal*

Accounts of 'collapsed' African economies abound. Uganda was once in this category and, despite a number of years of sustained recovery under President Museveni, average incomes are still one-tenth below their peak at the start of the 1970s. 'How do people cope?' Part of the answer was given in a 1985 paper (Jamal, 1985) and refined in a paper under a section with the same title at the second Uganda Conference in 1989 and published in *Changing Uganda* (Jamal, 1991). The two papers showed the vast changes in household survival strategies and pointed to the resilience of agrarian economies where subsistence agriculture is still the mainstay for a majority of the population. In this chapter I want to look at the quantification of the economic decline in much greater detail, using GDP data stretching back to the 1960s, with a view to establishing trends in incomes as well as income distribution. Secondly, I shall look at the poverty situation around 1990 based on the Household Budget Survey of 1989/90. Finally, the two pieces of analysis will be brought together to look at trends in poverty. All these are 'new activities': economic decline has so far not been fully analyzed in its proper context, and the HBS has yet to be extensively used. Conclusions and policy implications will be discussed in the final section. Three appendices contain the technical details – on statistics, poverty lines, and export pricing.

ECONOMIC COLLAPSE: INCOMES AND STRUCTURES

The quantification of economic decline in Uganda, particularly in terms of income shifts, remains sketchy. Part of the reason is that data are often lacking and, when available, unreliable. Yet a reasonable picture can be pieced together from the more usual GDP figures, suitably disaggregated, combined with data on wages and agricultural prices. Procedural details are given in Appendix 5.1 and results for selected years reported here for discussion.

*The author is Rural Sector Specialist at the International Labour Organization, Geneva. The views expressed, however, are in his personal capacity. Thanks are due to Teddy Brett, Martin Doornbos, Walter Elkan, Ian Livingstone, Erisa Ochieng and Ritve Reinekka for constructive comments on an earlier draft.

Growing out of poverty

Figure 5.1 shows the various phases in the progress/regress of incomes in Uganda, with real per capita GDP used as the indicator, broken down by its agricultural and non-agricultural components. Up to the early 1970s incomes were increasing steadily, with GDP growth managing to stay above population growth in all years. As is generally accepted, 1972 was the turning point. In the next eight years, aggregate GDP fell by 19 per cent, which translated to a decline of *44 per cent* in average terms. Sustained recovery can be said to date only from the late 1980s, with GDP growing at an average 6 per cent per year between 1987 and 1995. But even then the 1995 average income was still around one-tenth below the peak in 1970. To put it differently, if the economy manages to maintain its 6 per cent per year trajectory it will only be at the turn of the century that average income will regain its 1970 level, whereas, had the growth rate of even 1961–9 been maintained (5.6 per cent per year), average income should have more than doubled.

The differential trends in agricultural and non-agricultural incomes, due it may be pointed out, to a collapse of the urban economy between 1972 and 1980 combined with continuing high rates of internal migration, meant that the rural/urban – or more accurately agricultural/non-

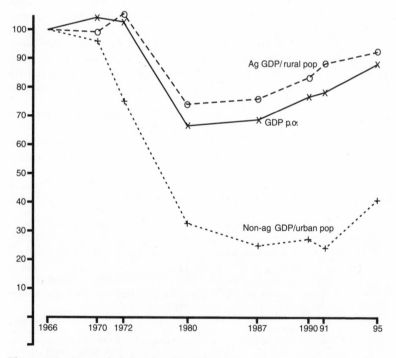

Figure 5.1 *Income decline and incline, 1966–95*
Source: Tables 5.AI.2 and 5.AI.3

agricultural – gap narrowed considerably up to 1991, but thereafter widened quite sharply as growth picked up in the towns. Given that agricultural incomes were much lower than non-agricultural incomes – and still are – the implied redistribution of income up to 1991 was in the 'right' direction, although we should note that quite a large part of this came from simply a 'collapse' in urban incomes rather than redistribution *per se*. Yet there was an aspect of the latter as food prices increased much faster than the general cost of living and as cash crop prices increased – or more strictly, were increased – much more than warranted by external prices (see Appendix 5.III). Thus agriculture's terms of trade improved and some of the increase in farm incomes came at the expense of urban dwellers. Unfortunately, it came mostly at the expense of wage earners, whose wages fell by as much as 85 per cent between 1972 and 1984 (Jamal, 1991, Table 5.4). Urban income distribution thus turned against the wage earners; by 1987 the average non-agricultural income was over seven times higher than the minimum wage and at least four times higher than the average wage.[1] *Prima facie* this implies a maldistribution of income – from wages to profits. Trends after 1991 were unmitigatedly in the direction of greater inequality – rural-urban as noted, but also intra-urban as wages did not increase anywhere as fast as the non-agricultural GDP (almost 9 per cent per annum, 1991-5).

One other gap features heavily in any discussion of income distribution in Uganda – the North-South divide. In the economic decline, cotton, which was practically the only cash activity in the North of Uganda, was wiped out as ginneries broke down and prices fell. The decline in cotton also affected the peripheral South – i.e. Jinja and Mbale – but they were hurt even more by the collapse of the modern sector on the departure of the Asians in 1972. (The population of Jinja and Mbale actually declined in the 1975–85 period.) The core South, of course, suffered most from the collapse of the modern sector, while its farming sector was hit by the demise of cotton and price declines for coffee, but at least coffee production held up. After the mid-1980s, food sales began to increase to feed Kampala, and Kampala itself regained its stature as the foremost centre of economic activity in Uganda.

CHANGING STRUCTURES

It may be discerned that Uganda's economy now operates on a completely different mode from that of the early 1970s. Two changes in particular are noteworthy: (i) in the urban areas the economy has become informalized, in both monetary and numerical terms; (ii) in the rural areas the economy has shifted towards food production. Both shifts are distress-induced, although in both we may see some signs of optimism, certainly in the second.

Uganda is still one of the least urbanized countries in Africa, with just over one-tenth of its population classified as urban in the early 1990s compared with at least three times as many for sub-Saharan Africa as a whole. The starting base was low – less than 5 per cent urbanization at the time of independence – and rural-urban migration too has been relatively low.[2] But employment growth in towns was even lower, at times even stagnant. Most migrants ended up in the informal sector. Some very rough calculations show that, whereas at the time of independence only 10 per cent of the urban labour force could be attributed to the informal sector, this proportion had increased to 40 per cent by 1980 and to 65 per cent by 1990.[3] The economy became informalized even more fundamentally in monetary terms, with the total wage bill declining significantly as a proportion of non-agricultural income, and quite a large part of the rest going to the informal sector. In the rural areas also there was an 'informalization' of sorts in that the locus of activity shifted away from cotton and coffee which were traded formally to food crops, which were either not traded, being consumed on the farms, or traded through informal channels.

Table 5.1 can be used to indicate the outlines of the informalization process, apart from other vital structural changes. In 1967 the wage bill came to 22 per cent of total GDP or 31 per cent of monetary GDP. Equivalent figures are not available after 1977 but an estimate can be

Table 5.1 Structure of GDP, 1967, 1981 and 1990
(1967, old shillings million, 1981 and 1990, new Sh.m.)

	1967	**1981**	**1990**
Agriculture	2706	1558	819709
Non-monetary	1437	868	510017
Staples	1100[a]	698	388146
Monetary	1269	690	363273
Cotton	286	)	)
Coffee	451	) 44[b]	) 26049[b]
Staples	160	310	196828
Livestock	237	265	97556
Wages			
African	701		
Non-African	396		
Operating surplus			
African	389		
Non-African	600		
Parastatals	170		
Total GDP	4962	2665	1537098
Non-monetary	1437	980	510017
Monetary	3525	1685	1027081

[a] Estimated. [b] Mentioned against 'cash crops' in the source.
Sources: Uganda Government: *Statistical Abstract, 1967*, for 1967, with estimates as derived in Jamal, 1976a and b. MPED, 1992b for 1981 and 1990. Only the main items are shown under monetary agriculture. Figures for 1967 are in old shillings, the rest in new shillings (=100 old shillings). As only yearly proportions are being derived the different currency figures may be shown together.

attempted based on the number of wage employees and the average wage. The wage force in 1981 was around 350,000 and each wage earner earned (old) Sh.20,000 per year. Both these are generous estimates. The wage bill was thus new Sh.70 million, compared with which the monetary GDP was estimated at (new) Sh.1,685 mn – wage share 4.2 per cent. In 1990 wage employment was still 380,000.[4] The average wage had climbed to Sh.72,000 per year, yet the wage bill (Sh.25.5 billion) came to just 2.5 per cent of monetary GDP. The point is that, even with the most liberal estimates, the share of the wage bill is not likely to climb into double figures, a far cry from the 30 per cent range in 1967.

As for 'informalization' in the rural areas, as the table shows, in 1967 cotton and coffee generated *58 per cent* of the total cash income in agriculture, whereas by 1981 they (as well as other cash crops) contributed only 6.4 per cent and by 1990 7.2 per cent. The quantum of exports declined by two-thirds and producer prices dropped even more, accounting partly for the above figures. In the meantime, food crops in both quantity and prices experienced quite the opposite trends. In 1967 only 13 per cent of food crops ('staples' in the table) was traded, whereas in 1981 this share had increased to 31 per cent and in 1990 to 34 per cent. *Matooke* (plantain) prices alone increased by one-third in real terms between 1981 and 1990.

INCOMES AND POVERTY PROFILE, 1990

In this section we shall derive an incomes and poverty profile of Uganda at around 1990 with the help of the Household Budget Survey of 1989/90. Three caveats should be noted. The HBS was conducted during a period of political unrest and some districts such as Kumi and Soroti (Eastern Region), and Gulu, Kitgum, Kotido, Lira and Moroto (Northern Region) could not be enumerated. Thus, the figures for these two regions are partial. Secondly, the survey reported expenditures without any correction for price differentials among regions and between monetary and non-monetary consumption. However, a rough calculation indicates that these price differentials were narrower than might be expected[5] and hence, as a first approximation, and considering the use to which such data can be put, the 'raw' figures may be utilized to provide an indicative picture of living standards across the country. The third caveat is of a more general nature, relating to the accuracy of data thrown up by an HBS. Prudence would require that the resulting figures be considered no more than indicative.

Table 5.2 shows the class distributions as well as average household and per capita expenditures[6] in the regions and main towns. Turning first to the expenditure figures, for Uganda as a whole the average monthly household expenditure was estimated at Sh.34,468, with the rural-urban differential 1: 1.7, i.e. urban areas had 70 per cent more expenditure than rural areas. In per capita terms, the equivalent figures were Sh.6,328 and 1: 2.1. As noted, GDP figures show considerably more rural-urban inequality, signifying that urban incomes were

Table 5.2 Distribution of households by monthly per capita expenditure by regions, rural/urban and Kampala. Also total number of households, persons, and average expenditures, 1989/90

Monthly p.c. expenditure	Central			Eastern			Western		
('000 shillings)	Total	Rural	Urban	Total	Rural	Urban	Total	Rural	Urban
0–5	33.4	41.1	7.4	58.9	62.7	16.6	39.4	40.8	17.1
5–10	36.5	38.4	30.5	27.2	26.9	29.8	41.4	42.4	27.1
10–15	13.4	11.0	21.4	8.0	6.8	20.6	12.4	11.9	20.6
15–20	8.0	5.1	17.7	3.7	2.5	17.7	3.8	3.5	9.8
20–30	4.5	2.3	11.9	1.3	0.6	9.3	1.9	1.1	13.1
30–40	2.6	1.3	6.8	0.5	0.4	1.7	0.5	0.0	8.5
40+	1.6	0.8	4.3	0.4	0.1	4.3	0.6	0.3	3.8
Memo items									
Households	1065257	819683	245574	671987	615809	56178	866508	816191	50317
Persons	5660563	4571951	1088612	3517153	3272324	244829	4918952	4692050	226902
Expenditure (sh/m)									
Households	41334	36477	57546	25856	23695	49548	36621	35813	49723
Persons	7779	6514	12990	4940	4462	11364	6451	6228	11025

Continued opposite

Table 5.2 *(cont'd)*

Monthly p.c. expenditure ('000 shillings)	Northern			Uganda			Kampala
	Total	Rural	Urban	Total	Rural	Urban	
30–5	68.3	69.4	57.5	44.6	49.2	13.4	5.0
5–10	25.7	24.8	34.3	34.8	35.5	30.2	29.0
10–15	4.5	4.6	2.9	10.9	9.6	19.9	20.9
15–20	1.0	0.9	2.3	5.1	3.5	15.6	19.9
20–30	0.5	0.3	2.0	2.6	1.3	11.0	12.7
30–40	1.0	0.0	1.0	1.2	0.5	5.9	7.7
40+	0.0	0.0	0.0	0.8	0.4	4.0	4.8
Memo items							
Households	283664	258204	25460	2887416	2509887	377529	199435
Persons	1629485	1490637	138848	15726735	14027544	1699191	868658
Expenditure (sh/m)							
Households	22652	22087	28380	34468	31645	53346	59944
Persons	3943	3828	5207	6328	5662	11853	13763

Source: MPED, 1991, Tables 1.13, 1.17, 1.21, 1.25 and 1.29

under-recorded in the HBS. The Central Region led the country, with the highest household expenditure – around Sh.41,330 – followed by Western, Eastern and Northern Regions. Among the cities, background figures show that Entebbe came first (Sh.70,295), followed by Jinja (Sh.66,117), Kampala (Sh.59,944; Sh.13,763 per capita), Masaka (Sh.57,234), Mbarara (Sh. 51,147) and Mbale (Sh. 48,459). The Gini coefficient on data uncorrected for price differentials is of the order of 0.35–0.4 for both rural and urban areas and falls to around 0.3 on the corrected data, signifying that the top 10 per cent of the population accounted for 30 per cent of the total expenditure, while the bottom 30 per cent had 10 per cent.

What can be said about poverty? Obviously at a per capita income (in 1990) of Sh.94,000 (equivalent to 13 kg of sugar per month[7]), everyone in Uganda, except the top 5 per cent, must be considered poor. For the purposes of analysis, however, we have to try and capture the core poor and this can only be done by defining a poverty line – and an austere one at that. Those falling below this line could be considered poor in an absolute sense. I have indeed chosen a very basic poverty line – in fact two, one costing a minimum food basket and the other a food + non-food basket. The procedure is discussed fully in Appendix 5.II. Different regional food poverty lines were computed to reflect regional diet patterns. The poverty lines were set against the expenditure distributions derived from the HBS (Table 5.2) to obtain estimates of poverty. Table 5.3 shows the resulting poverty lines and poverty incidence figures.

First, it may be noted that although we are costing a 2,200 calorie food basket (food poverty line), its price varies from a low of Sh.1,590 for the rural North to Sh.3,990 for Kampala. There are price differentials for the same commodity across regions – and even within the same region;[8] but the bulk of the difference arises from the diet chosen – millet-based in the North and *matooke* (cooking banana) -based in Kampala. Each millet-calorie costs only one-fifth as much as a *matooke*-calorie.

In the rural areas the incidence of food poverty was estimated at around one-quarter. The North, despite its low 'income' figures, had about the same amount of food poverty as the Central Region, a reflection of the low cost of the millet-based diet. Background figures show that Apac and Nebbi were the poorest districts in the north and Kamuli in the east. The districts excluded from the HBS – Gulu, Kitgum, Kumi, Soroti, Moroto and Kotido – would also be found to be food-deficient. In the urban areas 10 per cent or so of the population could be counted as food-poor according to the above definition of poverty. Kampala had only 4 per cent food poverty. The high incidence of food poverty in the rural areas is somewhat unexpected, given the general impression of food self-sufficiency in Uganda. Disturbed conditions in the Central and Northern Regions could well be held responsible.

When we expand the definition of poverty to include essential non-food items – again the most basic ones – the picture changes quite substantially. Around 35 per cent of the rural population and 16 per cent of

Table 5.3 Poverty lines and poverty incidence, Kampala and regions, 1989/90, and poverty line, Kampala, March 1992

	Poverty line (Sh. per capita per month)		Poverty incidence (% of households)	
	Food	**Total**	**Food**	**Total**
Kampala	3990	7980	4	23
Central				
Rural	2730	4095	22	32
Urban	2850	5700	4	12
Eastern				
Rural	2460	3690	31	46
Urban	2850	5700	10	21
Western				
Rural	2610	3915	21	32
Urban	2910	5820	10	21
Northern				
Rural	1590	2385	22	33
Urban	2280	4560	26	32
Memo item:				
Kampala,				
March 1992	8550	17100		

Source: Appendix Table 5.AII.2.

the urban population are now shown to be in poverty. Kampala had just under a quarter of its population in poverty. Since rural areas comprise over 88 per cent of the total population, poverty is very much a rural phenomenon in Uganda, with over 90 per cent of the total poverty.

POVERTY TRENDS

How did poverty change? Quite evidently, based on trends in incomes established in section I, urban poverty was much lower at the start of the 1970s – in fact even non-existent on the above definition of poverty – while in the rural areas too it was lower, although not by as much. Urban wage figures attest to the first assertion. Thus at the start of the 1970s, 60 per cent of the monthly minimum wage would purchase sufficient calories from *matooke* for an average family, whereas by 1990 the whole of the minimum wage would purchase only one week's supply. In the rural areas subsistence (or non-monetary) production held up pretty well and cushioned the fall in agricultural cash incomes. The urban situation is worth analyzing further for its insights into the changing nature of poverty in Uganda. Figure 5.2 will be used for this.

In 1964 the minimum wage was Sh.150 per month, and what could be called an average unskilled wage somewhat higher at Sh.175. This

Growing out of poverty

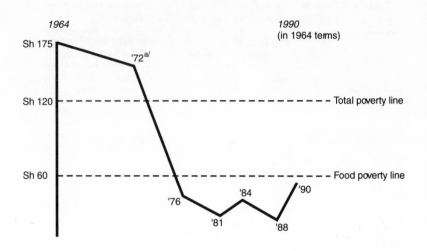

Average unskilled
wage = Sh. 175 p.m.

Consumption survey[c]
Food = Sh. 80
Milk, meat, fish = Sh. 25
Calories = 7,422 for 3.36
  members
For 4.36 members[e]
Food poverty line: Sh. 60
Non-food poverty line: Sh. 60

Average unskilled
wage = Sh. 15,000 p.m.
(Sh. 52 in 164 terms)[b]

Poverty line[d]
Food = Sh. 17,400
Non-food = Sh. 17,400

Figure 5.2 *Average real unskilled wage, 1964-90, and a comparison of 1964 and 1990 wages against Kampala household poverty lines, 1990, in 1964 terms.*

Source and notes: Explained in the text.

[a] Approximate movement of real minimum wage. Source: Jamal, 1991, table 5.4
  and updating.
[b] Inflation: 1964 = 100; 1990 = 28,850.
[c] Refers to MPED, 1965.
[d] Poverty line for a family of 4.36 members from Table 5.AII.2.
[e] Expresses 1990 poverty line in 1964 shillings.

82

kind of wage afforded quite a reasonable standard of living, gauged from a consumption survey conducted amongst unskilled workers in Kampala in 1964 (MPED, 1965). Average expenditure was found to be Sh.158 per month, of which one-half went on food. The total number of calories obtained was 7,422 and hence a family of 3.36 was being supported. Sixteen per cent of the total expenditure was devoted to meat, fish and milk, for a calorie contribution of 4.8 per cent; in other words, the average unskilled wage was high enough to afford the more proteinous, but also more expensive, foods. Even 'hotel food' figured in the wage earners' outlay, not to mention bread, tea, and sugar (which, along with the dairy products, were deliberately excluded from our consumption basket in 1990). Our basic diet in Table 5.AII.2 would cost only Sh.46 for the 3.36-member family or Sh.60 for a 4.36 family, while the minimum non-food basket would cost another 60 shillings. Thus a monthly expenditure of Sh.120 would bring the same sort of standard of living as the poverty line of Table 5.AII.2. As the average (unskilled) wage earner earned Sh.175, he enjoyed a standard of living 1.45 above the poverty line. In 1990 the average unskilled wage had risen to Sh.15,000 per month, but this was still less than even the food basket (by 14 per cent) – a 'killing wage', as it is often called in Uganda.

The question we ask ourselves is how much did average *household* income fall? The 1990 wage was only 30 per cent of its value in 1964 but, as I argued in my 1985 paper (Jamal, 1985), by the time we get beyond 1975 we can no longer speak of a 'wage earner household' because the average urban household becomes multi-occupational, straddling the formal as well as the informal sectors and the rural as well as the urban. Members start trading on the side and households start to grow food in the garden and to acquire supplies from rural-based kith and kin. To equal the 1964 average wage the household income has to reach Sh.50,000 – i.e. over three times the 1990 average wage. This does not seem likely: living standards have visibly fallen in Kampala. To equal the poverty line, the household income has to reach Sh.34,800 – i.e. over twice the minimum wage. This could well be the case. The average income for the bottom 80 per cent of the urban population in the HBS – the average of which may be identified with the 'average' urban household – came to Sh.38,500. Of this, Sh.15,000 would be from wage income. The rest would have to be made up from: (i) informal sector trading; (ii) urban farming; and (iii) food remittances from rural-based families. The importance of these activities for urban families is now fully accepted (Obbo, 1991; Maxwell, 1994), though how much in shilling terms the various 'survival strategies' actually contribute has not been quantified.[9] Neither is it known whether all urban strata can equally access these survival strategies. If we accept the figure from the HBS for the bottom 80 per cent of Kampala's population as corresponding to an average figure, this would imply a decline of 30 per cent in average low-income households compared with 1964.[10] Based on a hierarchy of needs – staple foods, clothing, rent, transportation, superior foods, household durables, entertainment – a 30 per cent decline would preclude of all expenditures beyond transportation.

The situation seems to have improved since 1990.[11] Private sector wages have in fact been increasing since 1988 and the trend has continued after 1990. By 1992 the typical unskilled wage in the industrial sector was Sh.35,000, a gain of 20 per cent in real terms over 1990. The poverty line at March 1992 prices was put at Sh.74,556 per household (Table 5.AII.2).[12] Hence, in keeping with the rise in real wages, some improvement is also indicated in the 'poverty gap' – a decline from 57 per cent to 53 per cent. But it is still a 'killing' wage.

In the rural areas, as we had noted, incomes fell much less than in the urban areas. By the same token, if we find 35 per cent rural poverty in 1990, in the early 1970s there would still be poverty – unlike urban areas – though at a lower level (20 per cent or so based on the sort of absolute poverty line used here). The unfortunate fact is that, just as in the urban areas income declines were experienced by the poor (the wage earners), so in the rural areas the least favoured (the North) suffered the most. We had estimated poverty in the North at around one-third in 1990. Casting back the income to the higher 1960s level, we would certainly find much less poverty compared with 1990. In the South we can be more sanguine. Incomes have declined much less than in the North and poverty levels therefore have not increased as much. The North-South finding is something new and no doubt future researchers will examine it carefully.

CONCLUSIONS

The economy of Uganda we are dealing with now is totally different from the one that had been carefully nurtured after independence and that existed till the early 1970s. One word summarizes the trends – 'informalization'. The alleged 'aristocracy of labour' has been smashed and the Asians have gone (some are now returning). Their place has been taken by the informal sector which has expanded both numerically and monetarily in relation to urban incomes. In the rural areas, export crops, once traded through the formal channels, have declined to a shadow of their former quantities and even more so in terms of incomes. Their place has been more than filled by food crop sales. Quantities have increased in response to increasing urbanization and prices have increased even more.

The overriding context of these changes is, of course, the economic crisis that engulfed the country for almost a decade and a half after 1972 and the ravages of which still persist. Poverty levels have increased sharply in the urban areas, although much less so in the rural areas because of the basic strength of the food sector. Whether income distribution improved is difficult to say. On the one hand, the narrowing rural-urban gap should be seen in a positive light, but when decomposed further, a large part of the decline in urban incomes centred on the wage earners. As a result, income distribution shifted away from wages. Some of this shift could have benefited the informal sector.

84

Changes in poverty patterns in Uganda

The important questions are, of course: (i) what kind of research agenda is suggested, and (ii) what are the implications for policy formulation? The establishment of research priorities should be seen not as an academic exercise *per se* but as a prerequisite for policy-making. The fact is that, although some broad outlines of the structural characteristics of the Ugandan economy can be discerned, very little concrete is known about how an informalized economy functions. In fact, all existing models assume rather rigid categories – urban/rural, formal/informal – carrying notions about income distribution and income transfers, for example, as mediated by rural-urban terms of trade. Now it is less and less accurate to assume that any increase in urban wages comes at the expense of farmers, because both categories exist within the same family. In fact, we need to know much more about household responses to changing relative prices, and for this we first need the basic details on the characteristics of present-day Ugandan households.

All these building blocks could be used to answer the second question we posed – the implications for policy formulation. What we need to establish, given the context of informalization and the present-day context of structural adjustment, is what the sources of growth in the Ugandan economy are. In the past it could be assumed that agricultural exports provided the main growth but this is now no longer self-evident. The export base has contracted and so have prices (despite the mid-1994 coffee boom). What kind of gains can be expected from pushing traditional exports, as is the basic premise of structural adjustment programmes? In the face of – up to recently – falling international prices, how far can increasing internal prices be justified? In the past it could also be assumed that import-substituting industrialization would provide the basis of growth in the urban areas, facilitating the transfer of labour out of agriculture. The industrial sector has now virtually collapsed and the current philosophy of liberalization does not augur well for its rejuvenation. Yet the economy *has* been 'de-agrarianizing' as evinced by high rates of urbanization. The informal sector is where labour – and incomes – have gone. We need to know a lot more about the dynamics of this sector to assess its potential for growth. More will have to be done to enable the sector to play its role in employment generation, given its now pre-eminent position in the urban areas.

It may be noticed that we have said nothing about poverty alleviation policies, as would behove a chapter on poverty. The reason for this is, of course, that poverty in Uganda is a *development* problem. The very fact that over 85 per cent of the population work on the farms and the rest, for practical purposes, in the informal sector, and that incomes in both sectors are generally low, requires that poverty be attacked through broad-based development. This is not to argue for a *growth* strategy but for a *development* strategy involving all sections of the population. In particular, the smallholders in the outlying regions have to be integrated into the economy by increasing their access to markets

Growing out of poverty

and to agricultural inputs. Similarly, the vast numbers in the informal sector have to be helped through subsidized inputs, credit and training facilities. The job is arduous. The Ugandan people will be up to it.

Appendix 5.I
Statistics

It would be true to say that statistics suffered even more than the economy during the 'economic collapse'. Once the provider of annual series on employment and industrial production and of the *Statistical Abstract*, bringing together diverse data on GDP, agricultural production, cost of living, etc., the Statistics Department now manages to produce only the GDP figures and cost of living indices in the *Key Economic Indicators*. The occasional reports – e.g. *Patterns of Income, Expenditure and Consumption of African Unskilled Workers* in the 1960s – are conspicuously absent. The GDP figures are published without any of the background breakdowns – wages, operating surplus, rent – which used to be routinely available. The HBS of 1989/90 recently published is a major step forward. And no doubt things will continue to improve with the return of growth and social stability.

The following four tables give the basic data used in the text to draw up the picture of economic decline. Table 5.AI.1 shows the splicing of the GDP series to get us back to 1961. Table 5.AI.2 gives the breakdown between agricultural and non-agricultural GDP and between cash agriculture and non-monetary agriculture. Table 5.AI.3 gives the corresponding rural/urban population breakdown and Table 5.AI.4 the cost of living index from 1968 to 1992. Updating to 1995, as done in Figure 5.1, is based on the following annual rates of growth for 1990-95: total GDP 6.6, agriculture 3.8, nonagriculture 9.0; total population 3.2, agricultural 3.0, nonagricultural 5.2. Estimation is involved in the construction of each of the series and the procedures are explained in the notes, along with a mention of alternative figures available.

86

Changes in poverty patterns in Uganda

Table 5.AI.1 Total real GDP, 1961–91 (1966 prices) (Sh.m.)

	Series 1 (1966 prices)	Series 2 (1987 prices)	Series 3 (1966 prices)
1961	4626		
1962	4786		
1963	5229		
1964	5510		
1965	5792		
1966	6112		1961–80
1967	6296		as for
1968	6440		Series 1
1969	7146		
1970	7226		
1971			
1972	7542		
1973	7496		
1974	7509		
1975	7357		
1976	7411		
1977	7527		
1978	7181		
1979	6376		
1980	6115		
1981	6351	180763	6351
1982		191530	6729
1983		205817	7231
1984		192340	6758
1985		196272	6896
1986		197466	6938
1987		210694	7403
1988		226958	7974
1989		243814	8566
1990		254291	8934
1991		264196	9282

Notes: Series 1 is based on 1966 prices. The sources are: MPED, 1970 and 1982 and World Bank, 1988; Table 2.1. Series 2 is from MPED, 1992b, Table 6, with 1987 prices. The switchover is made at 1981 to connect up with series 1 to obtain series 3 as the full series for 1961–91 based on 1966 prices. The figures should be seen not in absolute terms but as indices, and as such the base year used for prices is immaterial.

Growing out of poverty

Table 5.AI.2 Agricultural and non-agricultural GDP and cash and non-monetary agricultural GDP, 1966–91 (1966 prices, Sh.m.)

	GDP			Agricultural GDP	
	Total	Non-agricultural	Agricultural	Cash	Non-monetary
1966	6112	2716	3396	1525	1871
1970	7226	3381	3845	1696	2149
1972	7542	3324	4218	1876	2342
1980	6115	2481	3634	1540	2094
1987	7403	3061	4342	1962	2380
1990	8934	3878	5056	2317	2739
1991	9282	3773	5509	2386	3123

Notes: Source as for Table 5.AI.1, with splicing also done similarly. 'Agricultural' includes livestock, forestry and fishing, and 'non-monetary agriculture' includes also construction and owner-occupied dwellings. Non-monetary agriculture *per se* dominates, with normally over 90 per cent of the total.

Table 5.AI.3 Population of Uganda: Total, urban and rural, 1959–91, selected years ('000s)

	Total	Urban	Rural
1959	6537	294	6243
1961	7050	336	6714
1966	8515	467	8048
1969	9535	572	8963
1970	9783	602	9181
1972	10298	668	9630
1980	12636	1011	11625
1981	12952	1070	11882
1982	13276	1133	12143
1983	13608	1119	12409
1984	13949	1269	12680
1985	14298	1344	12954
1986	14656	1422	13234
1987	15022	1505	13517
1988	15398	1593	13805
1989	15783	1687	14096
1990	16178	1786	14392
1991	16583	1890	14693

Notes: Population censuses were conducted in 1959, 1969, 1990 and 1991. Figures for total population against these years are from the censuses. Inter-censual rate of growth was applied for the other years (1959–69, 3.8 per cent p.a.; 1969–80, 2.6 per cent; 1980–91, 2.5 per cent). Urban percentage is available for 1980 (8 per cent) and 1991 (11.4 per cent). The implied inter-censual rate of growth (5.85 per cent) was used to obtain urban population in the intervening years. For 1959 and 1969 it was assumed that the urban population's

Table 5.AI.3 *(cont'd)*

share was 4.5 and 6 per cent respectively and the implicit inter-censual rate of growth (6.9 per cent p.a. 1959–69; 5.3 per cent 1969–80) was applied for the intervening years. Rural population was obtained as a residual.

N.B.   A population series for 1981–90 with a rural breakdown is available in World Bank, 1993b, Vol. III, Table 2. This series seems faulty: there are years (e.g. 1984, 1985, 1987) when the rural population grows faster than total population, so that urban population (as a residual) declines. Reverse migration at the most occurred in the 1970s and in any case was not built into the World Bank model, which used a rural population growth of 2.15 per cent p.a.

Table 5.AI.4 Cost of living index, 1968–92, selected years

	Series 1	Series 2	Series 3	Consolidated
1968	119			1.235
1970	146			1.518
1972	164			1.505
1978	1546			1.607
1980	5474			56.9
1981	9618	100.0		100.0
1982		120.1		120.1
1983		158.2		158.2
1984		222.3		222.3
1985		597		597
1986		1508		1508
1987		4327		4327
1988		12105		12105
1989		24282	100.0	24282
1990			133.1	32320
1991			170.4	41380
1992			259.8	63080

Notes: The cost of living consolidation is obtained by splicing three series, with the common points shown. Series 1 is from MEPD, 1970 and 1982, with Jan. 1961 = 100. Series 2 is from World Bank, 1988: Table 6.8. Originally Aug. 1981 was 100 but was changed to 1981=100. Both series 1 and 2 pertain to Kampala low-cost index. Series 3 is from MPED, 1992a, with Sep. 1989 = 100. The series is for 'Kampala' unspecified.

N.B.   (i) A consolidated series for 1982–92 is available in World Bank, 1993a, Table VIII.2, said to be provided by the Statistics Department. The implied percentage changes differ from the ones above, particularly for 1988–89 when the World Bank shows 61.4 per cent increase whereas we have (from Statistics Department) 100 per cent.

(ii) The cost of living index differs greatly from the GDP deflator, which can happen, but the differences seem too great to be probable.

Appendix 5.II
Poverty lines and poverty

Initially poverty will be defined in terms of 'food poverty', with 2,200 calories per capita per day chosen as the threshold, usually taken to be the minimum intake necessary to maintain normal active life. As 2,200 calories may be derived from any combination of foods, a breakdown has to be stipulated, with a deliberate bias towards cheaper foods to capture the core of poverty. 40 per cent of calories were set to derive from the basic staples (*matooke*, millet, sorghum), 25 per cent each from maize and beans, and 10 per cent from oil. To highlight the diversity in regional diets – but even more to capture the price differentials – four separate consumption baskets were used, with *matooke* as the staple in the South, millet in the North, and a combination of millet and *matooke* in the East and West (Table 5.AII.1). Meat and milk were excluded, not because of any nutritional judgement, but simply because really poor people cannot afford them. The poverty baskets chosen were costed at prices as obtained from the Household Budget Survey and then compared against expenditures in the HBS.

The fact that we are using regional poverty lines is important to emphasize in relation to price differentials. A Uganda-wide poverty line would yield a misleading picture of poverty, particularly as between the North and the South since the northern staple – millet – is a much cheaper source of calories than the South's *matooke*. For example, at prices found in the HBS, an expenditure of Sh.23 per day would suffice to purchase 2,200 millet calories in the Northern Region, whereas Sh.130 would be needed for *matooke* in Kampala. A *matooke-*

Table 5.AII.1. Composition of regional food baskets
(% of total calories and calorie values)

	Kampala & Central	Eastern	Western	Northern	Calories per kg[a]
Matooke	40	20	20	–	890
Millet	–	20	–	40	2683
Sorghum	–	–	20	–	2900
Maize	25	25	25	25	3088
Beans	25	25	25	25	3200
Oil	10	10	10	10	9000

[a] Reflects bundle of food as purchased – for example, maize in the form of on-the-cob, grains and flour. Source for calorie values: USDHEW and FAO.

based poverty line, or even a national poverty line, would exaggerate the extent of poverty in the North.[13]

Table 5.AII.2 shows the derivation of the regional poverty lines (1989/90 prices). A poverty line for Kampala at March 1992 prices is also shown. The calculations proceed as follows. Price per kg is obtained from the HBS. Calorie value of the food items is obtained from Table 5.AII.1. From these, price per calorie is obtained, and then the cost of the specified number of calories. For example, as we see from Table 5.AII.1, a kilo of maize would yield 3,088 calories. Price per kg (Kampala) being Sh.186, price per 1,000 calories was Sh.60. Maize is slated to provide 550 calories per day in Kampala, hence its cost would be Sh.33. Similarly for the other staples. In Kampala the daily cost of food for an average person (2,200 calories) would be Sh.133, or Sh.3,990 per month. For an average household (4.36 members) the cost would be Sh.17,400.

To obtain another perspective on poverty, the table also computes a total poverty line. Here an assumption is made that in the urban areas essential non-food items require the same expenditure as food (i.e. food expenditure constitutes one-half of total expenditure) and in the rural areas 50 per cent as much (i.e. food expenditure constitutes two-thirds of total expenditure).[14] The two poverty lines are set against the respective regional expenditure distributions (Table 5.2) to obtain the incidence of food and total poverty.

Appendix 5.III
Export pricing and 'urban bias'

Uganda was often cited in the literature as a country where the agricultural sector had been penalized to subsidize the wage earners. Export taxes and marketing board surpluses were the vehicle for this. 'Urban bias' reigned. In the last 20 years urban wages have fallen and export taxes have been abolished. In fact, unnoticed by many, price increases induced by devaluations have put internal price trends for export crops far out of line with external trends, to the extent that agriculture may even be 'subsidized'.

Table 5.AIII.1 shows the prices of cotton and coffee on the internal and external markets, along with the appropriate deflators. Three years – 1972, 1980 and 1990/91 – may be highlighted to capture the trends. Between 1972 and 1980 the real price of cotton and coffee fell by around 85 per cent, whereas the external price of cotton held its own and that of coffee actually increased (by 33 per cent). Since in 1972 there

Table 5.AII.2 Costing of a 2,200 calories poverty line. Also total poverty line and poverty incidence, Kampala and regions, 1989/90. Additionally Kampala, March 1992

	Kampala	Central rural	Central urban	Eastern rural	Eastern urban	Western rural	Western urban	Northern rural	Northern urban	Kampala, March 1992
Price per kg (sh)										
Matooke	53	19	26	16	30	19	36	–	–	99
Millet	–	–	–	87	75	–	–	39	41	–
Sorghum	–	–	–	–	–	115	143	–	–	–
Maize	186	160	170	112	165	112	72	57	172	450
Beans	189	143	144	111	133	140	149	72	71	393
Oil	600	800	600	850	650	700	750	700	800	1650
Cost 2,200 calories/day (sh)										
Matooke	52	19	25	8	15	9	18	–	–	98
Millet	–	–	–	14	12	–	–	13	14	–
Sorghum	–	–	–	–	–	17	22	–	–	–
Maize	33	28	30	20	29	20	13	10	31	80
Beans	32	25	25	19	23	24	26	12	12	67
Oil	15	20	15	21	16	17	18	17	20	40
Total	133	91	95	82	95	87	97	53	76	285
Total food per month	3990	2730	2850	2460	2850	2610	2910	1590	2280	8550
Total poverty line per month	7980	4095	5700	3690	5700	3915	5820	2385	4560	17100
Food poverty incidence (%)	4	22	4	31	10	21	10	22	26	–
Total poverty incidence (%)	23	32	12	46	21	32	21	33	32	–
Memo items										
Household size	4.36	5.60	4.43	5.31	4.36	5.75	4.51	5.77	5.45	4.36
Total food/household/month	17396	15288	12625	13063	12426	15008	13124	9174	12426	37278
Total poverty line/household/month	34792	22932	25250	19595	24852	22512	26248	13761	24852	74556

Sources: Price per kg from background data supplied by the Statistics Department. Cost per day as explained in the text. Household size from the household budget survey tables. Poverty incidence obtained by setting the poverty lines against distributions in Table 5.2.

was an element of taxation in crop pricing – through the export tax – by 1980 this increased hugely. The mechanism was the exchange rate. In 1980 farmer's prices were still being converted at Sh.7 to the dollar, whereas everybody else was obtaining Sh.50 on the black market. Without any further calculations we could say that farmers were being 'taxed' to the extent of 86 per cent because of the overvalued exchange rate alone. The trends after 1980 were equally dramatic. Between 1980 and 1990/91, the domestic price of cotton increased almost *6.4-fold* and of coffee three-fold, whereas on the external market cotton's price fell by 32 per cent and coffee's by 72 per cent. These divergent trends can again be attributed to the exchange rate – this time the devaluations after the mid-1980s. Farmers could be given a higher shilling price for their produce. Some of this could be accommodated by abolishing the

Table 5.AIII.1 Producer and New York prices for cotton and coffee, and Uganda cost of living and MUV index, 1972–92

	Producer price (Sh/kg)		Cost of living (1981 = 100)	New York price (US cents/lb)		US manufacturing unit value index
	Cotton	Coffee		Cotton	Coffee	
	– (unprocessed) –			– (processed) –		
1972	0.0125	0.012	1.51	34.3	45.2	37.3
1973	0.0130	–	–	56.1	49.9	43.4
1974	–	–	–	57.9	58.7	55.4
1975	0.019	–	–	45.1	61.1	62.0
1976	0.019	–	–	68.0	127.6	64.0
1977	–	–	–	61.6	223.8	66.3
1978	0.03	–	1.61	57.6	147.5	70.9
1979	0.06	–	–	62.1	165.5	80.7
1980	0.06	0.07	57	81.3	147.2	91.6
1981	0.3	0.35	100	72.0	102.9	100.0
1982	0.4	0.5	120	60.0	111.0	101.2
1983	0.6	0.8	158	68.4	124.1	102.1
1984	1.2	1.3	222	68.2	138.2	103.6
1985	2.25	3.1	597	58.7	121.2	102.8
1986	4.0	8.5	1508	52.7	148.2	103.8
1987	19	24	4327	63.5	102.3	105.6
1988	80	60	12105	57.4	95.1	113.1
1989	130	60	24282	64.2	75.7	116.0
1990	195	100	32320	71.8	55.0	117.5
1991	300	165	41380	70.7	49.8	117.9
1992	340	210	63080	–	–	119.4

Source: Producer prices from usual Uganda sources; cost of living from Table 5.AI.4; New York prices from IMF: *International Financial Statistics Yearbook*, various years; price for 'Uganda coffee' and 'US 10 market' price for cotton; MUV from IMF tablets for USA. MUV reflects the price of Uganda's imports.

export tax and squeezing the marketing margins, but as internal prices have continued to increase consistently while external prices are falling, there is now a possibility that farm prices are being 'subsidized'. Certainly this seems to be the case for cotton, as table 5.AIII.2 shows.

First some preliminary remarks may be made *à propos* 'percentage of export price returned to the farmer' type of calculations. One cannot take the export price and compare it with the farm price because the two prices are for products at different stages of processing – export price for lint and farm price for seed cotton. Hence, processing and marketing charges have to be deducted – items (ii) to (vi) – and prices have to be reconverted to equal stage of processing (item x).[15] Finally the open market rate of exchange has to be used to avoid the type of result obtained for 1980.

What we have then is that one kg of lint valued at $1.57 in New York was worth $1 before ginning, or Sh.780. Converting to seed cotton yields Sh.236 per kg of seed cotton. Adding the value of seed and subtracting transportation charges, the farmer could be paid Sh.234 for his kilo of seed cotton. He was actually paid Sh.247. In 1991 with a lower price of lint in New York, the farmer was paid a higher shilling price for seed cotton. A clear subsidy is implied.

Table 5.AIII.2 New York/producer price chain for cotton (per kg), 1990/91

(i)	New York	$1.57
(ii)	Less transport	0.27
(iii)	At ginnery	$1.30
(iv)	Less marketing	0.02
(v)	Less ginning[a]	0.16
(vi)	Financing[b]	0.12
(vii)	Value of lint pre-ginning	$1.00
(viii)	Exchange rate (Sh/$)[c]	780
(ix)	Value of lint pre-ginning	Sh. 780
(x)	Convert to seed cotton at 0.33	Sh. 236
(xi)	Add value of seed[d]	Sh. 23
(xii)	Less primary society charges	Sh. 10
(xiii)	Less transport from primary societies	Sh. 15
(xiv)	Value of seed cotton to farmer	Sh. 234
(xv)	Producer price for seed cotton[e]	Sh. 247

Source: New York and producer prices from Table 5.AIII.1, averaged for 1990/91. Other coefficients from World Bank, 1991b: Table 2.

[a] Ginning cost estimated by World Bank at $30 per bale (400lb).
[b] From World Bank, 1991b.
[c] Bureau exchange rate for 1990/91 from World Bank, 1993a: Table VI.3.
[d] At $35,000 per tonne. Total seed cotton tonnage is converted to seed (at 0.67) and then costed.
[e] Average for 1990/91.

Notes

1. As wages collapsed the minimum wage became less and less representative of the average wage received by unskilled workers because of supplements added by way of in-kind bonuses – food in the canteen, group transportation, etc.

2. 5–6 per cent per annum as an average since independence compared with 7–9 per cent recorded in most other African countries. In the second half of the 1970s some towns – Jinja, Gulu, Masindi, Njeru, Arua, even Kampala – actually declined in population because of the prevailing civil unrest and the breakdown of urban amenities. Growth rates (percentage per annum) of the four largest towns between 1969 and 1980 were: Kampala, 3.2; Jinja, -0.7; Mbale, 1.7; Tororo, 0.5. Compared with this, the overall population growth rate was 2.8 per cent. It may be noted that the figures are for 1969–80. Up to 1972 the towns were growing at 5–6 per cent per annum, so that between 1973 and 1980 all towns (including Kampala) registered lower growth rates than the natural population increase, implying reverse migration (MPED, 1982, Table 1.26). Since the mid-1980s, urbanization has again speeded up.

3. These calculations are based on expressing non-agricultural wage earners as a percentage of the urban labour force. Wage figures are available as a series till 1977 and thereafter some sporadic figures are available – e.g. MPED, 1989. Obviously the figures obtained are rough estimates, derived simply to establish broad trends. It may be noted that with the passage of time even the 'wage earners' themselves became 'informalized' – especially those in government employment – as they devoted an increasing proportion of their time to activities 'on the side' to make ends meet.

4. MPED, 1989, obtained 378,227 as the total of wage employees in 1989, made up of 244,195 workers in government, 53,593 in parastatals, and 80,439 in the private sector.

5. For example, taking the Kampala price level as 1, the Entebbe index was found to be 1.16 and that of the Eastern Region's rural areas 0.74. Thus, Entebbe's 'real' expenditure should be scaled down by 86 per cent and Eastern rural's topped up by 35 per cent to make the three expenditures/incomes comparable. It may be noted that later in the poverty analysis region-specific poverty lines will be used, hence price differentials will be 'built into' the estimates.

6. It may be noted that, as often happens with household budget surveys, the Uganda HBS of 1989/90 reported figures for expenditure rather than income.

7. Price of sugar: Sh.585 per kg. Some other prices (per kg): bread, Sh.700; salt, Sh.160; soap, Sh.420. Source: MPED, 1992: Table 18. It may be remarked that often it is more meaningful to obtain 'real' GDP figures in this way since individual prices are almost always going to be more accurate than the cost of living index, especially when a long series is involved requiring splicing. To illustrate, in 1968 GDP per capita was Sh.722 and sugar cost Sh.1.43 per kg. Therefore, 42 kg could be purchased per month. Hence a decline in 'real income' of *69 per cent* is implied. GDP figures from Table 5.AI.1 give a much smaller decline – 22 per cent. It may also be noted that compared to the GDP per capita figure of Sh.94,000, the HBS yielded Sh.76,000, which should be considered fairly close, especially considering that in one case the figure relates to incomes and in the other to expenditure.

8. For example, compare rural North and urban North. For the *same* food basket, based around millet, the cost varies by 43 per cent, reflecting rural-urban price differences. Once again it is worth reiterating that while poverty lines differ intra- as well as inter-regionally, so do expenditures, since the same price data are utilized to derive expen-

Growing out of poverty

diture figures. Hence for poverty analysis prices are already 'built into' the estimation procedure: the same prices occur on both sides of the equation – in the poverty line as well as expenditure figures.

9. Particularly in terms of urban farming we need to know what percentage of calories the town *shamba* produces. In my 1985 paper I mentioned that in the 1960s urban budget surveys had shown that Kampala obtained 20 per cent of its food supply (in terms of calories) from within and that in the 1980s this figure quite likely doubled (Jamal, 1985: 35). This statement has been queried by Maxwell (1994: 1). Ten years later we should be able to refute such estimates with figures – or else accept the general thrust of the observation, which was something new in 1985, that Kampala did become significantly 'ruralized'. It is also worth mentioning that the situation in the mid-1980s was quite different from now. Transport was heavily disrupted and insecurity rampant, preventing supplies from reaching Kampala. In the 1990s there is still urban farming (as confirmed by Maxwell, 1994) but much more of the bulky staples now reach Kampala than in the early 1980s.

10. It may be noted that this is a much smaller decline than that given by non-agricultural incomes per capita. What the two figures imply is an equalization of incomes: in 1964, because of the Asian presence, the average non-agricultural income was much less representative of low-income households than it became after 1972.

11. Another household survey is available for 1992/93 – the Social Dimensions of Adjustment Integrated Survey. Simon Appleton (1994), in work-in-progress, reports that this survey implied that average (real) household income had fallen by 38 per cent compared with the HBS of 1989/90. He rightly expressed scepticism. Indeed all income series – wages and agricultural prices (see Table 5.AII.1) – indicate an improvement. Was the HBS of 1989/90 the more inaccurate one by overestimating expenditures or did the SDA survey underestimate hugely? As noted in Note 7, the HBS average expenditure figure was in fact lower than GDP per capita, so there is no question of overestimation. The two figures were actually pretty close, allowing for savings, for a judgement that the HBS, 1989/90, was fairly accurate. However, caution is never out of order in using HBSs.

12. It may be noted that while the cost of living increased by some 94 per cent, the poverty basket increased by 114 per cent. This is because the food items in the food poverty line experienced higher price increases than the general cost of living.

13. It may be noted that the World Bank in its 1992 mission (World Bank, 1993a) opted to use a global poverty line – in fact two, Sh.6,000 and Sh.3,000 per capita. These are arbitrary lines, set respectively at 4/5ths and 2/5ths of the average HBS expenditure, said to be Sh.7,512 per capita per month. There are problems with this procedure: (a) the HBS yields Sh.6,328 as the average income per month (it has to be calculated): monthly household income was Sh.34,468 (Tables 1.11–14, as well as summary table 1). Household size (from Table 5.2) was 5.45. Hence per capita income = Sh. 6,328. (b) A shilling figure has no meaning for poverty studies until it is articulated in 'real real' terms – command over a particular basket. (c) A Sh.6,000 (or Sh.3,000) poverty line for whom? For Kampala, it is at 43 per cent of average expenditure; for the rural North at *157 per cent*! (d) Because prices differ inter-regionally, a Sh.6,000 poverty line for Kampala would not purchase the basic poverty line of Table 5.AII.2, while for the Northern Region it would constitute practically a 'middle-class' basket. No wonder such a high incidence of poverty was found for the rural North – 81 per cent (Sh.6,000 poverty line) or 42 per cent (Sh.3,000 poverty line). It may be noted parenthetically that the author was on a parallel UNDP mission to Uganda and sat in on several brainstorming sessions with the World Bank when the methodology for poverty lines was being discussed. I did expound on mine and showed why a global poverty line simply would not work. So much for giving free inter-agency advice! The World Bank in its 1997 *World Development Indicators* reports a figure of 55 per cent poverty for 1992/93.

14. Effectively this means that whereas in Kampala, non-food needs would cost Sh.3,990 (per month), in the rural areas of the Central Region they would cost Sh.1,365. Whether the assumption is realistic can only be answered by asking – do Sh.3,990 in Kampala and Sh.1,365 in rural Central Region purchase equal non-food baskets? 'Rent' and fuel would be cheaper in the countryside, transport to work non-existent; clothing would be dearer, but by and large we can see that some equalization is possible.

15. One kg of seed cotton yields 0.3 kg of lint. Therefore Sh.780 per kg of lint = Sh.236 per kg of seed cotton.

SIX
Urban agriculture: unplanned responses to the economic crisis

Daniel G. Maxwell*

The crisis of institutional breakdown, economic mismanagement and civil conflict which characterized the life of Uganda from the early 1970s until the mid-1980s was particularly felt by the residents of Kampala (Obbo, 1991; Jamal and Weeks, 1993). Bigsten and Kayizzi-Mugerwa (1992) note that a major response to the economic crisis at the household level was to diversify income-generating strategies beyond formal employment, trade or wage labour. While some of this diversification has taken place through the informalization of commerce and small-scale manufacturing, much of it has resulted from increased labour by urban women (Basirika, 1992). Among a variety of other activities, urban farming has been increasingly practised, predominantly by women.

Many of the effects of the crisis have been heightened by the impact of economic restructuring policies in the late 1980s and early 1990s. These have increased food prices, cut social programmes and subsidies to the poor (Loxley, 1989), led to further reductions in real civil service wages and retrenchment in civil service employment (Chew, 1990), and in some cases to scaled back private sector employment (Mamdani, 1990). Pinstrup-Andersen (1989) refers to Kampala and suggests that urban production of food for home consumption may buffer or mitigate the decline in household food security associated with both the crisis of the formal economy and the policies of stabilization and adjustment. The source to which he refers is Jamal (1985), who noted that the proportion of the city's food supply being produced within the city doubled between 1972 and 1985. Bigsten and Kayizzi-Mugerwa (1992) make somewhat the opposite claim, suggesting that farming in Kampala is not 'serious' and that no one is going to feed themselves from their 'makeshift farms' in the city.

* Land Tenure Center, University of Wisconsin. I would like to acknowledge the excellent research assistance of Gertrude Atukunda in the collection of data presented in this paper, and comments on earlier drafts of this paper from Aili Tripp and Jane Collins of the University of Wisconsin, and Emmanuel Nabuguzi of Makerere Institute of Social Research. Funding for this research came from a Fulbright-Hays Fellowship, and from the National Science Foundation, USA. I am also grateful for the institutional support of Makerere Institute of Social Research during fieldwork.

98

Urban agriculture: unplanned responses to the economic crisis

Although there has always been some farming in Kampala (Southall and Gutkind, 1957), 'urban agriculture' is virtually an oxymoronic concept to urban planners in Uganda. Complaints about the contemporary 'ruralization' of Kampala are not infrequent (Bibangambah, 1992), and it is widely believed that only the most recently arrived migrants from rural areas practise farming in the city. Only comparatively recently has urban farming in Africa been systematically researched (Sanyal, 1985; Rakodi, 1988; Mvena et al., 1991; Freeman, 1991; Maxwell and Zziwa, 1992; Sawio, 1993). Most of this research portrays urban farming as a household survival strategy, one of the many ways in which urban families have redeployed their labour and resources in the struggle to survive in an increasingly hostile environment.

The results of the present study indicate that farming within the city of Kampala spans a continuum from a literal survival strategy for some to large-scale, lucrative investment of capital for a few. It is largely the effort of urban women to provide, for themselves, their children and their households, some degree of food security at least partially separate from cash incomes and markets. Under some circumstances, it also provides a source of income. Rapid urbanization, the precipitous fall in real incomes, and the informalization of the city's economy are all very real forces driving the need for a new source of food, but so too are intra-household dynamics governing access to and control over resources. These findings challenge previous perceptions about the practice of urban agriculture, and the extent to which it can be understood or characterized as a household strategy.

All data presented in this chapter were collected in Kampala between November, 1992 and October, 1993. In-depth case studies of 44 households were carried out, as well as a two-round, random sample survey of 360 households in three areas of the city which included anthropometric measurement of all children under the age of five years for nutritional assessment purposes. Focus group discussions were held in eight areas of the city, and some 80 key informants were interviewed.

URBAN AGRICULTURE IN KAMPALA

Two different kinds of agricultural production are taking place in Kampala, and two different trends can be noted with regard to both household participation in agriculture and land use for agricultural purposes. There are a relatively small number of commercial farmers within the city, producing primarily for sale to the urban market. The vast majority of urban farmers produce primarily for home consumption, though they may sell varying amounts of their produce depending on the need for cash, sources of income, and the intra-household distribution of income. This latter group was primarily the subject of this study.

With the exception of the small, commercially-oriented group, urban agriculture in Kampala represents the phenomenon referred to

99

by Mingione (1991) as semi-proletarianism, or relying on a measure of both labour market participation or petty trading and home production for direct consumption. There are two distinctly different forms of agriculture within the city. The first, occurring within the central city, the older suburbs, and City Council housing estates, represents a long-term movement away from sole reliance on the labour market in both the formal and informal sectors of the city's economy for livelihood, with increased effort over time devoted to production for direct consumption. The other, occurring within the newer suburbs and the peri-urban areas within the city – areas in which farming has always been a prevalent activity – represents movement towards either the labour market or informal trade, but a reluctance to become entirely dependent on either.

Agricultural land use is most evident in peri-urban areas that were incorporated into the city after Kampala and Mengo were merged in 1968. In the centre of the city, very small-scale agricultural land use is occurring in places where aerial photography as recently as the mid-1970s shows open spaces, utility accesses, parks, public lands and private yards. The most recent estimate for the city puts agricultural land use at 56.1 per cent of its total land area (GTZ/Department of Physical Planning, 1992). Crops grown in Kampala are largely staple food crops: cassava, *matooke,* beans, maize, sweet potatoes and cocoyams, in descending order of prevalence. Vegetable crops and fruit trees are also grown; and a limited number of commercial producers grow coffee and even vanilla beans in the city. Among livestock producers, poultry raising (for both meat and eggs) is most common, but cattle, small ruminants, pigs, rabbits and other micro livestock are raised as well.

The common perception among current residents is that farming began inside the built-up area of the city in the mid-1970s in the wake of the Amin regime's economic war. A UNICEF study, carried out in the aftermath of the 1979 war against Amin, determined that emergency feeding programmes were not needed and one of the major reasons cited was the high percentage of low-income families who had begun growing some portion of their own food in the city (Alnwick, 1981). Large numbers of people began farming in the city at three different times. The first of these groups have always been engaged in farming and the areas where they live have gradually been incorporated into the city. The second group began farming in the mid-1970s, around the time that city residents began facing declining real incomes. A third group began in the late 1980s. While this third time period corresponds with the beginning of the policy impacts of structural adjustment, it also corresponds with dramatically improved security in the city, making possible activities that were too risky to carry out prior to 1986. Respondents listed both as reasons for beginning to farm in the late 1980s.

An estimated 35 per cent of households in the city are involved in agriculture. Given that the average size of urban household engaging in farming in the city is considerably larger than the mean for the city as a whole, this implies that urban agriculture directly affects the livelihood or diet of something like half of Kampala's residents, and indirectly affects an even greater proportion. The vast majority of all major agricultural activities are carried out by women, although, in a majority of households interviewed during the survey, the land for cultivation was obtained by men. Similar but slightly lower figures apply to livestock production. The most commonly cited immediate reason for farming is the need to provide a source of food for the household. The major constraint to farming in the city is access to land. Underlying the practice of urban agriculture in Kampala is the fact that it is technically illegal, though bylaws banning the practice are only erratically enforced and have little impact on farming.

ANALYSIS OF HOUSEHOLDS

The first question to address prior to an analysis of urban agriculture, is whether the household can legitimately be viewed as a unit of analysis. A second question arises in the analysis itself. Given that urban farming is largely the work of women, can urban agriculture be understood as a strategy mobilized by a household or larger unit? Or is it strictly to be understood as the work of individuals? Are women's reasons for farming primarily rooted in forces external to households such as declining real incomes, or in internal struggles over access to, and control over, resources?

Regarding the first question, Kampala respondents repeatedly expressed views of what they considered to be their own households in terms of those persons whom the collective identity (the household) is responsible for feeding. Such definitions of the household came from both male and female respondents, from a diversity of ethnic groups, and from people who had been in Kampala for varying lengths of time. With the exception of the small group of commercial farmers in Kampala, *all* respondents said that provision of food was the major single reason for farming in the city. Therefore, the argument in this chapter is that if the household is defined to some significant degree by food and the responsibility of the collectivity to assure the access of individual members to food, and if food is the major reason for farming in the city – it is both methodologically and theoretically impossible to ignore households in any analysis of urban agriculture, however messy, imprecise or unwieldy it might be.

Regarding the second question, some contemporary authors (e.g. Basirika, 1992) correctly attribute much of contemporary female labour in Kampala's informal sector to the economic downturn of the 1970s and 1980s, and to the policy impacts of structural adjustment. However, a review of earlier literature on Kampala indicates that well before either structural adjustment or the economic war of Idi Amin, domestic and gender relations in the city were undergoing profound changes. One of the major points of contention in the struggle over the redefinition of these relations was the independent access of women to sources of income (Southall and Gutkind, 1957; Obbo, 1980). This would imply some historical continuity in evolving gender relations somewhat in spite of, or at least in addition to, changes brought about by recent economic hardships.

Reasons for farming. While maintaining access to food was listed as the most prevalent reason for farming by Kampala respondents in both the case studies and the survey, there were differences between males and females. Men tended to justify urban farming in terms of an over-arching cultural imperative, but women were much more blunt about why they farm. The consistency of this trend was striking, among both farming and non-farming informants, and among husbands and wives in households where the wife was farming. In the words of two male respondents, the first a retrenched civil servant, the second an elderly casual labourer:

> Even though I was working for government departments, the whole of my life is farming. And when I got that wife of mine, I found that she too took farming as her life. We couldn't afford to cater for those children with only the money from my employment.

> With us Africans, you cannot stay without farming. Farming is a very important issue. When you get a *kibanja*, you have to grow crops.

Women's views were typified by the comments of a young mother with no formal employment, and a low-income slum dweller self-employed as a beer brewer:

> [I farm] to get enough food for my children.

> I want to make sure that I don't just **wish** to eat something when I cannot afford to buy it.

Men tended to invoke a cultural rationale for why farming is predominantly a women's activity. Two men, both civil servants, expressed commonly held beliefs:

> Look at our wives – no matter how educated they are, they still want to dig!

> My wife wants to see something growing.

Time and again, male respondents, while eventually acknowledging a 'needs' imperative for urban agriculture, would explain its presence in the city in terms of women's cultural expectations of themselves. There is some support for the views of male respondents and the customary practices of the various groups who now inhabit Kampala, but numerous forces including urbanization have led to the breakdown of customary roles (Mair, 1940; Obbo, 1980).

Patterns of engagement in urban farming. Almost without exception, whether in the older part of the city or in the peri-urban areas, when people currently engaged in farming were asked if they would like to stop farming if they were offered a different job with the same monetary remuneration, the answer was no — an indication of the importance of farming. Nevertheless, the logic of farming's incorporation into the economic strategy of the household or individual lifestyle varies greatly.

At least four major categories of household logic emerge from an analysis of some 40 case studies. A small group of urban farmers produce mainly for the urban market, and can be described in terms of a *commercial* logic. By far the largest number raise poultry but other forms of commercial production can be noted. This group tend to be reasonably wealthy and have access to commercial credit. A second group, found mostly in the peri-urban parts of the city, gain the majority of their livelihoods from agriculture, and so can be described in terms of a *self-sufficiency* logic. But it is largely production for home consumption rather than for sale; hence the title of self-sufficiency, although this should be taken to mean self-sufficiency mainly in terms of basic foods. Needless to say, this group have access to fairly large amounts of land, usually on the basis of customary tenancy. A third group can be characterized as farming to achieve a *measure of food security*. The majority of both their food and income comes from non-agricultural sources, but farming is an important activity nevertheless. The last group farm because they have *no other means*. Often single women with children recently widowed or abandoned by their husbands, farming is a last resort against starvation for this group.

The 'measure of food security' category is by far the most common. One or more members of a household have gained access to some land – either within the compound on which their house or flat is located, or elsewhere – and someone within the household is producing food on it. But the amount of food produced does not constitute the majority of what the household consumes. Within this group, there are two different patterns in the way in which household-produced food is used: one is supplementary use of such food, largely when seasonal crops are harvested; the other is reserving such food for emergencies when other sources of supply dry up.

The logic of supplementary usage is fairly straightforward. The urban market supplies food for most of the year, with the exception of the time around the harvest of staple crops, as expressed by this working mother of four children:

> Now, since the season is not bad, food has been in plenty. We are getting a lot of potatoes now from our garden. We are not buying [food].

Such households tend to have at least one member employed elsewhere. Food from farming represents a source of income. A retired clerical worker whose pension benefits were rendered meaningless by inflation in the 1980s, expressed it like this:

> We may spend about two weeks without buying food. We even praise God for that. But when we go to the market, we can spend about 15,000 or 20,000 Shillings [US$ 15–20] within two weeks. Therefore when you grow crops it sometimes saves you from buying food in the market.

103

The logic of reserve usage of food from farming is more complex, and may be explained by a diversity of factors. One is simply erratic or unreliable household income. Another has to do with household dynamics and the need to have a source of food in the event that the primary income-earner does not provide money to buy food. Again, in the words of two women who farm:

> This food is like a reserve. This food helps us when money is scarce or you have no money in your pocket. You can go and harvest your *mayuni* and also eat the leaves as *etimpa* [sauce].

> There is likely to be a time when I may . . . find myself without any money to buy food. Then I can just go to my garden and get some food for my children.

In some cases, land used by these households for farming may be owned by someone in the household. Another common case is that a woman in the household (the wife, daughter, or female head of the household) may gain access to land on her own basis through borrowing, renting, 'squatting' or purchasing the use of it. Producing some amount of food for the household increases the food security of the members of the family for whose welfare she is responsible, as well as permitting her to put her own cash income to other uses.

It is particularly these women farmers who insist that they would never stop farming in exchange for a job which, in monetary exchange values, remunerates labour at the same rate. First, food is a form of income less easily expropriated by other members of the household than cash. Secondly, in some cases these women may have cash income from informal businesses which rely on farming for inputs, preparation of food for sale being the most notable example. One woman who had gained access to a sizable area of land in Kitante valley through the informal purchase of land-use rights expressed it like this:

> I was lucky [that there are workers at a construction site nearby]. I prepare this food and sell it to them. I come here [to my garden] in the morning, get food [sweet potatoes and cassava], prepare it and sell it. After eating lunch, I come here again and cultivate.

Third, farming is a task that fits in well with other work expected of women – especially child care and food preparation, as stated emphatically by this mother of three children:

> Of course I cannot stop this farming . . . You may get another job when you do not have anyone to leave at home. Who would cook and look after these children? You would still need to do both.

This is not to imply that women farmers in this category do not hold other jobs. Many do, both in informal commerce and as wage earners. However, unless a family is wealthy enough to be able to afford domestic help, having outside employment is in addition to, not instead of, these roles.

Urban agriculture: unplanned responses to the economic crisis

In a sense, the 'no other means' group is a more extreme form of the one just mentioned. They are low-income, food-insecure and land-insecure households. This group is often forced to sell some of what it produces to meet other expenses. It is this aspect which distinguishes this group from the 'measure of food security' one: the latter can usually afford to eat the food they produce; the 'no other means' group is often forced to sell some, even if they do not have enough food to eat themselves. These households are often not sufficiently well-connected to gain access to land other than by 'squatting' on it. This means that they are often subjected to eviction without compensation. Farming, for this group, constitutes a 'survival strategy' in the most literal sense.

Income and decision-making. While there is wide variation in responsibility for purchasing food and providing the money to purchase it, the preparation of food is still the responsibility of women. As a result, it is women who are expected to see to it that food is put on the table. As noted, this is a common reason for women's involvement in farming in the city. The point was reiterated in a focus group discussion with married women:

> Q: In those households where there is both a husband and a wife, who of the two is responsible for ensuring the availability of food?
> R1: The wife.
> R2: I am the one responsible for food in my home. It is up to me to decide what to eat and to ensure that it is available.
> R3: It is the same with me. I am responsible for seeing that there is food in the home.

Wide variation was also noted with regard to pooling income. But only about 15 per cent of the households surveyed could be described as income-pooling. Where women had independent sources of income, the provision of food usually became their responsibility:

> Q: So you and your husband [both] earn income. Do you decide together how to spend it?
> R: No, each one of us decides on our own what to do with the money.
> Q: Are you solely responsible for food procurement?
> R: Yes.
> Q: Does your husband contribute to meeting the expenses of the household?
> R: No.

Survey results indicate that men are responsible for purchasing food in only one-third of the households where women have independent income. In households where women had no apparent independent sources of income, responsibility for ensuring that food was prepared remained with the women:

> Q: Would we call that [provision of food] a man's responsibility since he is the one who provided the money?
> R: No. He doesn't give you that money for food only. He gives you one lump sum and tells you [you are responsible for the household]. So it is a woman's responsibility.

In households where both spouses generate incomes and pool them to meet expenditures, the household logic is self-evident. But non-pooling households, where the wife did not report any wage labour or trading, present something of a paradox. Wives in this category have no separate income, but reported that each spouse spends independently of the other. This category contains the greatest number of married women interviewed in the survey.

However, when the issue of farming is brought into the analysis, several things quickly become apparent. Of all married women respondents who claimed to have no separate incomes and no access to a household pool of income, nearly half engage in farming. A much higher prevalence of reserve usage of food was noted among this group than in the overall sample. The impact of income-pooling does not arise in such stark terms in female-headed households. A higher prevalence of supplementary usage of food was noted in such cases, although some income-generating activities available to single, low-income women (brewing and distilling, for example) provide income so erratic that reserve usage was noted in this group as well.

Quotations and statistics alone do not tell the full story about multiple motives for farming or the dynamics of the struggle over household resources. Provision of food is the major reason for farming, but it is clear that in many cases farming also provides a source of income for women, if only on an emergency or occasional basis.

The impact of farming. As a strategy for protecting food security and nutrition, farming appears to be very successful. Individual variation is considerable. But, on average, children in households where some food is produced by urban farming show significantly lower levels of malnutrition than do children in non-farming households, particularly among low-income groups. Multivariate analysis suggests three factors in this relationship: food sufficiency, dietary adequacy, and the amount of time mothers can spend on caring directly for their children.

In the very low-income group, roughly the same amount of money is spent on food/person/day at the household level. But, in farming households, food from farming is also available, resulting in significantly higher levels of food security. For the low-income group (often referred to as the 'working poor'), which constitutes the majority of Kampala residents, indicators of food security do not differ significantly between farming and non-farming households. But the money spent on food/person/day is much less in farming households, indicating a significant saving on food expenses. In middle- and upper-income groups, the difference between farming and non-farming households in both food security and nutritional status is not significant. Dietary adequacy, particularly in terms of micro-nutrients, is associated with urban farming across all income groups. The amount of time mothers are able to spend caring directly for their children is also positively associated with their nutritional well-being, and statistical evidence suggests that, at least at certain times of the year, women who farm have significantly more time to devote to child care than do women engaging in wage labour or in informal trade.

A picture emerges of great variation in urban households, in terms of their composition, internal dynamics, economic strategies, and the delicate balance between the internal struggle over resources and the external struggle for survival. Within this variation, however, several themes may be noted.

One theme is that of contemporary women facing economic circumstances which leave them responsible for the provision of food for their families without, in many cases, access to the means to do so adequately. They may have little real voice in the allocation of their husband's income to household needs, to say nothing of their own personal needs, and no access to an independent source of cash. This has already been mentioned as a major rationale for engaging in farming. On the other hand, some women reported beginning to farm because of the rise in inflation and the drop in real incomes that affected Kampala wage earners in the 1970s and 1980s, even if it was primarily their husband's wages that were affected at the time.

Another difference was noted in the rationale for farming as expressed by men and women. Men often explained farming in terms of a cultural imperative for women, whereas women expressed it in much more pragmatic terms. An apparent paradox also arises regarding claims made about sales: most respondents claimed not to sell any of their produce and only to sell livestock to raise cash for emergencies. Yet a picture clearly emerges that farming represents for many women some means of economic self-reliance. It appeared that many married women had good reason for letting their husbands believe whatever they wanted to about their motivations for farming; that in fact, women had good reason to keep their economic activities less than fully reported to their menfolk.

CONCLUSION

Certainly no single explanation can be offered for the incorporation of farming into the activities of contemporary urban households in Kampala. However, the research reported here suggests that the need to farm is driven at least as much by the internal dynamics of households as by external forces such as declining real wages.

Is farming to be considered a 'household strategy?' Clearly, in terms of the imperative to provide a secure source of food, whether for supplementary or reserve usage, the household is the social unit within which the imperative springs. In terms of the allocation of labour and other resources required for agricultural production, as well as the manner in which production is controlled, the issue is less clear-cut. A variety of factors are involved. These include the division of both labour and responsibilities within households for providing food; control over other income and other resources; and the degree of joint decision-making, both about short-term spending and longer-term investments.

To be sure, all these factors are subject to the influence of external forces. But, in urban areas in Uganda today, farming is largely an effort by women to control a source of food which is required for the survival and well-being of persons for whom they are responsible. Except for those with no formal education, farming represents less the exclusion of women from other kinds of economic activities than an effort to protect or supplement other income, and to protect their sources of food from the unpredictable nature of wage labour and informal trade in the city. The logic of farming in the city, then, varies with the circumstances of the people who, individually or as a household, engage in it.

PART THREE
TRANSFORMING POLITICAL
REPRESENTATION

SEVEN
The challenges of constitutionalizing politics in Uganda

Goran Hyden

In the middle of 1995 Uganda completed a seven-year-long constitutional reform process which started with the appointment of a constitutional review commission in 1988 – the Odoki Commission named
after the high court judge who chaired it. Following the elections in
1994 to a Constituent Assembly, the latter met for a period of about
eighteen months to deliberate on recommendations put forward in
the Odoki Commission's report. The Ugandan experience of constitution-making is unique in at least two respects. The first is the length
of time it has taken to complete the process. Although constitutional
reviews in other countries are known to have taken a long time – for
example the 1968 Constitution of Sweden took twelve years to work
out – the time allotted to this exercise in Uganda has no equivalent in
Africa. The second aspect is the domestication of the constitution-
making process. It involved consultation of the people through hear-
ings and submissions to the Odoki Commission and it involved locally elected representatives deliberating on the issues in the Constituent
Assembly. Although similar exercises have been conducted in
Ethiopia and Eritrea, Uganda was the first African country to embark
on it.

The purpose of this chapter is to reflect on the experience of trying
to constitutionalize politics in Uganda. Ugandans themselves have different views on the experience. Some are very satisfied with what they
regard as the democratic character of the process used in arriving at
the new constitution. Others are disappointed, arguing that the views
of the minorities have been largely ignored. This account is an attempt
to look beyond these particular viewpoints and to assess what has been
achieved, and to identify the challenges that exist in putting the constitution to good use for the whole of Uganda in the future. It will deal
less with specific details of the constitution than with the broader issues
that the whole exercise of constitution-making raises for Uganda as well
as the rest of Africa. The chapter addresses the following questions: (i)
what is a constitution? (ii) how constitutionalizable is Ugandan politics?
(iii) where has the constitution-making taken Uganda? and, (iv) what
are the challenges and opportunities facing the various political group-
ings in the immediate future?

WHAT IS A CONSTITUTION?

The purpose of a constitution is to provide a framework of rules within which politics will be practised. Constitutions differ in terms of how much they try to cover, but the essential components of all constitutions refer to the relations between rulers and ruled and the rights and duties of a citizen vis-à-vis the state and other citizens. Compared to most of its counterparts elsewhere in the world, the 1995 Uganda Constitution is quite extensive and covers more ground. In order to understand what the pros and cons are, it may be helpful to think of a constitution as being at one and the same time both a set of normative rules and a map of power relations in society. The first is the idealist dimension of a constitution, the second its realist dimension. No constitution can survive for long as a workable instrument unless it satisfactorily covers both.

The constitutional debate in Uganda has reflected the inevitable tension that exists between these two dimensions. President Yoweri Museveni and the National Resistance Movement have not only consistently argued that Uganda needs a constitution which responds to the challenges of the country's particular legacy of sectarian violence, but they have also been very concerned to make sure that the constitution-making process itself is democratic. In this respect, Uganda has taken a very different approach to constitutional and political reform from that of most other African countries. For example, the governments in neighbouring Kenya and Tanzania have shown little interest in engaging in any form of constitutional reform which involves groups outside the ruling party. By opening up the process of constitutional reform to the society as a whole, the leaders of Uganda have sought legitimacy not only from within their own ranks but also from other circles. By adopting this approach, however, these same leaders have also taken the risks of being challenged by others in terms of which principles should guide Ugandan politics in the future.

In the African context, this is a form of political courage rare among leaders. The experience has taught the NRM many lessons, the most important being that it is a political force in its own right which can survive without recourse to its military wing. Whatever one might say about the formula for the 1996 presidential and parliamentary elections, they did confirm to the leaders of the NRM that the political constellations in the country have definitely changed in its favour. Because the NRM has been in the driver's seat throughout this exercise, it has all the time been concerned with finding a constitutional formula that bears a Ugandan imprint. This very ambition has exposed the leadership to criticism from the opposition which has found inspiration from the universal declarations of human rights and practices adopted in other parts of the world. In adopting this universalist stand, the opposition has often appeared to take the moral high ground vis-à-vis the NRM. It has tried to shame the Movement into compliance with norms that other civilized states already practise. It keeps portraying the present leaders as no better than Amin and Obote, whose human rights records in Uganda are seen by all as particularly bad.

The NRM has yielded very little ground to the opposition in debates on at least the more crucial issues such as the form of government (decentralization versus federalism) or of political system (no-party versus multi-party), and has fallen back on the rationale of the realist dimension of constitution-making, that the final document must be grounded in the society it is meant to serve.

It is fair to summarize that, at the end of the constitution-making process in 1995, the differences over whether the idealist dimension should be allowed more influence over the realist dimension, as the opposition insisted, had not been resolved. Disenchantment with this state of affairs – most dramatically expressed by the walkout in the Constituent Assembly before the vote on whether to retain the movement system or not – has been particularly widespread in circles representing the old political parties, Uganda Peoples' Congress (UPC), Democratic Party (DP), and Conservative Party (CP). While these sentiments are fully understandable given the limited influence opposition representatives have had on major constitutional matters, this stalemate between the NRM and the opposition also raised the question of the kinds of expectations of constitution-making entertained in African countries nowadays.

HOW CONSTITUTIONALIZABLE IS UGANDAN POLITICS?

African politics has been variably described as 'personal rule' (Jackson and Rosberg, 1982),'prebendalist' (Joseph, 1987), or 'patrimonialist' (Hyden and Bratton 1992). In all these characterizations the notion is implied that the private realm is more important to the ruler than the public realm; that the person in power is more important than the role he occupies; and that the leader is above the law. All these qualities are the opposite of what is usually associated with constitutional democracy, the model towards which Uganda, like other African countries, has been striving in recent years. In short, politics in Africa is particularly difficult to constitutionalize — a tough and elusive beast to tame.

It might be argued that Uganda has suffered some of the worst consequences of the type of rule described above. The 1962 Constitution, adopted on the eve of independence, was essentially a compromise product worked out between the various Ugandan parties active at the time and the British Government, the colonial power. Constitution-making in those days was aimed primarily at grabbing rather than sharing power. The actual text bore little relationship to the political aspirations of the new Ugandan leadership. Because it was never really internalized by the Ugandans, it would have been of no great significance when it was abrogated by Prime Minister Obote in 1966, had it not been for the removal of the Kabaka of Buganda as President of Uganda at the same time. The outcry had less to do with the actual sus-

111

pension of the constitution than with the fact that one leader was making himself supreme at the expense of another. Patrimonialism could not be effectively practised in a system of shared leadership, and as it emerged as the key feature of Ugandan politics from 1966, the constitution lost its significance as a normative guide for political behaviour. Uganda fell into a pattern which Okoth Ogendo (1993), with reference to the African continent as a whole, has described as having a 'constitution without constitutionalism'.

For twenty years Uganda suffered the disastrous consequences of a system of rule in which there were no limits to the exercise of power. During this period the country went through no less than seven different regimes, all of which ignored the rule of law and left people without a sense of personal security and power. Many Ugandans were forced into exile and those staying on withdrew from politics, leaving the politicians to conduct their business without any accountability. The fact that the tyrannical rule during these twenty years had largely been exercised by leaders from ethnic groups in Northern Uganda using political parties to divide and rule the groups in the South, was to have an important effect on subsequent political developments.

The accumulated disenchantment with corrupt and dictatorial rule caused some educated and politically militant southerners under the leadership of Yoweri Museveni to challenge the system by beginning a guerrilla war in 1981. After five years in the bush, during which his troops gradually gained control over Western and Central Uganda, they were able to take Kampala in early 1986, replacing at that time the weak government of General Tito Okello. Committed to an alternative form of regime, in which popular participation, if not popular sovereignty, featured prominently, the Museveni government extended to the whole of the country a system of 'resistance councils' which had originally been set up in the liberated areas. These councils, which have operated in a hierarchical fashion all the way from the village to the national level since 1986, were established during the guerrilla war under the auspices of the NRM. In order to ensure as broad-based a regime as possible, Yoweri Museveni co-opted other groups, right, left and centre, into his movement. At the same time, most activities of other political organizations were suspended. Political participation was possible only under the auspices of the NRM — a virtual no-party situation. This limitation meant that some groups which had been particularly critical of Museveni's rise to power, notably northerners organized in Obote's UPC, were very reluctant to participate in the new regime. With time, especially after Museveni's government opened the doors to drawing up a new constitution, most UPC supporters accepted participation on the terms set by the Movement. Pockets of resistance continued, however, especially in the North, as soldiers from the defeated army of Tito Okello took to the bush to fight the Museveni government under a variety of different leaders and motivations.

The challenges of constitutionalizing politics in Uganda

The philosophy underlying Yoweri Museveni's approach to reforming Ugandan politics seems to have been that civil society cannot be trusted to lead Uganda forward unaided because it is still parochially divided along ethnic or religious lines. Basing his argument on the experience of politics during the first two decades of independence, he considered that pluralist politics would only have the effect of reinforcing these divisions moving Uganda backwards rather than forward. His position is that, above all, the economy needs to be developed so that social classes and social and economic issues become the foundation on which future politics rest. To this effect, Museveni embraces the structural adjustment policies because they do indeed tend to create class divisions in society. For this same reason, however, he is in no hurry to bring political parties back. He wants to see a further transition of at least five years during which his NRM continues to control politics. Only if people agree in a referendum, now most likely to take place in 2000, will parties be reinstated after this transition period. Yoweri Museveni is less sure than the opposition – and representatives of the donor community – that the return of party politics is a blessing for the country. He attaches more importance to the role of social structures and he does not think that politics can be used to shape society at will.

Because the suffering in Uganda had been so widespread and deep, it was not difficult for Yoweri Museveni to gain support initially for his claim to start a new chapter in Uganda's post-independence political history. His call for respect for human rights and the investigation of past abuses, as well as his ambition to promote popular participation in government affairs through the system of resistance councils, were seen as steps in the right direction, however, by a vast majority of Ugandans. The establishment of a constitutional commission was viewed as another move which would take the country to a new level of governance at which individual freedom would be respected and peace among Ugandans secured more firmly.

Looking back at the past ten years or so of Ugandan politics, it is clear that one of the ironies of the NRM victory is that it raised the level of expectations among Ugandans so high, in terms of what could be done to change the country's politics, that many people now see what has come out of the constitution-making process as a disappointment. Many Ugandans cling to the expectation that constitution-making can reshape the political landscape dramatically. Such an expectation is quite unrealistic. There is no doubt that the NRM has changed the quality of politics in Uganda considerably, but features of the old system have survived. These are evident in the positions taken by the opposition, which by and large feed on the same ethnic and religious divisions that structured Ugandan politics before 1986.

But traces of the past are also to be found in the actions of the NRM. The notion of politics as a 'zero-sum game' in which winner takes all, is evident in the approach which the NRM takes towards government. Patronage continues to be part of the way of governing. These obser-

113

vations are not made in any moralizing fashion, but rather as a reminder that there are limits to how much a political system can actually be changed over a relatively short period of time. Ugandan governance has been transformed in many important respects, notably in terms of popular involvement, deregulation, and decentralization. But there are other areas where changes will not come immediately and where practice will therefore continue to diverge from promise. These areas include inter-group relations and civil and political liberties, both of which continue to be threatened by civil violence, involving rebels or bandits as well as units of the National Resistance Army or the more recently created Local Defence Units. That is why work in the human rights field continues to be important in Uganda and a priority for all those who hope to help Ugandans to build a society characterized by both civic freedom and civic peace in future. The encouraging thing in the present situation is that, although the NRM still sets some limits to work in this field, there is no outright harassment of individuals or organizations active in the field as is the case in some other African countries.

WHERE HAS CONSTITUTION-MAKING TAKEN UGANDA?

Drawing on the notion of constitution-making having both an idealist and a pragmatic dimension, it may be helpful to try to understand where Uganda finds itself as a result of the political reform process that the country has been through since 1986. The most important aspect of constitution-making is to regulate state-society relations. This has two dimensions. The first is the representative one: how are individuals and groups in society to articulate their views in the public realm? This may also be called the 'input' side of politics. The second is the governance dimension – the output side – which deals with how the state is organized and government is constituted to carry out its business. With regard to both, the NRM and the opposition have taken divergent positions. The former has largely insisted on an inclusivist position, according to which, at least in principle, all citizens are expected to participate in politics on an equal basis under the overall umbrella of the Movement. The latter, in contrast, has throughout maintained an exclusivist position, whereby its representatives argued that people should be free to organize whichever groups and parties they wanted to. They should not be forced to co-operate with those whom they do not like. Diagrammatically these two positions are indicated in Figure 7.1, where they can be found in the upper left and lower right corners respectively.

As suggested there, the two positions are diametrically opposed to each other and the question that faces Uganda and the various actors involved in making its constitution work in the future is how far they are able to arrive at positions fostering greater unity as opposed to greater polarization. I am suggesting here that Uganda is at the crossroads: it could return to its former sectarianism or it could close its ranks and develop a new consensus about where it wants to go in the future. These two positions are represented in the lower left corner and the upper right corner respectively in Figure 7.1. The former represents essentially a return to a 'negative' form of politics in which winner takes all and loser gets nothing. This zero-sum form of politics would probably reverse the positive trend that the country has experienced in recent years, both economically and politically. The latter, by contrast, would enable the country to graduate to a new order, in which consensus about the basic rules of politics would be respected and stability would be strengthened. It is clear that the second route is the more difficult one because it requires a certain amount of give-and-take that Ugandan politicians are still finding quite foreign. Being in power, it seems, means taking full advantage of that position at any cost. A perspective which stresses that there are short-term concessions to be made in order to make long-term gains, has yet to be internalized by political leaders in Uganda.

The crucial question which faces Ugandans as they approach the turn of the century is whether they can avoid falling into the sectarian trap and thus avoid renewed violations of human rights and potential bloodshed. Will the leaders on both sides of the political divide face up to the challenges of enhancing the positive developments that the people, by and large, have experienced during the past ten years?

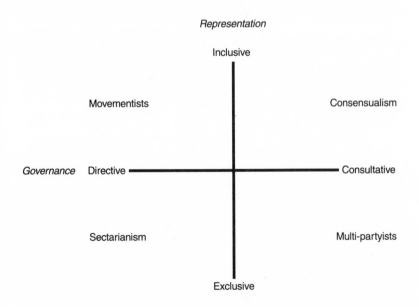

Figure 7.1 *Dimensions of constitution-making*

115

Transforming political representation

THE CHALLENGES OF BUILDING DEMOCRACY

The challenges to the NRM are many, but foremost among them is the task of retaining its position as an inclusivist organization. The whole rationale of a movement is that it is open to every one and thus serves as a catalyst of change for society as a whole. That is how the NRM originally came to power and acquired legitimacy across the country. President Museveni likes to compare the movement to a river which is being constantly recharged by the water from its tributaries, and at the same time loses some through evaporation and its use by human beings, animals and plants, with some of it coming back in the form of new rain. In short, his view of the movement is one of constant renewal. This perception of the movement has been questioned in Uganda for two major reasons. The first is that, as the constitution-making process began, the Movement had to take positions on critical issues on which there was bound to be more than one position. In short, the very act of constitutionalizing politics put the NRM in opposition to other political currents in the country, notably those represented by the multi-partyists and federalists. As this process of making the constitution unfolded, it became increasingly difficult for the Movement to retain its inclusivist image. Those holding a different opinion from it on critical issues came to the conclusion that it was no different from any other political party, and that the NRM leadership should recognize that fact.

The other reason why Yoweri Museveni's organization has come under increasingly critical scrutiny is the general difficulty of retaining political energy within an all-embracing movement as time passes. Movements build up their strength while in opposition rather than in power. The NRM tries to be part of both state and civil society at the same time. This generates contradictions which are not easily resolved, and where the tendency often is for its association with the state to take precedence in finding a solution. This leaves behind an image of the movement as more exclusivist than inclusivist. Thus, the task of renewal becomes more difficult, and there is a tendency for the river to dry up, to continue with Yoweri Museveni's own metaphor. This problem is well known from the history of other societies which have attempted major social or political transformations; and it is clear that in Uganda, too, the NRM is a victim of the very expectations it has created for itself. For this reason, it is not surprising that some leading members in the movement advocate the need for a transition to another system. Even Museveni himself, in a nine-page letter to NRM supporters in the Constituent Assembly on 21 June 1995, suggested that the NRM should be ready to transform itself into a new kind of political organization to compete for political power, should circumstances change during the next five years. This is the closest he has come to indicating that a return to multi-party politics may in fact become reality by the turn of the century. The likely effect of such a transformation would be to make the movement more like any other political party and thus more exclusivist

116

than inclusivist. This is the tension that the movement and the country as a whole, will have to learn to live with during this period of transition. Living up to expectations of itself as an inclusivist organization, while simultaneously preparing for political competition in the more distant future, is likely to prove a hard test for Yoweri Museveni and the NRM. It could wear down the legitimacy of the movement as an instrument of national integration unless new ways of bringing others on board, in the interest of national unity, are adopted.

Challenges to the opposition are also serious. Many leaders of the existing political parties seem unwilling to recognize that a majority of Ugandans are likely to have strong and continuing reservations about the return of political parties. Their memory of how party leaders have behaved in the past is such that they have a legitimate fear that multi-party politics might plunge the country into chaos and reverse the economic progress many ordinary Ugandans have enjoyed in the past decade. A recent study of perceptions of democracy among Ugandans, both elite and non-elite, in four districts (Hoima, Kampala, Lira and Luwero) seems to confirm this orientation (Ottemoeller, 1996). One of the major findings is that Ugandans tend to asssociate democracy more with individual freedoms, e.g. free speech, than with the right to organized political expression. In short, there is a considerable body of opinion in Uganda for whom the current political set-up, which amounts to competition and openness within the overall framework of a one-party system, is quite legitimate at least as long as there is freedom of speech and regular elections are held.

In the light of widespread doubt about the wisdom of returning to a multi-party system, it seems reasonable, if the country's voters so decide in the referendum on that issue in 2000, that such a return should be accompanied by legal and other measures to regulate political behaviour and make party leaders more accountable to their own members as well as to the public at large. Yoweri Museveni's leadership code is one step in that direction but, judging from the experience of Tanzania, it is not enough. A broad-based public commission, representing all political organizations, would be another means of ensuring that a new code of ethics is developed for political leaders in Uganda.

Such a commission would have to deal with such issues as what kind of criteria should guide the formation and composition of political parties, and what guidelines should be adopted for partisan debates. Past politics in Uganda suggests that parties tend to become based on religious or ethnic affiliation, and it would be desirable to come up with a formula that minimizes or mitigates these tendencies. This can be done by insisting on proof of support among broad segments of the population at the time of registration as well as in actual elections. This issue, however, could also be handled in a broader context of electoral legislation. For instance, a system of proportional representation has many of the qualities that reduce sectarianism, and instead encourages consensus across party boundaries. In many respects, such a reform would be a natural course of action for Uganda, if it wants to avoid a return to the divisive nature of past politics (Hyden, 1994). The fact that this particular system of electoral representation has been most ardently advocated by Dr Paul Semogerere, the leader of the Democratic Party and Museveni's chief contender in the 1996 presidential election, should not be allowed to stand in the way of a closer scrutiny of it. Whatever Ugandans decide to do eventually, however, reforming political behaviour is one item of unfinished business that the country must return to at some time during the next few years. The more broad-based and open an activity is, the more legitimate, and thus more effective, it is likely to prove.

The greatest difficulty Ugandans face in taking on this kind of reform is how to make political leaders more interested in, and capable of, transcending narrow self-interests and short-term gains. Although members of the Constituent Assembly developed skills in political compromise in creating the new constitution, their concern about the character or quality of the public realm was often limited and a vision of a substantively different future was lacking. The constitutional debate was at times of high quality but it is not clear how much it leaves behind a legacy of firm principle. The rather brash character of the constitutional debate in Uganda in recent years in which the foremost objective has been to 'trash' the opponents at any cost, often with exaggerated and highly personal arguments, suggests that Ugandans still have a considerable way to go before respect for the rule of law, and tolerance of people of other political persuasions, are properly institutionalized. As long as these qualities are missing, it is understandable that the political opposition to the NRM should be reluctant to accept its decisions, even when passed with a sizable number of votes. To them, tyranny of a minority has been replaced by tyranny of the majority.

Fortunately for Uganda, there are a good number of politicians who are capable of elevating constitutional and political debate to a level where narrow self-interests may be transcended in the interest of more worthy objectives. The outcome of the transition, for which seven years of constitution-making have laid the foundation, will depend on how much influence these particular politicians are allowed. The country's social and political fabric is still fragile. It may still be ripped apart very easily. For this reason, it is important that those allowed to set the tone of public debate in Uganda separate the private from the public, the short-term from the long-term.

CONCLUSIONS

Nobody can deny that the constitution-making process in Uganda has been more democratic than in most other African countries. The very fact that the country adhered to the principles of broad-based consultation helped legitimize politics after the many years of earlier alienation. It would be wrong, however, to look upon the dissolution of the

118

Constituent Assembly and Yoweri Museveni's confirmation as President by popular vote as the end of a process. It is rather the beginning of a new chapter. Now the greatest challenge is compliance with principles which enable Uganda to move towards consensualism rather than sectarianism in its public life. Many of these principles are not necessarily enshrined in the new constitution but inherent in what might be best termed civilized political discourse, that is, respect for the views of others and readiness to treat politics as a positive-sum rather than a zero-sum game. The seven-year effort to constitutionalize Ugandan politics has made a contribution towards this and it is likely that Uganda would have been worse-off without it. In this respect, the process has had a value in and of itself. Nations take years to build. The optimistic and often naive assumptions about nation-building which prevailed during the early years of independence are now gradually giving way to more realistic ones in which people realize that political development, like economic progress, only comes with concerted effort over a long period of time.

Although this effort must be led by the Ugandans themselves, friends of Uganda in the donor community have an important role to play. They can help the country strengthen its democratic structures and practices by nudging government and other political actors in a positive direction. This requires a careful balancing between consistency in positions on key issues and sensitivity to the sovereignty of local actors. A majority of Ugandans are rightfully proud of the constitutional process that they have been through recently and it is important that their sense of ownership of the task of reforming politics in the country is not violated unnecessarily by outsiders. Donors can also play a helpful role by assisting Ugandan civil society to get more involved in the political reform process. It is understandable that the focus of attention in the recent past has been on the form of government and principles of governance. As important in the long run, however, is the strengthening of institutions outside government, because they too are an integral part of the process of making the country more democratic. The field of human rights is still in need of much improvement in Uganda and efforts aimed at strengthening respect for such rights – both civil/political and social/economic – deserve continued and increased attention. Such support in the long run is as important as that given in recent years to the constitution-making process.

EIGHT
Local women's associations and politics in contemporary Uganda

Aili Mari Tripp

While Uganda has pursued critical debates about multi-partyism at the national level in the Constitutional Commission and the Constituent Assembly, other related debates have been going on over freedom of association and associational autonomy in the day-to-day politics of local communities. These community debates have been less conspicuous but they are every bit as important as the national debates because they affect the way that people interpret, struggle over and put into practice notions of participation in a new political order.

There are some important institutional changes taking place within Ugandan society, changes in who gets to participate, when and how. This is because there are some fresh actors on the scene who are taking advantage of new political spaces. They are also bringing new concerns to bear. In Uganda these roles are played out within Parent Teacher Associations, in district level development associations, in self-help health committees, in popular theatre groups, and in the many local women's associations formed since 1986. Debates are not only taking place at the Nile Hotel's International Conference Centre in Kampala. They are going on in everyday life, in communities, and in local struggles over access to resources. And, in some of these dialogues, new rules and ways of thinking are emerging about how government relates to the society it seeks to govern.

Local women's associations, for example, are concerned with the autonomy of association and the limits of participation within the local context. Women in some cases are challenging local authorities to permit them greater access to resources and community leadership. As long as large sections of society like women, who make up over half of the electorate in Uganda, are excluded from leadership and participation, the process of reform will be incomplete. Legal reform and constitutional change are necessary components of any movement towards political liberalization. For changes in the rules at the national level to have a lasting impact, there needs to be a simultaneous movement away from paternalistic, authoritarian and undemocratic structures at the local level.

In order to understand these transformations at the local level, I carried out a series of studies of community conflicts primarily involving

120

women's associations and various levels of the Resistance Council system before the inauguration of the new constitution.[1] This account is based on fieldwork conducted in the summer of 1992 and between January and July 1993. With the help of several enumerators, I also carried out a cluster/stratified survey of 1,142 randomly selected citizens (80 per cent women, 20 per cent men) in the urban centres of Kampala, Mbale, Kabale and Luwero (Luwero and Wobulenzi townships), looking at political and associational participation.[2] In addition, I interviewed leaders of national women's associations, women parliamentarians, academics and various government officials to get their sense of changes at the national level.

'WHEN THE JAWS DO NOT COME TOGETHER THEY CANNOT BITE'

In Uganda, women's associations are an important force, not just because women number half the population, but because as a group they have been most supportive of the NRM and yet most fiercely independent of it. In fact, in the districts surveyed, gender emerged as a better predictor of party affiliation than ethnicity or religion. This is important, given the high politicization of ethnicity and religion in the country.

Because of past instability, economic crisis, and the austerity measures connected with structural adjustment, people have sought numerous strategies, as individuals, neighbourhoods and communities, to raise incomes and to provide social and welfare services. At the local level one finds rotating savings clubs; community development associations for building roads, schools, clinics, wells; church committees for community improvement; local health committees; digging groups; burial societies and many other such organizations. Women are especially active in these organizations. Some women's groups are unregistered and loosely structured. Many others are registered with a church body, as a co-operative or with the National Association of Women's Organizations of Uganda (formerly the National Council of Women) under some other heading. Even informal unregistered groups frequently have a constitution, procedures for changing their leadership, and mechanisms to ensure financial accountability and keep strict records of their finances. Groups with little formal education sometimes enlist an educated daughter of one of the members to keep their records.

While associations like burial societies and digging groups are not new, the majority of women's associations have emerged since 1986 both at the national and local levels, taking advantage of the stability that grew when the NRM came to power (National Council of Women, 1991). In Kabale, which has the highest concentration of associations of the four towns surveyed, there were almost five times as many associations formed in the five-year interval between 1988 and 1992 as in the previous five years 1983–7. In Luwero only one organization was reported to have been formed in that area during the years of turmoil

(1983–7), while half the organizations there were set up during the following five years. Between 1986 and 1988, national-level associations like the Uganda Women's Effort to Save Orphans (UWESO), Action for Development (ACFODE), Uganda Global Network on Reproductive Rights, Uganda Women's Finance Credit and Trust Fund (UWFCT) were either formed or reactivated. While these formal non-governmental organizations emerged to take advantage of the new political spaces created by government, the impetus for many local-level groups was the need to meet economic needs and to fill gaps in public services which the local government was unable to finance (Kabukaire, 1992: 40).

The main organizations women were involved in were income-generating, handicrafts, cultural (music, drama, dance), religious,[3] and credit and savings associations. Women also participated in welfare groups, e.g., groups serving orphans and associations for people with special needs, like the blind or physically disabled. In areas like Kabale where two-thirds of the urban dwellers farmed, digging groups were especially popular. Many associations additionally participated in community self-help initiatives of various kinds, such as buildings, roads, wells, and assisting rural women's groups with various skills. However, most groups were multi-purpose. Men were more likely to be in single-purpose organizations, and, in particular, to be found in co-operatives, sports clubs and burial societies. They were less inclined to join religious organizations.

Women surveyed reported that the main successes of their groups were the provision of tangible benefits to members in the form of income, services or equipment (with which to generate income). Providing education, assisting the needy and developing their local area were also seen as major accomplishments. Lack of funds, difficulty in finding donors, and getting members to pay dues were the most frequently mentioned problems. Women saw low attendance at meetings as a problem, along with objections by husbands. Men often did not approve of their wives belonging to a women's group because they feared the women would gossip, group activities might detract from housework, and the women might come in contact with other men – and new ideas.

When asked why they joined organizations, women mentioned most frequently that they wanted to help one another, work and share together, learn new skills, improve their standard of living, and earn money. One of the members of a group named 'give of yourself' explained that under difficult circumstances 'It is important that you first give of yourself and think of others and then of yourself . . . You cannot survive if you only rely on yourself, we all need one another.' Others saw strength in joining forces. This was reflected in the name of one Pallisa group *Agali Amo:* 'when the jaws do not come together they can not bite' (Mulyampiti, 1993). Local groups averaged between 20 and 30 members.

Groups tended to be formed along gender lines. In Luwero, Mbale and Kabale women were twice as likely to join an all women's group as men to join an all men's group; and in Kampala, women were three times as likely as men to be in a same-sex group. Men, on the other hand, were more likely than women to be in a mixed same-sex group. In contrast to the strict gender segregation of associations, in urban areas both men and women were more likely to be in mixed ethnic and mixed religious groups, and women more so than men. Women saw this as an important break from the past when they tended to affiliate along narrower lines. One reason for the change is that economic crisis has given urban women added impetus to find new bases of association beyond the religious and ethnically based groups which were more common in the past (Tripp, 1994: 107–31). The main way the groups raised funds was by collecting dues from members, selling products, performing at cultural events, and (in Kabale) digging in other people's fields. In Mbale, assistance from outside the group was negligible. In Kampala and Kabale, one-quarter of the groups received outside assistance, whereas in Luwero almost one-third of the groups obtained outside funding. Religious-based organizations were the main ones receiving funding, which generally came from the national church body to which they were affiliated.

Women fiercely defended the independence of these associations and often deliberately kept them small, informal, invisible and unregistered, in order to make sure that they did not lose control of them to an outside regulatory or governmental authority. When I asked one member of a Kampala savings club why her group was unregistered when they might be able to apply for credit if they registered, she replied:

> These organizations will collapse if they become formalized. We work so well informally. We have no office. Everything is nice and simple. The minute we become formal we will collapse. The minute we try to get credit, we will become a shambles. The group is based on trust, mutual confidence, flexibility. You do what you want, the organization is yours. What would we do if we registered? We would have to have a location, an office, and we can't afford that. We would have to get registered and do the proper paperwork. Who would have time to go around and do all that? We are all working women. Then they would want us to be a cooperative and we do not want that. They would want a fee and we can't afford that. We just want things nice and simple.[4]

WOMEN AND POLITICAL PARTICIPATION

While defending this kind of associational autonomy, women are perhaps paradoxically also seeking new avenues for participation and engagement in the political arena. The women we surveyed reported dramatic changes in women's status after 1986, attributing the biggest changes to female participation in politics, standing for office, becoming leaders in government and society, and being able to express themselves publicly to a greater degree than in the past. Similarly, three-quarters of the women surveyed saw female leaders as equally or more effective than male leaders. Related to their gains in politics, women have conveyed a general sense of accomplishment since 1986, typically commenting that 'women have developed,' 'they are no longer backward,' 'women have more confidence in themselves,' 'women have started their own businesses,' 'they have become financially independent of men,' 'women work harder than they ever did,' 'women can involve themselves in any kind of occupation,' and 'women are no longer restricted as they had been in the past'. The pattern in the women's responses was striking, whereas men were more tentative about the changes women had experienced. In Kampala, for example, four times more men than women saw *no* change in the position of women.

These survey results suggest that women themselves had been responsible for many of the changes that have occurred since 1986, as women's organizations and leaders repeatedly pressed the NRM government to make good its promises to place women in responsible positions. In 1994 there were two women Cabinet members, three ministers and one deputy minister. A woman held the key position of Minister of Agriculture.[5] Seven out of 32 Permanent Secretaries and five out of 38 District Administrators were women. Women were also represented on national commissions and parastatal boards. In the National Resistance Council, 34 (15 per cent) of the seats were reserved for women; two women had won their seats in direct elections against male aspirants, one was nominated by the President, and two were 'historical' members associated with the NRM. While in 1994 women clearly did not constitute half the parliamentary body, their representation had improved significantly from 1980, when there had been only one woman out of 142 members of parliament. Similarly, if the 1994 Constituent Assembly elections are any indication, women are becoming less apprehensive about competing directly with men, i.e., 36 women ran in open contests against male candidates.

RESISTANCE COUNCILS AND WOMEN'S ASSOCIATIONS

One of the arenas in which women's interests and those of the NRM came into most conflict was within the Resistance Councils. It is here where one sees most clearly both the necessity of autonomous association and the limits of participation when Resistance Councils dominated local government. Resistance Councils were initially designed to be organs of the people, of the state, and of the NRM – at the same time. As organs of the people, they were intended to be the key arena for popular participation and were expected to hold civil servants and the state accountable to the people. At the same time, the RCs were under the jurisdiction of the Ministry of Local Government while serving as the political organ of the NRM. Political party activity and campaigning remained officially suspended (Ddungu, 1989; Mamdani, 1988a).

Local women's associations and politics in contemporary Uganda

The 1993 Local Government (Resistance Councils) Statute was an important step in devolving power and financial autonomy to local authorities, replacing the centrally appointed District Administrator with the elected Chairman of the District Council. Following the 1993 Statute, Resistance Councils were to become even more important as participatory vehicles promoting local involvement in security, carrying out self-help projects, planning and implementing development plans, collecting government revenue, mediating in local disputes, performing judicial functions and overseeing the provision of educational, medical, water and road services outside the jurisdiction of central government. While these are vital measures in enhancing local control and decision-making, the extent to which they are intended to subsume all local participation will blur lines of accountability and narrow further opportunities for popular participation. The focus on the Resistance Councils and local government as the main vehicle for participation in the earlier years of Museveni's government may also have limited coalition building among the various interests in Ugandan society. As Mamdani (1988, 1993a, 1994) and Ddungu (1989) have pointed out, in the past the focus on RCs delayed the development of political parties capable of combining various societal interests. It limited the possibilities for making politics issue-oriented rather than personality-oriented. Furthermore, it limited freedom of assembly and expression by making residence the main basis for political participation in Uganda. Although independent associations generally operated freely during Museveni's first years, the impulse to contain participation within the Resistance Councils acted as a constraint on their asserting their own interests separately.

One measure of the capacity of Resistance Councils to fulfil this participatory role was the extent to which they effectively represented competing interests within society. For example, critics have questioned how representative RCs were for women. In talking about women as a sector, it is important to recognize that women themselves represent varied and often competing interests. The Women's Secretary at village level is elected by all citizens in the locality and therefore may not necessarily be representative of the interests of the majority of women in the area, especially where men still make up the bulk of the population. Some have found instances where male villagers purposely promoted younger more timid women, 'a pretty face', or women who they knew would not challenge male authority during campaigns for the women's secretaryship. At other RC levels, all positions, including the Women's Secretary at the district level, were elected indirectly by an electoral college from a lower level, and the women's representatives in the National Resistance Council (NRC) were elected by the District Resistance Councils. By the time one reached the elections for District Resistance Council and the NRC, the electorate became overwhelmingly male, making women's representatives in such indirect elections 'less likely to function as representatives of women at large, and more likely to function as representatives of NRM to women at large' (Mamdami, 1993).

In spite of this limitation on women's representation, in all four towns surveyed increasing numbers of women voted with each successive RC election from 1987 to 1989 and 1992. By 1992, an average of three-quarters of the women voted in the four towns surveyed, with only slightly more men voting than women. In contrast, in the earliest RC elections there were instances in which men were elected as women's representatives, e.g., Bushenyi (Ddungu and Wabwire, 1991:40). By 1992 the situation had changed considerably and women were paying more attention to the women who ran for RC positions. Survey respondents reported that one-third of RC1 committees in Luwero, Mbale and Kampala had as many as two women members, and close to a half in Kabale. Less than 10 per cent had 3 or more women members – with the exception of Luwero, where over 20 per cent of its RCs had 3 or more women members. Women's increased involvement in associations has also stimulated a greater involvement in local-level politics. In fact, women involved in organizations were more likely to be active in RC politics. In all four towns, roughly two-thirds of the women involved in associations actively supported and campaigned for particular candidates in the 1992 RC election.

But, beyond elections, women have had mixed experiences of participating in the RC structure. Around one-third of the women surveyed reported participating in all or most RC meetings, with Kampala having the highest participation rates for women. Men participated roughly twice as much as women overall. Tabitha Mulyampiti (1993) found in rural Pallisa that women's attendance at the RC1 level was slightly less than 50 per cent, but it was negligible at the RC2 and RC3 levels. The reasons given for not attending had in large measure to do with opposition from husbands. Those women who did attend meetings tended to remain silent. Those who spoke up at the RC1 meetings attended by Mulyampiti did not manage to get their concerns considered. A Pallisa RC Women's Secretary said that at one time all the men in her RC decided that women should not bother to attend the meetings since it interrupted their domestic chores and that men should attend on their behalf. The woman RC representative was able to argue and convince the men that women should attend the meetings. She felt that her opinion had been listened to. However, the fact that these men even contemplated such an action is evidence that they were not yet at a point where the participation of women could be taken for granted. One Pallisa RC Women's Secretary commented to Mulyampiti:

> We are still ignored by our fellow committee members, the men. Many of them still think that a woman's husband should decide on her behalf. The committee is also dominated by men and usually when I talk, they think – before I can complete my sentence — that I am trying to oppose them. They have even stopped calling me to the meetings.

Because of such limitations on women's participation and voice in the Resistance Councils, women prefer their own groups as arenas in which

126

to mobilize and influence public opinion and policy-makers, carry out community development initiatives, improve their living standards or express their own political views. One RC Women's Secretary in Kasubi, Kampala, openly admitted this, saying that it was hard to mobilize women through the Resistance Councils and she was trying instead to mobilize established women's associations in her area such as a local Munno Mukabi group, local chapters of the Catholic Women's Guild and the Mothers' Union, a women market vendors' group and several other local self-help groups. She put it explicitly:

> Women are not keen about the RC system but would easily come to a Munno Mukabi (self-help/burial society) meeting, one that involves issues pertaining to income-generation or religion. It is easier to organize women through their weak points by appealing to their values, to what they love and cherish rather than the RC system.[6]

Mulyampiti (1993) also found in rural Pallisa that, because of the limited opportunities for mobilization within the RC structure, women formed organizations outside it, often using RC women officials as mobilizers and heads of clubs. She found 59 women's clubs in Pallisa District with approximately two clubs in each sub-county, involving about 9,600 women. The groups were involved in horticulture, vegetable growing, food and cash crop farming, brick making, handicrafts, music, dance, drama and other such activities. Like the women I surveyed, the main aim of groups in Pallisa was to improve living standards, gain access to credit and property, earn money to pay school fees and health fees, market their produce, learn better farming methods and acquire new skills in cooking, handicrafts and tailoring. The groups were also arenas for expressing opposition to various forms of oppression and appealing to policy-makers through dance, drama, and poetry, especially on issues of land ownership, to which women have little access in this area. They also used these cultural forms to raise public awareness of problems of widows' inheritance and lack of rights to retain control of their children.

Because of the limitations on participation within the Resistance Councils, local women's associations became even more important to women as arenas for mobilization. Perhaps ironically, women were found to be more possessive about their independence from the RC system than men, yet, according to my survey, they also tended to be more supportive of the NRM than men. To better understand this dynamic, it is helpful to examine a case study involving a dispute between a women's market co-operative and a Resistance Council in Kampala. The conflict brings into sharper focus some underlying issues, including (i) the limits of participation and representation within the Resistance Councils; (ii) the importance of autonomous organizations to maintain accountability and responsiveness within the Resistance Councils/Local Government system; and (iii) the importance of these associations as a source of pressure for changes in political norms and institutions on the grounds of inclusiveness, participation, and leadership.

KIYEMBE MARKET WOMEN

In 1983, a group of ten women street vendors, most of whom were widows from Luwero, formed a co-operative, the Kiyembe Women's Co-operative Savings and Credit Society. They obtained a plot of land and started a women's market at what is known today as Kiyembe Market in Kampala. Like the majority of women's organizations in Kampala, it was a multi-ethnic, multi-religious association independent of any political party affiliation even though its leader had been a *muluka* chief under Obote 2. By 1986 the co-operative had 107 members and the market had nearly 290 vendors. They deliberately kept it as a women's market because of their past experiences of losing control and resources when they had collaborated with men.

Their problems began in 1985 during the Lutwa Okello coup, at which time their market was looted by soldiers who stole both goods and money. Soon after the NRM came to power, the Kampala City Council announced that it was taking over all markets and the RC5 Chairman issued an ultimatum to market co-operatives that they should close down their societies or face a six-fold increase in daily fees paid on their stalls. The losses they had incurred a year earlier during the looting placed the Kiyembe women in an especially vulnerable position and the Kiyembe Women's Co-operative was left badly divided.

Then in 1987 some male vendors who had been employed by the women started what they described as 'a rebellion against the women' in order to gain control of stalls for themselves. One of the leaders of the rebellion was elected chairman of the market RC1 and remained in that position for four years. The RC5 chairman, who, according to the male vendors, was colluding with them, declared the following year that from the day he made the announcement those selling at the Kiyembe stalls would become the owners. Many of the women had hired young male employees because they had other household responsibilities, and they therefore lost not only their stalls but also their goods. More importantly, they lost control of the market.

The male vendors, led by the RC1 chairman and by their own Kiyembe Vendors Association, claimed responsibility for the takeover and justified it by saying that they did not want to be under the control of women. They argued that the co-operative was a UPC organization, an accusation the market women vehemently denied. When the women tried to regain their stalls, the young men beat them with sticks and bars, threatening to kill or imprison them, but the women refused to back down or be intimidated. The RC1 tried to force the women out of its office at the market but the women have refused to leave to this day. The male vendors at the market felt that the RC was helpful in solving their problems and that they had good working relations with it. The women, on the other hand, had nothing to do with the RC. They were convinced that they had lost control of the market because they were women. Mary Kaikara, leader of the co-operative, put it bluntly: 'They took our property because we were women'. This was confirmed by both the RC1 members and the former RC5 chairman, Wasswa Ziritwaula, who (according to several market women) had told them that he had never known a market to be owned by women and did not see why only women should have control of the place. The women did not consider the market RC a legitimate institution, even though the co-operative chairperson held the position of Women's Secretary. Clearly the interests of the male vendors and of the women co-operative members were at odds and each discounted the legitimacy of the other, the men on the grounds that the women had controlled the market exclusively as women, and the women's co-operative that their property and rights had been illegally misappropriated.

By 1994 it was clear that the Kiyembe Co-operative had done all it could on its own to reclaim the stalls and was taking steps to find a new market for the women. The women had appealed to the town clerk, the District Administrator, the Minister for Women and later to the Ministry of Community Development – but to no avail. They had also sought legal assistance from the National Council of Women and the Uganda Women Lawyer's Association (FIDA), but without success. The institutional weaknesses of these intermediary organizations made them incapable of supporting the cause of the Kiyembe market women, even though representatives of the NCW and FIDA made it clear that they thought the women had a just cause.

Nonetheless these Kiyembe women, despite some bitter experiences under the NRM, expressed their support for the political changes made after 1986, once again showing the complexity of women's relationship to the political order. They were still generally supportive of the NRM government and felt that it had opened up new possibilities for women. As one Kiyembe market woman put it:

> Women are becoming politically active and involved in the same affairs as men . . . Women are so effective as leaders and work harder than men so as not to be counted as failures. We attend political education training together with men. Women can even lead the men in this.[7]

The Kiyembe conflict demonstrates how important it was for the women to have an autonomous base from which to mobilize and to express their interests, because the Resistance Council (now known as the Local Council) represented the dominant interests of male vendors in this particular case. The Kiyembe women wanted control of the market because past experience had led them to believe that, if they shared control with men, the men would take over. Given the fact that at this time most public institutions at the local level were controlled by men, such a view was not unreasonable. The fact that the leader of the women's co-operative held the position of RC 1 Women's Secretary made no difference to the women's capacity to defend their interests, because of the predominance of men on the RC Committee.

AUTONOMY OF WOMEN'S ASSOCIATIONS AT THE NATIONAL LEVEL

Finally, struggles for autonomy are occurring not only at the local level. They have also had a national dimension, starting in the post-colonial regimes of Amin and Obote. Amin established the National Council of Women by presidential decree in 1978 to serve as an umbrella organization for independent NGOs. However, independent organizations were effectively curtailed during Amin's tyranny. Under Obote's second presidency (1980–5), the National Council of Women was subject to the manipulations of the Women's Wing of the UPC (Tadria, 1987:88). Many Ugandan women activists nonetheless attended the 1985 UN Decade for Women meeting in Nairobi as individuals and not as part of the official delegation led by President Obote's wife. They returned inspired to revitalize women's organizations in Uganda and to create new and autonomous ones. The Nairobi conference coincided with the coup that overthrew Obote, after which the NCW organized a peace march in Kampala, in part to assert its future autonomy from the UPC.

The coming to power of the NRM allowed women greater latitude to mobilize. Women's groups were encouraged to push for the formation of a Ministry for Women, which became a reality in 1988. Although women's associations have flourished under the NRM-led government, the NRM made constant efforts to control the mobilization of women at the national level. It established an eleventh directorate, the Directorate of Women's Affairs, at the NRM Secretariat, to be in charge of political mobilization (Boyd, 1989: 106–17). Although short on resources and not very visible in the women's movement, the Directorate carried on despite continual standing feuds with the Ministry for Women and in particular with the National Council of Women, which functioned as a parastatal body until 1993. The Directorate was allegedly responsible (although it never took the credit for it) for pressuring the Ministry for Women into redrafting and submitting to the National Assembly a National Women's Council statute repealing the 1978 act that had created the NCW. It also forced the Council to change its name to the National Association of Women's Organizations of Uganda (NAWOU) and to become a non-governmental organization, thus ending the possibility of its continuing to receive financial support from the Ministry. The Directorate was probably anxious to undermine, if not close down entirely, this organization, given its origins under the Amin regime and its more recent attachment to the UPC government of Obote. In its place a new 'National Women's Council' was to be formed with a name almost identical to the former NCW.

Even though most organizations, including the NAWOU, supported the repeal of the 1978 act and the creation of an independent umbrel-

130

la organization, officials at the Ministry for Women, NAWOU leaders, and other heads of women's organizations, were critical of the way in which the Directorate intervened to get the bill passed and the Council to change its name. The new National Women's Council was to be made up of women's councils at the village, parish, sub-county, county and district levels under the direction of the Ministry for Women, which would appoint the Secretary. The NRM claimed that these councils would enable it to reach all women because the independent women's organizations did not mobilize the majority of women. It remains to be seen whether the NRM has the capacity and resources to make the women's councils a reality in future. National women's organizations are adopting a 'wait and see' attitude, unwilling to be overtly critical of any gesture on the part of the government to encourage women's mobilization, but at the same time wary of the NRM's apparent attempt to control women's participation and incorporate it within a NRM political framework.

CONCLUSIONS

The proliferation of women's associations in both rural and urban Uganda provides a useful lens through which to examine the context and limits on autonomous collective action in the country. Here we have suggested how in concrete situations these local women's groups could engage and disengage the state at different levels and at different times. Women were at one and the same time taking advantage of new political opportunities afforded by the NRM regime, while also taking advantage of the autonomous spaces they had carved out for themselves and their organizations earlier, both to exert pressure in order to make the public realm more inclusive and participatory and to carry out their activities undisturbed. In some cases, they kept their distance to make sure their activities were not politicized or used to advance sectarian causes, in order to keep their primary focus on mutual economic and welfare concerns cutting across party, religious, and ethnic lines.

In the case of Kiyembe, the women's co-operative was the base from which market women sought to defend their interests. At the same time they were threatened by male vendors whose interests dominated the RC1. Without an autonomous base, the women would not have had a forum from which to express their particular interests, while also revealing some of the limitations of the Resistance Councils as representative of all. For the successors to Resistance Councils to be effective, representative and accountable to the population under their new names as Local Councils, it will be important to have associations independent of them and capable of acting as a check on their activities.

Ugandan women have adopted complex and seemingly contradictory strategies. In Kampala, Luwero, Mbale and Kabale, women were more likely to oppose multi-partyism than men. Generally they are reported to have been pleased with the NRM's encouragement of

131

women's opportunities in the political arena. At the same time, women jealously guard their associational independence. Basically, they seem to be keeping their options open. They want to make sure they do not lose their associational strength should Uganda again slip back into internal strife in the future. But throughout their various initiatives in recent years, women have demonstrated the importance of organizational autonomy that complements, challenges, and holds accountable local political structures, parties and government.

Notes

---

1. I am grateful to Rebecca Mukyala and Juliet Kiguli for their conscientious and tireless help in researching the Kiyembe case study.
2. Special thanks to Juliet Kiguli, Rebecca Mukyala, Primrose Naloka, Norah Kagambirwe, Mary Betubiza, Peace Kakira, Enid Rwakatungu for their assistance in carrying out the survey.
3. Common examples of religious groups include chapters of the Protestant Mothers Union or Catholic Women's Guild.
4. Interview, E.N., 2 June 1992.
5. The Ministers included Victoria Sekitoleko, Minister of Agriculture; Dr. Specioza Wandira-Kazibwe, Minister of Women in Development, Youth and Culture; Betty Okwir, Deputy Minister for Labour and Social Welfare, and Betty Bigombe, Minister of State in Prime Minister's Office for the Pacification of the North.
6. Interview, Mrs. Ssebawato, 18 June 1993.
7. Interview, J.K., 10 February 1993.

N I N E
Towards the empowerment of women:
a critique of NRM policies and programmes

Mary R. Mugyenyi

> Our policy aims at strengthening the position of women in the economy by
> raising the value and productivity of their labour and by giving them access
> and control over productive resources. By productive resources I mean
> land, capital, credit, seeds, fertilisers, tools, water, energy, education, infor-
> mation, etc.[1]

Developing Uganda takes men and women. Gender should therefore be
on the agenda of the development dialogue more so in Uganda where:
women constitute a 53 per cent majority of the population; they contribute 80 per cent of agricultural labour (the main income earner of the
economy) and 90 per cent of the domestic labour; and are almost exclusively responsible for the health and nutrition of their families and communities. Development requires a peaceful environment and a recipe
for promoting it in Uganda, if it is to bring about equity not only
between different ethnic and religious groups, but also between men and
women. Inequity breeds conflict, and conflict undermines development.

This chapter makes a critical evaluation of the National Resistance
Movement's policies and programmes in the light of women's empowerment. 'Empowering women' is conceptualized here as systematic
change towards gender equity or the process of weakening structures of
female subordination. The chapter assumes that state ideology affects
men and women differently, and that gender plays a significant role in
determining ways in which men and women participate in economic,
social and political activities. Men and women have different interests
and concerns based on their respective socio-economic statuses and on
the different roles they play within the household, the community, and
at the state level. Government policies and programmes therefore affect
them differently. Government programmes which ignore gender differences weaken the status of women and the welfare of their families.
It is therefore essential to examine the gender implications of policies
and programmes in order to achieve development aims.

In relative terms, the NRM government has shown commitment to
raising the status of women through positive policies and programmes.
The NRM pro-woman approach has been influenced by a number of
factors. In the first instance, distinguishing between the NRM's inter-
nally conceived gender policies and the mandatory policies of such

dominant world bodies as the World Bank Programme for the Alleviation of Poverty and Social Costs of Adjustment (PAPSCA), the United Nations and its agencies and other international organizations is not always easy. Secondly, the women's emancipation drive in Uganda is part of the World Wide Women's Movement, particularly after the UN Decade for Women (1975–85) and the Nairobi Forward Looking Strategies. Women in Uganda, in liaison with women elsewhere and with the support of the international community, have pressed for equal opportunities with men. The NRM came to power soon after the United Nations had responded favourably to international pressures in this field. Thirdly, the NRM's relatively pro-women policies might also have been inspired by the significant contribution that women as combatants, intelligence personnel, and support staff had made during the guerrilla war that brought it to power (Byanyima, 1992:136). Lastly, women have numerical strength as voters and supporters and it is beneficial to the government to have their support in elections and in the implementation of development projects.

The prevailing relative peace and stability in Uganda in recent years has made it possible for people to organize and to speak out. Women's organizations and clubs have mushroomed in numbers. Affirmative action has been taken in the education of women at university level and in politics through women's representation, first in the Resistance Council (RC) System and more recently in Local Councils. The appointment of women Ministers to key ministries, and the formation of a Women in Development Ministry, now merged with Youth and Culture, are further good gestures by government. In general terms, the NRM government has provided an enabling environment for women's emancipation activities. But to what extent have the women used their opportunities? How far can the government empower women?

WOMEN'S EMPOWERMENT

The term 'empowerment' has been used extensively in varying ways. For example, development organizations refer to empowering people in the sense of involving the poor in development activity. Feminist scholars (Antrobus, 1989; 207), (Kabeer, 1994: 224) have asserted that the term empowerment loses its political meaning when it is used as a substitute for integration or participation in development activity prescribed from above. They define empowerment as a bottom-up process in which less powerful people generally (women, the poor), have control over their lives. Empowering women should not be seen as involving women in agricultural production well calculated to take advantage of their free labour. Neither is it about targeting women for government or donor aid, based on their survival needs. Empowerment policies should start by addressing factors that prevent women from taking control of their lives. It should not be equated with having a few women in high positions. It is about weakening structures of gender discrimination. We can say that women are becoming empowered only if we see

134

change in the structural factors that create and sustain gender inequality, and that women's 'strategic interests' are being met. This change will give women an equal chance with men rather than favour just a few lucky or exceptional women.

Empowerment is a process; and the main point is not to draw a line between empowerment and disempowerment, as neither can be quantified. But change at the following levels could act as an indicator of empowerment: individual, socio-economic, political and organizational empowerment.

Individual empowerment:
(a) Conscientization – when the individual understands gender as a way of ordering society and human relations, rejects patriarchy as a form of exploitation, and puts forward arguments for women's rights as a form of human rights.
(b) Breaking the 'dependency syndrome' – self-reliance, rediscovering one's own sense of dignity and reaffirming confidence in one's own capacity to solve one's problems.

Socio-economic empowerment:
(a) Improved welfare relative to men (in income, access to social services, education and training opportunities, employment opportunities, etc).
(b) Access and control of the factors of production on an equal basis with men.

Political empowerment:
Participation in decision-making at all levels from the household to national leadership.

Organizational empowerment:
(a) Women's capacity to organize
(b) Women's position compared with that of men in mixed organizations.

OBSTACLES TO WOMEN'S EMPOWERMENT IN UGANDA

In broad terms, gender inequality in Uganda is reproduced through the paternal family and kinship systems; religious institutions which preach domination of the woman by the man; and an education system that stereotypes girls and boys into careers based on traditional roles and is reinforced by the state ideology through state policies and the legal system.

A close look at NRM policies reveals a number of obstacles to the women's emancipation movement in Uganda. The fundamental problem is that individuals are often not aware of the manifestations of patriarchy and its pervasiveness because it is intrinsically rooted in our value systems, beliefs and thinking processes. Hence, questioning patriarchy invariably means challenging values and beliefs. Policy-makers, who are mainly men but also women, hardly realize that they are practising gender discrimination. For example, development planners often speak of 'gender-neutral' policies. But how can development policies be neutral when the order of society is not? For example, is it possible to have gender-neutral policies in education when in actual fact boys and girls have unequal chances in getting education and training? Can it be possible in agriculture where even when women contribute much of the needed labour, they have little control and ownership of the factors of agricultural production (land, technology, information and training, etc.)? The so-called gender-neutral programmes and policies are 'gender-blind' policies. Gender-blindness in planning has negative implications for the overall achievement of development goals and not just for women.

> The costs of ignoring the needs of women are uncountable population growth, high infant and child mortality, weakened economy, ineffective agriculture, a deteriorating environment, a general divided society and poorer quality of life for all.

> This lack of recognition [and] neglect deprive the whole society of the benefits of higher economic activity which it would enjoy if women's work was recognised and supported. It also denies the women the status they deserve through their significant contribution to the development of the country. Women therefore continue to be the most socio-economically disadvantaged group in the country (Gertrude Byekwaso in Abid, 1990: 2).

There is a gap between what is said on paper and in rhetoric and what is practised on the ground. For example, agricultural credit schemes targeted at women have mostly ended in men's bank accounts. Examples include the Uganda Commercial Bank's Rural Farmers Scheme, where only 35 per cent out of a 60 per cent target for women was received by women, and the Bank of Uganda Development Finance Scheme where only 4 per cent of the funds was received by women. Lack of transparency and rampant corruption in the public sector frustrate some potentially good programmes for women. It is common practice to add women to development project proposals to meet the donors' requirement for women to be involved in development activities. However, it does not necessarily mean that the acquired funds will benefit women in general. They may well be diverted, as deemed necessary by decision-makers who are mainly men or elite women.

There is often conflict between modern law and cultural practice and expectations. One such example is in property ownership and inheritance. According to the law, a wife equally with a husband is entitled to 15 per cent of the spouse's estate at death. The practice, though, is that in the majority of cases a man inherits all of his wife's property, while culture dictates that a woman does not inherit from her husband at all. Where there is conflict between cultural unwritten laws and the written modern law, the cultural laws take precedence (Mugisha, 1992: 14).

There are no statutes that prevent a woman from acquiring property but according to custom, property acquired during marriage belongs to the husband. If a woman leaves her husband, she may have to leave most of her property. Traditionally, women are not their husband's automatic heirs. In some districts if a husband dies and the wife has only young children, she may be allowed to continue to occupy the house and work the land. In other areas she may be forced to leave or to marry a brother or other male relative of her late spouse (UNICEF, 189: 75).

Cultural custom in Uganda has undermined women's potential and limited their participation and contribution to national development. Culture is used to justify keeping women subordinate. Gender inequality, manifesting itself in prejudices, stereotypes and discriminatory practices, is still justified by cultural and religious explanations.

Cultures are never static but change in response to the needs and circumstances of society at a particular time. The beliefs and values of our hunter-gatherer forefathers and mothers could not possibly be maintained in our age of commercialized agriculture with complex market forces and arrangements. There are many aspects of our cultures that are valuable and give us identity as a people – language, food, dress, recreation, etc. But we must not hesitate to change those aspects of the culture that are anti-progress or which keep sections of our society subordinate to others. The same logic applies to other less privileged members of the population: the disabled, minorities, and the poor. Willingness to change and to adapt will not only benefit women but also enable society to cope more effectively with the present demands of development.

Lastly, although the government has taken many steps towards empowering women, it has never been committed to addressing gender discrimination at the domestic level. The domestic sphere is considered 'private' and outside political intervention. However, this is a serious omission because the so-called private issues (domestic violence, division of labour, property ownership and inheritance, wife inheritance, alimony, sexual violence, brideprice, child custody) apply to all families in Uganda and affect all girls and women. They are manifestations of a power imbalance between men and women in society. State legislation and monitoring are essential to redress imbalance in the domestic sphere. It is at the family level that the structures of gender subordination are rooted; where the socialization of girls and boys takes place; and where society's values and stereotypes are formed. This is the foundation level at which empowerment must begin. It is the gender bias in the household that is reproduced at the state level. Unless the government becomes committed to eliminating gender inequality at the domestic level, other policies in the context of empowering women will remain superficial. Empowering women should not be perceived as simply involving women in development activity but most importantly, as Antrobus (1989: 201) puts it, as building an infrastructure in which women can have control over their lives. The foundation for this infrastructure is the household, and it is at the household level that meaningful empowerment will begin.

POLITICAL EMPOWERMENT
Politics has been defined as the exercise of power in the public sphere. The public sphere for many societies is a man's domain while the private and domestic sphere is assigned to women (Bystytzienski, 1992: 2; Randall, 1987: 11; Burack, 1988: 274). This is the case in Uganda as women are mainly confined to the domestic realm as mothers and housewives.

Traditionally in Uganda, men wielded more political power and influence but women were not entirely excluded from politics. For example, in the kingdoms of Southern Uganda, women occupied important offices like chief princess, queen mother, and regent. They also conducted religious ceremonies, important rituals and advised the king (Nyinya-Mijinya, 1989: 2; Doornbos, 1978: 4). The Western style of leadership during the colonial period was based on the Western gender division of roles and stereotypes. The teachings of Christian and Muslim emissaries further deprived women of their political responsibilities. The post-independence period from 1962 to the early 1980s saw women's political participation reach its lowest level in Uganda.

The NRM government through the Resistance Council (RC) system puts in place an infrastructure to provide individuals and local communities, women included, with a chance to participate in politics and decision-making. Each Resistance Council at each level elects a nine-member committee, one of them a secretary for women. The Women's Secretaries at the RC5 level were also members of the District Resistance Council (DRC). Women in each district also elect a representative to the National Resistance Council (NRC) or parliament, altogether totalling up to 38 members of parliament. Apart from the women's seats, women contest open elections against men. Another example was the Constituent Assembly elections, where 9 out of 31 women successfully contested seats for the CA against men. There were altogether 51 women delegates out of 284 in the Constituent Assembly.

The extent to which women utilize their opportunities to the full in the political field has yet to be established. There is evidence to show that women's political activity is still restricted by their lack of confidence; disapproval from their partners; intimidation by male counterparts; fear and lack of time to perform tasks (Mulyampithi, 1994: 140). The RC committees had many responsibilities without remuneration, which reduced their effectiveness. Also important to note is that the RC's powers were limited as real power lay in the parent ministries, particularly in the Ministry of Local Government.

Women have also been elected to high office in the Ugandan government and the parastatals. The recent appointment of a woman vice-chair in the Constituent Assembly demonstrated the government's commitment to making women's voices heard more clearly and definitely in politics. However, in comparative terms, women are still underrepresented in decision-making positions in Uganda.

Table 9.1 Women in decision-making

Post	Female	Male	Total	Female %
Cabinet	2	20	22	9
Ministers				
of State	1	9	10	10
Deputy				
Ministers	2	9	11	18
Permanent				
Secretaries	7	35	42	17
Under				
Secretaries	16	45	61	26
District				
Administrators	5	34	39	13

The creation of a Ministry for Women

In realization of the need to involve women in the mainstream of development, as well in recognition of their contribution to economic production, the NRM government established a Ministry for Women in Development (WID) in 1988. The stated objectives of the Ministry were to bring women into the mainstream of all aspects of development activity. Following the public restructuring exercise of 1991, the Ministry became a department of Women in Development, under the broader Ministry of Women in Development, Culture and Youth (WIDCY). The WID department consists of five divisions: Planning, Legal, Education and Training, Research and Non-governmental Organisations (NGOs). The department monitored gender-balanced policy formulation, programme planning and implementation across sectors.

The department has conducted several successful programmes including the recently completed programme of educating and encouraging women to participate in the constitution-making exercise; gender policy implementation in each sectoral Ministry; and several gender sensitization workshops and conferences. On the other hand, the department was handicapped by: budgetary constraints, limited personnel, failure to co-ordinate women's activities countrywide, and the general marginalization of the department and its work. The merger with Youth and Culture may well imply stereotyping women as custodians of culture and child issues. But still more importantly, the merger has meant a further financial and human resource reduction in WID work. Given the state of the Ministry, and because of neglect of and resentment at WID policies, the influence of the WID department on the sectoral ministries has yet to be established. Sectoral ministry policies still reflect gender bias.

Women in the army

Women are mostly absent from the higher ranks of the National Resistance Army (NRA). Mrs Nalweiso is the only woman to be a senior officer in the NRA and a member of the army council. There is not a single woman in the army high command. Yet information about the war in the bush which brought the Museveni government to power, as provided by video tapes, personal stories and literature (Byanyima, 1992: 136), indicates a substantial presence of women soldiers. Where are these heroes now? Interviews I conducted among senior army officers indicate that: many of the women fighters left the army after the guerrilla war because they were frustrated by male harassment and discrimination within the army itself; some became wives of the male fighters and were withdrawn from the army by their husbands; the rest were sent to the Women's wing of the army in Bombo and subsequently retrenched during the recent demobilization exercise. We do not know the status of women in the lower ranks of the army and can only speculate about the welfare of wives and girlfriends of soldiers in the barracks. Women's biological nature is given as the major reason for their failure to progress within the ranks of the army. However, the army could be made more woman-friendly and more conducive to female participation.

Education and training

> A woman is a very crucial person in society. If we could succeed in educating a woman, we could kill many birds with one stone.[2]

Illiteracy among women is high (40 per cent) compared with men (26 per cent) (Uganda Demographic and Health Survey, 1989). The government has acknowledged the importance of educating women. Affirmative policies in favour of women's education include the 1.5 bonus points to female candidates at university entrance level since the 1990/91 academic year. The purpose of the policy is to correct gender imbalances in management and decision-making by increasing the number of skilled women graduates. Secondly, a department of Gender Studies was established at Makerere University in 1991, with the objective of producing gender-knowledgeable men and women who will direct gender-aware planning and implementation in government and non-governmental organizations.

These are well-intentioned and useful policies, but a number of issues need to be put into perspective based on available information about women's education in Uganda. Statistics (UNICEF, 1989; MOE, 1990; ACFODE, 1989) have shown that the factors responsible for female illiteracy and in particular female school drop-out are: school fees and parents preference for boys' rather than girls' education if a choice has to be made; female children's involvement in domestic chores; early marriages and the need for brideprice from girls; teenage pregnancies and lack of support by the education system. These constraints to girls' education cannot be addressed only from the post-secondary level of education onwards. For example, affirmative action is needed both at the primary level and the early secondary levels where the majority of girls drop out of school. UNICEF (1989) estimates indicated that about 44 per cent of all pupils in Uganda's primary schools are female, but at secondary level they constitute only 26 per cent dropping still further to 16 per cent at post-secondary level.

The Education White Paper does not seem to recognize the need to take specific measures in favour of women's education and assumes a 'gender-neutral' educational system. This could lead to further gender imbalances in education in future. There is need to provide skill training to women and to increase female intake in the existing technical colleges. The paucity of vocational training institutions which accept women students further compounds the problem for women. Female school drop-outs have little choice before them except marriage or the most basic forms of employment. Educated females do not have to be restricted to careers like nursing and home management which tend to be low paid. Women, like men, need skills that will make them self-reliant, facilitate personal entrepreneurship, and give them better chances in the job market.

Finally, as mentioned already, the government needs to protect women from discrimination imposed by cultural practices – such as the preference for boys' rather than girls' education; early marriages; brideprice; and the unequal gender division of domestic work – which deprive girls of further educational opportunities.

ECONOMIC EMPOWERMENT

Empowering women economically is vital to female emancipation and to national development. So far the NRM government has not shown much interest in this area. Women are predominantly dependent on their male next of kin (husband, father, brother)economically. Dependence on men deprives women of influence in family and community matters; ties them to unpleasant male relationships for their sustenance and the survival of their children; it also limits their productive capacity. The following are some of the major economic areas where government action is needed:

Means of production and income

Women in Uganda lack control and ownership of resources of production. For example, they own only 5 per cent of the land. Culture and the present law (the Succession Act, section 2) dictate that property inheritance is through the male line. Because women do not own the capital and land on which they work, they have little control over the product of their labour. After all, their labour is assumed to have been paid for by the brideprice at marriage.

> Although women do a very large proportion of the work for both cash and food crop production, men usually control the cash crop marketing and the generated income. Women have more control over the proceeds from the sale of food crops than cash crops, but the relative price of traditional foods is very low. (UNICEF, 1989: 77)

141

Women lack security for bank credits and also information and training in agriculture as extension services are normally targeted at the male head of household. Female-headed households are very vulnerable. Women's economic deprivation in Uganda has not changed much since the NRM came to office.

Women are under-represented in wage employment (only 17 per cent in professional and 5.8 per cent in administration and managerial jobs). Constraints to women's participation in the labour market include: lack of skills; prejudice against women on the part of employers; sexual harassment; and difficulties in time-budgeting between official and household roles (Mwaka, 1993: 12).

Employed women dominate the low-paid jobs of domestic work, teaching, nursing and secretarial work. They are also concentrated in the informal sector (Basirika, 1992: 15) in petty commodity trade where profit margins are very low. The majority of Ugandan women are located in the agricultural sector where they rarely control cash crop incomes. The most exploited women employees, however, are those in domestic work where there is no protection regarding a minimum wage or working hours. This group of young females, most of whom tend to be either destitute or orphans (aged 10–20), are exposed not only to work slavery but to abuse by employers. Government legislation is urgently needed in terms of a minimum wage and regulation of working hours and conditions.

VIOLENCE AGAINST WOMEN

Violence against women is rampant in Uganda in the form of rape, physical harassment, domestic violence, and mutilation of female sexual organs (circumcision among the Sebei and pulling of the labia among several Bantu tribes). Society trivializes domestic violence as a private issue and the government has ignored appeals about domestic violence against females. Battered as well as sexually abused women find too much of a stigma in reporting it, hence most cases of violence go unpunished. Women need firm government commitment to protecting them against violence. This would be in line with the second of the NRM's 'Ten Point Programme', issued upon its assumption of power in 1986, i.e. security of all persons in Uganda and their properties.

STRUCTURAL ADJUSTMENT POLICIES AND WOMEN

Since 1987, NRM economic policy has been more or less guided by the World Bank/IMF structural adjustment programmes. Understandably, the economy needed restructuring and stabilization measures were needed to correct the economic chaos at the time. However, when structural adjustment was conceived and implemented in Uganda, hardly any consideration was given to the vulnerability of disadvan-

142

taged groups like women and the poor. The implementation of the Programme for the Alleviation of Poverty and Social Costs of Adjustment (PAPSCA), the precise impact of which is still to be assessed, came in as an afterthought when the harm had been done. Women bear the bulk of the adjustment costs within the family and the community, because of their particular responsibilities and status in the community. Studies have shown that the welfare of women in Uganda has been negatively affected by SAP (Basirika, 1992; Evans, 1993; Obbo, 1991). Below is a summary of their impact on women in Uganda.

Production

Women have had to step up agricultural output to meet increased export demand and to make a living in the face of higher costs. Increased production is often not matched with availability of markets, storage facilities, extension services, credit facilities, information and training. As a survival strategy, women in the urban areas have crowded into the informal sector where they are involved in petty commodity trade with very narrow profit margins.

Social services

Given the general division of labour between men and women in Uganda, reduction in government social spending shifts extra burdens on to the women. Women's unpaid labour relieves the state of social responsibility. For example, women look after the sick in the absence of government medical care, and their own health is at risk particularly in the AIDS era. Women's education is adversely affected as girls are the first to be withdrawn from school when parents fail to pay school fees.

Environment

Adjustment policies are sometimes pursued at the expense of the environment. For example, the drive to produce for export induces over-cultivation of land or even encroachment on marginal lands and forest reserves (Kisamba-Mugerwa, 1991a: 10). Environmental deterioration affects women most because they interact more with the environment through collection of water and firewood and also land cultivation.

Food security

Emphasis on production for cash has shifted land and other resources from production for food to production for the market. This poses the danger of food insecurity particularly during the dry season, as food is no longer stored for the next season but is sent to the market. Women as home managers feel the effects of this dangerous situation most.

CONCLUSIONS

It is not the intention of this chapter to underestimate the work done by the NRM government in empowering women. Neither should the achievements of women through their own efforts be underrated. The analysis of women's associations in Chapter 8 shows convincingly how much women can achieve by organizing themselves. The purpose here has been to clarify the issues affecting women's empowerment and to identify areas for further action. I have looked at the main government policies, particularly affirmative action in favour of women, and revealed gaps in each of them. I have also indicated vital areas in women's emancipation where the government has failed to show firm commitment: legal protection; protection from backward cultural practices; domestic violence; and economic deprivation. Lastly, I believe that the effectiveness of government policies will depend on the women themselves; on their capacity to make demands on government; on their capacity to define their needs and interests: on their ability to organize and take advantage of the new political and economical environment inaugurated by the National Resistance Movement in 1986; and not least on their ability to make full use of the strong position guaranteed to them in the 1995 Constitution.

Notes

---

1. Museveni Yoweri Kaguta, 'Speech by the President of the Republic of Uganda on the Occasion of the Closing of the 1st Conference on Women and Health', in 1989, reproduced in *Agenda: a Journal About Women and Gen*der **No.6**: 10.
2. President Yoweri Museveni's speech on Women's Day, 8 March 1990: 2.

TEN

Indigenous NGOs and political participation

Susan Dicklich[1]

Uganda is now at a critical juncture in its political and economic development. Given the past political trauma that characterized the country and the near disintegration of the state under Milton Obote and Idi Amin, the political, economic and social space has widened of necessity to incorporate autonomous self-help organizations and NGOs to fill the vacuum left by the former regimes. The regimes of Amin and Obote induced an 'exit' from the formal economy and a general avoidance of state institutions by a wide range of groups and occupations. Ordinary Ugandans have had to fend for themselves, relying on organizations outside the state rather than the state itself to provide basic necessities.

Since 1986, the National Resistance Movement has been in power with a mixed system of direct participation and representation. The current restructuring of the economy sponsored by the International Monetary Fund and the World Bank has encouraged the liberalization of economic space. The state is retreating from its responsibilities to provide basic social services, such as health care, education, sanitation and basic security, leaving this space open for other actors to occupy. Consequently, there is competition for political and economic space with increased participation by non-state actors. Indigenous non-governmental organizations are one set of actors.

Foreign and indigenous[2] NGOs have flooded Uganda since the National Resistance Army (NRA) stormed into Kampala in January 1986. The 'invasion'[3] of NGOs has affected almost every sector and region of Ugandan life, although some districts, such as Rakai (badly hit by the AIDS virus), Luwero, and Kampala have higher concentrations of NGOs. This flood of NGOs[4] and NGO activity has produced varying degrees of cynicism and optimism. The increasing number of 'briefcase NGOs',[5] however, tends to give all NGOs an unsavoury reputation, whether deserved or not.

NGOs in general are deemed important because of their efficiency in addressing the needs of service provision and poverty alleviation. They are often positively characterized as having a labour-intensive approach, a focus on community participation, and a non-hierarchical decision-making structure, as well as being flexible and adaptive to the locale they are operating in, and more cost-effective than government (see Kwesiga and Ratter, 1992: 13). NGOs, and civil associations in particular, have also been lauded by neo-liberals as one of the key vehicles of empowerment,[6] the development of a strong and vibrant civil society[7] and democratization. It is suggested that NGOs can provide independent centres of power to check the abuses of central and local authority and thus procure greater accountability from the regime (Bratton, 1989; Korten, 1990); pluralize the institutional environment; and give voice to popular demands and help promote a popular culture (Chazan, 1993: 282).

However, even though NGOs pluralize the institutional environment and provide for economic and, in some cases, political empowerment, this does not automatically translate into political participation or power within the institutional set-up. NGOs have to be examined in relation to the state structure and the openings that are both fought for by autonomous organizations and relinquished by the state.

Are NGOs, as the neo-liberals and the radical populist approaches argue, vehicles of empowerment, the development of a strong and vibrant civil society and democratization? What role can (and do) NGOs play in political empowerment and democratization in the current political economy of Uganda, given the contextually limiting and facilitating factors as well as the shortcomings of the NGOs themselves? It is this problem which concerns this chapter.

Focusing specifically on indigenous, intermediate NGOs,[8] I argue that although individual NGOs are very important in Uganda in terms of service provision and poverty alleviation, and although some individual NGOs have been quite successful in political advocacy and political empowerment, the overall prospects for the NGO sector in engendering political empowerment and participation and encouraging the long-term development of a democratic civil society are poor. Intermediate NGOs offer weak prospects for engendering political empowerment and participation. This is because of their own internal organizational and capacity problems, their dependence on external funding, and their lack of co-ordination. Even more limiting are the environmental constraints NGOs face, especially the politics and economics of survival, the state regulation of NGOs, and the nature of political participation in Uganda under the Resistance Council (and Local Council) system.

This argument is mainly based on field research conducted in Uganda from August 1992 to June 1993.[9] I focused on 5 indigenous, intermediate NGOs representing a cross-section of Ugandan society regionally, ethnically, economically, politically and with regard to gender. These included two human rights NGOs: Ugandan Human Rights Activists (UHRA) and the Foundation for Human Rights Initiative (FHRI); a women's NGO: Action for Development (ACFODE); a developmental NGO: Uganda Rehabilitation and Development Foundation (URDF); and a political NGO: Foundation for African Development (FAD).[10] All of these NGOs can be classified under Korten's term, 'voluntary organizations' (Korten, 1990: 2). In order to appreciate what NGOs have accomplished to date, their historical role in Ugandan politics and economics should first be examined.

THE ROLE OF NGOS IN POST-COLONIAL UGANDA

During the colonial period, most NGO activity was restricted to humanitarian and missionary causes. The Churches played a key role in this regard, although there were other organizations such as Sanyu Babies Home, the Mothers' Union, Uganda Red Cross (1945), Catholic Relief Services, and St. John's Ambulance Brigade that offered a variety of services, including relief, welfare, education, family welfare, youth services and child care (Mugira, 1991: 12–13; de Coninck, 1992: 11). On the political level, trade unions, co-operatives, urban associations and political parties helped to expedite independence through their strong opposition to colonialism (de Coninck, 1992: 11).

With independence in 1962, the Ugandan state became more involved in education and health services, although the churches remained significant actors. The fact that indigenous NGOs were not very active during the post-colonial era, in part reflects the repressive political situation as well as the new social/cultural climate in Uganda. The churches were particularly significant during the Amin regime when most other NGOs either fled the country or cancelled their services, because of the severe repression.[11] With the overthrow of Amin, foreign NGOs returned, focusing mainly on disaster relief. For example, more than 50 foreign NGOs were involved in the 'Karamoja emergency' and later in operations in the West Nile region and the 'Luwero Triangle' (de Coninck, 1992: 13). Most indigenous NGOs were linked to a foreign NGO or church during this time. It is only recently that indigenous NGOs have become more key social actors.

Given the past history of civil war and internal strife, it is perhaps not surprising that Uganda does not have a well-developed and strong 'civil society'. Years of repression and mistrust have undermined the development of strong autonomous organizations. In the past, association had been restricted mainly to organization along kinship lines or on a self-help rather than a nation-wide basis. However, in recent years the number of indigenous NGOs has skyrocketed. This phenomenal growth must be understood within the context of the re-awakened interest of foreign donors in Uganda rather than as the establishment of relative political stability.

No complete record of NGOs is available, but it is estimated that there are more than 700 registered NGOs operating in Uganda nowadays, both foreign and indigenous. A study commissioned by the Ministry of Finance and Economic Planning, and funded by the World Bank, found that of 703 organizations that applied for registration by December 1992, 15 had 'relief' as a primary main activity, 430 'development', and 258 had some 'other'. Of this last category, 248 had 'evangelism' as the 'primary subsidiary activity' (Kwesiga and Ratter, 1993: 10). These do not include the hundreds if not thousands of indigenous grassroots associations that have not registered with the NGO Registration Board.[12]

NGOs have become very important because of their number as well as their involvement in many crucial services. For example, the estimated aggregate annual expenditure of NGOs in Uganda (foreign and indigenous) for the fiscal year 1992/93 was US\$ 125 million (Kwesiga and Ratter, 1993: 11), almost equal to the expected World Bank contribution to the Rehabilitation and Development Plan for the same year. What impact have NGOs had on their target groups and the wider community in terms of empowerment, given the political and economic environment in which they operate and their own organizational constraints?

THE POLITICS AND ECONOMICS OF SURVIVAL
For the average Ugandan, the politics of survival in the past translated into a withdrawal from politics in an attempt to escape state terror. Anything considered minimally political would bring undue attention and possible retribution from the state. To a certain extent, years of war have created a culture of suspicion and fear, which has placed even NGO motives and activities under public scrutiny. Consequently, many NGOs, especially those that can be considered 'political' in any way, are regarded as having ulterior motives and objectives. The state is also very suspicious of NGO activities, especially those that are considered to be 'political' (Matembe, 1993: 130). Although the Resistance Council system has helped to re-politicize Ugandans, there still seems to be a reluctance among them to embrace organizations that may somehow antagonize the regime.

The composition of many NGOs has also caused suspicion and cynicism. Many NGOs are composed of elite persons, often bureaucrats or professionals who have discovered NGOs as an alternative, lucrative source of income. Most civil servants are unable to make even a 'living wage' in government jobs. Consequently, with the influx of donor money, many civil servants have turned to the NGO sector for personal profit. Because the private sector is still very weak, and because the state has lost its former attractiveness, many have switched to NGOs instead to further their ambitions. The extent to which NGOs are characterized by self-interest and greed varies, with some just 'briefcase NGOs' and others engaged in important work. However, promise of foreign travel (to seminars, etc.), upcountry travel, networking, subsistence allowances and other perquisites associated with being a member of an NGO, often tend to overshadow any strictly 'voluntary' motivation for involvement.

Because of state withdrawal from the provision of basic services, and the consequent economy of survival that has developed, many NGOs are being pressured into dealing with poverty alleviation (not eradica-

148

tion), and the provision of basic social services like primary health care, education and sanitation, instead of empowerment and advocacy. These are not mutually exclusive pursuits, but they do serve to divert NGOs to a more reactive rather than proactive focus. The willingness of the NRM regime to allow NGOs to multiply, especially NGOs that are engaged in poverty alleviation and service provision, suggests that it is an indirect beneficiary of NGO activities as well.

Although state-NGO relations may be either conflictual or consensual, NGOs acting as alternative service providers operating in an environment of political and economic survival often serve to give the regime added legitimacy and to fill gaps where state-initiated service provision has lapsed (if it even existed in the first place). This is particularly the case in Northern Uganda where the state is only minimally present and regional/ethnic animosities still flourish. The state has thus come to rely on the service provision and poverty alleviation offered by foreign and indigenous NGOs, and has increasingly attempted to integrate NGOs into its national development programme.

FORMAL STATE REGULATION AND CONTROL OF NGOS

The main method of regulating and controlling NGOs is through the NGO Registration Board which was established in 1989, under the NGO Registration Statute (Uganda Government, 1989).[13] The Board is overseen by the Ministry of Internal Affairs (rather than the Ministry of Planning and Economic Development), which suggests that the state is more concerned about security issues pertaining to NGOs than development issues. The stated objective of the statute is [t]o provide for the registration of NGOs, to establish a board for that purpose, strengthen its functions and role in considering applications for registration, monitoring and guiding the programmes and activities of NGOs in Uganda . . . (Memorandum-NGO Registration Bill, 1989).

The Board has the power to reject NGO applications (S.9(a-c))[14] and deny renewal or approval of operations as well as demand that an NGO make a written report to the District Administrator 7 days in advance before contacting people in the District (Section 12 (9)). This is part of the NRM attempt to integrate NGOs into its national plan. Under Section 5 (1) (a) of the statute, every organization is required to submit with its application for registration under the statute a written work plan for the consideration and approval of the Ministry responsible for planning and economic development.

Similarly, under Section 14, (4), NGOs are obliged to carry out their business operations in consultation with the District Development committee in the area. However, for the most part, the NGO Registration Board's powers have been *de jure* rather than actually carried out in practice: the government simply does not have the resources adequately to monitor and control NGOs. Regulation and

149

control tend to be haphazard and not very effective, resulting from a lack of resources and incompetence rather than a lack of desire to control the activities of NGOs.[15]

The national-level regulation of NGOs is meant to complement local regulation, whereby District Administrators and Resistance Council officials are supposed to keep a watchful eye on NGO activities. NGOs are posited as having a 'complementary' relationship with the RCs/Local Councils. For example, RCs/Local Councils often ask assistance of NGOs because of their resource constraints. The RC/Local Council will identify a problem and suggest a policy, and the NGO will help to implement it.[16] Many NGOs are actually quite dependent on local councils for the mobilization of groups to attend meetings and the identification of local problems, as well as identification of resource people. In this sense, the relationship between NGOs and the RCs/Local Councils is not competing, but complementary. However, it remains complementary only so long as the NGO remains within the acceptable parameters defined by the regime, and linked to the national development plan.

DEGREE OF NRM TOLERANCE

Although the NRM regime has relied 'more on the carrot than the stick' to co-opt individuals and groups under its broad-based rule, there seems to be a tacit understanding as to the limits of non-compliance with NRM policy which will be tolerated. This explains why some NGOs prefer to remain apolitical and non-confrontational. NGOs and individuals within NGOs which have stepped beyond the acceptable limits have received strong warnings from the regime. For example, the former executive director of the Uganda Human Rights Activists (UHRA), Lance Seera-Muwanga, was detained without trial for 13 months in 1987, under the Public Order and Security Act, because he gave an interview to a journalist from an African news magazine that was critical of the NRM regime. This significantly muzzled the future aggressiveness of the organization, which now channels its concerns through the office of the Inspector-General of Government. UHRA now views itself as having an 'educative role in human rights, rather than being a pressure group'.[17]

A more moderate warning was given to the UHRA by the District Administrator (DA) of Entebbe, when he addressed a paralegal workshop for UHRA at Entebbe. The DA called on members of UHRA to serve as 'mediators and peace creators' and to avoid 'political gains'. The government commended the work of UHRA and encouraged them, but warned them not to 'misuse their forum for political gains' (Nkwenge, 1992: 3). In other words, the government was willing to support the UHRA's activities as long as they did not get too political.

Similarly, the Foundation for African Development (FAD),[18] an organization closely associated with the Democratic Party, has been accused by President Museveni of not heeding the NRM's advice to let the transition period be a time of 'national recuperation' allowing the population to chart their own future through the constitution-making process (Bakunzi, 1992: 3). These warnings serve to remind NGOs of their subservient and tenuous position in Uganda. Anything that is deemed critical of the regime is often classified as 'sectarian' and 'destabilizing'. These pronouncements serve to undermine the legitimacy of NGOs that confront issues deemed too political by the regime. Many NGOs fear to become 'political' because of possible repercussions from the regime. FIDA-U (The International Association of Women Lawyers, Uganda branch), for example, does not focus on politically sensitive issues like the detainment of women in military barracks, but prefers to remain in areas that will not bring it into confrontation with the regime.[19] The NRM regime has made clear how much dissension it is willing to tolerate, particularly with the more traditional 'political' non-state actors, such as political parties, the media and trade unions (see Dicklich, 1993).

THE NATURE OF POLITICAL PARTICIPATION IN UGANDA

The RC system provided the foundation for the NRM claim to grassroots democracy. The RCs (RC 1–5), now renamed Local Councils, have become an important source of mobilization and self-help, of security and defence, of leadership building (especially with women), and are important in bringing together people of different ethnicity and religion to work together for their mutual benefit. Every individual belongs to a village-level (or cell in Kampala) council. As a member of that village, he/she has the obligation to participate in the local council, although participation has drastically diminished in certain areas of Uganda.

The RC/Local Council system is composed of 5 main levels: 1 (village or cell level in Kampala), 2 (parish), 3 (sub-county), 4 (county), 5 (district). Increasingly, however, RCs were bureaucratized and limited by state policy from above (see Ddungu, 1989; Makara, 1992: 92; Mamdani, 1993b). For example, RC1s had little power and influence beyond the very local level in the RC system. Under their new name of Local Councils, they still have no finances and no real policy-making power above the very local level. Often, directives come from above (District level), and are filtered through to village level, rather than rising from the grassroots upwards. There tends to be a heavy top-down emphasis on political participation. This significantly circumscribes the degree of autonomy that the lower levels have, as well as any groups that are outside of the system.

Political participation can be defined as ' . . . action which is directed at influencing (controlling, changing, supporting or sharing in) policy making and or execution in a political structure' (Hayward, 1973: 594). Midgley further differentiates between four modes of political participation: the anti-participatory mode, the manipulative mode, the incre-

151

mental mode and the participatory mode (see Midgley, 1986: 39–44). The manipulative mode of political participation can be used to describe the situation under the NRM regime. It is identified as a situation where

> ... the state supports community participation but does so for ulterior motives. Among these are a desire to use community participation for purposes of political and social control and a recognition that community participation can reduce the costs of social development programmes and facilitate implementation ... Co-optation may also occur because the state seeks to direct participatory aspirations through alternative mechanisms which it has established and which it regards as legitimate and satisfactory. Although the state does not oppose community involvement, it seeks to neutralize spontaneous participatory activities hoping to channel them through established mechanism (Midgley, 1986: 41).

The established mode of political participation in Uganda is via the Resistance Council (now Local Council) system. Although the NRM regime has established other democratic institutions and engaged in other reforms (see Dicklich, 1993) it seems firm on the maintenance of the council system as the main vehicle of political participation. It will not compromise on its existence. The Director of Mass Organization and Political Mobilization, NRM Secretariat, illustrated the limitations of political participation in the NRM system.

The NRM government is the best pluralist system; it allows people to organize themselves in different groups but not to take power. Some groups have limited selfish interests; however, the movement does not allow these groups with different interests to organize and exercise power together.[20]

In other words, the RC system allows for political participation, but filtered through councils at the RC 1–5 levels. If groups are deemed 'political' the regime, advocating a broad-based and inclusionary mode of participation, attempts to bring them in line with the NRM.[21] The First Deputy Prime Minister and National Political Commissar stressed the parameters of popular power within the new system under decentralization:

> ... the central government representative [former district administrator] will not be accountable to the RCs nor will they become accountable to him. They will only be accountable to the central government ... to make sure that the 'national interest' is being looked after the DAs ... will make sure that the RCs [i.e. LCs] assert their power, **but in the proper manner** [emphasis added].[22]

Within this framework, NGOs 'fit' into the local council system as facilitators of NRM objectives, not as alternative sources of power. NGOs will be tolerated by the regime as long as they continue to function in an apolitical and non-confrontational manner.[23] The degree of latitude they have is conceded by the NRM regime. The best illustration of this is the NRM reaction to, and subsequent banning of, the National

Organization for Civic Education and Election Monitoring (NOCEM). NOCEM was made up of a 14 indigenous NGOs, including the human rights organizations (UHRA, FHRI), FIDA-U, and the Uganda Law Society, which focused on civic education and closely monitoring the progress of the Constituent Assembly elections held in March 1994. The Honourable Eriya Kategaya, the First Deputy Prime Minister, called the NGO leaders of NOCEM into his office prior to the elections and castigated them for being 'too political'. NOCEM was consequently banned by the CA Commission from engaging in further civic education because it was going beyond what was considered acceptable by the regime.[24]

In addition to the 'environmental' constraints facing them, most NGOs in Uganda tend to have a non-confrontational and apolitical agenda; the regime has therefore been able to integrate them into its development plan fairly easily.

THE CHARACTERISTICS OF INTERMEDIATE INDIGENOUS NGOS IN UGANDA

NGOs have been praised for their ability to reach the 'poorest of the poor'. Indeed, they have penetrated areas in Uganda that the state has not even been able to reach.[25] They have played a crucial role in poverty alleviation and service provision. The bankrupt and corruption-ridden public sector and the nascent private sector could never have achieved the same degree of effectiveness or efficiency as NGOs have (see Brett, 1993a: 297). This alone, however, does not provide a firm foundation for political empowerment or for the development of a democratic and strong civil society.

Most NGOs in Uganda are inward-focused, small, relatively young, dependent on foreign donors for their survival, apolitical, and weak on NGO co-ordination. Because of this, they do not offer a strong, autonomous power source that will help keep the regime accountable, or provide firm grounding for the development of a democratic civil society.

The fact that many NGOs are urban-based and headquartered in Kampala, whereas over 80 per cent of the population are rural, results in a lack of real grounding with the grassroots. Participation by the beneficiaries therefore tends to be somewhat *ad hoc* and haphazard, even in the most effective NGOs, like Action for Development (ACFODE).[26] In other NGOs, participation by the targeted beneficiaries in decision-making and programme implementation appears to be much less than expected (see de Coninck, 1992: 111). If there is not ample opportunity for participation in the organization and in its programmes and policies, this undermines the self-help and empowering potential of NGOs.

Furthermore, the heavy reliance on foreign donors for continued survival often places NGOs in a position where they are more accountable to their donors than they are to local people. Many intermediate-level NGOs therefore become virtual 'middle-men' in the facilitation of aid money between foreign donors and grassroots groups. This does not help to 'empower' people, but often serves to create a new kind of dependence on foreign aid.[27] It also weakens the NGOs because this dependence creates long-term instability and lack of continuity in programme planning.

Because most intermediate-level NGOs are urban-based, heavily dependent on foreign funding and therefore accountable to foreign donors more than to their own constituencies, their projects have tended to concentrate on problems which produce quick results for foreign donors (see de Coninck, 1992: 10). Consequently, most programmes focus on more concrete objectives like safe water provision, primary health care, income generation (for example, piggeries, mushroom planting, group farming), and credit, rather than more intangible pursuits such as political empowerment. There are exceptions, however, with the women's NGO, Action for Development (ACFODE) being one of them. It is one of the most successful advocacy groups in Uganda (see Tripp, 1994: 115–17).[28] Their advocacy, however, has been based almost exclusively on gender-related issues, and on issues with which the NRM regime has no real dispute.[29]

Other NGOs tend not to adopt an advocacy role because they are closely connected to the regime. For example, URDF (Uganda Rehabilitation and Development Foundation) was formed by a number of NRM sympathizers in 1986 and has a number of high-level NRM officials on its national board of directors. It focuses on non-contentious and regime-supporting projects,[30] citing an aversion to political or confrontational issues.[31] It is characteristic of an NGO that is service-provision-oriented, filling in the social and economic spaces from which the state has withdrawn. The state gains legitimacy from such NGOs in that they perform the duties/tasks that the regime itself does not have the capacity to perform. However, if NGOs do not build themselves up as autonomous power sources, they will not be able to provide a check on abuse of the regime's powers, nor will they be able to keep it accountable.

DEGREE OF NGO CO-ORDINATION

The heavy reliance on foreign donors also instils a spirit of competition rather than co-operation among NGOs. Many NGOs end up competing for scarce funds rather than co-ordinating efforts to make the greatest impact. This, for example, is the case with some women's NGOs, like ACFODE (Action for Development) and FIDA (Uganda Association of Women Lawyers) which have similar programmes in legal networking, but do not work together. The Acting Executive Secretary of FIDA, when asked about co-ordination efforts between FIDA and ACFODE, stated 'if ACFODE has a legal programme in one district, we do not interfere . . .'.[32] Instead of co-ordinating their efforts, these two organizations have often duplicated them.

Similarly, the Uganda Human Rights Activists (UHRA) and Foundation for Human Rights Initiatives (FHRI) are two human rights organizations that do not effectively co-ordinate their efforts and often compete for foreign support.[33] FHRI, the newer of the two organizations, is attempting to become a co-ordinating NGO for human rights-related organizations. It has met with varying degrees of resistance from other human rights NGOs, since it does not yet command an established position of legitimacy.

There have been other efforts to co-ordinate NGO activities. For example, there are a number of NGO co-ordinating bodies that tend to focus on specific sector projects, such as UCBHA (Uganda Community-Based Health Care Association), UCOBAC (Uganda Community-Based Association for Child Welfare) and NUDIPU (National Union of Disabled Persons in Uganda). DENIVA (the Development Network of Indigenous Voluntary Associations) attempts to '... develop and maintain the highest levels of self-regulation among NGOs ... provide guidelines on national development policies and play an advocacy role to the government on behalf of indigenous NGOs' (DENIVA, 1990: 13). It has not been very successful, however, in providing a strong forum for NGO co-ordination and organization.[34] Overall, NGOs remain a very fragmented and unorganized sector in Uganda.

Even when organizations do engage the regime directly or indirectly, there tends not to be a co-ordinated effort, thus limiting the amount of influence the organization has vis-à-vis the state. Given the lack of co-ordination, competition, dependence on foreign funding for survival, and the relative youth and apolitical focus of most NGOs in Uganda, the NGO sector is not currently capable of bringing pressure to bear on the state and keeping it accountable. The fact that NGOs exist and that they are engaged in some advocacy and empowerment projects is, however, a positive sign.

PROSPECTS FOR NGO ENGENDERED EMPOWERMENT AND DEMOCRATIZATION

Although NGOs are vital in Uganda from the perspective of service provision and poverty alleviation, they have not become vehicles of political empowerment or the development of a democratic civil society. There seems to be a tenuous relationship between the regime and NGOs. The regime recognizes that it needs NGOs, and consequently attempts to balance its need for help and its need for controlling the political and economic climate in Uganda. The NRM has been able to maintain a fairly non-confrontational policy with regard to monitoring and controlling NGOs, but this has been mainly due to the fact that most NGOs have been non-confrontational and apolitical. NGOs are not meant to be bastions of democracy in Uganda: the RC system, at least at the very local level, is. As long as this is the case, NGOs will be sidelined as facilitators of foreign and state agendas, not the people's agendas.

It is probably premature to draw any concrete conclusions about the democratic potential of NGOs in Uganda. This will depend not only on the internal structure of NGOs, but also on the wider political climate. In order for NGOs to become bastions of democracy and vehicles for the development of a more vibrant civil society, they must keep the regime accountable and act as a watchdog of people's rights as well as bringing pressure to bear on the government. There is an urgent need, therefore, for better NGO co-ordination of their efforts and the establishment of indigenous sources of funding as well as genuine participation by beneficiaries in NGO programmes. Unless NGOs become better organized and co-ordinated, their efforts will remain mainly stopgap, with little prospect for the development of a strong democratic civil society in Uganda.

Notes

---

1. The author would like to thank Rhoda E. Howard, Aili Mari Tripp and Richard Sandbrook for valuable comments on an earlier draft.
2. Although it is often very difficult to distinguish between foreign and indigenous NGOs, indigenous NGOs will refer here to those NGOs that are composed of Ugandan nationals, working for Ugandans, and operating in Uganda.
3. For example, one newspaper article entitled 'NGOs invade Kumi' examined the influx of NGOs in Kumi district, *Weekly Topic*, 5 March 1993.
4. NGOs will henceforth refer to indigenous NGOs unless otherwise stipulated.
5. Dr Elizabeth Madraa, the Director of Aid Co-ordination, Prime Minister's Office, referred to these briefcase NGOs as 'one pajero, one briefcase, one project house in Muyenga NGOs'. The pajero, an expensive four-wheel drive Mitsubishi vehicle, is considered a symbol of wealth in Uganda, while Muyenga is one of the more exclusive residential areas in Kampala. (Interview with Dr Madraa, 17 November 1992)
6. Empowerment can be defined as '. . . a multifaceted process[which] involves transforming the economic, social, psychological, political and legal circumstances of the currently powerless' (Sandbrook, 1993: 2). However, there are two key components of empowerment; the development of a sense of efficacy in the individual and a group's ability to influence the political and personnel decisions of government or powerful institutions.
7. The term civil society is problematic because it is used to define just about everything outside of government. For the purposes of this chapter, the term will be used to refer to associations and groups that are consciously autonomous from the state and active in promoting their groups' interests as well as broader societal interests, often in contest with the state.
8. NGOs can be defined as mainly voluntary, not-for-profit organizations that are largely, if not entirely, independent of government (Paul, 1991: 3; Nerfin, 1987; Brown and Korten, 1991: 49). Intermediate NGOs can be classified as those NGOs that are not grassroots self-help organizations, but organizations that have a more outward national focus, bridging the gap between the grassroots and the state.
9. This chapter is based on a wider study, Dicklich (1994).

156

10. My analysis examined two levels of NGO effectiveness: state level and local/target group level. At the first level, I focused on whether the NGO affected public policy formulation on behalf of its target group and the wider community. Did the NGO advance group or individual interests that were distinct from state policies, or did it lobby for changes in state policies that affected its constituency? In other words, did the NGO provide an alternative, autonomous (potential if not actual) power base from that of the state? At the second level, I examined whether the NGO made a significant political and economic impact on the everyday lives of the target group and the wider community. The above information, in addition to other data collected, was used in assessing whether these particular NGOs and the broader NGO sector can have a positive effect on the development of a democratic civil society and polity in Uganda.

11. The churches were not immune to this repression either, most vividly portrayed by the murder of Archbishop Janani Luwum on 16 February 1977.

12. There are 2 key recent works on Ugandan NGOs: Brett (1993) examines the service-provision potential of NGOs and their effectiveness relative to the first and second sector, and de Coninck (1992) examines 4 case studies on the successes of NGOs in poverty alleviation.

13. Prior to 1989, NGOs were registered under two statutes: either the Companies Act or the Trustees and Incorporation Act. Other methods of NGO regulation include the Aid Co-ordination Secretariat, Office of the Prime Minister; and the External Aid Coordination Department, Ministry of Finance and Economic Planning.

14. NGO applications for registration under the NGO Registration Board require a written recommendation from the RC1 chairman in the region of operation, as well as an endorsement from the RC2, RC3 Chairmen and the District Administrator (DA). This excessively bureaucratic process often results in not only a lot of money being 'eaten' in order for an NGO to be registered, but also a lot of time wasted.

15. The Board has to a certain extent controlled which NGOs it deems acceptable and which its deems questionable. For example, DENIVA, a co-ordinating NGO body that was perceived as a 'rival body' to the NGO Registration Board, was considerably delayed in obtaining its formal registration. (Interview with Mr. Livingston Sewanyana, Executive Director of Foundation for Human Rights Initiatives, 13 November 1992).

16. Interview with Mrs. Gertrude Njuba, Director of Mass Organization and Political Mobilization, NRM Secretariat, Kampala, 9 March 1993.

17. Interview with Mr. S. Bukenya Kasaato, Executive Secretary, Uganda Human Rights Activists, Kampala, 18 January 1993.

18. FAD was established in 1979 and operates in the field of training and education cum development services.

19. Interview with Mr. Remmy Kasule, Former President of the Uganda Law Society, Kampala, 10 May 1993.

20. Interview with Mrs. Gertrude Njuba, Director of Mass Organization and Political Mobilization, NRM Secretariat, Kampala, 9 March 1993.

21. This is especially the case with other non-state actors, such as political parties.

22. Interview with Honourable Eriya Kategaya, First Deputy Prime Minister and National Political Commissar, Kampala, 15 October 1992.

23. The NRM's reaction to political parties is similar. Political parties are allowed to exist but are not allowed to be active in politics outside of the co-opted RC system. For example, on two separate occasions, the Democratic Party Mobilizer Group (DP mobilizers) attempted to hold rallies in Uganda (May and November 1993) which were suppressed by armed police. Similarly, the Ugandan Peoples' Congress attempted to hold meetings in Mbale in early 1993 but was prevented from doing so by police and RC officials in the area.

24. Personal communication by Judith Geist, USAID Kampala.

25. The NGO record in poverty alleviation and service provision has not been flawless, however. A recent study on Ugandan NGOs argues that, in fact, many NGOs have failed to undertake any detailed analysis which would identify the 'poorest of the poor' group and help to cure the causes of their poverty rather than just addressing the symptoms (de Coninck, 1992: 107). In addition, de Coninck found that '... most programmes with an "economic focus" are characterized by the lack of attention given to

the issue of social differentiation . . .', resulting in some of the most needy being effectively by-passed. Similarly, another study found that the more educated the individual or group, the more likely it was that the NGO would consult them. Men were also consulted 67.6 per cent of the time more than women (Kwesiga and Ratter, 1993: 43). This last point is particularly disturbing, given that there are 8,203,300 women in comparison with only 7,869,200 men in Uganda (World Bank, 1993a: 158) with more women in the rural areas as well as more involved in actual production and work.

26. For example, an ACFODE needs assessment trip to Mbarara and Kasese Districts, 6–10 December 1992 attended by the author, was characterized by lack of organization, minimal input from the intended beneficiaries and a very rushed atmosphere. Three different counties were targeted for a Woman and Health Needs Assessment. In Kazo county, a large assembly of women and men awaited the ACFODE team, but the parallel desire to include men in the discussions backfired because many women were hesitant to talk in front of their spouses or relatives. Much time was spent on political speeches made by members of the various RCs, and not enough on consulting the women about their problems. Because the political speeches lasted longer than scheduled, the needs assessment based on a general questionnaire was rushed through. More time could have been spent encouraging the women to speak out about their problems rather than having ACFODE talking to the women. In Kabatunda-Busongora county, the last ACFODE destination, the meeting took place in a very small RCI office (because of the rain) and included 10 men and only 2 women. The questionnaire was rushed through, with the women in particular not really consulted. The majority of people stood outside in the rain, peering into the office. The follow-up on programme success also tended to be weak. There is, however, a substantial amount of participation within the organization itself, evident in the monthly meetings of the general membership.

27. A lot of time, effort and money is spent on training individuals and groups in writing proposals that are needed in order to secure donor funding for various projects.

28. Even though ACFODE considers itself an apolitical organization, it has been instrumental in lobbying the government for the establishment of a Ministry of Women in Development, a Department of Women's Studies in Makerere University and the establishment of a women's desk in every Ministry. It has also been integral in empowering women at the grassroots level, for example by educating them about their rights in relation to customary law, in organizing them into self-help groups, and in sensitizing the government to the needs of women.

29. For example, many ACFODE programmes focus on sensitizing women (and men) to the injustices suffered by women, due to culture, economics and politics. The NRM, in 1986, launched a programme to make women more aware of their rights and increase their political awareness (Baliwa, 1986: 5–6). The pursuits of ACFODE and the NRM regime are therefore complementary rather than competing. This can partially explain why ACFODE has been so successful in lobbying the government on women's issues.

30. For example, URDF has engaged in an 'integrated rural development' programme which includes establishing primary health care, low-cost housing, skills development for youth and women, income-generation programmes and carpentry workshops. It has also been involved in the rehabilitation of the Masaka Technical Institute.

31. Interview with Mr. Bernard Masooko, Uganda Rural Development Foundation Officer, Kampala, 5 February 1993.

32. Interview with Mrs. Mary Kabogoza, Acting Executive Secretary, FIDA, Kamapala, 20 November 1992.

33. FHRI was formed by a former executive member of UHRA. The origins of FHRI may explain part of the lack of interaction between the two organizations, but the fact that they are both competing for the same donor funding exacerbates the differences.

34. DENIVA also published the first Directory of non-governmental organizations in Uganda.

ELEVEN
Decentralization policy: reshaping state and society

Anthony J. Regan

Under the National Resistance Movement government in power since January 1986, Uganda is one of the few countries in Africa seeking to change the state/civil society equation. The NRM aims not only to transform the state into a less dominant and more accountable institution, but also to encourage the emergence of a wide range of political and economic forces which can help to control future state action. Analyzing decentralization policy in terms of these aims in a brief chapter such as this has obvious limitations, as neither the theoretical issues nor details of the policy can be explored in any depth. Nevertheless such analysis is useful in terms of highlighting broad areas of strengths and weaknesses in the NRM decentralization policy. Perhaps more importantly, as the policy is a vital part of the broader NRM strategy for Uganda, analysis of its impacts should also provide insights into the possible long-term prospects of achieving its aims.

PERSPECTIVES ON STATE, SOCIETY AND DECENTRALIZATION IN AFRICA

State and society

There is wide agreement that the present crisis in Africa is to a large extent a crisis of the state. The state has played too pervasive a role, originally because there was 'no realistic alternative to it as the mobiliser, organiser, and manager of resources' (Ghai, 1993: 51). There is less consensus on either the goals or the prescriptions for change. However, many observers are optimistic about the positive roles civil society might play in limiting state power. The emergence of increasing numbers of NGOs and signs of popular protest since the late 1980s tend to be seen as evidence of an emergent civil society.[1]

There is, however, little certainty about the origins and roles of civil society, even in its home, Western Europe.[2] Less still is understood about civil society in Africa. It is seldom spelt out how it might 'develop' to the stage where it can limit state power, nor exactly how it might play such a role. Woods (1992:97) argues that the principal indicator of a 'developed' civil society is the manner in which individuals and groups 'articulate a set of norms which affect the way the state functions

159

and how other groups will interact'. In Africa, civil society 'is still threatened by the particularism of ethnicity and atomistic actions'. The 'relatively unarticulated character of economic differentiation on the continent' is a significant factor, for while the economic base 'does not determine whether civil society exists . . . it does influence the rate and manner in which class interest will intersect with normative claims in the Western European tradition'.

Woods's interesting analysis tends to assume that the goal for Africa is civil society on the model of Western Europe. A wide range of political, economic and cultural forces, however, shape the specific roles and relations of states and societies even in Western society (Fukuyama, 1994). If civil society is to become more important in Africa, much the same will be true there. Common factors such as ethnic divisions, the limited economic base and the still pervasive role of the state, will tend to shape a distinctive African form, which may also work in different ways and have different consequences from civil society in Western Europe.

It is also the case that civil society in Africa may not necessarily limit state power on the model of the 'developed' world. Experience in Asia should warn against what Ghai (1995) terms 'over-romanticisation of civil society', for it is not only the state that abuses human rights:

> . . . massive violations also take place in and through civil society, sometimes with the connivance of the state, and frequently reflecting feudalistic and patriarchal dimensions of culture. Social conflicts, particularly those stemming from ethnic or caste differences, have politicised and militarised civil society in many states.

STATE AND SOCIETY AND DECENTRALIZATION POLICIES

Decentralization in its myriad forms has been the subject of much interest in Africa in the 1990s, a reaction against the general failure of attempts from the 1960s onwards to promote development through strong and centralized bureaucratic states. Democratic sub-national government is seen as a major contributor to the emergence of a strong civil society. Diamond summarizes the position of many observers:

> Civil society provides an especially strong foundation for democracy when it generates opportunities for participation and influence at all levels of governance, not least the local level. For it is at the local level that the historically marginalized are most likely to be able to affect public policy and to develop a sense of efficacy as well as actual political skills. The democratization of local goverment thus goes hand in hand with development of civil society as an important condition for the deepening of democracy and the 'transition from clientelism to citizenship' in Latin America, as well as elsewhere in the developing and postcommunist worlds (1994: 8–9).

160

An additional issue emphasized in some decentralization studies is the role of strong sub-national centres of power in keeping the central government accountable.

There is, however, little experience of long-term political decentralization in Africa. Deconcentration of administrative capacity – 'administrative decentralization' – rather than political decentralization has been the pattern since the end of the colonial era. Further, the uneven experience of political decentralization in developing countries elsewhere (Rondinelli et al., 1983; Ghai and Regan 1992) suggests the need for care in making assumptions about the sustainability and outcomes of political decentralization in Africa.

STATE, SOCIETY AND DECENTRALIZATION IN
UGANDA TO 1986

State and society

Uganda is divided along overlapping and complex religious, ethnic, regional and economic lines. Of particular importance are ethnic/regional divisions (the 'North' – areas north and east of the River Nile – versus the 'South') and religion (Catholic versus Protestant). Each is important largely because of associated patterns of access to political and economic power since early colonial times. In the late and post colonial periods, these divisions were manifested in party politics. The Democratic Party tended to be a vehicle for the Catholic elite of the South and the Uganda Peoples' Congress played a similar role for the Protestant elite of the North. In their struggles for state power, elite fractions have mobilized support around these ethnic and religious divisions, thereby both deepening and masking cross-cutting economic divisions.

The state has been a dominating force. Initially it filled the lack of 'mobiliser, organiser and manager of resources' identified by Ghai (1993: 51). As it became the major source of political power (through patronage) and economic advancement for the elite in the post-colonial era, its pervasive role became self-sustaining. At the same time, as an instrument of advancement of the interests of particular elite fractions and their clients, the state and its agencies perpetrated terrible abuses of rights.

Civil society in Uganda has been weak. The factors alluded to by Woods (1992: 97) and the long periods of repression by the state all had their impact. Repression also prompted a variety of forms of resistance,[3] however, and alliances between a range of groups and interests. The NRM itself, as an alliance of a range of political interests, was originally forged in the fire of that resistance.

Indeed, developing Woods's analysis, we could say that resistance to repression contributed to the development of some basic norms affecting the way the state functions and the way in which groups interact, norms which to an extent cut across ethnic and class divisions.

161

Arguably, the reasonably high level of national support enjoyed by the NRM reflects the extent to which such norms have become more widely established. If so, the basis may have been provided for civil society to play an increasingly important role in Uganda in future.

Decentralization to 1986

Uganda experienced administrative (rather than political) decentralization from the beginning of the colonial period until the NRM came to power. Appointed 'chiefs' were at all local levels 'the bedrock of administration' throughout this time (Uganda Government, 1987: 12). The extensive power of the chiefs has been described as 'decentralized despotism', because of the combined legislative, executive and judicial authority they exercised, the use of administratively driven, unwritten customary law and the use of force (Mamdani, 1994b).

Limited political decentralization operated in parts of Uganda from the early 1950s to the early 1960s, primarily in the form of district councils. But from independence onwards the powers of the councils were reduced and legislative changes facilitated central control, culminating in the Local Administration Act 1967 under which councils became largely appointed bodies. Gertzel (1988) has described how they became not only instruments of central and party control, but also sources of patronage and personal enrichment, trends for the most part reinforced under the Amin and Obote 2 regimes. Hence the limited political decentralization attempted prior to the NRM had relatively little impact on either the state or civil society.

NRM STRATEGY FOR TRANSFORMATION OF STATE AND SOCIETY

Decentralization policy is but one of a number of NRM policies implemented as part of a political strategy intended to bring about fundamental change in state and society. That strategy is based on the NRM's analysis of the basic forces at work in Uganda, and in particular of the sources of the earlier destructive post-independence conflict.

The starting point of the strategy was the incorporation of as many groups as possible in a government of national unity to operate for a strictly limited interim period (initially to be limited to four years). Several factors contributed to this choice. In terms of territorial control, the NRM was in a relatively weak position when it came to power (Mamdani, 1988a: 1168) and so had to avoid conflict with as many potential opponents as possible. Further, its analysis was that elite-dominated sets of interests had been contending for state power since Independence, manipulating and deepening the sources of conflict in the process. Hence, in the short term, peace could best be achieved by incorporating the contenders for power in government.

To achieve longer-term change, the NRM needed political space in which to implement a broad package of policies seeking to resolve conflict and reform the country. The government of national unity helped create the space, for, together with strict limits on political party activity, it restricted the political room for movement for old political actors, many of whom were its potential opponents. Their room for manoeuvre was also restricted by the populist appeal made over their heads by many NRM policies, and in particular the village-based resistance council (RC) system and constitution-making processes which involved an unparalleled degree of popular involvement.

Although not explicitly described by the NRM in this way, the broader package of NRM policies can be analysed in terms of their intent both to transform the state and to develop civil society. A number of NRM publications, the NRM's 'Ten Point Programme' (Museveni, 1985) and others (e.g. NRM, 1990; 1991; Museveni, 1992: 28–35), indicate that essential to the NRM strategy were the aims of reforming and reducing the pervasive role of the state and of increasing democratization.[4]

Democratization is intended to contribute, together with other policies,[5] to the creation of new political forces in Uganda. The aim is to reduce the intensity and importance of the old political divisions, and so reduce the opportunities for major political forces to 'capture' state power. The combined effect of these new forces should be sufficient to limit state power.[6]

Many commentators have made criticisms of the NRM which highlight contradictions and weaknesses in its analysis of state and society as well as the strategy based on that analysis and its implementation. These are matters which can only be summarized in this chapter.

Corruption and inefficiency in government are apparently accepted by the NRM together with obstruction of the implementation of some of its policies (an example is the leadership code introduced under a 1992 statute, but never implemented). Some policies apparently directed towards democratization incorporate contradictory elements involving considerable government control. Examples include policies on national and local women's and youth organizations as well as the potentially high degree of central control retained under the 1992 decentralization policy.

Such problems are largely a consequence of a contradiction inherent in the NRM strategy. As the key player in a government of national unity, the core elements of the NRM must co-operate with leaders of the very elements which (on the NRM's analysis) derive their political strength from manipulation of the ethnic and religious divisions which the NRM seeks to transcend. Hence its relative political weakness requires the NRM to co-operate with those most likely to suffer – in political terms – from the changes it seeks. It was presumably because of its relative weakness that the NRM made no attempt to seek alliances with more progressive elements of the old forces by requiring prior acceptance of a minimum political programme (Mamdani 1988b: 1168). Without such a policy, however, it has been forced to move slowly with its partners, attempting to bring them along with each major change. In so doing, much corruption and mismanagement is accepted as the price of co-operation. At the same time, awareness of the opposition it faces, even from its partners, tends to push the NRM to seek tight control of the process of change.

OVERVIEW OF NRM DECENTRALIZATION POLICY

NRM decentralization policy was implemented in two main stages. The first began with the establishment of the RC system from 1986–87 onwards, and was given a legal basis in statutes passed in 1987 and 1988. The second stage announced by the President in October 1992 is still being implemented.[7]

Only central features and problems of the policy of particular relevance to the change of state and civil society can be outlined here.[8] The focus is on the hierarchy and selection of membership of RCs, their functions and resources and their local powers.

First stage – The RC statutes of 1987 and 1988

A five-tiered system of local government was established under the 1987 statute. Councils consisting of all residents were established at the village level (approximately 100 households). Each elected a 9-member village resistance committee to manage local affairs. For the next three levels of councils and committees (parish, sub-county and county), the committees from the level below form the council which elects the representatives. The district council (RC5) is made up of two persons elected from each sub-county and town RC, together with a woman representative elected from each county and municipality.

Elections were used to establish RC committees on a piecemeal basis in much of the country in 1986.[9] Country-wide RC elections were held in 1989 and 1992, resulting in much competition for positions and the replacement of many committee members at all levels.

However, the method of voting by lining up behind candidates rather than secret ballot, and the indirect election of committee members above the village level by electoral colleges of ever decreasing size, have been criticized. The former is said to open the voting process to pressure, and the latter is said to dilute democratic control, with people in the lower-level RCs having no sense that they can control the RC5 (Burkey, 1991). The Odoki Commission agreed in general with these criticisms, although it did suggest that voting by lining up might continue for the lower-level RCs (Uganda Government, 1993b).

With an estimated 45,000 village councils[10] there may be in excess of 400,000 people serving in elected offices in the RC (now renamed the Local Council) system – an impressive rate of direct participation in government when considered against a total population of about 18 million. The democratic nature of the system is enhanced by the powers that councils at all levels have – and are prepared to exercise – to recall committee members unable to perform the functions of office or breaching laws or public trust.

164

Decentralization policy: reshaping state and society

The basic functions of the committees below the district and municipality levels are: to manage all manner of local problems, including monitoring of administration in their area, reporting instances of maladministration, corruption and misuse of government property; and to act as courts dealing with a wide range of mainly civil matters. At the district and the municipality levels, councils have the functions already mentioned together with the limited functions that district and municipal authorities had exercised since the 1960s.

While district level and municipal RCs and successor Local Councils have the fiscal and staff resources available to district and urban councils prior to establishment of the RC system, the lower-level RCs were provided with no resources under the 1987-8 statutes.[11] While they had no legal powers of direction, however, they did tend to hold their chiefs far more to account than before.

Lack of funding has been a serious problem at all levels, but especially at the lower ones, where committee members have carried out onerous and time-consuming duties with no provision for remuneration save for minimal amounts paid to RC3/LC3 committee members. Yet most observers agree that there continues to be a surprisingly high level of commitment from councillors, although there are some moral problems in parts of the country (Burkey, 1991: 53).

Control of staff and funding under the 1987 statute was further complicated by the creation of new and confused lines of authority. Division of responsibility between the chairman of the RC5, the senior public servant (the district executive secretary or DES) and the 'political head' of the district (the presidentially appointed district administrator or DA), was confusing. While the DA tended to dominate, limited local popular legitimacy and local resources restricted his or her actual power. Conflict and muddle were inevitable.

Second stage – the 1993 statute

Apart from maintenance of the multi-tiered RC system virtually unchanged below the district level, major features of the second stage of change involved rationalization of confused lines of authority at district level; transfer from national ministries to district control of significant levels of functions, staff and revenue; statutory guarantees of base levels of grant revenue to rise with increases in national revenue; and measures for district accountability and national control. In combination the measures result in a dramatic change in the responsibilities and standing of district and large urban councils, but do little for the lower level RCs. Furthermore, analysis of the arrangements exposes areas of potential concern, especially in relation to the security of the basis for the exercise of the increased responsibilities of district and urban councils, and hence of the future autonomy of local governments.

The RC system of 1987 had been expected to be no more than a starting point for the NRM decentralization policy, and a Commission of Inquiry sat in the same year to recommend the details of further developments. The delay of six years was caused largely by its novelty (for Uganda) and lack of precedents for what was being attempted; strong opposition to further decentralization from conservative political elements (local administration had been an important source of patronage to previous regimes); and opposition from ministries fearing loss of power and importance if significant functions, funding and staff were to be decentralized.

By 1992 a series of committees had hammered out the details of the policy. More importantly, the NRM now had the confidence to proceed in the face of opponents. A high level of support for further decentralization had been maintained and there was clear support for further decentralization evident in most parts of the country.[12] In the lead up to the Constituent Assembly elections planned for 1994, the NRM saw the opportunity for bolstering its electoral support by strengthening the popular decentralization policy. It was also hoped that strengthening district governments during 1993 and 1994 might to some extent pre-empt development of strong support for a federal system of goverment in the old kingdom areas, and so reduce the problem expected to be involved in dealing with the twin issues of traditional monarchies and federalism in the Constituent Assembly.

The 1993 statute dealt with the confused lines of district authority by giving the RC5 chairman clear control of administration through powers to direct the DES. The DA became Central Government Representative (CGR), still appointed by the President, but with far less responsibility than before. Unfortunately, there was still room for confusion and conflict about the CGR's powers over the district authorities.[13]

Numerous functions previously carried out by the national ministries were then transferred to the districts,[14] together with control of associated staff and funds. Well over half of public service personnel and as much as 30 per cent of the national government's recurrent budget were ultimately to be transferred to district control.[15]

One of the most significant changes was to make public servants directly answerable to RCs at all levels. Parish and sub-county chiefs were to be 'subject to directions that may be given by the Resistance Council that has jurisdiction over the parish or sub-county', while all other chiefs and public servants carrying out decentralized functions were to be answerable to the DES, who is in turn responsible to the RC5.[16]

The provisions providing legal guarantees for the funding and therefore the autonomy of the district are also of central importance. First, much new district funding was to be transferred in the form of grants – block grants maintaining recurrent costs of transferred activities at pre-transfer levels, and equalization grants assisting less developed districts to improve development to national average levels. Second, the districts were to share in the expected improvement in national budgetary performance over coming years through provision for total district grant funding to increase as the national recurrent budget performance improved.

166

Various measures sought to ensure accountability of what would be relatively well resourced district and urban councils. Tender boards and public accounts committees were required in each district. Financial regulations were to be set by the national government.

There are several considerations underlying the inclusion of measures permitting national control of local governments, and they also underlie other aspects which limit the latter's autonomy. First, they were included as a response to opponents of decentralization. Second, they reflected the general tendency of the NRM – already noted – to keep control of political processes. The powers in question apply to RCs at all levels and include powers to suspend councils and committees, to disallow laws, to impose conditions on and withdraw grants, and to modify the appointment of senior district and urban officials.

While the 1993 statute greatly increases the status of district and urban councils, it pays little attention to the problems of lower level councils (other than providing that 50 per cent of revenues collected at the RC3 level are to be retained there). Relations between various levels are likely to be a continuing problem. Already tending to be dominated by local elites (Burkey, 1991), the relatively well resourced district councils may tend to become the focus of decentralization. They will have little to gain from strengthening the still lower levels of local government, as that would tend to be at the expense of the districts (in terms of functions and resources). Already too remote from the lower level councils to be influenced by them, district councils may well have even less reason to concern themselves with the problems of lower levels if, as proposed by the Uganda Constitutional Commission and others, all levels of local government eventually become directly elected.

There is a range of complex problems and uncertainties involved in the 1993 arrangements. Some have already been touched upon (the CGR's role and the wide national powers of intervention in local government). Limits of space prevent the mention of more than a few key additional issues, most of them related to the lack of a secure legal basis for the arrangements and the extent of national government ability to assert a high degree of control over what is being transferred to the local level.

First, not only is the law long and complex, but it includes six schedules which contain well over half of the provisions on all aspects of local government, including detail on the internal organization of district and lower level councils, staffing and funding arrangements and the core functions of district and urban councils. But the schedules provide little security for local governments, as they can be amended by the Minister for Local Government, with the approval of Cabinet, without even being tabled in the legislature.[17]

Second, there is little security for the district and urban councils in the arrangements for the transfer of powers and functions. A few are listed as district and urban council functions in the schedules to the statute, but most are being transferred with no clear legal basis. They could easily be re-claimed by the national government, together with associated staff and funding (resulting in reduced grant funding). Hence a secure basis is lacking for the grant arrangements as well.

Third, scepticism and opposition from key national government agencies are likely to result in less than full implementation of the policy. Already in 1994, there was uncertainty over implementation of the grant arrangements by the Ministry of Finance. It would not be surprising if some extra-legal administrative control were maintained in the long run.

Indeed, while grant arrangements are a major step forward for the districts, the statutory requirements could be circumvented in various ways. Not only can services be transferred back to the national government, but it is also the case that the formula for minimum grant levels is tied only to the size of the national recurrent budget, and so could be largely defeated by moving funds for national recurrent activities out of the recurrent budget and under the separate budgetary processes for development (or capital) expenditure.

More generally, the limited financial and personnel resources available in the country as a whole when compared with the massive tasks involved in, and the high popular expectations of, decentralization pose serious concerns. While a small and highly committed decentralization secretariat is overseeing the implementation of the reforms, it lacks the personnel and funding resources needed to carry out the enormous tasks involved. There will certainly be many instances of poor performance, maladministration or corruption, as district and urban councils struggle to implement decentralization policy. Ammunition will thereby be provided to the many opponents of decentralization and the reforms may be put at risk. A greater commitment of government and donor resources to the implementation of decentralization may be required.

Impact of the Draft Constitution and the 1995 Constitution

The *Draft Constitution*, which contained detailed provisions on government at local level, was not only the starting point for debate in the Constituent Assembly, but also quite difficult to change. Hence its provisions on local government may easily provide the constitutional basis for future decentralization, with all statutory provisions having to be consistent with the new Constitution.

Although based on views submitted to the UCC from 1989 to early 1992, the *Draft Constitution* was finalized late in 1992, just after the NRM decentralization policy was announced, and a year before that policy was refined into the statutory form of November 1993. As a result, the UCC proposals did not reflect developments in thinking on decentralization evident in the 1993 statute.

Experience in other countries shows that constitutional protection for federal and lesser forms of decentralization can be a crucial factor in the stability of such arrangements, especially when they face considerable opposition (Ghai and Regan, 1992). There seems little doubt that the NRM's decentralization policy since 1993 will have a negative impact on a range of interests in Uganda. These include the old political parties, conservative monarchists, and many senior national government civil servants. Hence a key aim of constitutional arrangements intended to provide support for NRM decentralization policy should have been to protect key aspects of local government arrangements.

The *Draft Constitution* did provide constitutional protection for district councils, far beyond that offered to other forms of sub-national government under prior Uganda Constitutions.[18] It went so far as to give district councils a role in the process for amendment of key provisions of the Constitution, including that on the core principles of decentralization.[19]

Unfortunately, however, the bulk of the *Draft Constitution's* provision on local government was muddled with detail which would have been better provided by way of normal statute. It failed to deal with a number of matters of fundamental significance such as guaranteeing: the existence of the levels of councils and committees below the district (the most democratically significant of them);[20] basic funding arrangements; division of responsibilities; and the degree of control the national government should have over the exercise of functions at local level. It is the way in which such matters are statutorily defined, however, that tends to determine the degree of autonomy of local level governments. In the absence of constitutional limits, the national government has great latitude to restrict or do away with that autonomy.

The guaranteeing of both the autonomy of local level governments and the existence of the lower level governments is of particular importance to the long-term sustainability of the beneficial impacts of decentralization on state and society. While it may ultimately depend on the level of political support for the system rather than legal protections, there seems little doubt that legal protection could be an important factor in future political conflict about decentralization. At present, the existence of the RC system (and its successor councils) is protected by statute law. As statutes can be changed with relative ease by the national Parliament, the degree of long-term protection for decentralization is limited.

Despite having been given insufficient attention in the Odoki Commission it would still have been possible for such issues to have been put high on the agenda of the NRM in the Constituent Assembly debates. But key NRM figures were giving only slight attention in the Constituent Assembly debate to the future of the RC system. Instead the major importance of the issue related to negotiations over federalism in general and over the federal position of Buganda in the new Constitution in particular sought by Baganda traditionalists. In the finally agreed Constitution promulgated in October 1995 there is, as a form of compromise on the federal issue, an opening for traditional entities as it is stated that two or more districts are free to co-operate in areas of culture and development (article 178). But Buganda succeeded in extracting an even greater concession. Apart from the recognition of Buganda as a distinct entity it is written into the Constitution that 'the districts of Buganda shall be *deemed* to have agreed to co-operate on the coming into force of this Constitution' (article 178, clause 3, italics added). Although a district may decide to withdraw from the co-operation it remains to be seen whether the special clause on Buganda is just cosmetic or it represents 'the seed of federalism' (Mukholi, 1995: 52).

The Constituent Assembly, however, left no doubt regarding the continuation of the decentralization policy with the district as the basis for local government. In the Constitution the existing RC system in the districts is endorsed, but it is left to Parliament to decide on lower local government units. This means that the local government system below the district is still dependent on statute law. Certain names of institutions and individuals have already been changed. Resistance Council/Committee (RC) has been changed to 'Local Councils/Committees (LC), and 'RC5 Chairman' to 'District Chairperson', for example – but the details of decentralization policy at the lower levels have still to emerge.

IMPACT OF DECENTRALIZATION ON STATE AND SOCIETY

Decentralization policy has certainly had significant impacts on the state. It is less clear what has been achieved in relation to civil society. The more important issue, however, may be the sustainability of the decentralization policy.

Decentralization and the state

By any measure, the NRM decentralization policy has had a remarkable impact on the state in Uganda. The extension of popular control over local government and the transfer to local (district) control of significant personnel and financial resources of the centre involve dramatic reversals of twenty years of centralized and undemocratic control of the state.

Mamdani (1993b, 1994b) has argued that the most significant contribution of the NRM to Uganda has been the establishment of popular control over the local state – the chiefs – through the RC system. The power to hold them accountable under the 1987 statute has become one of direction in 1993. Undermined in 1987, their previous position of almost unlimited power had been destroyed by 1993. As long as the RC system or successor councils are in operation it will be very difficult for the chiefs to be woven back into the web of political patronage developed earlier. The 1993 statute has, of course, gone beyond the chiefs to bring many other public servants also under political control at district level.

The RC system has helped constitute a new kind of state for Uganda, where elected representatives of the people not only direct the local state but also act as intermediaries in many of the dealings of the people with other state agencies.

170

Decentralization policy: reshaping state and society

Concern has been expressed that the RCs have become too close to the state, and so have tended to become state agencies rather than those of the people.[21] There was concern that the RCs were becoming either or both administrative or/and political adjuncts of the state – administrative adjuncts in that their duties were being increasingly defined by the state officials, and political adjuncts in that they could be removed from office if they came into conflict with the state (e.g. Mamdani, 1988b: 1176; 1988c: 44). By 1994, the concern went further; in defining the movement system, the *Draft Constitution* was accused of 'incorporating local RCs into centralized state structures' (Mamdani, 1994b: 15).

It is suggested, however, that if RCs or their successor councils are to exercise the legal powers which to some degree provide them with their local authority, they must derive it from state authority, and so they are, to an extent, state organs. The key issue is the degree of autonomy they enjoy in the exercise of their powers. Central aspects of autonomy include the extent to which their long-term existence is guaranteed, and the degree to which they exercise those legal powers free from direction and control by state functionaries and by higher levels of government.

As pointed out earlier, neither the 1993 statute nor the *Draft Constitution* provided adequate protection for the autonomy of the RCs and the 1995 Constitution has not meant any change for the succeeding Local Councils. Given the intensity of opposition to decentralization likely to develop and the lack of clear attention to constitutional and other mechanisms which might give some measure of protection to the system, there must therefore be some concern about the sustainability of the impact of decentralization on the state.

Decentralization and civil society

The key issue in the strengthening of civil society is the sustainability of the full range of NRM reforms. Although it seems clear that the NRM has maintained popular support in much of the country,[22] it also relies on military strength to retain power. The NRM strategy on changing the nature of the political forces at work in Uganda recognizes that, without such change, its state reforms may not be sustainable in the longer term, especially once a multi-party political system is operating. A civil society capable of limiting state action would act as a brake on any tendencies towards a return to the role the state played from the 1960s to the early 1980s.

As a result of village-level RCs, there has been a remarkable degree of democratization in Uganda. As powers to decide matters closely affecting people at the local level have been given to the local councils, all people in Uganda are able to participate in the making of decisions about matters that affect them and a significant proportion do in fact do so. They can be mobilized at the local level in relation to a wide range of issues. The various local councils can act as an interface between state

171

and society. Not only can people articulate their needs, there are also opportunities for a two-way flow of information and ideas.[23]

The involvement of hundreds of thousands of people in the work of such councils and committees means the exercise of powers of decision-making, policy-making and recall of all leaders who fail to meet expectations. This must contribute to increased understanding of the state, and of how ordinary people can deal with and influence it. All this experience will contribute to strengthening common norms about political leadership and the way in which the state operates.[24]

Of course involvement in the RC system and its successor councils is occurring together with other developments which will also tend to contribute to common norms, and so may have significant impacts on the development of civil society in Uganda. These include the wide-spread public contributions to the constitution-making processes, wider political activity surrounding the Constituent Assembly elections, debate in that Assembly, presidential and parliamentary elections in 1996 under the new Constitution, the emergence of new political and other organizations seeking to influence state action in various ways and the expansion of a vigorous and critical mass media.

It is, of course, impossible to quantify such impacts at this stage. There is as yet little evidence of a 'developed' civil society in Uganda of the kind envisaged by Woods (1992). There is in fact evidence of the continuing strength of the old political forces, and of their ability to make use of new structures like the RCs and their successor councils. For example, the RCs in the 'Buganda' area were used in 1993 and 1994 to mobilize support for a much more substantial re-establishment of federal kingdoms in the country than has so far been achieved.

Indeed it remains problematic whether a civil society of that kind can be encouraged by state policy alone. If the economic base of a society is of great importance to civil society of the Western kind, then that kind of civil society is unlikely to emerge without economic change of a kind and scale at present unimaginable in Uganda. The direct contribution political decentralization can make to such economic change is, of course, limited.

CONCLUSIONS

The NRM has set itself broad goals of changing both the role of a previously dominant and oppressive state and the nature of political forces in Uganda in such a way that not only will conflict to control the state be less likely, but also society will change in ways which may enable it to limit the actions of the state.

Decentralization is one of a number of policy initiatives directed to achieving these difficult goals. The policy has unquestionably changed the Ugandan state, bringing it under popular control to a degree that is remarkable by any measure. Although the impact is difficult to measure at this stage, it seems likely that the policy has had some impact in strengthening civil society. The difficulty of quantifying that change highlights the need for caution in assessing the many claims made since the fall of the Berlin Wall about the potential role of civil society in Africa.

As to whether the change brought about by decentralization is sustainable, the full possibilities of civil society are yet to be seen, but it remains a fragile development. On the other hand, decentralization policy has adverse impacts on a range of interests in Uganda. They can be expected to seek to undermine or oppose the policy either during the period the NRM remains in power under the new Constitution or under any later multi-party political system after 2000. In those circumstances, legal and constitutional protections for key aspects of decentralization policy may offer some support for political forces also supporting it. There are, however, some weaknesses in the protections offered by the 1993 statute and the new Constitution.

Notes

---

1. Many academic observers are cautious. In a survey of popular protest and political reform in African countries after the fall of the Berlin Wall, Bratton and van de Walle found little evidence of the emergence of effective forces 'aggregated across the full breadth of civil society'. Based in the urban bourgeoisie, protest sought to 'protect corporate privilege', being 'a conservative reaction against economic austerity' (1992: 440).
2. For references to a representative sample of literature see: Jeffries, 1993; Diamond, 1994.
3. Examples include the struggles of various groups to maintain a critical press even during the pressures of the early 1980s under Obote 2.
4. Policies directed towards reform of the state include: improved accountability through new institutions – the Inspector General of Government and the Human Rights Commission – and improved performance of bodies such as the Auditor-General and Public Accounts Committee; greater control of, and discipline for, the security forces; privatization; and public service reform.
5. They include: privatization and economic liberalization policies (which create room and opportunities for a range of interests – mainly economic – to develop independent of direct control by the state); encouragement of a richer associational life, in the promotion of associations of women and youth at all levels; active involvement of the population in the unprecedentedly populist constitution-making process.
6. This analysis of the NRM policies is derived from both a range of NRM publications already referred to and from personal communication with a number of senior NRM figures during 1993 and the first half of 1994. I am grateful to the editors of this volume for updating my discussion.
7. See The Resistance Councils and Committees Statute, 1987, The Resistance Committees (Judicial Powers) Statute 1988 and The Local Governments (Resistance Councils) Statute 1993, hereafter referred to as the 1987 statute, the 1988 statute and the 1993 statute respectively. The 1993 statute repealed the 1987 statute but reproduced most of its essential features.

173

8. The RC system, inclusive of well documented problems, has been analyzed in detail elsewhere. See for example, Uganda Government 1987; Oloka Onyango, 1989; Ddungu and Wabwire, 1991; Burkey, 1991; Kasfir, 1991; Brett, 1993b; Nsibambi, 1993, Uganda Government 1993b, ch. 18; and Brett, 1994. Following approval of the new constitution in 1995, RCs were succeeded by Local Councils.

9. The RCs had been operating in NRM controlled areas for several years before the NRM took over national power, and were established administratively even before the 1987 Statute was passed.

10. This figure derives from the final report of the Uganda Constitutional Commission (Uganda Government, 1993a: 517). Lower estimates are sometimes given, Brett (1993: 25) gives a figure of 40,0000 based on very rough figures of 38 districts with approximately 1000 RCIs in each.

11. Administrative arrangements permitted sub-county RCs to retain a proportion of the tax revenues collected on behalf of municipal and district councils, and all lower-level RCs derived some revenue from 'unofficial' fees for the administrative and maintenance services they provide.

12. The UCC, for example, reported strong support for the system and for the idea of constitutional protection for strong local government (Uganda Government, 1993b).

13. The statute provides for the CGR not only to 'take precedence over all officials in the district', but also to be responsible for defence and security (other than the police) and to tender advice to district and urban RCs on national issues.

14. In mid-1994, it was planned that most of the functions in respect of the following broad areas of responsibility would be transferred from the relevant national agencies: trade and industry; agriculture; lands and housing; education and sports; health; information; labour and welfare; internal affairs; natural resources; women and youth; and tourism. Most of the wide ranging responsibilities previously coordinated by the Ministry of Local Government were also to be transferred.

15. Unofficial estimates provided by officials of the Ministry of Finance and Economic Planning and Ministry of Public Service in March 1994.

16. Local Governments (Resistance Councils) Statute 1993, sections 30(1) and 34(6).

17. Section 47(2) of the 1993 statute permits the schedules to be amended, replaced, altered or revoked in this way, in contrast to section 47(1) and (3) under which regulations made under the statute must be tabled in the legislature which can then amend or revoke the regulation. It seems likely the requirement for tabling in and possible amendment by the legislature was also intended to apply to instruments made in relation to the schedules, and may have been omitted by error. If so, it is a serious omission which should be rectified.

18. The sole exception is the position of the traditional kingdoms under the short-lived 1962 Constitution.

19. Under section 289, ratification by two thirds of all district councils is required in addition to the votes of two thirds of members of Parliament before all provisions on human rights as well as other key provisions can be amended.

20. The narrative volume of the UCC's Final Report expressed concern about the lack of major emphasis on other than the district level in the NRM's new decentralization policy announced in October 1992 (Uganda Government, 1993b: 490). It also recommended adoption of the following aim as a principle to be followed: 'to decentralise to all levels of local government, from the district to the village' (*ibid.* 494). But in the process of translating narrative and recommendations into the *Draft Constitution* there was a change in emphasis, so that the principle stated in s.201(2)(b) of the draft is:

> decentralisation shall be an objective applying to all levels of local government and in particular from higher to lower local government units. (Uganda Government, 1993c: 91)

The *Draft Constitution* made a number of references to 'lower level' local governments and local government units, but nowhere defined those expressions. This is also the case in the new Constitution. It was therefore open to later statutes to recognize or withdraw recognition from levels below the district level.

Decentralization policy: reshaping state and society

21. As early as 1987 the Commission of Inquiry into the Local Government System expressed concern that the RCs should not be regarded as 'organs of the state' or 'organs of the movement' but rather as 'democratic organs of the people' (Uganda Government, 1987: 22).

22. The outcomes of the Constituent Assembly elections of March and April 1994 provide evidence in this regard – see Geist, 1994 and Kasfir, 1994.

23. The fact that 9,521 – or almost 25 per cent – of the approximately 40,000 village-level RC committees made written submissions to the Uganda Constitutional Commission in the 1990–92 period is a striking example of the potential of the mobilizing power of the RC system.

24. It is the lower level councils which involve the largest proportion of people in decision-making. Hence if the impact decentralization policy has on civil society is to be maintained, attention should be given to providing guarantees of the continued operation of, and material resources for, those levels.

TWELVE

Land reform in the making

Mark A. Marquardt and Abby Sebina-Zziwa

There are two general approaches to land tenure reform. The first views land reform as the breaking up of large estates and redistributing land in accordance with distributive justice. The second views land reform as an integrated and co-ordinated programme involving a comprehensive policy covering the revision of legislation, ownership, and increased security of tenure, in addition to other measures to assist farmers such as improved credit systems, better marketing facilities, agricultural extension services, and general education.

Uganda has a long history of a spatially diverse set of laws and social systems governing its land tenure. While legally, since the promulgation of the Land Reform Decree of 1975, only two systems of land tenure exist in Uganda (leasehold and customary tenure), in practice a complex mixture of land tenure systems (including customary, leasehold, freehold, and mailo[1]) continues to function throughout the country. In recent years, the government has taken an interest in simplifying and unifying the nation's land tenure system. Given the sensitivity of the topic and the experience of the 1975 Decree, the government has chosen not to rush the process, but has allowed ample opportunity for research and debate. During the course of the exercise, issues have moved from general to specific, from emotion to administrative reality with a recognition that the evolution and implementation of land tenure are a continuing process. One major result in the still ongoing process has been the inclusion of paragraphs on land tenure in the new Constitution of 1995. But important issues like women's rights to own land are still in need of further consideration.

BACKGROUND

Prior to the promulgation of Idi Amin's Land Reform Decree of 1975, Uganda had four major types of land tenure: customary, leasehold, freehold, and mailo. Customary tenure represents the bulk of landholdings. An individual's access to and use of land are determined by the customary rules of the tribal group to which he belongs. Leasehold tenure, a more formalized means of access to land, has generally applied to grants of state land to non-citizens and urban tenure.

176

Freehold tenure is of limited extent, found mainly in the former Ankole, Toro, Kigezi, and Bugisu Districts. Mailo tenure is limited to roughly 9,000 sq.km. of central Uganda.

Since its introduction in Buganda mailo land has been the subject of continual controversy and misunderstanding. Following the original allocations in the early 1900s, a lively land market developed allowing means of access to titled land to those having the means to purchase it. At the same time individuals who were occupying the land as customary tenants at the time of the allotments became tenants of the new landowner. Other tenants were encouraged to move on to mailo land by the owners who saw 'rental' payments as a source of labour and income. The Busuulu and Envujjo Law of 1927 formalized this landlord-tenant relationship and guaranteed ample security of tenure to the tenants with respect to occupancy, inheritance, and protection against eviction as long as the Busuulu and Envujjo payments were made. That these payments had not been altered until they were abolished under the 1975 Decree meant in effect that they had become of symbolic rather than economic value and also that a deadlock over land rights evolved between the landowners who possessed *de jure* freehold over the parcels and their tenants who enjoyed *de facto* freehold.

The Land Reform Decree of 1975 radically altered these relationships. The Decree vested title of all land in Uganda in the state. Individual freehold and mailo titles were reduced to leaseholds. Customary tenants on state land and mailo tenancies were reduced to tenancies on sufferance. The Decree also extended the scope of public control over land transactions and the ability to impose developmental conditions on land.

However, the Decree has not been effectively implemented. Mailo and freehold titles have not been converted to leaseholds, customary tenants on state land continue to enjoy an adequate level of security of tenure, and relatively few instances of evictions of mailo or customary tenants have occurred. There are no public records of why the Decree has not been enforced. However, there are a number of possible explanations including the entrenchment of mailo land in the Constitution, the effective nationalization of private property without compensation (conversion of freehold and mailo titles to leaseholds), the inability of the Ministry responsible to implement the Decree, and the lack of consultation prior to enactment.

In view of the existing confusion over land law, in 1989 the Agricultural Policy Committee and the World Bank commissioned Makerere Institute of Social Research, in collaboration with the Land Tenure Center, University of Wisconsin, to undertake a study on land tenure and agricultural development with the main purpose of analyzing the land tenure systems operating in Uganda and to make recommendations on changes in land tenure policy. Three policy objectives have guided the analysis:

Policy imperatives

i) a land tenure system should support agricultural development by ensuring that the system is flexible enough to enable progressive farmers to gain access to the land,

ii) a land tenure system should not force people off the land, particularly those who have no other way to earn a reasonable living or to survive,

iii) the law should provide for the evolution of a uniform system of land tenure throughout the country.

PROBLEMS AND DILEMMAS IN LAND TENURE REFORM

While there was a general consensus of opinion on the priority of agricultural development, and also on necessary safeguards for tenants, the question of a uniform system of land tenure raised a number of issues for discussion. Ten issues were identified as crucial for the tenure reform process:

Uniformity of tenure: As discussed earlier (Kisamba-Mugerwa, 1991), Uganda has a multiplicity of tenure systems which has led to confusion and insecurity. Confusion over *de jure* and *de facto* land tenure rights has resulted in a recognition of the need to regularize the system. The general consensus for a uniform tenure system has existed for some time. The problem has been: which system?

Freehold tenure: It became clear during the study that a general consensus existed that freehold tenure should be the uniform tenure system for Uganda. In general individuals recognized the advantages of titles to land. However, what appeared to be the people's greatest concerns when committing themselves to this tenure system were the implication and speed of its introduction. If, on the one hand, immediate conversion to freehold is not administratively feasible, how are rights to be protected in the meantime? How are issues of traditional clan and family control of land holdings to be addressed?

The recommendations and the proposed legislation address this in two ways. While they propose that freehold tenure should be the uniform tenure system for Uganda, they recognize that conversion to that system is going to take a long time. In the meantime it is essential that existing rights should be protected and secured. No one will be forced to convert to freehold tenure if they believe that their existing tenure rights are adequate for their needs. Thus, as part of the decentralization exercise, the establishment of adjudication committees is proposed to ensure individual rights are not extinguished without the individual's consent.

Non-citizen ownership of land: Experience has shown that for a long time ambiguity in both policy and law has, on the one hand, left land in Uganda exposed to acquisition by foreigners and, on the other hand, limited access to certain groups of citizens. The Land Transfer Act (Cap. 202) makes reference to 'African' and 'non-African', while the Public Lands Act, 1969, talks of an 'African citizen of Uganda'. It is dif-

178

ficult to identify who an 'African' is; and decided cases reflect this difficulty. The majority of respondents stressed that the ownership of land in Uganda, especially rural land, should be based on citizenship rather than race.

Decentralization of the Land Registry: There is great demand and support for decentralization. There is increased public awareness of the value of individual title, and individuals are willing to come forward for titles. During consultation there was unanimous support from respondents for decentralization to take place. However, the demands for setting up more land registries raise questions of how soon and how far decentralization can be effected. Given the limited resources available, decentralization requires consideration of which functions, services, and activities can be decentralized and to which level without causing problems of administrative capacity and guarantees of the integrity and physical security of the land register.

Non-Governmental Organizations (NGOs): Despite the stringent measures put in place to co-ordinate and control the activities of NGOs, there is still widespread suspicion about the intentions of some NGOs. We noted divided opinion on the question of whether or not NGOs should own land in Uganda, particularly rural land. This seemed to be based both on the 'citizenship' of the NGO and the intentions of the organization. Generally, it seems to be felt that local or Ugandan NGOs should be allowed to acquire freeholds, while foreign NGOs should only be allowed to lease land.

Role of the Minister: Present legislation, which gives certain powers to the Minister responsible for land, has caused concern to the general public. Reservations were expressed about entrusting decisions with respect to land, which may be far reaching, in the hands of a single individual. Respondents noted that ministers vary in character and integrity and such powers could be abused by a single individual. The majority view is that a body should be set up to replace the Minister in the exercise of these powers.

Urban tenure: In 1989 it was recommended that leasehold tenure be retained in urban areas, and it was provided for under Clause 2 (2) of the draft Tenure and Control of Land Bill (1990). A number of reasons were advanced to support this position based primarily on concerns about the requirements of more rigorous planning, control, and direction of development and re-development, and ensuring an annual flow of revenue to urban authorities through rental payments.

However, a number of arguments have also been advanced supporting the granting of freehold titles in urban areas as well. These include existing tenure status (towns such as Kampala, Mukono, Lugazi, and Mityana are already on mailo land); future tenure status (urban expansion in future will extend the boundaries of urban land into freehold tenure areas); equity (it is hard to justify relegating higher-value urban investments to leasehold tenure, when lower-value rural investments are granted freehold titles. Similarly urban popula-

179

tions would be limited to leaseholds, while rural populations would enjoy higher tenure status); corruption; and existing legislation (the Town and Country Planning Act, 1964) gives wide powers to controlling authorities to plan and direct development within their jurisdictions on all types of land, no matter how it is held.

These arguments discredit the pro-leasehold arguments for development controls. If the town and country planning legislation currently in place is not enforced, how can urban authorities argue that leasehold conditions will be any more effectively administered? They also reflect a desire to avoid inequities in access to comparable forms of tenure for all citizens wherever they live.

Common property: Since common property resources are resources to which access is shared by members of a community, conversion to freehold tenure presents a problem regarding eventual ownership. Common property regimes are structured ownership arrangements, with management rules, membership identity, incentives to follow acceptable resource use, and sanctions to ensure compliance. Yet, if a uniform system of freehold land tenure is adopted in Uganda, the question arises of who would own these resources.

Similarly, communities which have traditionally had access to these resources have established rules and customs which define rights of access and management to them. However, these rules and customs break down as a result of changing legislation, population growth, changing resource use as a result of changing economic opportunities, etc. If the tenure rules change, should the control of these resources remain with the communities deriving the most direct benefit from them or should it be placed in the hands of a higher administrative authority? District sources were of the opinion that ownership should be vested in local authorities and management should be vested in the same local authorities or the communities with technical support.

There is a dearth of information on common property resources in Uganda. Rather than propose legislation concerning the ownership of these resources, and recognizing that the process of conversion to freehold would of necessity be slow, there is an opportunity here for further research to be undertaken on common property management regimes to provide the necessary data to formulate appropriate government policy concerning these resources. It is therefore desirable that common property resources should continue to be treated as customary tenure rights and be protected much like individual customary tenure rights. By continuing to treat these common property rights as customary tenure rights presumably the 'community' would protect their common property resources from being lost through acquisition by an individual or individuals from outside the community. Similarly, the community should be able to continue to manage the resources and, through appropriate education campaigns, develop sanctions against their abuse.

Land reform in the making

Free land market: The first policy objective stated that the land tenure system should support agricultural development. It is often suggested that land is more productively distributed and utilized if it is a marketable commodity.

It should be noted that a market in land has existed in parts of Uganda for nearly 100 years. Immediately following the allocations of land under the Uganda Agreement of 1900, subdivision and sales of these allotments began. In 1953 a researcher at Makerere reported that in his two study areas over 50 per cent of the mailo owners had purchased (rather than inherited) their land. The 1989 MISR/LTC land market study found evidence of land sales being accepted throughout the areas of eastern and southern Uganda.

Discussion of a free land market with a view to proposed legislation has been within the context of titling as a mechanism to facilitate its evolution. However, a free market in relation to the sale of land is often feared as a factor that would fan speculation and could serve to push most of the land into the hands of a few well-to-do members of society at the expense of the majority of the people and of national development. Another concern is the likely sale of land by the very poor, who sell progressively more and more of their only income-generating asset in order to pay school fees, taxes, and brideprices, and eventually become landless.

The above fears have some justification. Land markets can hardly be free from speculation, nor can landlessness be avoided in a socio-economic situation that is in transition towards a monetized economy. However, given the advantages of allocating land to farmers with the greatest resources to utilize it, the land market should be encouraged. District consultations registered an overwhelming response in favour of encouraging the development of a free land market. However, at the same time there was concern that, while a free market should evolve, safeguards needed to be put in place to guard against irresponsible sales of land by the cash-needy. The proposed law had included stipulations that would require the parties to a proposed sale to obtain a recommendation from the sub-county adjudication committee. This recommendation would be given after the committee had satisfied itself that the seller had consulted his/her immediate family.

Ceiling on land holdings: While there appeared to be a general consensus on the evolution of a free land market, almost equal concern was raised concerning the imposition of a ceiling on the amount of land that an individual could own. It was recognized that the two issues and the resulting conclusions were contradictory, yet there did not seem to be any mechanism for resolving them. This question was perhaps the most difficult to address and most clearly demonstrates the need for continuing dialogue in the evolution of tenure policy as emotion gives way to pragmatism.

While the imposition of a ceiling is not workable, a number of arguments for establishing a ceiling on landholdings need to be considered.

181

Policy imperatives

These are based on two major concerns: land speculation and land-lessness. It is argued that the imposition of a ceiling would limit the amount of land speculation. It is also argued that the imposition of a ceiling would limit the level of concentration of land holdings in the hands of a few members of the community and thereby ensure that land would be available for everyone. Great concern was expressed that if there were no ceiling the resulting unrestricted acquisition of land through a free land market would lead to a significant number of landless people.

In a country such as Uganda, which has widely varying climatic conditions and levels of population density and variations in land-use activities which dictate different minimal sized holdings as realistic economic incentives for investment, a uniform ceiling on land holdings is obviously both illogical and unworkable. A multitude of ceilings is even less workable. Similarly, if a ceiling is established, an administrative structure must be developed to monitor compliance with the ceiling. This would entail the development of a system of land records that would be able to identify landholders and the amounts of their holdings throughout the country at any given point in time. It would also necessitate a process of vetting all land transactions to ensure that the stipulated ceiling was not being exceeded.

These are some of the problems associated with setting a ceiling on land holdings. However, if it is not technically or administratively feasible to introduce and manage a ceiling on landholdings, what mechanisms can be introduced to avoid or control land speculation and slow the process toward landlessness completely? The amount of land is finite and, as long as populations continue to grow and economic opportunities change, societies will eventually be confronted with segments of the population becoming landless, some by force of circumstances and others by choice. A role of government is to establish policies which encourage the development of alternative, non-agricultural economic opportunities for such people.

LAND REFORM AND THE CONSTITUTION-MAKING PROCESS

Work on land reform has all along been part of the constitutional debate, and suggestions for a new land policy figured inevitably in the Draft Constitution submitted to the President by the Constitutional Commission in December 1992.

In the Constituent Assembly which sat from 1993 to 1995, land tenure became one of the three most controversial issues, only superseded by the question of federalism and the position of Buganda, on the one hand, and the choice between the movement and a multi-party political system, on the other (Mukholi, 1995: 48 ff.; Hansen and Twaddle, 1994).

In the end the Constituent Assembly shelved the idea of a uniform system for the time being. Instead it chose as its point of departure the

182

prevailing pluralistic system and wrote into chapter 15 of the Constitution that land ownership shall be based on four tenure systems: (i) customary; (ii). leasehold; (iii) freehold; and (iv) mailo. The longer-term policy is expressed more indirectly, 'Customary and leasehold may be converted into freehold'. It follows that in due course Parliament will have to pass the necessary legislation in order to establish rules and procedures for the transition to freehold as the dominant mode of land ownership in Uganda.

Gender issues and property rights

Little consideration has been given in the discussion of tenure reform to its potential impact on women. While it is widely recognized that women make a significant contribution to agricultural production in Uganda, their tenure rights are fragile. The determination and protection of property rights have increasingly become an issue as a result of the internal struggles of the recent past as well as the increasing impact of AIDS on the population. The analysis of property rights in a gender perspective is therefore important in order to formulate appropriate land reform legislation that will be sensitive to its negative and positive impacts on that segment of society.

At present, in the absence of laws and statistics putting a value on their contribution to the local or subsistence sector, women are not considered equal partners and equal sharers of the property accrued in a marriage. They tend to become victims in times of instability in the home. The state's legal stand on inheritance in Uganda can be said to be progressive in the sense that it recognizes the devolution of property through statutory as well as customary law. This is not the case in several other African countries.

Would a restructured family law in Uganda evolve into a stable productive base? Such a question leads to deeper issues related to gender and inheritance practices in a country with diverse cultural values and beliefs. A strong family law dictates new norms, attitudes, and practices regarding property transfers. The newly promulgated Constitution does state that laws, cultures, customs or traditions which are against the dignity, welfare or interest of women or which undermine their status are prohibited. But this is not enough. The so-called discriminatory laws, cultures, customs, and traditions must be spelled out by Parliament in order to avoid ambiguity such as exists in the 1972 Succession Act. Wives' rights to property accrued in marriage need to be explicitly indicated as well as those of a woman's exclusive control of the property after the death of her husband. This calls for registration of mortgageable property in both names. It can also be pointed out that all property is potentially subject to links forged between legitimate marriage and inheritance.[2] This is evidenced by the significant correlation between the type of marriage and men's traditional knowledge about inheritance, attitudes to ownership of assets in the household, women's land ownership, and equal inheritance. In practice, however, kin relations often invoke customary practices to legitimize heirship by children born to other unions.

It appears that the idea of all children of the deceased being equal inheritors is widely acceptable, thus getting round the legitimate marriage requirement. It is perhaps precisely this practice that led to the inclusion of all children as inheritors of their father in the 1972 Succession Act. This, however, further complicates the issue of the form and type of marriage and has brought about more conflict than it has solved. It also encourages loose unions, thus further eroding the legitimate wives' commitment to household development.

Widespread ignorance of statutory law about inheritance, coupled with varied traditional practices, is the root problem facing widows, girl-orphans and children in general. Since the new Constitution prohibits discriminatory customary and traditional laws and practices in relation to women, it should also put in place machinery through which local authorities can work hand-in-hand with household members to promote the peace and development of the household.

It is recommended that, in the short term, it would be plausible for NGOs to emulate and/or support the legal aid clinic and FIDA to encourage will-writing throughout Uganda. NGOs and the Ministry of Women, Youth and Culture should also increase their efforts to further empower women economically. However, many problems currently facing female-headed households are a result of previous unbalanced and/or unfair distribution of property within the family setting. Thus the long-term solution to this problem is to enact strong laws accompanied by the machinery to enforce them, particularly on the distribution of property between couples. Secondly, a strong civic education programme on family property rights should be launched.

Notes

---

1. Mailo tenure, which is unique to Buganda and a small part of Bunyoro, was created by the Uganda Agreement of 1900 under which land in Buganda was divided between the Protectorate Government and the Kabaka, chiefs, and other tribal notables. The word *mailo* was derived from the square mile unit of measurement used in the allocation of this land. Mailo land is akin to freehold in that a land title is issued and the interest in the land goes on in perpetuity.
2. We owe this insight to the work of Jane I. Guyer.

THIRTEEN

Developing a population policy for Uganda

Edward K. Kirumira

Almost invariably, any report on Uganda's population status begins by stressing the paucity of demographic data in the country. The first systematic counting started with the 1948 Population Census; subsequent censuses have been carried out in 1959, 1969, 1980 and 1991. These efforts had varying levels of coverage and content. Uganda was omited from big surveys like the World Fertility Survey (WFS), and the first rounds of the Demographic and Health Surveys; it was only in 1988/9 that a Demographic and Health Survey was conducted in the country. Systematic collection of vital statistics is also a recent phenomenon in Uganda, although the Births and Deaths Registration Ordinance dates back to 1904. This provided for voluntary registration by the native population. It was only in 1973 that registration was made compulsory. Since then, the coverage of vital statistics has improved but is still far from adequate.

The reasons for this state of affairs are several. The most important is that policy-makers have often failed to recognize how far their immediate concerns – slow economic growth rates, poverty, unemployment, national security and defence, food deficits – have been affected by past population growth and how continuation of present population trends will compound development problems in the future. In several instances, government officials have actually adopted the opposite view, namely, that lower population figures have been the problem especially with regard to slow economic growth rates.

Secondly, the population question has been, and remains, a sensitive issue in Uganda. Discussion of it has been unduly politicized. As a result, much analysis has adopted a numerical perspective largely shaped by successive governments'·interest in the 'political arithmetic'.

Thirdly, there has also been a general failure to see family planning as a component of a comprehensive population policy, rather than as its equivalent. The two have been assumed to be synonymous.

DEMOGRAPHIC INDICATORS
Uganda's population is largely rural, with 89 per cent of the people residing in the countryside. Recent population estimates stand at 16.6 million people, representing an inter-censal growth rate of 2.5 per

cent, down from 2.8 per cent registered between 1969 and 1980 (Ministry of Finance and Economic Planning, 1992a: 31). Significant changes have also occurred in the composition of the population over the years. For instance, socio-demographic changes have resulted from displacement due to wars as well as searching for economic survival. Acute population growth, because of a persistently high fertility rate and a relatively high mortality rate, have brought about further changes in people's fertility expectations, migration patterns and reaction to morbidity and mortality.

The sex ratio has declined from 101.8 in 1969 to 96.1 by 1991; there were also slightly more males than females in 1969 than is the case now. According to the 1991 Census, the proportion of children below 15 years is 47.3 per cent, almost half the population. Other changes have included increasing pressure on land; increasing population density over time, rising from 48 in 1969 to 85 persons per square kilometre in 1991. Career aspirations have also changed, leading to ever changing mobility patterns and new modes of residence, obligations and ties with family, kin and other social, economic and political groups.

Changes have been observed in overall patterns and general demographic indices between and across generations, gender and ethnic groups. Overall, however, fertility remains high and the population of Uganda portrays a disproportionately high percentage of the youthful age groups. This implies that a relatively large portion of young people enter the reproductive age group and, at the other end, only a small percentage move out of childbearing through ageing. Table 13.1 gives a comparative picture of the population pyramid between 1969 and 1988/89.

Table 13.1 Aggregate age structure (1969, 1980 and 1988/89)

Age Group	1969 Census	1980 Census	1988/89 DHS
0–4	19.45	19.4	20.45
5–9	14.3	15.2	15.5
10–14	11.75	12.7	13.0
15–19	10.05	10.5	10.65
20–24	8.6	8.75	8.65
25–29	7.25	7.15	7.05
30–34	6.05	5.85	5.6
35–39	4.95	4.8	4.6
40–44	4.15	3.95	3.7
45–49	3.4	3.25	2.9
50–54	2.8	2.6	2.35
55+	2.4	1.81	2.7
Total %	82.4	84.35	85.5

Source: Statistics Department, Ministry of Finance and Economic Planning

The 20–39 age groups indicate a drop in overall percentage representation. All subsequent age groups show a consistent drop in their percentage representation of the total population, except for a slight increase for the above-55 category. Note that the total percentage representation for the 0–39 age groups has steadily increased over the last 20-year period, with adverse implications for the population doubling over time, and still more so for public service provision. '. . . Hence, despite the apparent falling [overall] growth rate, there is still a need to control population increase' (*ibid.*).

RELIGIOUS AND ETHNIC CONSIDERATIONS
Much as the population question has been talked about in Uganda – for various reasons – there have been few efforts to address it systematically. Population issues have often been addressed unsystematically in terms of religious and ethnic perspectives.

The religious concern was dominant in the early post-independence period and manifested itself in political alliances and counter-alliances as well as in political parties at the time. It is not surprising therefore that, although religion is often taken to be an important factor in Uganda, in the population censuses that have been conducted in the country actual percentages of religious denominations are seldom made public.

The ethnic diversity of the country has played a major role in further politicizing discussion of population growth in Uganda. Ethnic belonging and allegiances have often determined the fate of successive governments. The 1961/2 debates on Buganda's claim to a special status in post-independence Uganda were based, for example, among other things on its population as a single ethnic group vis-à-vis other ethnic groups.

The Obote 1 and 2 regimes demonstrated distinctive patterns of ethnic allegiance. Other governments have demonstrated other patterns. Proportional ethnic representation in the national army is still being discussed in both private and public fora. Provision of facilities like schools and health care, which under normal circumstances are measured against the ratio of population served, have more frequently been measured in terms of how many of them were Catholics or Protestants.

The ethnic consideration manifested itself clearly in the Census exercise of 1980. Political parties participating in the December 1980 elections had ethnically defined strongholds. It is an open question whether the population counts of quite a few areas were either inflated or deflated to justify the demarcation of constituencies shortly before these elections. Some critics argue that similar dynamics were not wholly absent in the more recent 1994 Constituency Assembly elections, with the emphasis here being played out intra-ethnically. Ethnic arithmetic bedevils the political arena in Uganda and its influence underlies government perceptions of population growth and policy develop-

187

ment. The politics of population growth has therefore been played out in terms of the power-sharing potentials of regional, ethnic, religious and interest groups' rather than in terms of the overall impact of population growth on national development.

EXTERNAL INFLUENCE

The reluctance of successive governments to give direct and massive support to population policy and programmes has meant that outside assistance has been vital in the planning and designing of the programmes. Training personnel for the implementation of programmes has also had to rely heavily on external funding. The international definition and interpretation of the population problem have thus influenced the process of population programme efforts in the country considerably.

For a long time, international pressure has favoured population control, citing the 'unacceptably' high population growth rates in developing countries. Funding has therefore favoured anti-natalist programmes. This has often pitted the governments of developing countries, in general, against international agencies, with the former being highly suspicious of the motives and concerns of the latter. This has still further politicized the debate on population growth.

Of late there has been a shift, with the emphasis being given to maternal and child health. The gender perspective has also gained ground. The 'Women in Development' initiatives in Uganda, for example, received significant increases in external funding, especially from 1987 onwards.

The politics of funding has thus complicated the population problem in Uganda still further, with policy and programme managers anxious to support or develop those programmes that can attract quicker and better funding. Most funding for the AIDS epidemic over the last decade should be seen in this light.

OPPOSING VIEWS

It is worth noting that the population debate in Uganda is also peculiar in that, much as the emphasis may be placed on the stand of the churches, for example, it is virtually impossible to characterize opposing views. The churches, government and public opinion are equally likely to adopt pro-natalist as anti-natalist positions.

Secondly, population policy is currently a side issue even for the feminist and anti-natalist activists in the country. One therefore has a situation where, on the one hand, there are no doctrinaire, fully committed pro-natalists, and, on the other hand, the pro-natalist position may be characterized as pro-natalism by default.

POPULATION POLICIES

Population policies comprise deliberate attempts by government to affect the size, structure, or geographic distribution of population. In practice, it is difficult to make a clear distinction between those measures that influence population growth deliberately – that is, directly – and those that influence it indirectly through the side effects of other policies. Sometimes measures designed to reduce the problems caused by population growth are also described as population policies (King, 1974).

There has been much debate on what a population policy should entail. Centrally at issue in contemporary debates are conflicts regarding the ends to be pursued, and the means to be employed in their pursuit. Bok argues that population policies basically serve two aims: first, to stem the growth of the world's population; second, to counter the poor health, lack of reproductive choice, subjugation, and poverty of so many members of the world's present population (Bok 1994: 19). The means employed to attain the objectives remain controversial, concerning both their efficacy in achieving the intended aims and their moral legitimacy. In general, however, it can be argued that population policies address the following issues:

– the processes of change,
– the emerging systems of social relations;
– financial and resource allocation;
– the division of labour and task assignment;
– responsibilities, duties and obligations to individuals; and
– the social environment within which people find themselves.

Furthermore, most population policies mainly address the question of fertility and are only indirectly concerned with mortality and migration matters. In most instances, mortality reduction policies are subsumed under health care provision policies.

In Uganda, population problems were first seriously recognized in the country's Second Five-Year Development Plan (1966–71):

> . . . In Uganda, population pressure as such is not the critical problem it is in many developing countries. However, the high growth rate does mean that a large proportion of the population is in the school-age group, which makes the education burden much greater than in most wealthier countries, which experience lower population growth . . . Growth in output and employment of nearly 3 per cent per annum is necessary in order to maintain per capita standards and hence for increasing per capita income an even higher rate of growth has to be achieved [p. 6].

However, before the coup which brought Idi Amin to power, the first Obote government had no policy to reduce the rate of population growth and had little interest in a national family planning programme, let alone a comprehensive population policy. Population growth was not regarded as a serious problem and birth control was politically sensitive in view of ethnic tensions within the country at the time (Miller, 1971b; Stamper 1977).

In the Third Five-Year Plan, 1971/2–1975/6, one chapter was devoted to the country's demography. Because of the then economic, social and health problems arising from the high birth rate, planners now supported a family planning programme. Although substantial declines in fertility could not be expected, they hoped that Uganda's population would decline to about 3 per cent per annum by 1979. The following quotation from the Plan summarizes the government's attitude toward population policy at the time.

> ... Government's main interest at this stage is to make people fully aware of the potential benefit of child spacing to their own family welfare, and to make available to those families who actually demand it, the means for regulating their sizes. In all this, every care will be taken to ensure that the programme is not conducted with detriment to the culture and morals of our society [p. 76].

At that time, although the Family Planning Association of Uganda (FPAU) was seen as the main agent for implementing government policy in this field, it was envisaged that the Ministry of Health would gradually take over responsibility for the family planning programme throughout the country. To date, it is arguable whether this policy has yet been implemented. Nowadays neither the FPAU nor the Ministry of Health appears to be in sole charge of the national programme. Integration of family planning services provision and health care is more or less left to the discretion of individual District Medical Officers.

The 1980–81 proposals

Governments have failed to be clear on family planning policy, because of perceived opposition from religious and socio-cultural interest groups. Successive governments have been keen not to antagonize religious groups, especially the Roman Catholic Church, in this respect. They have also lacked sufficient grassroots political support to risk encouraging far-reaching policies on family planning issues. Policymakers seem to think that any mention of population policy development will automatically force them into the muddy waters of family planning programme issues that they are reluctant to touch.

The 1980 population and health proposals were a reflection of this situation. The proposals provided for the integration of family planning services provision with other government facilities. The lead in family planning provision, however, was given to the Family Planning Association of Uganda (a non-profit-making organization based on volunteers) and the government opted only for indirect involvement at the policy level. In fact only one clause in the proposals directly mentioned population regulation; the rest were health-oriented. The policy proposals in the document included:

- support of family planning for demographic reasons;
- integration of family planning with health services;
- population growth targets;
- extension of family planning services; and

190

– family planning information, education and communication (IEC) activities in government and private facilities as well as at community level.

No mention of any desired population ethos, such as an ideal number of children or ideal family size, was made in the proposal. No motivation or incentives were drafted into the proposals either.

Even with such lukewarm proposals, the policy was unable to pass the Parliament of the day. No government official was prepared to risk debating population-related proposals when the December 1980 general elections were only months away. After these elections, there were other more urgent national issues to deal with, like the National Resistance Army(NRA) that had just gone to the bush or the political dissent that threatened Parliament throughout the Obote 2 regime. In fact, during this period, more than in any other period in the history of Uganda, numbers became absolutely critical to both government and the guerrilla forces.

Legal impediments

A number of government policies continue, directly or indirectly, to promote the exact opposite of was proposed in the 1971/2–1975/6 Third Year Plan and subsequent documents on population policy. Thus a number of legal enactments, in various fields of the public sector, are by default pro-natalist. For instance, allocation of housing: the more children you have the more points you get, and if you are single it is almost impossible to get government or institutional housing. To date, this has not changed. The period between 1981 and early 1987 is a blank sheet as regards serious efforts to develop a population policy in the country.

CURRENT STATUS OF POPULATION POLICY DEVELOPMENT

It should be noted that successive governments have offered very little in terms of social services to the population. For example, the Uganda National Household Budget Survey (1989/90) found that 67.21 per cent of all types of household dwellings were owned by individuals [Statistics Department, MFEP, 1993]. Another 14.74 per cent included other buildings like huts, garages and all 'unconventional' dwellings suggesting that this percentage also did not include dwellings provided by government. Formal education, which is a major concern in Uganda, continues to be partly privately funded, even in government schools, through Parent Teacher Associations (PTAs). Governments have found it hard to agree upon a population-regulating policy but this may change with projected help for 4 children per family.

Since 1987, with the introduction of the Economic Recovery Programme, this imbalance is being slowly addressed. However, macroeconomic policies prioritized economic recovery in the produc-

191

tive sectors. The social services sector, covering primary health care, water supply and sanitation, education, and family planning, has received less initial attention. The Rehabilitation and Development Plan earmarked only US $221 million, that is 17.2 per cent of total national expenditure, as planned expenditure on social services over the 1987–91 period.

With the stabilization of the economy, at least at the macro level, it is hoped that this situation is beginning to change. As a result, a number of measures have since been put in place to work towards the promulgation of a National Population Policy. These include the formation of a Population Secretariat under the Ministry of Finance and Economic Planning.

International agencies have also stepped up their funding for population programmes in the country, with a strong emphasis on Maternal and Child Health in addition to Family Planning (MCH/FP) programme activities. The Country Population Programme of the UNFPA, UNDP, UNICEF and USAID agencies all underline this emerging emphasis. Recently the Danish, Swedish and Japanese governments as well as several non-governmental organizations have joined the efforts towards a comprehensive national population programme in Uganda.

New policy guidelines for Maternal and Child Health and Family Planning were launched in March 1993. These established national benchmarks for training providers, managers and policy-makers within a primary health care framework. The most important aspect of these guidelines was that access to family planning was established – for the first time directly by government – as a basic human right. The guidelines also include provision for sex education and contraception for adolescents. They do not deal, however, with the generally disapproving attitude of the providers towards adolescent sexual activity, an attitude which is essentially hostile to adolescent clients.

A culmination of all these efforts has been the formulation of a Draft Population Policy and the proposed establishment of a National Population Council to ensure implementation and monitoring of the population policy [MFEP, 1992a: 32]. The National Population Council has since been officially launched. In the Preamble to the draft policy document, it is stated in part that,

> ... Government has formulated an explicit National Population Policy to evolve a society that is both informed and conscious of population and development issues at all levels. To address the identified population concerns in a comprehensive and multi-sectoral manner and in line with government's decentralization policy, the thrust of the Population Policy is to promote intervention programs designed to improve health, nutrition, education, and the environment. Further, family planning, as a basic human right, shall be promoted to play a key role in reducing the proportion of high risk pregnancies and births, ensuring child survival, enhancing the status of women, raising the levels of income of individuals and families; alleviating poverty; and ultimately improving the quality of life and the standard of living of the people.

The formulation of the draft policy has not, however, been as smooth as this statement implies. The time it took the Population Secretariat to put together the document and the amount of money that went into its composition were both enormous.

The government's stand on population growth has not made the process any easier. Issues like the government's attitude towards the use of condoms, its perceptions of the most desirable current overall population of the country and a number of other population-related issues, all remain far from clear. Some government sources, for example, still argue that the country has lost a lot of people because of both civil strife over the past 25 years and the AIDS epidemic. Other arguments, based on the persistence of large pieces of uninhabited land, also continue.

With the exception of maternal and child health and control of the AIDS epidemic, the question of 'how' in government population policy is not clearly addressed. Furthermore, although it is committed to social development and improvement of the quality of life, the Draft Population Policy does not spell out the linkages between population issues and broader developmental concerns which are so aptly pointed out in the Preamble.

However, one of the strongest points in favour of the document is its assessment of the current population situation in the country. Its analysis of how population factors have a major impact on the attainment of development objectives and targets is also well drawn out. The test for this policy document is therefore going to be how its analysis is translated into concrete policies and activities. This will depend heavily on the extent to which the government is willing to commit itself regarding the population problem in the country. The indirect apolitical approach to the policy development process is bound to yield only disjointed and disappointing results. A prerequisite for success will be the expansion of national development planning beyond the short or even the medium term, and the de-politicization of the population question. The policy formulation process has to address specific objectives, targets and time frames. It will have to lay out operational strategies, monitoring and evaluation procedures, the roles of various players and, above all, a concrete timetable for the achievement of desired outcomes.

FOURTEEN
AIDS and development in Uganda

Maryinez Lyons

> Good health both contributes to and is an objective of economic development (Martha Ainsworth and Mead Over).[1]

It is difficult to disaggregate cause and effect when discussing the relationship of good health to development. It is not so difficult, however, to see that poor health is one of the results of poverty and distress. The AIDS epidemic in Uganda is rooted in the decades of civil strife and devastation which ended in February 1986.

Since 1987, AIDS in Uganda has attracted significant donor interest and funding[2] and, in that sense, AIDS can be regarded as a motivating factor in many development programmes. A former head of the USAID health mission to Uganda suggested that by 1990 'probably about thirty-five per cent of the "self-money groups" coming to Uganda look at AIDS'.[3] We do not know how many non-governmental organizations exist in Uganda but by March 1993 there were more than 600 registered as working on AIDS, while hundreds remain unregistered – estimates range from 800 to well over 1,000. Clinging to their own agendas, these NGOs are neither co-ordinated nor supervised, but since at least half of health care provision is delivered by NGOs, it is important to identify and attempt to co-ordinate their activities.[4] By 1993 it was a widely-held view that

> AIDS is no longer a disease, but a huge multinational business in which international and local agencies as well as quack medicinemen are struggling to cash [sic] on AIDS (*New Vision*, 2 March 1993).

Apocalyptic generalizations like the following by the US Bureau of the Census (1993) have spurred donors into action.

> The cumulative effect of national AIDS epidemics will be staggering. Government health programs and facilities, with meager budgets already stretched, will be unable to cope with the numbers of people with AIDS and other HIV-related illnesses ... Economic growth will be encumbered by increased morbidity and decreased productivity of HIV-infected workers and many others will be unable to enter the work force because of care-giving responsibilities among families (p. 68).

The concept of 'development' is often imprecise, ranging in meaning from the immediate repair of existing, but damaged, material structures to the planning and implementation of totally new structures and systems. By 1993, Uganda had experienced a wave of international aid to the health sector which can be more appropriately described as rehabilitation of past structures rather than development of new policies and implementation.[5]

AIDS is significantly altering the disease pattern in Uganda. The rehabilitation of a health system inherited from colonialism with its emphasis on curative, urban-based hospital care, already of questionable value in a poor country, will become increasingly inappropriate as HIV-infected people fall ill. Patients are younger and some diseases which were formerly diminishing, like tuberculosis, are recrudescing alarmingly. AIDS is a chronic disease which means for most patients periods of quiescence punctuated by a number of illness episodes ranging from mild to severe. Medical services are seriously overstretched as AIDS-related patients increasingly monopolize beds and limited supplies of drugs. A 1990 study at Mulago Hospital revealed that in one day 30 per cent of in-patient admissions were between the ages of 20 and 29.[6] Kitovu, a 200-bed mission hospital in Masaka, reported in the same year that 40–50 per cent of all admissions were HIV-related, while 70 per cent of the medical wards and the entire tuberculosis ward were occupied by HIV-infected patients. Nsambya Mission Hospital in Kampala, with 360 beds, had 70 per cent of its medical wards occupied by HIV-infected patients.

Let us now turn to the subject of the epidemic of HIV/AIDS and consider its relation to development in Uganda. First we need to survey briefly the nature of HIV and the extent of its presence in the country.

HIV/AIDS IN UGANDA

At present, scientists believe that most people infected with the human immunodeficiency virus will eventually develop AIDS, a fatal disease which affects mainly adults in their most productive years. It seems that the period of good health between the time of infection with HIV and the development of AIDS is on average between two and ten years. However, the time between infection and illness may be shorter in sub-Saharan Africa because of the generally poorer state of health of many people. Still, persons infected with HIV can remain in apparently good health for many years during which they can transmit the virus to others. In this way HIV can percolate unnoticed through a population.

In the Ugandan population of nearly 17 million at the time of writing, about 1.5 million people are estimated to be infected with the virus, that is 10 per cent of the total population or 20 per cent of sexually active men and women. Nearly 80 per cent of those infected are between the ages of 15 and 45, that portion of the population responsible for most of the production and reproduction of the nation. Uganda is still in the early stages of the epidemic in terms of both the spread of the virus and the development of AIDS.[7] With an estimated 250,000 to 300,000 cases to date, AIDS is already *the* leading cause of death of young adults. In 1990 in one sub-county of Masaka District just over 8 per cent of adults (aged 13 plus) were HIV-positive and within two years 23 per cent of them had died. This is a truly dramatic mortality rate in the world history of epidemics. In the words of Dr Daan Mulder

> Young adults infected with HIV-1 have a risk of dying which is *sixty* times the risk of the non-infected. More than 50 per cent of all adult deaths and more than 80 per cent of deaths in young adults are HIV-1 associated.[8]

The Uganda Ministry of Health AIDS Control Programme reported in 1993 that the sex ratio of AIDS cases was 1:1, but women tend to develop AIDS at younger ages than men. However, with regard to HIV infection, the sex ratio ranged between 1:1.2 and 1:1.4. Girls between the ages of 15 and 19 are five times as likely as boys to become infected. At the AIDS Information Centre in Kampala, a voluntary testing and counselling facility opened in 1990, and 35 per cent of women and 22 per cent of men have been HIV-positive. Between the ages of 15 and 19, 31 per cent of females were HIV-positive whereas only 13 per cent of males in that age group tested positive. The monitoring of ante-natal mothers is a good indication of infection rates in a cross-section of the general population. Already high by the mid-1980s, infection rates among pregnant mothers in Kampala were about one in four by 1994.[9] In 1993 Nsambya Hospital reported 30 per cent of ante-natal mothers to be HIV-positive, while a study based at Mulago Hospital reports that in the early 1990s 29 per cent of ante-natal mothers were HIV-positive.[10]

Finally, as the rate of disease progression in Uganda has been shown to be about twice that observed in industrialized countries, a significant proportion of the estimated 1½ million infected could become ill in the near future. We must ask how this epidemic will affect the future development of the country.

Multisectoral nature of the epidemic

By 1991, Ugandan leaders recognized that AIDS would affect far more than the health of the nation. Every area of national life as well as the lives of millions of individuals will be touched by the virus. In the words of Manuel Pinto, Director-General of the Uganda AIDS Commission:

> The HIV/AIDS epidemic will impact on Uganda's social and economic fabric well beyond the next 30 yearsThe virus is transforming the demographic and epidemiologic map, not only of Uganda, but of Africa as a whole. It has a major impact on the development of human resources, on the ecology, on the coping mechanisms of households, families and communities, on orphans, widows and widowers, on farming systems as well as industrial and handicraft production, and on trade and commerce.[11]

While initial research attempted to unravel the epidemiology of the disease, more recent studies explore the multi-sectoral and economic impact of AIDS.[12] It is anticipated that 'national capacity-building efforts may be imperiled and decline in income is expected to affect the

196

balance of payments' (Topouzis, 1994: 2). This will have serious implications for any country, but for a poor country in the process of rehabilitating its basic infrastructure, the added burden of a widespread, fatal epidemic disease is indeed unfortunate.

Development resources

Resources required for the development of a country include human and financial capital, stability and time. HIV/AIDS will affect the development of Uganda through its impact on each of these sectors.

The first and perhaps most important resource of a nation is its people, its human capital. If they are healthy, stable, informed and have a reasonable life expectancy, a nation might also reasonably expect to progress.

As stated earlier, an HIV-infected individual may have many years of relatively healthy and productive life ahead; nevertheless, it would be unrealistic to anticipate a normal life expectancy, thus many productive years will be lost to HIV/AIDS. Life expectancy in Uganda, already one of the lowest in the world, is currently 47 for males and 50 for females.[13] Demographers speculate that, because of AIDS, by 2010 the life expectancy of Ugandans will be in the region of 35 to 45 years instead of the 48 to 55 years anticipated without AIDS (World Bank, 1991c: 15). While life expectancy rates are not to be taken as the literal number of years an individual may expect to live, they are an important economic indicator when compared to other national aggregates, and often affect development policy decisions in areas such as long-term funding. Demographers use the concept of 'discounted healthy years' to measure the impact of disease on an economy. The benefits of averting a single case of HIV are high compared with other diseases. For example, avoiding a case of HIV saves 19.5 years compared to 3.7 years for malaria or 7.1 years for tuberculosis. Discounted healthy years are the years saved per person through the aversion or prevention of a specific disease (Over and Piot, 1992).

A country with a decreasing life expectancy caused by increasing young adult mortality may not be an attractive prospect for long-term financial investors and may therefore attract only short-term investors. In fact, the 'National Operational Plan for HIV/AIDS/STD Prevention, Care and Support, 1994–1998' has predicted such a shift in investment priority (Uganda AIDS Commission Secretariat, 1993: 1). This could have serious implications for the type of development proposals which can be realistically tabled in Uganda.

Population

In spite of Uganda's high fertility rate of 7.3 children per woman, HIV/AIDS will affect population growth although not as dramatically as some early demographers (Roy Anderson, for example) predicted. The aggregate rate of increase (difference between the crude birth and death rates) will not drop below 2 per cent in much of sub-Saharan

197

Africa and it is now believed that a national adult HIV seroprevalence of about 50 per cent or more would be required to cause population rates to become negative. Experts vary in their estimates of the long-term impact of the epidemic on Uganda's population but one study made a powerful impact on President Museveni in 1990 and was instrumental in decisions to address AIDS as a multi-sectoral issue.[15] The 1990 Census reported a population of sixteen and a half million. The demographers projected a potential population of 32 million by the year 2015 *if* HIV is controlled whereas, without effective intervention in its spread, the population would be in the region of 20 million. That would mean a loss of 12 million people plus the added burden of 5 to 6 million orphans[16] resulting from the death of AIDS victims.[17] This will be a significant reduction in the expected population in spite of the very high fertility rate. Already high rates of infant mortality (117 per 1000) and child mortality (180 per 1000) will rise. While not every child born of an HIV-positive mother is infected with the virus, it seems that about 35–40 per cent are, while it has been shown that pregnancy very often activates HIV in women who then progress more quickly to AIDS and death.

Dependency ratio

Perhaps more significant than the contentious issue of the impact of AIDS on overall population size is its impact on the dependency ratio, i.e. the ratio of young and elderly dependants per working adult in a population. The Household Budget Survey of 1989/90 classified household members under the age of 18 and over 55 as dependants. This ratio is particularly significant in Uganda where AIDS affects the very age group supporting dependants. According to the most recent Census in 1991, the present population of Uganda is 16½ million. Half the population is, in demographic terms, dependent, that is **below** the age of 15. (Most of this age group is free of HIV.)[18] There is only one working-age adult for each child, whereas in most developed countries the ratio is more likely to be 2 or 3 adults per child.[19] Dependency ratios vary according to economic status. Over half (52 per cent) of the members of poor households are dependent, whereas only 38 per cent of the members of non-poor households are classified as dependent.[20] While AIDS will affect all classes of society, it will impact more upon the poor who possess fewer resources and fewer adults with whom to cope.

Some analysts argue that dependency ratios may not increase dramatically owing to the effects of AIDS mortality which will increase among children as well as adults of working age. But already the numbers of destitute and orphaned children has attracted national and international attention, and it is clear that orphans will constitute a major social problem. Statistics vary widely, however, and there may be at present between 400,000 and 1,100,000 orphans in the country, of whom at least 115,000 have resulted from AIDS.[21] The Uganda AIDS

Commission estimates that the number of orphans created by AIDS will be multiplied fivefold by the year 2000.

The implications for national development of increasing numbers of children without the care and guidance of adults is serious indeed. Several development initiatives have taken note of this issue. Uganda's National Plan of Action for Children and UNICEF's programme, SCFA (Save Children from AIDS) are examples (MFEP, 1992; UNICEF, 1992).

Labour force: quality and quantity

AIDS will affect the population of Uganda in a number of ways but some consider that 'the main channel through which the epidemic will affect the economy is the size and quality of the labour force' (World Bank, 1991c: vi). Considerable time and investment are required to produce and educate precious human capital. There is already good evidence that one of the first effects of AIDS on families is the necessity to withdraw children from school. School fees constitute the single most desired, yet most difficult, expenditure for the vast majority of Ugandans. Education will suffer from both the deaths of teachers and the inability of surviving adults to continue paying school fees for children.

Productivity will be affected in both the formal and informal sectors and in a variety of ways. The episodic nature of HIV-related illnesses means that phases of illness will be interspersed with periods of decreasing productivity. A study of some fifteen firms including transport companies, banks, a hotel, a brewery, a mill and a sugar estate revealed that absenteeism is already a serious problem. Many firms report an increase in AIDS-related mortality since the mid-1980s and an increase in health costs. For example, Uganda Railways has lost 10 per cent of its staff of 5,600 to AIDS in the past few years, while the corporation's annual hospital bill rose from US $69 per patient in 1988 to US $300 per patient in 1992, a rise attributed in large part to AIDS-related illnesses.[22]

Development planners must take into account the impact of AIDS on future levels of technical and professional personnel such as engineers, teachers, nurses and doctors. Investment in precious human capital is central to the future development of the nation; planning efforts should therefore incorporate the potential impact of the epidemic when projecting manpower needs and the educational requirements to meet them.

Losses will result, with lowered output by individuals still able to work but weakened by illness. This is an area difficult to quantify in most cases; but it will be real loss. Another difficult area to quantify is the loss of labour of those individuals, who, although not ill themselves, miss work time because of the need to care for kin who are ill. Some attempts have been made to quantify the impact on productivity of time lost in attending funerals, but far more productive time is spent caring for the increasing numbers of sick relations. It is difficult to assess the future impact of the epidemic in terms of output per capita and, even if it were possible, economists point out that

199

modelling effects of AIDS on GNP per capita obscures the overall detrimental impact on the development process. The impact of AIDS on unquantifiable human and social dimensions and on quality of life indicators [infant, child and maternal mortality] are concealed by looking solely at macroeconomic indicators (World Bank, 1991c; 35).

Women, agriculture and development

National income account variables exclude the contribution of the 'informal' labour of women in the household and in agricultural production. Four-fifths of the population depend on agriculture for survival but it is women who underpin the national economy through their agricultural production which is 'the engine of growth of the Ugandan economy (World Bank, 1993a: xvii). It accounted for 67 per cent of GDP in 1989, and over 95 per cent of Uganda's foreign earnings derive from agricultural products. Women constitute 70 per cent of all agricultural labour and produce 80 per cent of food.

Recalling that women suffer higher rates of HIV infection, it is likely that AIDS will affect agricultural production.[23] Cultivation is labour-intensive; and in normal times few women can afford to employ extra help, a vital factor in farming systems utilizing virtually only a hoe.[24] A 1980 study revealed that in four districts of the country nearly 80 per cent of women were unable to employ labour (Jaensen et al., 1984), 85 per cent of cultivated land consisted of household plots of less than 5 hectares, and 85 per cent of these were cultivated with only a hand hoe and panga.[25]

Agricultural exports for 1992 dropped to one quarter of the amount exported in 1991. The explanation was a combination of drought and 'many unfulfilled barter deals' (*Weekly Topic*, 21 February 1992). Not mentioned, however, was the much more likely explanation – the impact of AIDS on agricultural production. FAO-funded studies of the potential impact of AIDS on agricultural production in Uganda, Zambia, Malawi, Rwanda and Tanzania predict that it will be necessary to switch to less labour-intensive crops which will affect household income and nutritional levels. In addition, livestock may be sold. As a consequence, items requiring cash such as school fees, medicines and additional foods, may become prohibitive (Kingman, 1991; Barnett, 1994).

The World Bank cautions that 'raising agricultural productivity, along with increased access to basic health and education, must take priority in the Government's spending program' if Uganda is to recover. It is clear that the future development of Uganda greatly depends on the role of women, yet their potential vulnerability to HIV infection and its effects places that future in grave jeopardy.

The health sector

From the mid-1930s until 1970 the government allocated a minimum of 6.5 per cent of the total recurrent and capital budget to health services, and by 1971 'Uganda had a level of health services far better than many developing countries.' (Scheyer and Dunlop, 1985: 27–9). The situation was to change dramatically. The sudden departure in 1973 of half of some 1,000 doctors contributed to the deterioration of formal health services and by 1985 health care delivery had reached a level of roughly half the early 1960s level.[26] Government expenditure on health fell from 5.3 per cent in 1972 to 2.4 per cent in 1987 (World Bank, 1989: 264). The real purchasing power of the health budget had dwindled to 6 per cent of the 1968–9 level. Of course, it was not only the health sector which disintegrated. For example, between 1972 and 1982 per capita income dropped 25 per cent, while consumer prices increased by 1200 per cent.[27]

Quality of life indicators are poor: a crude birth rate of 51, crude death rate of 22 and infant mortality rate[28] of 117. There is only one doctor for each 25,000 people compared with about one per 1,000 in the West (World Bank, 1993d: 208).[29] Annual expenditure for *all* health care is about US $6 per capita (*ibid.*).[30]

Since 1986, Uganda has experienced impressive rehabilitation and it is today a country very much in the process of 'development'. Significant capital and recurrent resources have been made available by international agencies and NGOs for the rehabilitation of the health infrastructure.[31] Rehabilitation, rather than development, has been the hallmark of much foreign aid for health; and the lack of co-ordination and consultation among agencies, or between them and Ugandans, has often resulted in inappropriate allocation of funding and effort.[32] In Uganda 'the transition from relief to development has been made with difficulty' (Macrae et al., 1993). AIDS is a serious obstacle to this transition.

The cost of AIDS – AIDS and poverty

AIDS is impacting heavily on the health care delivery system in Uganda. We have already noted that the disease pattern is changing and there is a clear shift towards younger patients. It is difficult to calculate with precision the cost of treating AIDS, for a number of reasons: individual illnesses vary in nature and numbers of episodes and the availability and cost of drugs vary. A rough impression of the potential cost can be gained from a 1990 World Bank study. Three components were factored in the cost estimate: typical AIDS-related conditions in Uganda; typical number of episodes of those conditions; and the costs for treatment per episode. The cost per episode of illness per patient, based on the least expensive drugs which are routinely supplied in the country, is roughly US $14 (Kadama, 1994). In 1994, total per capita expenditure on health amounted to $5.65 ($2.82 from government and $2.83 from private sources).[33] To put the impact of AIDS into perspective, it helps to compare the cost of a single episode of AIDS illness, US $14, with the parallel cost of a single episode of malaria, 20 cents (World Bank, 1991c).

Policy imperatives

By 1995 AIDS will cost US $2,273,555 annually if every patient seeks medical treatment. We know, however, that not every sick individual can, or will, seek medical treatment.[34] If only half seek care, AIDS will cost Uganda US $1,136,800 and drugs used for AIDS will represent between 8 and 23 per cent of the national drug budget.

As mentioned earlier, the government has recognized that AIDS is more than a medical problem and will impact on every sector of national life. This means that the response to the epidemic must be multisectoral. In spite of the fact that the virus has affected all classes of society, its spread can be linked to the widespread poverty and poor health status of the majority of the population. A per capita income of under US $170 makes Uganda one of the poorest countries in the world, with 70 per cent of the population living in poverty while 25 per cent are in absolute poverty (Obbo and Southall, 1990). It should be mentioned that Uganda spends much of its foreign earnings on debt servicing (US $100 million in 1994). As the Oxfam representative to Uganda has explained

> As things are, Ugandans are now paying the debt with their very lives . . . When you spend the money on debt servicing instead of medical services, then people who can't afford private treatment simply die before their time.[35]

It can be argued that poverty, not AIDS, is the issue to address in development planning. Rehabilitation of the health care delivery system, widely praised in the 1960s, is inadvisable in view of the number of people who are expected to suffer varying episodes of HIV-related illness over long periods. Mobile, home-based care units already operating under the aegis of private sector hospitals like Kitovu and Nsambya or TASO (the AIDS Support Organization) provide a more appropriate service for patients who thrive better in familiar surroundings of home and kin. Vertical health programmes, such as the essential drugs programme or the child immunization programme, are expensive, logistically difficult and narrowly focused. NGOs, donors and the government should combine their efforts and resources in the effort to contain HIV and to assist the millions of people who are already, and who will be in future, affected by AIDS.

CONCLUSION

This paper began by highlighting the relationship of AIDS to development. It ends by mentioning a growing concern that, added to the crushing burdens facing most Ugandans, AIDS will tip the balance of the national *will* needed for the moral, political, economic and social reconstruction of the country. Dr Joseph Konde-Lule, public health specialist and epidemiologist, underlines the widespread pessimism, which, in his view, will make it difficult to change people's behaviour.

> We Ugandans are getting too used to seeing death. We had the civil wars and now we have AIDS. People expect that anyone can die at any time.

He believes that the biggest challenge facing health workers may be the 'massive psycho-social trauma' experienced by the population which has led to widespread fatalism.

> When you see death so often, it becomes less traumatic ... people are becoming less and less sensitive towards others. Some people are becoming less prepared to plan ahead for they think they may die at any time ... [they think] I may as well just go ahead and enjoy myself.[36]

Such fatalism poses great difficulties for any government. AIDS in Uganda has become an issue of major political and economic as well as social concern. Armed with hard statistics and demographic projections, President Museveni has warned that 'the growing devastation of a range of national aspirations is very real unless something is done quickly' (*New Vision*, 26 June 1991).

Notes

1. This remark was made in 1992.
2. The author is indebted to the Institute of Commonwealth Studies, University of London, for much intellectual stimulation.
3. Interview with Paul Cohen, USAID, Kampala, 17 January 1991.
4. Interview with Dr. Donald Sutherland, former team leader of the World Health Organization, Uganda 6 June 1991. In Nebbi District, for example, some NGOs' work is so secretive that even beneficiaries are not allowed to see project documents. Some NGOs enter the district and begin operating without government health officials' knowledge. Ogen K. Aliro, 'Health 2000: the foreign actors in Uganda', *The Monitor*, 6–10 May 1994.
5. The Ministry of Health appointed a Health Policy Review Commission in 1987 and an updated White Paper of 1993 outlines a rehabilitation and recovery programme which includes some development planning.
6. One-day census taken in April 1990, World Bank, 1991c: 19.
7. AIDS, or 'slim disease', was first noticed in 1982 in the small fishing village, Kasensero, on Lake Victoria near the border with Tanzania. By October 1984, there was medical confirmation of AIDS in Uganda. The AIDS Control Programme began in late 1986 when US $750,000 was earmarked by the World Health Organization's Global Programme on AIDS, for use in Uganda. Funding was begun in the spring of the following year and by July 1987 Uganda had implemented the first AIDS campaign in Africa.
8. Stated on 3 June 1993, at the London School of Hygiene and Tropical Medicine, 'Magnitude and Impact of AIDS in Africa' press conference. Dr Mulder was Director of the MRC Research Programme on AIDS, Entebbe, at the time.
9. U.S. Bureau of the Census, 'Trends and patterns of HIV/AIDS infection in selected developing countries', December 1993. The presence of other sexually transmitted diseases facilitates the spread of HIV and high rates of syphilis have been reported among women attending ante-natal clinics at hospitals. Syphilis seroprevalence rates reported at:

	1991	1992
Nsambya Hospital	27.8	25.3
Rubaga	22.1	11.6
Tororo	30.5	26.6
Fort Portal	27.9	20.3

Source: USAID, May 1994.

Testing for the syphilis antibody during the 1988 National HIV Serosurvey revealed 17.5 per cent of random specimens were positive.

10. Dr Lawrence Murram, Case Western Reserve University project, Mulago Hospital, personal communication, 10 May 1994.

11. Hon. Manuel Pinto, opening comments at Workshop on Preparing for HIV Vaccine Evaluations in Uganda, Sheraton Hotel, Kampala, 9 March 1994.

12. Topouzis, 1994; Martha Ainsworth, *The Impact of HIV/AIDS on African Development* (World Bank, Washington, DC, 1993); Martha Ainsworth and Mead Over, *The Economic Impact of AIDS: Shocks, Responses and Outcomes* (World Bank, Washington, DC, 1992); Mead Over, *The Macroeconomic Impact of AIDS in sub-Saharan Africa* (World Bank, Washington, DC, 1992); World Bank, 1991c; Barnett, 1994.

13. The World Bank, 1993a; xiii, 155. It should be noted that the crude death rate of 20 per 1,000 is about twice the rate of an average low-income country, e.g. Kenya, a result not only of civil strife and AIDS but of generally poor health conditions. The principal killer of adults in Africa is malaria, not AIDS.

14. U.S. Bureau of the Census, 1993. The Bureau estimates that by 2010 the crude death rate in Uganda *without* AIDS would have been about 8 or 9 per 1000 but that *with* AIDS it will be 27 or 28 per 1000. Life expectancy in 2010 *without* AIDS would be about 58 years but *with* AIDS it is expected to be around 32 years.

15. The AIM (AIDS Impact Model) computer programme for presenting information about AIDS was prepared by John Stover for the Futures Group in collaboration with AIDSTECH/Family Health International. The Futures Group is a private firm of demographic consultants based in Washington and this project was prepared in collaboration with the AIDS Control Programme of Uganda and USAID/AIDSTECH.

16. There is much to be said about the assumptions and definitions upon which the models are based. In AIM, for instance, the definition of an AIDS orphan is a child under 15 who has lost its mother to AIDS. In many Ugandan societies, an orphan is a child who has lost *either* a mother *or* a father while some feel that an orphan is a child who has lost a father and *not* a mother. More careful social research is required before we can accept unquestioningly the results of mathematical models for projecting the impact of AIDS in Africa. John Stover for the Futures Group, 'AIM: AIDS impact model – a computer program for presenting information about AIDS', Washington DC, May 1991, p. 69. See Elizabeth A. Preble, 'Impact of HIV/AIDS on African children', *Social Science and Medicine* 31 (1990): 671–80.

17. Uganda's population in 1959 was 6,449,558 with an annual growth rate (AGR) of 2.5%. In 1969 it was 9,456,466 (AGR 3.7%) and in 1980 12,636,179 (AGR 2.8%).

18. 30 per cent of the total population [5,040,000] are aged five to fourteen.

19. A 1984 study of four districts found the following dependency ratios (based on individuals under age 20): Busoga: 1/3, Masaka: 1/4, Kigezi: 3/1, Teso: 2/1 (Jaensen et al., 1984). The findings of the 1990 Uganda Household Budget Survey highlight differences between rural and urban households. Rural adults are responsible for more dependants, although urban areas are not far behind.

20. 'Non-poor' had 11,810 Sh. per capita available for household expenditure whereas the poor had 3,485 Sh. and the 'poorest' 1,845 Sh.

21. The 1991 census identified 784,000 orphans or 10 per cent of children under the age of 15.

22. World Bank, 1993c: 3. (Based on report by the PANOS Institute, London, 'The hidden cost of AIDS', 1992).

AIDS and development in Uganda

23. The impact will vary from region to region. For example, a study which attempted to measure the economic impact of AIDS in Rakai and Masaka Districts found that abundant rainfall and crop patterns made these areas less sensitive to loss of labour (Barnett and Blaikie, 1992).

24. The few women who can afford to employ labour will find it increasingly difficult to locate available labourers, who are also succumbing to AIDS. This was recently reported by an official of Uganda Commercial Bank who also said, 'AIDS is a major factor in the near collapse of the rural farmers scheme' because 'many of the beneficiaries have died from the disease'. *Weekly Topic*, 29 January 1993.

25. Ministry of Planning and Economic Development, 'Uganda: population factors in national reconstruction and development' (Entebbe: [1989] 1990), p. 36. Twenty-six per cent of women own only a hoe (Jaensen et al., 1984: 172).

26. Between 1971 and 1987, it is estimated by the Ministry of Health that about 1,500 doctors fled Uganda for better pay and conditions elsewhere. Ministry of Health report, 1988. Many of the remaining medical workers had to 'moonlight' to survive.

27. In July 1985 the average monthly civil service salary was estimated to be US $21; by 1989 it was $10 while university professors received $25. In order to survive, nearly all income-earning Ugandans maintain other small businesses and practise subsistence cultivation. 'The tendency to take up several jobs (especially in the teaching and medical professions) leads to declining standards' (Brandt, 1987: 23).

28. Infant mortality rate is calculated on deaths between birth and age one year. Child mortality rate includes deaths between one and five years and all these rates are calculated per one thousand population.

29. Statistics do not reveal the real imbalances of health provision around the country. In Nebbi District, 400 km northwest of Kampala, there are four doctors for 325,815 people – one per 81,000 people.

30. 3.4 per cent of GDP is expended on health. In 1990, foreign aid provided US $46 million for health, covering 48 per cent of all government health expenditure. Government spending per capita in 1991/92 was 8 per cent of the national budget, but most of it went to the main government hospital, Mulago, and only 2.3 per cent was shared by other hospitals and health units countrywide. Ogen Kevin Aliro, 'Health for a Few, Death for the Rest?', *The Monitor*, 29 April – 3 May 1994.

31. A selection of agencies and health projects supported include:
EUROPEAN ECONOMIC COMMUNITY: Rural Health Rehabilitation Programme (southwest).
USAID: AIDS Programme including AIDS Information Centre, TASO; World Learning, Uganda AIDS Commission Secretariat, Ministry of Defence, Ministry of Health and various religious and community groups.
WORLD HEALTH ORGANIZATION: technical assistance in epidemiology; Information, education and communication re: AIDS; vaccine development; National operational plan for AIDS; funding for the Ministry of Health.
WORLD BANK: Sexually transmitted infections project; First Health Project (to rehabilitate nine government hospitals and certain health centres).
UNDP: Technical assistance; funding for Uganda AIDS Commission; STD Control; Mitigation of Social Impact; Institutional strengthening; Care for persons with AIDS; Microgrants projects. (Note: UNDP has designated 20% of its Uganda budget to be spent on AIDS.)
UNICEF: SYFA (Save Youth From AIDS); School health education programme; Expanded immunization programme (UNEPI).
WORLD FOOD PROGRAMME; Food for persons with AIDS and families.
UK Overseas Development Administration (now Dept. for International Development) Support for TASO; technical assistance.
DANIDA: Support for TASO and other community-based organizations; Essential drugs and equipment programme.
Other organizations active in HIV/AIDS projects include: AMREF; World Vision; Médecins sans Frontières; Médecins du Monde; World Learning; Care; and many others.

32. Under the present Rehabilitation and Development Plan, 1990 – 1994, there is some attention to the development needs of the health sector. In 1987 a Health Policy Review Commission was appointed and in 1993 a White Paper on Health Policy Review appeared.
33. Two-thirds of the government contribution is provided by external sources of assistance. The total, US $5.65, amounts to less than half the amount, $12, accepted globally as the minimum per capita expenditure for health care.
34. In Mukono District in 1992, 49.7 per cent of sick people treated themselves, 23.2 per cent attended private clinics and 27.1 per cent attended government or NGO facilities, *The Monitor*, 13–17 May 1994: 24.
35. Anthony Burdon, Oxfam country representative, quoted in *The Daily Topic*, 16 March 1994.
36. Interview with Dr Joseph Konde-Lule, Mulago Hospital, Kampala, 7 September 1990.

FIFTEEN

Who cares for the carers?: AIDS and women in Uganda

Christine Obbo

On 20 October 1987 in a statement to the UN General Assembly, Jonathan Mann, the then director of the World Health Organization, suggested that the Acquired Immunodeficiency Disease (AIDS) pandemic has three distinctive phases that can each be called an epidemic. First there is the HIV retrovirus infection whose long incubation period leads to its inadvertent spread. The second epidemic is when the immuno system becomes so compromised that the opportunistic diseases become fatal. Third is the epidemic of the social, economic and political reactions. In other words, the disease AIDS raises legal and human rights issues, and socially threatens tolerance.

In Africa, initial denials and the blaming of perverted others, such as traders, long-distance transport workers, and sex workers, waned as AIDS became undeniably a disease of families, affecting couples and children conceived after the HIV infections. Families rallied to provide care for the afflicted. In 1989, the Society for Women and AIDS in Africa (SWAA) described the dangers facing women as individuals, mothers, and carers as a 'Triple Jeopardy' (Panos,1990). SWAA stressed the increasing threat to women and the importance of women-centred HIV intervention and AIDS care programmes. Elsewhere women medical experts, who were often denied funding, were arguing that AIDS in women was a separate epidemic and that approaches to its control needed to be gender-specific (Cornea, 1992; Cotton, 1994). In Uganda cultural expectations and social practices exposed women and girls to HIV transmission. And poverty and male dominance prevented women from negotiating safe sex, particularly as, in the absence of a vaccine, the only hope of protection is the condom whose use depends upon the co-operation of men (Obbo, 1993).

This chapter suggests that in Africa we are soon going to face a fourth phase of epidemic, involving the deaths of infected carers, who are being infected because of ignorance and personal poverty. In addition, national poverty and privilege entitlements force many families to provide informal health care for family members. This task falls heavily upon the shoulders of women because of social and cultural expectations. In the case of AIDS women assume the role of nursing a disease that requires complex medical care for the patients and maximum

207

protection for the carers. The dangers of infection have been discussed in connection with formal providers of health care in hospitals in Western countries. But there has been virtual silence regarding the dangers faced by the invisible army of women health carers in African countries. This is because African women are seen to be coping as they do in every crisis.

The feminization of the AIDS epidemic is not good news for societies in which women are the chief producers of food and the universal nurturers. There is a dearth of information about problems encountered by African women. They are physically, psychologically and emotionally fatigued, in addition to being exposed to HIV infection. Health policies need to address both their current and long-term social and medical needs. Any intervention policy must promote the protection of carers without invoking fear and stigma that might lead to the neglect of patients. It should not be an impossibility to balance the rights and health of patients with those of providers of health care.

This chapter suggests that women's social roles as nurturers and health carers, within an informal and gendered health care system, subsidize the formal health care system when national poverty forces a government to adopt the proposals of international agencies. Women bear the immediate and long-term brunt when certain development policies are adopted. Examples are the World Health Organization's suggestions of accessible Primary Health Care provided by communities, and the World Bank and International Monetary Fund's Structural Adjustment Programmes, whose consequences are cuts in education and health services as well as civil service redundancies.

GENDERED INFORMAL HEALTH CARE

In 1981, the WHO Alma Ata Declaration called for 'Health care for all by the year 2000' and led to massive political commitment around the world to the 'Primary Health Care Approach'. Uganda joined other countries in formulating a national plan of action, and in promoting the formation of Community Health Workers' associations, consisting often of volunteers, as the key strategy for involving communities in improving people's health. This initiative aimed at shifting the emphasis from curative to primary health care, and reducing the disparity in accessibility and affordability between the rich and the poor. The Bamako 'Initiative for Primary Health Care and Maternal Child Health' further committed African governments, among other things: to promote the rational use of basic essential drugs; to accelerate the reduction of infant, child and maternal morbidity and mortality;to incorporate Primal Health Care policies within long-term plans and policies; and to take specific measures to ensure equity of access to Primal Health Care. The Alma Ata Declaration alludes to class as being important in health care delivery, but does not address the impact of gender. The Bamako Initiative is silent on both class and gender. Yet, as the present study suggests, in Africa there is a gender division of

208

labour and entitlements with regard to health care, and 'commmunity-based health care' is a euphemism for 'women-based care'. The user fee charged for medical services was also an outcome of the Bamako Initiative. However, women's relatively limited access to money compromises their ability to take care of themselves and their children adequately in cases of serious sickness.

This chapter is based on a total of sixteen months field work between 1989 and 1992. I started researching on AIDS in 1987 (Obbo, 1988). Between 1989 and 1990 I carried out field work in Rakai District in Uganda on personal and community coping mechanisms in the days of AIDS. I undertook participant observation and became involved in many local sufferings and rejoicings. I conducted questionnaires and informal interviews in 203 households, designed and delivered projectile questions to 58 secondary school students and engaged in participatory focused group interviews and impromptu discussions at weddings, funerals, market places, clinics, bus stops, shop verandahs, bars, Resistance Council meetings and court proceedings. The questionnaires were also worked on for two months with 207 workers of the Grain Mills factories in Jinja and Kawempe, and of Pepsicola in Kampala. In 1992, interviews and participant observation were carried out in 1,342 households in six Kampala suburbs (Obbo, 1992).

This chapter deals with one question from the survey: Who takes care of the sick in your home? This seemed to me a straightforward question to help access the distribution of health care responsibilities in the community. The possible respondents included: husband, wife, sister, neighbour, mother, father and relatives to be named. But the question proved to be complicated as both men and women claimed responsibility for taking care of the sick. When the nature of caring was probed: How do you care for the sick?, a picture of gendered care emerged. The men said that they cared for the sick by providing money, while their wives did the nursing. This assertion was made by rich and poor men in the towns and rural areas, and even by unemployed or casual workers whose food and rent were subsidized by the activities of girlfriends, sisters or mothers. Unmarried men claimed to give money to their female relatives to take care of the sick. Professional men and women had access to family health insurance provided by their employers. Most factory employees had access to first aid, and in theory their families had access too, but the women often found taking children to factory clinics too much of an effort. In the factories men were the most frequent clinic users (they seemed to be accident-prone when cutting glass and also suffered from strained backs). Both men and women frequented clinics for colds and malaria. In one factory a manager said that half the employees were casual workers because they had found that they were losing a lot through absenteeism by regular employees. The absenteeism of women was due to the sickness of family members, especially children.

Women said that they sought clinical care immediately only if they had cash, but that they were reluctant to initiate such action for them-selves or their children when they had no money to buy drugs or to pay for travelling to the clinic. Thus, in the absence of readily available cash, women and children relied on the first aid provided by kitchen herbal gardens and sought ways of raising money if the case was deemed to be serious. But when men got sick money was found to get them prompt clinical care. Speaking from experience women said that the apparent differences in the way family members sought and were accorded treatment were because, irespective of the nature of the afflic-tion, men made a lot of fuss groaning and demanding constant atten-tion. In addition, men hate herbal drugs unless they are absolutely guaranteed to cure them or poverty rules out access to medicines. In a focused group discussion women insisted that 'it does not look good if a man dies without treatment unless he is an orphan or a Munyarwanda (meaning male migrants to rural Buganda without fam-ilies in the past)'. Men explained their priority access to treatment as due to their being 'bread winners' or homestead heads (*nyinimaka*). Middle-class women who had access to medical insurance and nearby doctors and facilities sought prompt attention for all family members. Some of the women were described by one of the doctors interviewed as suffering from hypochondria because they could not even remem-ber their mothers' remedy of applying vaseline to the chapped lips of their children rather than take them to the doctor. Women with money are envied by poor women or women with niggardly husbands because they always 'look healthy. They do not have to endure pain until it becomes impossible to work and one simply has to lie down.'

AIDS AND THE DIVISION OF HEALTH CARE LABOUR AND CASH CONTROL

Three months after I started my fieldwork in Rakai three cases came independently to my attention because of the people's unanimous reac-tion to them. In the first two instances two young brides of three and five months deserted their husbands and accused them of marrying them in bad faith. Neighbourhood public opinion judged that the women were right; for the grooms to have developed 'AIDS' (a refer-ence to the AIDS symptoms of Kaposi's Sarcoma and oral thrush com-monly recognizable by most people because there were many AIDS patients in the area) in such a short time after marriage, they must have knowingly married the women after contracting it. The neighbours pointed to womanizing men who had married young girls in the hope of erasing their history, and men who said that having a young wife was as good as using a condom. There were allegations, similar to those one hears in other African countries, of people who deliberately infected others because they did not want to die alone. Rich men were suspect-ed of spending a lot of money on medication so that they looked nor-mal and enticed young women to sleep with them. In essays school boys accused older, particularly richer, men of infecting young girls who then passed on the virus to young men. Contrary to interpretations by outsiders who heard of the cases secondhand, no one in the community accused the women of abandoning their husbands. But outside reports by people who heard this story secondhand claimed that the women were deserting their infected husbands. The unsympathetic stance of the men seemed to stem from their knowledge of their fellow men and a concern for their daughters. The young people despised the educated, the rich and older men in general for setting bad examples by getting the disease in the first place while continuing with their sexual licence. Women, whenever they met, repeated the anguished cry of one of the brides: 'Who will look after me after I have taken care of you?' This echoed the general concern and predicament of women in AIDS afflicted households.

The third case involved a woman who one night raised the alarm usually reserved for alerting neighbours to a death. The neighbours came and, to their surprise, were greeted by the woman who was accusing her husband of being a murderer. It turned out that the husband was a trader. He had married and established another home, and the first wife felt that anyone who married in these days of AIDS without consulting his first wife was equal to being a murderer. She said that, since he had abandoned her and her children, they would accept it but, if he ever thought of dispossessing them, he would have to deal with the powers that be. The husband had been taken by surprise at his wife's reaction. This was apparently triggered when he arrived home late and demanded sex after dinner. Audience murmurs of 'She is right. UHHUN' left him in no doubt that his neighbours hated him and that his wife had bewitched them. He left before the neighbours, roused by the noise of the quarrel, went back to their beds. For weeks people shook their heads in wonderment. When asked, the men said that these days of AIDS were difficult times for men. The women admired the first wife's courage because they had not expected her to get away with it and stressed that women must use all possible means to protect themselves.

In Uganda it used to be said that the poorest man is one without a wife. Nowadays it is said that a doomed AIDS patient has no mother or sister or wife. Although men and women are infected on a 1:1 ratio, the patient needing help is male according to the current aphorism. From our study of six Kampala suburbs, we found that increasingly people who are ashamed to return to their villages, or who do not get on with their relatives, or who have no families in the country, are dying in town lonely and dependent upon the charity of their neighbours and workmates. Nevertheless, most AIDS patients desire, or are persuaded, to return to their villages to be looked after by their family, mostly in order to avoid the expense of transporting dead bodies from hospital. AIDS patients are cared for at home for between two years (as in the case of local traders, businessmen and district civil servants) and ten to

211

six months (in the case of urban returnees) and about four months in the case of women, who usually fall sick soon after giving birth (and whose AIDS symptoms are often revealed by autopsies). Despite the three-year campaign in the London *Sunday Times* newspaper arguing that AIDS patients are a drain on the time, personnel, medicines and money that could be more usefully used to treat older diseases like malaria which kill far more people than AIDS, AIDS patients are predominantly cared for at home. It is true that no one dies of AIDS. But the weakened immuno system causes victims to die much more easily from many traditional diseases that are termed opportunistic. HIV produces a dramatic disregulation and disfunction in the immune system. In Rakai people were dying because oral and often oesophageal candidas or thrush made it difficult to swallow food, or Kaposi's Sarcoma swellings in the stomach and intestines made it difficult to hold the food down, thus inducing constant vomiting and diarrhoea.

The impact of all this leads to death resulting from starvation which reduces the patient's weight to about 60 per cent of the normal weight of a human being. In the mid-1980s, during the early years of the epidemic, the US Center For Disease Control designated weight loss of greater than 10 per cent of body weight, associated with fever of more than 30 days or diarrhoea, as a criterion for establishing HIV infection even in the absence of AIDS symptoms. There is some doubt that the HIV virus is the cause of the current disease with the wasting syndrome, also known as AIDS (Slim). Some people point out that sick people, particularly those suffering from malaria, lose weight. Yet others fear that it is possible that all deaths are being branded as due to AIDS. All these are legitimate concerns.

Whatever is killing people by reducing them to skeletons may not be HIV/AIDS but a new disease that carers would prefer not to be nursing and patients are ashamed of suffering from because it is prolonged and causes compassion fatigue. In fact there is a new trend at wakes where disguised faces and bodies of people who have died of AIDS are displayed. At one funeral of an AIDS victim a pathologist was in attendance to administer injections to hold the departed person's face up. The educated relatives told the mourners that the deceased had died of Kaposi's Sarcoma, a medical term that no one bothered to translate just as no one translates 'cancer'. They would not have announced this had they known that this generalized internal KS is symptomatic of AIDS.

Women are the most important factor in AIDS care. The 'burdens' associated with care affect women physically because of the extra chores; financially because of the money spent on treatment; and emotionally as many carers' relations with patients become characterized by compassion fatigue and the risk of infection. The last factor is related to the first, of physical overload. Families were having dinner at 11p.m. or midnight which is late by traditional standards. Women often said that they wished the sun never set so they would be able to finish their chores. One consequence of long days of uninterrupted work is that women damage themselves when peeling food, collecting firewood, or gardening. HIV can be transmitted by exposing cuts to infected body fluids (except perhaps saliva). Scratches and cuts are to be expected if one lives by subsistence. No one usually makes a fuss about them. But their increased frequency with AIDS carers exposes women to body fluids as they wash thrush sores, attempt to clean ulcerated body rashes, and launder clothes and bedding soiled by vomiting and diarrhoea. In advanced stages of AIDS the patients are unable to get up or control their bodily functions.

One sign of the increased work burdens on women was that girls were falling behind in their school work, failing to pass exams and staying out of school because they were ashamed to repeat classes with younger children. One primary school headmaster, who reduced the fees for children from homes with afflicted fathers, noticed that this did not keep girls in school. He concluded that involvement in caring, and not absolute lack of school fees, was a major factor affecting girls' education. Interestingly, women seemed to be instinctively aware that caring exposes them to danger, because most of them diverted their children to household tasks that did not involve washing the patient or their belongings, and even when there was a soap shortage, pieces of soap were always available for children to wash their hands after touching anything soiled. Enmity developed between two village women because one found her daughter washing a patient's bedding in the home of the other. Exposing children to danger in this way was by popular agreement referred to as murder *(butemu)*.

Caring exacts a lot of emotional energy and often leads to compassion fatigue. Women who have children to mind, and other chores to attend to and complete, are not often 100 per cent attentive to the patient. Often patients get annoyed when responses to their calls are delayed. People are aware of this and advise carers not to be hard on themselves but to blame the disease that will not go away. It is commented that caregivers are people too, and it is unfair for someone to have to nurse for so long. Parents and immediate family members in Christian and Muslim homes may be opposed to treatment by traditional healers, but quite frequently patients will be rushed to diviners at the eleventh hour. Pressure from visiting relatives or neighbours has resulted in patients' murmurs being translated as 'Are you letting me die without treatment?' Money was always found to consult diviners about the emotional state of the patient, whether the patient was present or not. It is believed that the ghost of a person who dies in anger will cause illnesses including barrenness for survivors. The concern over the patient's wellbeing was a quest for assurance that the carer had done a good job and that the patient held no grudge against the carer. If the diviner found some ambiguity in the relationship then there would be the sacrifice of a goat or a chicken and herbs for washing, eating and drinking for the patient and carer, and sometimes other members of the family. Also, some women who had nursed a husband or a child felt nervous about nursing and being bereaved again. 'No one should have to go through so much again and again.' One woman who had lost two daughters becomes paralyzed down one side of her body every time she hears a Land Rover because she fears that it might be bringing her only surviving child.

In addition to hygiene concerns and spiritual/emotional well being, health caring involves money with which to buy medicines. Particularly if the patient is the husband, possible cures are sought and pain killers bought regularly. Nowadays cash purchases including food are essential in rural areas. Some widows manage subsistence on their own farms but others are forced to work for rich farmers. Most women outlive their husbands by six months to a year before they develop symptoms of AIDS themselves. Sick women manage as best as they can with help from their children. Unmarried women and widows may go to live with and be nursed by a sister. The lucky ones have a sister or female relative who is unattached and can come and stay with them in their own home. Others have to depend on the charity of neighbours or workmates. Women with AIDS worry about how to feed themseves and their children or whether they will die alone. And they rightly ask: Who takes care of the carers? The carers are expected by communities, society and the state alike to cope as they seem to have always done.

CONCLUSION

Home care subsidizes formal hospital care. Instead of leaving the whole burden to families, especially women, the government should assist women to carry out care more safely. The Ugandan government has committed itself to the Bamako Initiative which, among other things, requires the provision of financial resources to promote Primary Health Care. In a fourth AIDS epidemic that is going to affect carers, an epidemic that is going to be predominantly a feminized one, policy decisions need seriously to include measures for empowering people to protect themselves. AIDS/HIV may now be a disease of poverty, but history will never forgive us for professing ignorance in the face of clear danger signals.

SIXTEEN

Urban management: service provision under stress

Philip Amis

There has been considerable debate in sub-Saharan Africa in general and specifically in Uganda on the impact of structural adjustment policies. The debate has tended to focus on either a macroeconomic level or a household level. The former has been dominated by economists and has focused on whether the policies are working in terms of economic aggregates, while the latter, associated with a more anthropological approach, has focused on questions of household (and individual) incomes and resources. There is a critical research and policy lacuna at the institutional level which needs to be dealt with in order to understand the impact of the adjustment process over the long run. This lack of analysis at the institutional level is a major weakness of almost all the approaches to the adjustment process. This is relevant because institutions are the central building blocks of any economic development strategy.

The present study[1] focuses on two institutions associated with urban management and their performance under a period of adjustment. In the Ugandan context it is misleading to discuss institutions in terms of crisis when decay has been going on for at least twenty years. There has been a process of institutional decline in the public sector as individuals ceased to work effectively as they pursued other income-earning activities; a middle ranking civil servant (Assistant Secretary) in real terms earned only 5 per cent of his 1975 salary in 1988 (Chew, 1990). This study therefore seeks to determine the characteristics of the 'new animal' into which institutions in countries like Uganda have *de facto* evolved. The study is divided into three sections: the first considers the experience of Jinja Municipal Council, the second the contrasting experience of the National Water and Sewerage Corporation(NWSC), while the final section draws together some general themes and conclusions concerning urban management in Uganda.

JINJA MUNICIPAL COUNCIL
Jinja is Uganda's second largest urban area with a population of 60,979 in 1991. It was developed in the 1950s as a major industrial centre attracted to the cheap electricity associated with the construction of the Owen Falls dam. This was part of a policy by the colonial administra-

tion to develop an industrial and manufacturing capacity in East Africa; within Jinja this was mainly to involve the development of the textile industry (Southall, 1988: 57). Jinja is unusual as an African city in that it was planned as an industrial urban centre.

Jinja shows clear signs of physical planning with a well demarcated road and plot lay-out, an impressive level of infrastructure provision and an imposing Town Hall. There are clear indications that Jinja was influenced by physical planning ideas associated with the New Town movement. It is a debatable point whether this impressive level of infrastructure was sustainable in the 1960s without a substantial subsidy; it is clear, however, that, without a successful local economy, it was not. This problem was to be greatly exacerbated by the expulsion in 1972 of the Asian community who were particularly important in Jinja; indeed they were not only traders but formed the town's bourgeoisie. Jinja, perhaps more than any other urban centre in Uganda, was associated with the Asian community. Whatever the precise reasons, by 1991, with the exception of the main road to Kampala, Jinja, though pleasant, did show signs of major physical decay and lack of maintenance. Nevertheless in this hostile economic environment associated with extremely low wages and salaries Jinja Municipal Council (JMC) has managed to survive as an institution. This was primarily because it was able to exploit a buoyant source of income, namely, market dues and to a much more limited extent, Graduated Tax. In 1989/90 market dues accounted for 26 per cent of JMC's total revenue in previous years and the estimate for 1990/91 was in excess of 40 per cent. Graduated tax made up around 15–20 per cent of total revenue. Furthermore JMC is effectively completely autonomous in revenue terms of the Ugandan government. The collection of market dues has allowed JMC to tax one of the most dynamic and robust sectors of the Ugandan economy, namely, agricultural food production primarily for domestic consumption. In addition, it has also had access to taxing the informal transport (minibus) sector. This represents a successful example of taxing the 'informal sector'.

In Uganda's economic crisis these two sectors have in fact proved remarkably resilient, indeed the argument can be extended to assert that they actually expanded as a result of the economic difficulties. The clearest example was the switch to food crops from export crops, itself the result of political insecurity and inappropriate macroeconomic policies on farm gate prices and/or exchange rates, which has directly benefited JMC. In this shift JMC's gain has in many respects been the Ugandan Treasury's loss. As a result, JMC has been able to isolate itself in revenue terms from the almost total collapse of its industrial sector.

Astonishingly, JMC's total revenue in real terms increased at an annual rate of 187 per cent between 1987 and 1989/90 or, as 1987 may exaggerate the increase between 1988/89 and 1989/90, JMC's municipal revenue increased in real terms by 67 per cent. The Resistance Councils (RCs) have been actively involved in attempts to increase rev-

216

enue and step up financial management. This in part reflects their role as a public watchdog on the behaviour of local officers, but also the political reality that by increasing revenue and limiting (unnecessary) expenditure they will be able to increase the amount diverted to the capital fund spent on visible projects to 'repay' voters. In the recent past complaints about malpractice in the collection of revenue in markets have led in Jinja to some interesting innovations. Three times since 1988 the RCs have become directly involved in market revenue collection in order to attempt to ascertain the monthly revenue and establish an appropriate daily average. In 1988 the average daily market revenue in Jinja was 370,000 Uganda shillings, which leapt to 900,000 Ushs in February 1988 when the RCs participated in the process. How much this large discrepancy is to do with seasonal and daily variations and how much could be accounted for by non-collection of revenue and how much by embezzlement is not clear.

The RCs carried out a similar exercise in March 1990 and maintained a daily average of 400,000 Ushs in comparison with the Council's daily figure of 300,000 Ushs. However, the Treasurer countered that the RC average daily figure was in fact 377,540 Ushs while the revenue collectors' average daily figure was 346,750 Ushs, and that the discrepancy could be accounted for by religious and public holidays. Furthermore the previous week's average was 419,273 Ushs. This small example taken from the Council's minutes highlights the concern of the RCs and the Treasurer's Department to monitor revenue collection. That the RCs should be prepared to become involved in revenue collection is interesting politically as local politicians across the world like to distance themselves from tax collection. However, we should not overemphasize this. Their motivation is as likely to lie in controlling the administration and generating a surplus for capital projects as in encouraging taxation. Indeed the RCs in Jinja in 1991, with RC elections due in 1992, were apparently less enthusiastic about taxes.

Because of the hand-to-mouth nature of JMC's finances, the Treasurer's Department has effective control on expenditure. Its monthly Report to the Finance Committee on the implementation of the Council's policy involves a regular statement of income and expenditure. This is the major instrument of financial control and monitoring as it systematically compares the monthly figures with the budget estimates of revenue and recurrent and capital expenditure. Furthermore the Treasurer prepares a statement explaining the variances or the difference between the estimates and the actual monthly figures. This was routinely carried out on a monthly basis.

In addition, at the local RCs' request JMC has also introduced a Financial Management Sub-Committee to monitor the Council's expenditure and income further. In the prevailing circumstances this could be interpreted as an attempt by the RCs to control the Treasurer's personalized sanction on expenditure. A weekly statement of income and expenditure is produced by the Treasurer's Department

217

for the scrutiny of the Financial Management Sub-Committee; to produce such information regularly, given the circumstances of revenue
collection and the general condition of the Department, is an impressive achievement in itself. There is no doubting the RC's enthusiasm for
controlling expenditure. Nevertheless there is considerable room for,
and evidence of, misunderstanding and conflict in such a situation. The
officers see it as unwarranted and 'unconstitutional' interference in
their perceived role as implementors. They complained, for example,
that they were being asked to account for statutory payments JMC was
legally obliged to pay. Meanwhile, the RCs see it as a legitimate attempt
consistent with their perceived role of controlling expenditure and creating a capital fund for development projects. In conclusion, it is worth
noting that the officers and the RC members do have different primary interests. Thus the management are primarily concerned with the
continuing operation of JMC (the protection of the recurrent budget)
while the councillors or RC members are more concerned with the tax
burden and visible projects (namely, to expand the capital budget).
However, what is also clear is that there is a high level of accountability and a clear understanding on all sides of the relationship between
income and expenditure and the absolute necessity of maintaining the
latter. In this JMC as an institution has adopted an ambitious and brave
political strategy on increasing revenues to create capital rather than a
more conservative low revenue approach.

JMC has been the most successful municipality in Uganda in being
able to generate capital for development projects from its recurrent
revenue (there are no sources of credit or grants, so JMC's finances
are self-contained), and on a per capita basis it raises three times the
amount of revenue that Kampala raises. In per capita terms JMC
raises almost the same amount as Nairobi (Amis, 1992a). That after
twenty-five years of economic decline and with the complete collapse
of its economic raison d'etre (industrial production) Jinja can be
compared with Nairobi in terms of revenue collection is quite frankly
astonishing.

INSTITUTIONAL REHABILITATION: THE NATIONAL WATER AND SEWERAGE CORPORATION IN UGANDA

Water in Jinja is supplied by the National Water and Sewerage
Corporation (NWSC) which is an autonomous body set up in 1972.
The water supply was previously the responsibility of the local authority. As at June 1989 NWSC was responsible for the provision of water
in seven urban areas: Kampala, Jinja, Entebbe, Tororo, Mbale, Masaka,
and Mbarara. The NWSC has been subject to considerable support and
involvement by donors. There is clear evidence that this donor support
(Uganda Second Water Supply Project, World Bank-funded) has been
successful in rehabilitating the provision of water in Uganda's main
urban centres.

Urban management: service provision under stress

The NWSC is both centralized and decentralized in operation; thus the Jinja office is responsible for the local collection of revenue and operating maintenance, while headquarters in Kampala is responsible for the programme of rehabilitation and capital investment and the collection of revenues from large institutional debtors (parastatals and Ministries). Furthermore the finances and revenue collection of the local offices of NWSC are monitored monthly by HQ. Finally the maintenance of vehicles, which is often a major constraint on the delivery of services in Uganda, is done centrally in Kampala, to which all vehicles must be sent on a strict rotational timetable. The workshop in Kampala is extremely well appointed in contrast to the sorry state of the JMC workshop. As a result, the mechanics use the tools provided rather than their own, as was the case with JMC.

The atmosphere in the NWSC office in Jinja is in sharp contrast to that of other parastatals in Uganda. There is an efficient, punctual and committed workforce. The importance of cost recovery and the institution being self-financed was frequently mentioned by all levels of NWSC employees. Indeed the zeal with which we were told about the importance of such market mechanisms was reminiscent of the enthusiasm of 'born-again Christians'. This was the result of a deliberate policy to sensitize the NWSC workforce on this issue. Within Uganda NWSC is generally known as an efficient organization in the delivery of water, albeit at a high cost.

The water supply coverage in Jinja at 54 per cent of dwellings is amongst the highest in Uganda; furthermore the supply is continuous. The standard charge for metered residential connections (effective from June 1990) is 330 Ushs per cubic metre for premises connected to the sewerage system. In the unauthorized urban areas water is provided by public standpipes at 125 Ushs per cubic metre with a quarterly charge of 16,560 Ushs. Interestingly in these areas the local RC chairperson is registered as the owner of the standpipe, whom the community pay indirectly for water by contributions. In the unauthorized areas visited this system worked efficiently. There was some policy discussion about the idea of allowing the RC chairperson to sell water directly by the debe to the local inhabitants at a controlled price.

NWSC is notorious for its enthusiasm in disconnecting the water supply of non-paying consumers, not only private customers but also government parastatals. Indeed the only government agencies which NWSC would not disconnect were the Ministries of Defence, Internal Affairs and Prisons. This is no idle threat. There are many examples of local authorities and government agencies which have had their water supply disconnected. Indeed, the presence of one institution in Uganda aggressively pursuing a cost recovery approach has a significant knock-on effect on the financial behaviour of others; JMC admitted that the impact of the NWSC at the local level had encouraged it to collect some of its own revenues more energetically.

219

In summary, there is a considerable emphasis on financial self-sufficiency and effective cost recovery within NWSC. A considerable emphasis is placed on the routine sending out and payment of water bills and subsequent disconnection in the case of non-payment. In this there is a conscious attempt not to allow for any special cases. It is interesting to contrast this with the highly personalized nature of the operation of JMC.

It is the institutional rehabilitation of NWSC and its policies on human resources development and salaries and wages that are perhaps unique in the public sector in Uganda. Thus NWSC is attempting with some success a much discussed but rarely implemented strategy in Uganda, namely, the attempt by means of paying higher wages to achieve full-time attendance and commensurate levels of productivity. This also requires a much smaller-scale workforce. This is also the logic behind the present civil service reform in Uganda.

The strategy adopted by the NWSC has been to try and replace the many allowances which employees in the public sector receive with bonuses based primarily on attendance and performance. In addition to the performance bonus there are direct penalties for non-attendance. If an employee is absent for a single day (or is unreasonably late), he/she forfeits 25 per cent of his/her monthly bonus; two days late and the penalty is 50 per cent, and three days and the monthly bonus is lost completely. In addition, if an employee loses his/her monthly bonus three times then he/she loses his/her job. These attendance rules appeared to be administered rigidly and without exception, for example attendance at a relative's funeral or because of transportation problems (both of which are common in contemporary Uganda).

The logic implicit in the bonus scheme is that an individual is making a rational choice in missing a day's work and as such must be prepared to forfeit the earnings forgone. The impression given did suggest very strongly that the bonus system was administered fairly. Employees complained about it in principle but not about its actual implementation in practice. The result, according to the NWSC Personnel Officer, was 'a great impact'. This was confirmed by our general observation that there was full-time attendance of all personnel throughout the day. Indeed lunch time between 12.45pm and 2pm was clearly marked, with all the employees stopping and starting on time.

The main reason was, of course, the performance bonus which accounted for approximately 50 per cent of an individual's salary. As one respondent said, it 'mattered a lot'. It is interesting to note that performance-related pay, which is much discussed in the industrialized economies, often only concerns around 10–15 per cent of an individual's salary. In addition. it should be noted that there were differences in the amounts of bonuses paid. The system is more than a simple nominal performance or productivity scheme in which bonuses are *de facto* paid as an entitlement. (I have recently been informed that these bonuses are in fact increasingly being treated as entitlements and are paid like allowances.

The nature of human resource development in the NSWC is also considerably more thoroughgoing than in much of the public sector in Uganda. The project involved the establishment of a small Training Centre; the six trainers were individuals who had previous hands-on experience in the NWSC, and who then spent seven months training in the UK before becoming the nucleus of NWSC's Kampala Training Centre. The training covered: pump operation maintenance, mains service, leak detection, water and sewerage, management and supervision, and accounts.

By 1991 all the staff of NWSC had been through this training programme, and for some groups there had been a process of continual training often linked with the physical rehabilitation of the plant. In addition to being linked to the physical plant, the training laid specific emphasis on increasing employees' awareness of the importance of maintenance and cost recovery. These training courses were apparently popular; participants were paid a specific allowance.

In the NWSC approach to its labour force there are many similarities with the labour stabilization policies of the 1950s and 1960s used in East Africa by the public sector and large private sector firms. The NWSC has an established relationship and Joint Negotiation Committee with the East African Public Employees Union; this is apparently effective in settling disputes and misunderstandings.

In addition, for some grades of employee housing is directly provided. Finally, the NWSC will pay all the medical expenses of an employee's family. There was little doubt that NWSC offered its employees one of the most comprehensive packages in the Uganda public or parastatal sector.

In relation to wages and salaries, given the extraordinary complexity of their composition in Uganda, it is not really possible to make sensible comparisons. Nevertheless it was clear that working for NWSC was a sought-after job and that there was very limited turnover. One recent advertisement for a fairly low-level job resulted in 500 applicants; this is in sharp contrast to the high level of unfilled vacancies in JMC. Indeed we were informed in the Jinja office that wages were increasing in real terms and that 'morale was improving'.

In conclusion, the NWSC is an example of a successful programme of institutional rehabilitation based on the following: substantial donor support, an emphasis on maintenance rather than capital, enthusiastic water disconnections (sensitized by management), depersonalized routinized administration, hierarchical structure, training, and attendance and performance linked to bonuses. This rehabilitation has produced one of the most efficient organizations in the Ugandan public sector. The first few institutions are perhaps the easiest to rehabilitate; in the appalling overall state of the public sector, they can easily recruit the best and most committed personnel. Nevertheless the success of NWSC in the same hostile environment as other decaying institutions does show vividly that an analysis at the institutional level is significant.

FINANCE

Municipal authorities in Uganda have effectively become financially independent of the central government. This was not a conscious policy but resulted by accident from the distribution of taxes and revenue sources between the centre and the municipalities. The centre's revenue and expenditure position was so weak that it was unable to finance transfers to the municipalities, leaving the latter to try and sustain themselves through their own resources.

The clearest example is Jinja which is the most financially viable municipality, despite the total collapse of its industrial sector. It is possible to suggest the tentative conclusion that because of the buoyancy of municipal income sources municipal finances are in fact in a better condition than those of the central government. It is interesting to speculate whether a sustained economic recovery might reverse this unusual situation.

Nevertheless this has not been achieved without cost; in the absence of realistic rates the burden of municipal revenue is narrowly based and appears to be inequitable. To make an assessment of the impact of market dues and rents is complicated; the suggestion is that the incidence of such a local tax is being borne by a much wider group of consumers than might at first appear.

In this context of declining or non-existent financial resources, municipal authorities have been reduced to becoming 'revenue collecting animals' whose object is simply to sustain themselves. Indeed the emphasis in all the institutions visited in Uganda (NWSC included) on revenue collection to the exclusion of any discussion of expenditure and capital investment was very marked. Nevertheless, particularly for the municipalities, the question needs to be asked, when they are providing a minimal level of services, what function is local government performing in Uganda?

In one municipality (Kabale) 53 per cent of the total expenditure went directly on wages and salaries. While some of these wage earners are providing a service, given the very low level of wages in comparison to capital expenditure, this is a high figure and does support the argument that municipal authorities in Uganda are primarily self-sustaining organizations.

In general municipalities appeared to be politically responsive; this was particularly the case in Jinja where JMC was very responsive to the demands of the market traders. Furthermore the RC structure in 1991/92 did increase accountability although this seemed to be as much the result of unofficial adversarial 'party' policies as of the RC structure itself. However, the strength of the prevailing NRM ideology which effectively promotes a message of 'development before politics' should not be underestimated. Neither should the strength of the idea that the politicians/RC or Local Council representatives are responsible for monitoring and/or controlling the administration.

The local RC structures did facilitate urban administration by providing a vehicle for community aspirations and an organizational structure for the municipalities to 'negotiate' with. There were many instances of the local RC structure being successfully used to improve aspects of urban administration. This was particularly clear in the case of refuse collection points and the delivery of water in low-income areas.

In terms of expenditure (recurrent) in the municipalities visited the central departments of the Town Clerk and the Treasury were relatively well protected from economies. This is, of course, consistent with the revenue collection rather than service delivery emphasis of the institutions. By contrast, the departments of Engineering and Education were the weakest in terms of resources, technical manpower and capital equipment.

Service delivery

In service delivery three discernible trends were identified in response to the overall lack of resources. First and most simple has been an overall decline in the quality and quantity of provision; this was clearly the case with basic planning functions.

Secondly, some services have effectively become projects administered by the central government, often but not always as a result of donor intervention; the provision of health care, and, in particular, the establishment of the NWSC, is perhaps the clearest example.

Finally some services have *de facto* become separated from the public sector and are provided almost exclusively by the community and/or the public sector; basic education and the role of Parent/Teacher Associations (PTAs) are perhaps the clearest examples, but there is also evidence of this in primary health care (Brett, 1991) and more unusually in revenue collection. The result of these three trends has been to weaken the municipalities and to limit their involvement in service delivery and, by implication, to question their raison d'être.

Aside from these more general trends in service provision, the key bottlenecks in many services centre around the maintenance of vehicles and plant and the inadequacy of the workshops which are entrusted with their servicing and maintenance. The JMC workshop was 'borrowing' simple tools and basic plant from its own workers and from other institutions.

In the medium term such a situation is untenable; supporting or contracting out such services would seem to be more appropriate long-term strategies. At one level, given the resource weakness of municipal finances, this is inevitable. But it also reflects an attitude which underrates such activities. There were choices available in the relevant systems which partly operated against the importance of such maintenance functions. This appears to stem from two interrelated sources. The first is the well known tendency of most organizations systematically to undervalue the importance of recurrent expenditure and maintenance. Secondly, the pre-eminent position of Makerere University has a subtle but powerful tendency to undervalue the importance of such 'technical' vocations. This is particularly unfortunate and inappropriate in an economy where the major constraint appears to be the operation of vehicles.

Internal organization

The municipal institutions have metamorphosed themselves into different forms over the last twenty years. The municipalities visited suggest the following characteristics of being under severe and sustained stress.

First, in operational terms they are very dependent upon key administrative personnel, in particular the Town Clerk and the Treasurer. There is a complete lack of a middle tier in the administration. This 'structure' is primarily the result of the level of salaries and extra economic benefits. Thus the key personnel (Heads of Section) are in a position to obtain highly subsidized housing and transport; in many cases these may be provided gratis. In addition, their positions have local status which opens doors to their other business interests. As one high ranking local official put it in relation to a discussion [private] with a local Bank, 'they would not talk to me unless I was [position]'.

At present all these extra non-salary benefits go only to the highest officers, whereas the next tier down are much more dependent on their salaries. While impossible to quantify, these extra benefits could make these top officials relatively comfortable. Interestingly it was also argued that the lack of rewards for the next tier down were important contributing factors in corruption.

The second observation is that activities within the municipalities have become highly personalized and seem to be the result of individual negotiation rather than formal procedure. This is partly the result of the hand-to-mouth nature of the financial situation, but also of the complete lack of any intermediate administrative tier which would tend to limit the nature of the 'bureaucracy'. It is interesting to note that much of the effort of the RCs attempted to reimpose bureaucratic procedures on the key municipal officers; this was particularly clear in Jinja.

This personalized nature of the internal operations of the municipalities visited results directly from the smallness of their administrative structures. Again the critical importance of the absence of a middle tier, both in actual posts filled but also in quality and level of training, should be noted.

In this environment the annual budget process seemed to take on a critical importance. For officers and RCs alike it appeared to be the central, indeed the only, statement which approached what might be termed strategic planning. There is a slight paradox here in that, while the Annual Budget as a document was often referred to and used as an approximate plan for the forthcoming year, the actual day-to-day operation of the municipalities considerably reduced its importance.

A fourth observation about the internal organization suggests a tendency for individuals to be paid for individual tasks. This is partly the result of the extremely complex structure of allowances which has grown up. In addition, the impact of donor finance has in many cases considerably exacerbated this tendency by pulling (by offering considerably higher financial rewards) individuals out of positions in the administrative structure to work on specific projects.

This tendency is extremely clear at the central government level; indeed, this process has effectively destroyed the local administrative structures. This effective control of capital investment, together with the weakness of local administrative structures, has greatly limited local involvement in policy-making. Indeed, in the central government one anecdote clearly illustrates the pressures the rapid increase in donor finance and projects has put on key personnel. A Permanent Secretary, when asked why he worked on Saturday, replied 'it is the only day I can get my work done, as the donors do not work on Saturday'.

This trend, while very clear at the national level, is also apparent at the municipal level. Primary education and health have effectively been projectized, with all the resources and payments coming through a separate channel. In this situation municipal employees often deliver the services and are paid specifically for the task by the project. In some cases the payment is disguised as a 'training allowance' or 'transport allowance' but it is in reality a direct payment to ensure that a particular task is performed.

In general the project agency (usually donor-financed) is not really concerned with the impact of such payments on the general operation of the municipality. Indeed, it is usual that strenuous efforts are made, for understandable reasons, to isolate 'project' funds from the municipalities' other funds.

In this practice, and in Uganda in general, the donor position is contradictory if not openly hypocritical. At one level, alongside the IMF and the World Bank, donors support a policy of wage restraint and of ignoring local arguments about the impossibility of working productively on prevailing salaries. Meanwhile, in their private capacity and within projects, they fully acknowledge the link in designing all sorts of mechanisms to ensure that their Ugandan personnel will get sufficient remuneration to work efficiently. This will usually mean working exclusively on a particular task. Indeed, the effective 'going rate' to achieve this is the subject of considerable interest to the mainly donor expatriate community.

CONCLUSIONS

An important policy conclusion concerns the possible replicability of the success of NWSC, in particular the possibility of institutional rehabilitation by linking increases in wages to increases in productivity. This is the rationale behind the present civil service reform in Uganda.

The conclusion of the present study would suggest that increases in wages are a necessary but not a sufficient condition for successful rehabilitation. The success of NWSC depended upon a mutually reinforcing package of rehabilitation in terms of capital investment, maintenance, training and incentives as well as salaries. Indeed, without such packages and even perhaps with them, wage and salary earners in Uganda are likely to adopt a conservative strategy towards increases in earnings and still seek to maintain their well established multiple income sources as a means of security.

In relation to the Ugandan economy there is likely to be a multiplier effect in the rehabilitation process. Rehabilitation and the creation of financially viable organizations, like the NWSC, in general have a positive impact on other organizations' financial management and ultimate viability (e.g. JMC). Historically the reverse has also been true, in that unviable and irresponsible institutions encourage similar behaviour in organizations with which they come in contact. The Departed Asian Property Custodian Board is the most obvious example of the latter tendency.

Urban municipalities perhaps need to consider alternative forms of service provision as well as the traditional anglicized model. This model of direct service delivery is under threat in many countries. Indeed, this was also the case in the municipalities visited, where there was considerable interest in processes of tendering and subcontracting. This model, with a few key personnel co-ordinating a situation where the majority of functions are contracted out, is in fact an extension and rationalization of the institutional structure that has evolved as a result of economic and political pressures.

It is suggested that policy options for Uganda in the 1990s should adapt well established structures of *de facto* service provision by the community, private sector and household rather than beginning with public sector 'blueprints'. Nevertheless for the rehabilitation of Uganda's urban fabric in the medium term, the availability of capital for development projects is an absolute necessity, whether from donors or from some central government agency. The challenge is to design programmes which can absorb such capital without causing additional problems of institutional weakness.

Notes

---

1. The material for this study was gained in two separate visits to Uganda in May and September 1991 in collaboration with Edward Mugabi of the Uganda Institute of Public Administration. The study forms part of a larger study in six countries concerned with the 'Institutional Framework of Urban Government' funded by UK Overseas Development Administration (now Department for International Development) and the World Bank as part of the Urban Management Programme.

SEVENTEEN
The values of development: conceiving growth and progress in Bunyole

Susan Reynolds Whyte and Michael A. Whyte

Most economic or political paradigms of development define it as a process of structural change in which external forces shape and transform people's lives. In a recent volume on theory and practice in social research and development, Norman Long criticizes such approaches, arguing that both 'neo-Marxist' and modernization models '... are tainted by determinist, linear and externalist views of social change' (Long, 1992: 19–20). Long proposes an alternative – an actor-centred sociology of development that emphasizes the agency of individuals and local groups in shaping the pattern of social change. It is important, he argues, to attempt to develop theory 'from below', by examining the practices, cultural motivations and values of social actors. This is not just a matter of identifying the interests of a given actor (as if each position had a single fixed rationality), but of examining the repertoire of practices, statements and implicit meanings ('discursive means') that are available to people who interact and (perhaps) develop together (*ibid:* 25). What are the ways in which people explain to themselves what they are trying to achieve? (see map of Bunyole on p. 244.)

This may sound like a mere rationalization for doing the kinds of micro studies that anthropologists and other near-sighted researchers prize. Long implies that it is more than that. He wants us to cast development as something that is created by social groups, institutions and individuals, rather than imposed on passive recipients by a world system. This is a paradigmatic issue, and not just a question of micro versus macro levels. It opens the way for a discussion of an often neglected aspect of agency – the values that inform the agendas of social actors. This is not simply a micro matter safely left to ethnography. Careful reading reveals that development debates are shot through with statements about cultural values as motivating factors. Mazrui's (1991) discussion of cultural contradictions in structural adjustment points to the values of prestige and profit and redistribution to kin as motives for economic behaviour. Petter Langseth spoke of the need for '... a culture that rewards performance, honesty and a sense of public duty' at the conference from which this volume derives, John Munene spoke of morals, values and commitment in the teaching profession too – of altruistic motives, unity of purpose and individual calculations of profits and costs. The term 'participation' has become very popular in development circles – lip service, at least, to the idea of agency. If we are to take seriously the views and involvement of those people who are the subjects of development, then we must develop methods for analyzing the cultural values that inform their participation. In this chapter, we try to do that using the example of the part of Uganda we know best.[1] Before examining Nyole concepts and values, however, we must give some background information

DEVELOPMENT IN BUNYOLE

Bunyole is a county in Tororo District, inhabited by people who consider themselves a distinct ethnic group and speak a Bantu language most closely related to Lusamia. The county is heavily agricultural and densely populated, though the soils are of only moderate fertility. Bunyole had no traditional chiefs; the position of County chief was filled by Baganda until 1938. There are over 200 clans, and they are in practice equal. Inheritance is patrilineal; essentially no women own land or significant amounts of property.

Since we first began research in Bunyole more than twenty-five years ago, changes have taken place that might be termed 'development'. The number of secondary schools has increased from one in 1970 to eleven today. The Doho Rice Scheme area is locally referred to as 'little Europe' because of its money and iron roofs. The trading centre of Busolwe has become a town, with a hospital, rice mills, disco hall, 'compact' (tape cassette) shop and – in the words of a resident's proposal for an AIDS project – 'beautiful youths'. Brickmaking is a thriving activity these days and the number of bicycle taxis meeting the train at Busolwe station indicates the lively circulation of people and goods.

Yet in the midst of these signs of progress, many people say that they are poorer than ever. When we recently repeated a household survey in the communities of Bubaali and Buhabeba not far from Busolwe and its 'beautiful youths', we found that the material standard of living had declined slightly from its level nearly 30 years ago. Using bicycles, radios, and corrugated iron roofs as measures of prosperity, we found that families were slightly worse-off than they were when we surveyed the same villages in 1970. Structural paradigms of development, whether of modernization or neo-Marxist persuasion, would accommodate this seeming paradox in the principle that change is always uneven. In 'liberal' modernization terms, development trickles down from the North to Kampala to Doho and Busolwe and has not yet reached our survey villages. In more 'radical' formulations, the elite prospers at the expense of others; trading centres flourish by making profits out of the peasants. Development of some groups and localities requires the underdevelopment of others.

Another approach to development, not mentioned by Long, is demographic. We know that in the two decades between our surveys, the population of the county increased by 76 per cent, from 60,734 in

1969 to 106,678 in 1991 (Uganda Government, 1971, 1992). New schools, employment opportunities, trading activities and forms of crop production have had to keep up with a booming population. Development activities are said to be undermined by the growing population; new opportunities (to the extent they exist at all) do no more than permit living standards to remain the same. It could be argued that this too is a 'determinist, linear, and externalist view of change' in that it posits a factor that impinges upon a local community, beyond people's conscious choice. Although population growth is certainly a factor of a different order from capital formation or dependence on world markets, it has the linear virtue of being measurable.

People in Bunyole are well aware of the population increase and point to the number of Banyole who migrate to take up land in Busoga. But they still want many children so that their families may prosper. They are also conscious of the inequalities of development. 'We're working for the traders,' said one man. People remark that in the 'little famine' of 1992, traders in Busolwe made fat profits selling cassava, millet, and beans, which they had bought up at far cheaper prices at harvest time. But still they are pleased; such activity is evidence that Busolwe is developing.

In talking to people in Bunyole, including the RCs of the two villages we surveyed, we became aware that, for local actors, development has multiple meanings that may even contradict one another. In this chapter we shall argue that in the name of development people pursue at least three sets of values. It is the co-existence and interaction of these three kinds of values that provide the dynamic for 'development' in Bunyole and, we suggest, in rural Uganda generally.

WHAT IS DEVELOPMENT?

The word for development in Lunyole, *ohuhulahulana*, is an intensifying form of the intransitive verb *ohuhula*, to grow; perhaps the most accurate rendering in English is 'to progress'. It is etymologically similar to the Luganda term *okukulaakulana* defined as 'grow, develop, advance, go forward (e.g., in one's career)' (Murphy, 1972: 238). Although it is used in ordinary conversation, as exemplified below, it also has a special place in the political rhetoric of the Museveni period – in Lunyole as in Uganda's other Bantu languages. Politicians and donors are meant to promote *ohuhulahulana*. The term overlaps with others that also have the sense of progress and advance. For example, 'to stand up' (*ohwenyuha*) can imply accomplishment and improvement. The common phrase, *ohutina mumoni*, 'to go forward', has the same sense of progress and achievement, though with a possible implication of comparison or competition; thus it might also be translated 'to get ahead'.

The semantic range of these terms is very broad. Consider the following examples:

Development at the grass roots

'You will never develop unless you go to meetings. I call upon you to attend meetings and seminars when you are summoned' (the Honourable Member for Bunyole)

'In order to develop you must put up buildings on your land. You can't talk about development without buildings.' (the Honourable Member for Bunyole)

'Our children should study so that they can go forward' (clan leader)

'Bunyole is developed because it has a woman county chief' (RC3 Women's Representative)

(From informal conversations)

'The little market that has started at the crossroads has made our neighbourhood develop because now we have a place to drink *enguli* right here' (man aged 30)

'Nowadays Busolwe is standing up' (elderly retired teacher)

'Where there are *basungu*, there's development. People say we're developing because you are here' (man aged 40)

'The mediums for clan spirits should form an organization so that we can develop' (spirit medium)

'We need someone to pull projects to Bunyole so we can develop' (elite professional man)

'When I finished S6, I got accepted for Makerere, but I preferred to go into business so that I could develop myself' (young businessman in Busolwe)

'Should I only work for development here at the project without developing my home? How would it look if visitors did not find me well settled?' (Manager explaining that he had stayed home from the office in order to supervise work on the house he is building)

It seems to us that the concept of development as people actually use it spans from the development project, a clear prototype of development, to elements that could be translated as modernity, progressiveness and prosperity. Education, bureaucratic forms of organization with officers, modern amenities, fine houses and wealth are not just means to or signs of development; they are development. Do Banyole have a folk model of development comparable to those of policy-makers? Although the metaphors of growth (*ohuhula* is what children and plants do) and forward movement may seem to suggest a linear notion of progress, we do not think that this is implied in the Nyole idea. Experience in the dark 'time of regimes' showed that social and economic growth, like natural growth, was followed by decline. In general, most Banyole, like lay people anywhere, are not particularly concerned to explain development; they have neither a theory nor a consistent model of it. In daily life, considerations about determinism, teleology and lineality are not particularly relevant. What is important for ordinary people is that

230

The values of development

development expresses hopes and plans of achieving something. As an academic exercise, we can distinguish means, strategies, stages, and ends. But it seems to us more useful to enquire about how people pursue underlying values.

In order to analyze local concepts of development, we want to distinguish between three co-existing sets of values that constitute the way people talk about and practise growth or development in Bunyole. These are our analytical concepts; they do not correspond to Lunyole terms or categories. But they are derived from listening to what people say and observing how they proceed in many different contexts.

One value set might be called 'kin group prosperity'. To develop as a family, lineage or clan means to have many children, to attract wives and marry off sisters and daughters well. It means to have prosperity understood as the common property of the kin group and to be acknowledged and respected by other groups. Another set of values can be summed up as 'individual achievement'. To develop, or better, to get ahead, as an individual means to achieve wealth and power. This invariably involves contacts or long stays outside Bunyole, typically as a trader or through a career in the civil service or with some private organization. Friendship is part of this set of values, since individuals, not kin groups, form ties of affection and common interest with non-relatives. Finally, there are the 'universalist progressive' values of the common good that are usually associated with development. They include education, welfare, equity, social service and the religious values of Christianity and Islam. These values promote the well-being of social units more inclusive than the individual and the kinship group. In Figure 17.1, we show these value sets as having different shapes in order to remind ourselves that they are not directly commensurate with one another.

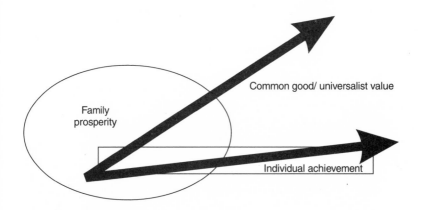

Figure 17.1 *A geometry of development values*

231

The development rhetoric of scholars, donors, and planners tends to focus on the universalist values as developmental. Some kinds of individual achievement are desirable, but private interest is seen as potentially anti-social. Familial values are mere culture or worse; terms like patriarchy, parasitism, nepotism and amoral familism express the negative views of these ideals.

From the local point of view, things appear differently. Development is a continuous and creative interaction between the universalist, the individualist and the familial. This interaction can be problematic; people speak fatalistically of how individual greed and family values undermine their efforts to develop. But the co-existing values can also form a positive synergy in which ideals and activities associated with one category help realize the goals of others. There can be resonance as well as dissonance between the kinds of values that people hold. In either case, these values are the basis of social action and interaction. They form the framework for an actor-centred analysis of development. In order to demonstrate these points, let us examine each set of values and its articulation with the others.

THE PAROCHIAL VALUES OF KINSHIP

Bunyole, like most rural areas of Uganda, has an economy and a social life that are heavily structured by kinship. For ordinary people, clan, lineage and marriage provide the framework of daily life and access to the most significant resources. Farming, the main source of livelihood, is largely a family enterprise. Land and labour are primarily available through kin and affinal relations. Likewise these form primary social identities for rural people. Family or clan is the 'we' for which spokesmen formulate a vision of hope and progress. Listen to the words of an elder as he dedicated sacrificial animals to the ancestors at a second funeral ceremony.

> We are begging here for wealth. We are begging here that all the children may study and learn. Here we too would like a motorcar to drive. Wherever we plant millet, wherever we plant sesame, wherever we plant sorghum, may it come quickly and soon. Here let us elope with women; we are begging here for facility in bringing wives. We are begging here for fertility: let us strike two by two, that we may hold a twin ceremony every day. Let us be well; you give us health and let us be free from illness.

This prayer follows a general formula for the invocation of blessings that represents kin group prosperity as consisting of growth in human and material resources. A family must be able to attract wives, produce many children and maintain the health of its members. Agricultural abundance is always mentioned, but Banyole do not think of agriculture as the source of the sort of wealth that could purchase a car. Affluence on that scale is attainable through education and employment or through success in business.

The *we* of kinship assumes a group that shares resources and shows solidarity – that is based on what Meyer Fortes (1969: 237ff.) called the

The values of development

'axiom of amity'. The kinship 'we' incorporates individuals: the success and property of one belong to all; the needs, difficulties and losses of individuals are ours, not his or hers. This is a discourse on the common good, but the community of which it speaks is a kinship one. Loyalties are the parochial, primordial ones of clan, lineage, affinity, and family. Our clan should develop, our children should go to school, our son working in Kampala should help us. Even honorary Banyole can participate in the 'we' of kinship development. When we recently celebrated the completion of our house on the land of Michael's adopted father, one of his clan sisters reminded Susan that 'you are our wife who married here and this is *our* house you have built'.

We have noted that kinship development has a human and a material side. Growth on these two fronts entails control over women and rights to their full reproductive abilities, as well as a positive interest in economic strategies that can increase the family fortune. Let us begin with gender.

The notion of family prosperity involves the acquisition of wives, which is accomplished through the exchange of bridewealth. Since the 1950s, there has been a ceiling on bridewealth set by a district by-law at 5 cows and 5 goats. Today people still state that this is the amount that should be given, although in fact 2 cows and 3 goats are considered a reasonable 'instalment' with the rest owing, perhaps to be paid by the next generation. Men and women agree that the payment of bridewealth is connected to the fact that men 'rule' women. In Lunyole, people speak of fathers and brothers as 'the owners of the girl' and a husband who has paid bridewealth is 'the owner of the wife'. There is thus a strong patriarchal element in kinship prosperity; in a sense women are a resource to be controlled and maximized. At the same time, however, the 'we' of kinship also includes women as group members, so that women like Michael's clan sister can say that other women are 'our wives'. Indeed, the solidarity of kinship is such that a sister for whom bridewealth was paid can with satisfaction say that she bought a wife for her brother.

Family development means acquiring multiple wives if possible. In our two survey communities, 20 and 25 per cent of men had more than one wife in 1993. For women this meant that 42 and 49 per cent had co-wives with whom they had to share their husbands' resources, attention and support. In one village, the rate of male polygyny remained unchanged from 1970 to 1993; in the other it fell moderately. Fathers usually provide animals for a son's first marriage, but subsequent ones are the responsibility of the individual son. Thus the desire to develop his family may be an important motivation for a man to engage in individual strategies of wealth accumulation.

The other means of developing a family is through children. Banyole mothers bear an average of eight or nine children, and the use of family planning is virtually nil. But the death of children is common. In Bubaali today, mothers have lost 27 per cent of the children they

233

have borne. This represents a fall from 39 per cent in 1970, yet parents and grandparents do not directly experience statistics. Indeed, given the population increase, funerals are just as common in any neighbourhood today as they were in 1970. Parents experience death as a constant risk, and therefore they say that they must have many children. In order for a family to go forward, wives must bear as many children as Hasahya the Provider sees fit to provide. The value of children disposes people favourably to many aspects of modern health care services and thus resonates with some of what we call universalistic values. At the same time, having many children makes it difficult to realize others of these values, such as education. The cost of schooling is one of the few accepted arguments against unlimited fertility.

Family development requires agricultural abundance and the accumulation of wealth. Farming in Bunyole is largely dependent on family labour and family capital. It produces for family consumption and also for cash to meet family needs. Recent changes in Nyole agriculture (M. Whyte, 1988, 1990) require consideration of the relation between gender, rice, and kinship values. Strict patrilineal inheritance means that essentially no women own land in Bunyole. In our surveys, in 1993 as in 1970, the only female household heads were widows holding land for their sons. When cotton was king, men, as members of co-operative societies, used to control the cash that it produced. Now food crops, many grown by women, are a more important source of cash. Nevertheless, family values dictate that women may only sell crops with the permission of their husbands and for specific agreed purposes. Thus it is almost impossible for women to accumulate capital with which they might engage in trading, for example. To the extent that women are economically more active nowadays, it is because hard times have made it more difficult for men to meet basic household needs and the requirements of school fees. Virtuous women work for the family, not for their own individual development. (The corollary – a wife who accumulates wealth on her own cannot be virtuous – also holds; men look with suspicion on wives' income and women in turn hide their income from husbands.)

Since the implementation of the Doho Rice Scheme in the 1970s, rice has become a very profitable crop. In 1992, the Scheme produced rice valued at 1.8 billion shillings. Twice as much again is grown in swamps outside the Scheme by farmers experimenting on their own. Rice farming is in some ways less congruent with family values than cotton was. It is less likely to be grown on land inherited from a father. Because it is only cultivated in swamps, men without swampland must rent or borrow it. It also strengthens the agricultural labour market, providing a form of farming that is not simply dependent on family labour.[2] For some men, rice forms part of a strategy of individual accumulation of capital that can be reinvested in more plots and the hire of more workers. Yet, for the majority of people, rice has not transformed the fundamental association of farming and family values. Not more than one

234

household in six grows rice. Many of those men who do so experience the conflict between family solidarity and individual endeavours. Family troubles – a death requiring extensive involvement in funeral rituals, expenditures for health care or the need for school fees – easily interfere with the finances and time commitments of rice farming.

THE VALUES OF INDIVIDUAL ACHIEVEMENT
Family development depends not only on farming but on access to the kinds of resources that successful members can mobilize. A kinship group needs eminent and wealthy individuals to act as representatives and agents of family advance. At a recent meeting of the Bagombe clan, for example, there was general agreement that the clan could not develop unless it could produce doctors, lawyers, engineers and other university graduates. Thus the universalist values of education are seen as a way of achieving progress for a kin group that is made possible through the accomplishments of individuals. The fact that only half of all children between 8 and 18 years of age are in school means that education is by no means taken for granted. It is something to strive for.

The values of individual achievement include the accumulation of private wealth, the ability to live an 'opulent' lifestyle with a fine house and smart clothes, the possession of power through money and position, and having contacts with other influential individuals. Individual achievement means the independence to use resources for your own benefit and enjoyment, according to your own priorities. At times individual achievement appears to threaten or challenge both family values of redistribution and the universalist emphasis on community welfare, equity and charity. At other times, individual achievement is seen as the motor for community development, whether community is conceived in kinship or in broader terms.

Individual achievement is an option not readily accessible to women. Although daughters as well as sons are sent to school, the number of adult women who use their education as a basis for employment is very small. In Buhabeba, the survey village with the highest rate of education and jobs, we asked about the years of schooling and present employment of all children of living mothers. We found that of 53 sons and 45 daughters who had left school, the sons had completed an average of 7 years of school, while the daughters had finished 6. Of these school leavers, 55 per cent of males were working in occupations other than family farming. The figure for females was 7.5 per cent. More striking was the finding that the 31 men who had managed to get jobs had an average of 8 years of schooling, while the 6 women who were employed had an average of 11 years. In other words, women had to be more educated in order to have a job.

In the 1950s and 1960s, it was widely accepted that individuals could get ahead by going to school and getting a job. The rural salariat enjoyed moderate prosperity. The old prayers that children should open their eyes and learn were first formulated at a time when civil servants had a steady cash income and provided a model of local success. But even then the really successful men were those who managed to get a job that gave access to resources outside Bunyole. Individual Banyole men who reached high positions in the East African Customs, in the President's Office, in ministries and parastatals, were prototypes for young men struggling to pass their exams with distinction. In this scenario, individual achievement was tied to educational accomplishment.

By the late 1970s this connection was no longer self-evident. Hyperinflation and the inability of the state to pay a living wage meant that the position of the rural salariat deteriorated sharply. Those who had advanced to influential positions could still parlay a government job into individual wealth. But they did so more as entrepreneurs than as educated civil servants. By the end of the 1980s, university graduates unable to find work in Kampala were coming back to try to scrape a living as teachers in local secondary schools. As one educated woman explained with bitter irony: 'Unschooled traders ask what advantage education brings (*Abasomi batusinga hii?*). They say we learned to read the sign that shows which bus is bound for Busolwe – but the bus is owned by an uneducated man.'

In the past few years, the growth of trading centres has witnessed to the values of individual initiative in Bunyole (Whyte and Whyte, 1992). New shops are going up, traders load lorries, pickups, and hired bicycles with rice, cassava and charcoal. In 1970 there was only a single motor vehicle in Busolwe. By early 1993 there were 15, 6 of them purchased in the first three months of that year alone, and 4 of these bought from profits made during the 'little famine' of 1992. Noting the difference between harvest and high season crop prices (e.g. 380 vs. 800 shillings a kilo for rice), people remark with resignation that trading is cheating (*ohusubula ohudulinga*). They also note with satisfaction that bicycles, iron roofing sheets, cement and the daily newspaper are now available in Busolwe. One no longer has to go to Tororo for them. In pursuing profits, traders provide services that are appreciated by the community at large – or rather, by those with enough money to take advantage of them. Just two miles from Busolwe, in the village of Bubaali, ownership of bicycles declined from 0.6 per home in 1970 to 0.4 in 1993; possession of even one structure roofed with iron sheets among the several buildings of a homestead went down from 0.6 to 0.2 per home in the same period.

Individual effort and achievement are recognized and praised in Bunyole. As in most of southern Uganda, people are continually 'thanked' for what they have done. 'Thanks for studying', a child is told on coming home from school. 'Well built!' or 'Thanks for building' is the acknowledgement to a person putting up a new house. Someone who receives a gift that has been purchased for cash should thank the giver for 'jobbing'. Even someone who buys something for his own use is thanked – *webale hupakasa* - well earned! Wealth is admired; individ-

uals are praised for their success. Cleverness and diligence are respected. A friend said of a neighbour who was an extremely hard-working
farmer that he felt deference for him, using the Lunyole term *ohutya*
meaning to fear/respect.

Ethnographic reports from other African societies suggest that the
accumulation of wealth is sometimes seen as achievable through super-
natural means. Johannes Fabian (1978), for example, has written of the
image of the mermaid in Zaire, who gives to those lucky enough to
meet her the secret of riches. In some cultures, wealth is seen as obtain-
able through the mystical exploitation of others, as when the Bakweri
of Cameroon associated affluence with zombies who were mystically
killed and made to work for the enrichment of their masters (Ardener,
1971). The moral economy of witchcraft often involves an image of limited good; where resources are seen as finite, the success of some is
always at the expense of others (Austen, 1993). The Nyole attitude
towards individual achievement contrasts with all of these. Although
people pray to ancestors and clan spirits for the blessings of success,
and although they explain falls from affluence in terms of mystical
intervention, by and large Banyole act as if success is available through
individual effort and talent. Because the arena in which people operate
is not a closed one, the notion that one man's triumph is another man's
loss is not particularly emphasized. The tendency is rather to hope that
a successful man will pull others up.

This brings us to the articulation between individual interest and the
social good, a relationship at the very heart of local views of development. When clans, lineages and families desire that their members
should study, have successful careers and get rich, it is because they
assume the 'we' of kinship. As a kinsman, the successful individual is
obligated to help others and redistribute wealth. Every modern
Ugandan knows the weight of these obligations, though we cannot
think of any research that systematically documents the significance of
this *de facto* programme of poverty alleviation in contemporary
Uganda. Paying school fees for poorer relatives, finding them jobs, setting them up in business, building houses for rural parents, giving
lodging to country kin who come to town to look for work – none of
this is seen by planners as development. But in local understandings of
making progress, growing, and getting ahead, these are essential parts
of the process of individual and family development. In one sense individual achievement is consonant with family growth and prosperity. In
another sense, the amity of kinship, or the 'economy of affection', is
antithetical to individual achievement.

People who have laid plans and embarked on strategies for their own
progress recount to one another tales of the impositions and demands
of their relatives. These stories are so common that one is tempted to
call this dissonance between kinship and individual efforts a dominant
narrative theme in daily conversation. A man who was building a house
and stored his cement at home, came back from abroad to find that his

brothers had 'borrowed' it. Another man was trying to earn a bit by providing injections for sick people, but he could never refuse free treatment to his sick relatives and was actually losing money because he had to give away all the injectables he bought. One version of these stories emphasizes the power that senior relatives have to curse those who fail to show respect and to provide gifts to elder family members. The moral line of these tales is that the ancestors are the power behind such curses and that senior relatives have rights over their younger consanguines. But they are also allegories of ambiguity (Jackson, 1982) in that many younger people wonder about the justice of demands made by relatives they see as greedy, undeserving and mean-spirited.

UNIVERSALIST VALUES

If individual achievement must be articulated with family values, on the one hand, it must also be related to the good of a broader, non-kin community, on the other. We use universalist values as a cover term for notions of the good of a group or category not defined in terms of kinship. We are thinking of the ideals promoted by the state and by the universal religions of Christianity and Islam that education, health care, social services and political participation should be available to all. Universalist values are associated with institutions; they assume that organization is the basis for progress and for the achievement of the social good. They appeal not on the basis of individual or family interest, but in terms of a commitment to wider goals sought by a 'community' imagined as a nation or a fellowship of believers, or experienced as a neighbourhood or a congregation. The belief that education should be a primary channel for inculcating values of the common good was expressed by Kajubi, who pointed out that Ugandan education is failing in its task of 'promoting a sense of national unity, economic development, self-reliance, social justice and equity, scientific and technological literacy, cultural values and a sense of mutual responsibility' (Kajubi, 1991: 322). Universalistic values, as expressed here, often have an altruistic flavour; one should serve the 'community' as a good citizen.

When we say that these values are associated with the state and with the religions of the book, we are not denying that ideals of the common good of 'communities', understood in non-kinship senses, existed in the pre-colonial period. But the forms of organizational rationality that underpin and promote these values were firmly established in colonial times and have been adapted to a multitude of purposes in a variety of contexts. Organizational form is not just a means through which to realize universalist values; it is itself a value – an ideal of relationship for common purpose. To organize is to develop. Choosing officers and identifying members is progressive and modern. Co-operative societies, women's groups, organizations of traditional healers and student associations are almost by definition developmental because they bring together non-related people for activities oriented towards a shared goal and a common good. Sports – village football clubs, girls' netball teams – are highly appreciated as forms of organization that bring pleasure to both participants and spectators. The introduction of Resistance Councils brought progress and modernity into every village; even aside from the values of democracy and political participation, they were developmental by their very structure.

For most people, schools, churches or mosques, and the lower levels of government administrative structures are the institutional channels through which universalist values were and are conveyed. Perhaps that partly explains the edifying style and the tendency to rely on leaders that characterize many efforts at development in this mode. Organizers often seem to be instructing people about their needs, informing them about policy, and speaking in a disciplinary tone about their behaviour. At the same time, they pass on moral advice and exhort people to participate in activities for the common good.

This didactic tone may relate to more than the institutional authority that forms a model for community development activities. Building a school or a church, running a successful women's group, establishing a clinic or bridging a swamp require patrons. For all the development rhetoric about grassroots participation and community involvement, few projects for the general good get far without sponsors. This brings us back to the relation between individual success and the social good.

An accomplished individual who keeps in touch with his rural home is under strong pressure to help his community as well as his family to get ahead. Some influential men, who live in Bunyole, or who come home regularly, assume the role of sponsors or patrons of projects for the common good. There are even a few women, living in Bunyole or members of the Banyole Development Association in Kampala, who are trying to promote community development. This can take the form of 'pulling projects' – persuading a donor to undertake or subsidize a project in Bunyole. There are several examples of this: the Christian Children's Fund project at Busaba and the European Union 'Microprojects'. One wealthy man sponsored projects directly by financing the building of a school, a church and the drilling of several boreholes out of his own pocket. It is the local elite, not representatives of the 'masses', who sit on the new management committees for health facilities. People who have got ahead as individuals are expected to lift not only their families, but also their communities, however these may be defined.

In the last year or so, a movement has grown up in Bunyole to build a causeway and bridge across the Mpologoma River to Busoga. This would put Western Bunyole about two hours closer to Kampala and facilitate the movement of people and goods to Iganga and Jinja. At the moment people walk bicycles or carry headloads across the railway bridge; motor vehicles must go by way of Tororo which is much further. Everyone agrees that a road connection would help Bunyole to develop. But where will the resources come from and who will organize it? Residents of Budumba, where the bridge would cross, have already contributed their labour clearing papyrus and beginning to bring in murram for the road. But without the support of powerful individuals who can attract a donor or persuade the government, the project will certainly fail. The head of the County Technical Institute has thrown himself into the cause and tried to mobilize the Banyole Development Association, an organization of Banyole working in Kampala. He exhorts the locals to do what manual labour they can, 'to show we are serious, because these days you have to help yourself before government or donors will assist – there are no handouts any more'. A committee has been formed and a bank account opened. People are being asked to contribute money and one Bunyole businessman has promised to put his lorry at the disposal of the project for some days. But no one believes that enough money can be collected by going from village to village.

A project to build a clinic and maternity home in Eastern Bunyole has revealed the same sort of dynamics on a smaller scale. The European Union is contributing manufactured materials – cement and iron sheets – while the local people are to contribute the land, labour and all local materials. This means in effect that a considerable amount of money must be collected by the women's group undertaking the project. Small contributions were given by many, but nowhere near what was required. The project would have failed had a few individuals not made very large contributions. At a meeting last year, discussion turned on how to bring in the remaining amount needed. One speaker suggested that collections should be made in every sub-county. But the director for women's affairs in the Banyole Development Association was pessimistic. 'It won't work,' she said. 'The only way is to get a few big people to contribute a lot.'

Thus the universalistic values of community service and the common good are often seen to depend on the commitment of individuals who have got ahead. The converse of this combination is that appeals to engage in developmental activities for the common benefit are often suspected on the grounds that the sponsor is actually out for private gain. Rumour had it that the man spearheading the causeway cause was actually using it as a platform to run for political office (in fact he did not stand in the recent elections). Leaders of women's groups say that husbands refuse to let their wives join on the grounds that they will only be working for the enrichment of the leader. Our point is precisely that motives *are* mixed. Doing well by doing good is an essential component of local development – and is essentially morally ambiguous.

A recent event in Busolwe illustrates the complex ways in which individualist, familial and universalist values interdigitate in local understandings of development. The hospital staged a ceremony to commemorate Kapere, the man who had given the land on which the hospital was built, by naming a ward after him. Speeches invited support for the hospital and more commitment to development; the hidden agenda was the problem of encroachment on the hospital land by entrepreneurs putting up shops along the perimeter fence. The ex-Member for Bunyole reminded us that Kapere was a farsighted man, though he was uneducated. At the age of 80 he gave a large piece of land for a project to benefit us all, although he could not hope to see it realized in his lifetime. The Bahyama (his clan) have been generous. The Bagunda and the Balunda (other clans heavily represented in the area) should follow their example. Kapere's son, back from Sweden, pointed out that he spoke as a representative of the family, but that the boundaries of his father's kin went beyond the biological family, and beyond clan, tribe and religion. (He thus gracefully alluded to and transcended the recurring conflicts between Muslims and Christians in the trading centre.) Unfortunately greedy people out to get rich have illegally taken up plots on the land his father gave.

The value of the common good, as represented by the hospital, was recognized and supported by the gesture of a single visionary individual. But the efforts of other individuals to achieve wealth were cast as antithetical to the good of the community. Kapere was taken as a representative of his clan to which he brought honour and respect, and appeals were made to other kin-based groups to follow the lead of the Bahyama. Thus Kapere as an agent of development was seen to embody and to have realized all three sets of values at once.

The intertwining of values, means, and ends is characteristic of local conceptions of development in many parts of Africa. Peel (1978) gives a fine example in his discussion of the Yoruba notion of 'enlightenment' (*olaju*). He shows how democratic education was considered a condition for prosperity and communal vitality. It became popular once it was seen as a precondition for individual career advance, which in turn was the basis for communal progress.

GETTING AHEAD AND GROWING TOGETHER: SOME POLICY IMPLICATIONS

Development involves the realization of family prosperity, individual achievement and the common good. Sometimes these values are in dissonance, as when people whisper that the leader of the women's group is pocketing the proceeds from the sale of the group's handicrafts. Often they are seen as consonant, as when a woman trained as a Traditional Birth Attendant strives to establish a business on the basis of her new credentials. This is not, as some health planners might claim, a failure of altruism and commitment, but rather an attempt to realize other values together with the universalist ones of community service and professionalism.

Universalist values are not simply imposed upon local communities from the outside. They *are* local values, deeply entwined with those of individualism and family progress. Families go forward through individual members who act as agents of a kinship group. Sometimes these agents have their own agendas which diverge from and conflict with

241

Development at the grass roots

those of the family. Yet it is striking how often individual actors and
families do support one another. In the same way, religious activities,
social service and development projects succeed best if they are consonant with the values of individual achievement and family progress.
This way of looking at existing development ideas can raise relevant
policy issues for both government and NGOs in today's Uganda.

1. The state and the value of professionalism

Privatization, decentralization and user fees for services are the order
of the day. The civil service is being reduced significantly and the role
of the state in local affairs is changing. From the point of view of local
people in Bunyole, privatization of health care or education can per-
fectly well be seen as a congruence of values of the common good and
individual achievement. But while certain kinds of services are easily
commoditized, other functions cannot be privatized. We think of our
friend Titus, a nurse, who gave up his private clinic to try to survive on
farming and a civil service salary. He longs to go on an up-grading
course, not necessarily because he would make more money, but
because he would like to develop his professional skills. Living far from
town, he never hears about these courses.

Titus's idealism, his commitment to the universalist values of profes-
sionalization and science, are an important part of his own self. Such
commitment, never total yet never insignificant for Bunyole, where he
works, is part of development and it is undermined when further pro-
fessionalization is blocked. The investment needed to maintain professional identity is small but, we suggest, the rewards for individuals and
communities may be significant. Indeed, the many diligent Tituses in
Uganda can be said to legitimize the state. The system of professional
training is itself an example of universalist values; it also provides individuals with motivation for universalist action, as is evident in the role
of professional individuals in taking initiatives for the common good.
By continuing training and support for the many unsung professionals
in the countryside the state in turn legitimizes itself, at the same time
facilitating the realization of universalist values.

2. Gender, family values, and the role of the state

We have suggested that the local conception of family prosperity
involves growth through wives and children. Women are subordinated
as individuals to the values of kinship, and their efforts are directed at
the well-being of the family. Opportunities for women to realize the
values of individual achievement are limited indeed within the local setting. There are practically no independent Banyole businesswomen or
traders in the county (and there is much speculation about the
Baganda women who come to trade rice). A few Banyole women have
made careers based on educational achievement, but mostly they are
working outside of Bunyole. We do not see any possibility that this will
change without strong state promotion of the values of equity and open
opportunity. Mazrui, writing of privatization and the market, has

242

pointed out that a shift to more equitable gender relations demands state intervention to bring about 'cultural adjustment'. He writes: 'Classical privatization and laissez-faire would simply permit worsening conditions of marginalization for women. Progress towards female entrepreneurialization would be aborted or retarded . . .' He calls for intervention by an 'activist and enlightened state' to release the market 'from some of the shackles of tradition and cultural prejudice . . .' (Mazrui, 1991: 365). In the terms we have presented here, local values are not just shackles but constellations that contain some opportunities for change. The argument that the individual achievements of wives, daughters and sisters might benefit the family, supported by the appeal of universalist values of equity and welfare, could well be acceptable.

3. The role of individual initiative in public affairs

Individual initiative is evident in business ventures and the furtherance of business interests that provide valued services. Private clinics and drug shops, criticized by health planners, are extolled by local people. Busolwe businessmen finally repaired the bad spot on the Busolwe-Tororo road themselves, after years of waiting for the Works Department to install the culverts that lay beside the road. Trading may be cheating, as the Lunyole saying goes, but traders provide services for the common good.

The notions of community control and community participation are justifiably popular today, yet, from our point of view, they are misleading. We have argued that local conceptions of how development works focus on individuals rather than communities as agents. The tendency to expect 'big people' to attract donor-funded projects and to make generous contributions reflects this allocation of responsibility and authority to successful individuals. Those who are strong should lift others. In some ways this emphasis on patronage is inconsistent with the universalistic values of democracy and equality. It is certainly anathema to the externalist expert or project manager, who reads it as 'mere' patronage. Yet such patterns are another pathway linking family and individual values to universalist goals. For local people this is also 'development' with the added advantage that it often works.

243

Notes

1. We carried out our first field work in Bunyole from 1969 to 1971 (26 months). Since 1987 we have undertaken shorter periods of research, separately and jointly, amounting to about 8 months in all. Most of the recent research has been carried out within the framework of the MISR-University of Copenhagen Enhancement of Research Capacity Programme. We are grateful to this Danida programme for financial support.
2. In the Doho Scheme alone, we reckon that at least 100 million shillings a year are paid to labourers. This is a conservative estimate based on the assumption that half of the plotholders paid 25,000 sh. a year for labour – a reasonable figure according to records collected from plotholders.

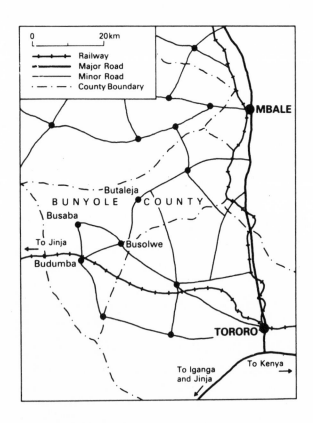

Map 2 Bunyole County

EIGHTEEN
The Holy Spirit Movement's New World:
discourse and development in the North of Uganda

Heike Behrend

Ideas of progress and development emerged during the eighteenth and nineteenth centuries in Europe during the initial stages of industrialization and capitalism. They were part of a teleological concept of history which optimistically promised mankind a better future. Karl Löwith, a German philosopher, suggested that this teleological concept of history was nothing more than the old, now secularized, Christian notion of salvation, which found its clearest expression in the Marxist concept of communism as the fulfilment of history (Löwith, 1953). However, the twentieth century did not do much to fulfil such promises. Instead, we experienced the worst catastrophes, finally leading to a radical critique of history as a process of progress and development.

During colonial and post-colonial times the ideas of progress, development, and salvation were brought to Africa. While in eighteenth and nineteenth century Europe the concepts of progress and development were to some degree open-ended to the extent that the future or the telos of history was unknown, the meaning of progress and development in Africa changed substantially. The so-called developed countries themselves now became the telos of development for the so-called underdeveloped world. The discourse of progress and development helped to impose Western hegemonies and left little room for strategies for the independent development of post-colonial societies.

As a result, the outcome of colonial and post-colonial development policies was underdevelopment, resulting in the marginalization of societies, cultures, and human beings (Mudimbe, 1988: 2,4; Meillassoux, 1993). Post-colonial African societies, rather than being one step in the imagined 'evolutionary process', became the locus of paradoxes that radically called into question the moralities and implications of development (Mudimbe, 1988: 5). These paradoxes not only betrayed simple models of progress and continuity but also underlined the complex entanglement of local and global processes.

Thus, one of the paradoxes of development is that, despite the attempts to impose Western rationality on Africa, we nowadays find a proliferation of various religious discourses, centring around spirits, spirit possession, and witchcraft. It seems that, in contemporary Africa, political issues are increasingly expressed in religious discourses. To gain or conquer the central power, i. e. the state, religious discourses are invented. Thus, not only the Marxist-trained guerrillas of the Zimbabwean African National Liberation Army (ZANLA) worked together with spirit mediums during the war of liberation (Lan, 1987), but also RENAMO in Mozambique used spirit mediums to fight against the enemy and witches (Roesch, 1992). And the NAPRAMA movement, which emerged at the beginning of 1990 and fought alongside FRE-LIMO, was led by a man possessed by various Christian spirits (Wilson, 1992). Increasingly, prophets and spirit mediums, rather than politicians and party leaders, seem to be leading the new movements and cults as well as inventing their own religious discourses. In addition, it also seems that the post-colonial governments, for example in Gabon (Löffler, 1983), in Cameroon (Fisiy and Geschiere, 1990), and in Benin (Elwert, 1984), have increasingly resorted to witch-hunts in order to stabilize their own power and to finish off their opponents.

However, we should not interpret this as a regression or a recourse to pre-colonial 'traditions' but as a reaction to and expression of modern transformations. In a dialogue with God, the gods, or other forces, Africa is inventing its own modernity (Bayart, 1993: 12). While Western discourses of development mainly concentrate on economics and politics, African discourses, especially in the rural areas, centre on healing not only the individual but also the social body, and on morality and its opposite, immorality. Thus we might, for example, interpret the immoral economy of witchcraft as an expression of the failed dream of development (Comaroff, Jean and John, 1993: xxv).

In the following discussion I hope to show that an approach to development focusing on economic maximization and neglecting the religious and moral aspects will be incapable of understanding events in present-day Africa. Especially in countries devastated by war, like Uganda, the reconstruction that takes place at the local level will not be understood without taking into account religious discourses and practices that try to heal individuals and society. Terence Ranger, for example, has written about the Zimbabwean desire for healing after the atrocities of the liberation war. In order to be cleansed, guerrillas resorted to both spirit mediums and to priests of the *Mwari* High God cult. These priests also asked Mugabe and Nkomo to come for national cleansing and repentance; in addition the Roman Catholic church explored the rites of exorcism in order to stop the cycle of violence (Ranger, 1992: 705–6).

Recently in Northern Uganda, in Acholi, a series of prophets have emerged to organize resistance against the central power, the government of the National Resistance Army (NRA) of Yoweri Museveni. In 1985, a young woman called Alice Auma from Gulu in Acholi was possessed – from a local perspective – by a previously unknown Christian spirit named Lakwena. His mission was 'to help as a doctor'. Under the guidance of this spirit, Alice established herself as a spirit medium and set up a new cult of affliction, working as a healer and diviner. In August

1986, in a situation of internal and external crisis (Behrend, 1992), the spirit asked his medium to stop healing and instead organize the Holy Spirit Mobile Forces (HSMF) to wage war against the government, witches, and impure soldiers. She recruited many former soldiers from the Uganda National Liberation Army (UNLA) and the newly formed Uganda People's Democratic Army (UPDA), another resistance movement which, like the HSMF, was fighting against the government. After the first military successes against the NRA, other segments of the population joined her: peasants, pupils, students, teachers, businessmen, about a hundred women, from different ethnic groups, mainly Langi, Teso, and Jopadhola. Under the leadership of various spirits, she marched with between 7000 and 10,000 men and women towards Kampala. Near Jinja, about 50 km from Kampala, she and her soldiers were defeated by the government troops. Many of her soldiers died or were injured. She crossed into Kenya, where she supposedly remains.

Even after the HSMF suffered the decisive defeat of October 1987, the fighting did not cease. The spirit Lakwena took possession of Alice's father, Saverino Lukoya, who continued to fight with the rest of her soldiers until 1989. Then the spirit possessed Joseph Kony, a young man, who continues the struggle in the north of Uganda to this very day (Behrend, 1993).[1] (See map of the administrative divisions of Uganda p. 260.)

The Holy Spirit Movement waged war against the government of Yoweri Museveni. However, the HSM's war must also be seen as a consequence of preceding wars. Its war was a war against a war, one attempting to cope with the never-ending cycle of violence and retaliation. Although itself generating violence, despair, and death, the HSM nevertheless tried to end this cycle of violence and to heal not only individuals but also society. To this end, the HSM invented a religious discourse which attempted not only to reconstruct the economy and effect political change, but also to create a new moral order and thus reconcile the people.

However, the HSMF waged war not only against an external enemy, the NRA government, but also against internal enemies: against rival resistance movements like the UPDA and the Uganda People's Army,[2] against witches, i.e. pagan spirit-mediums and men and women accused of practising witchcraft, and impure soldiers. Thus, destruction[3] was not only directed against the government troops but also against people in Acholi who were held responsible for all the evil in the world. A war within a war took place, expressing not only class tensions but also gender and generation tensions.[4]

The HSM's discourse was, as mentioned already, essentially a religious and indigenized Christian discourse. It stressed moral rehabilitation: 'the causes and the solutions of all the problems of Uganda can be biblically explained and resolved by turning to Our Lord Jesus Christ and becoming God-fearing people.'[5] The HSM was organized into a military and a civilian wing both led by the holy spirit Lakwena as

247

Chairman and High Command. The civilian wing was divided into the Frontline Co-ordination Team and the War Mobilization Committee, whose duties were to:

provide moral education to the people wherever they go
preach the message of the Lakwena, of love, unity, and repentance, to the people
provide moral and political education to the troops
solicit moral and material support for the people
perform other duties.

This enormous stress on moral education in the HSM's discourse can only be understood in the context of the crisis to which the HSM tried to provide an answer. For the people in Acholi, this crisis was seen above all as a moral crisis.[6]

As far as I was able to find out, there were two discourses that attempted to explain this moral crisis in Acholi from a local point of view. At the heart of the first discourse, primarily conducted by the elders, stood ideas of purity and impurity that had their origin in lapses from the moral order. At the centre of the second discourse, conducted by everybody, but especially by women,[7] stood ideas of witchcraft and sorcery. Each discourse was in some way connected with varying interests. The discourses were also part of strategies to keep or gain power.

When in 1986 the NRA succeeded in overthrowing the Okello regime, thousands of Acholi soldiers fled home to the North. There, in Acholi, a power struggle began between the young soldiers and the elders who used 'Acholi tradition' to subject the young soldiers to their authority. For these elders, the soldiers who had returned to Acholi were the root of all evil. They had become *internal strangers* (Werbner, 1989), alien to those who had remained at home. During the civil war, they had plundered, tortured, and murdered (especially in Luwero) and had become 'of impure heart'. Because they had killed, they brought *cen*, the revengeful spirits of those killed, to Acholi, thus threatening the lives of their relatives at home. However, it was not actually the killing that violated the moral order. In pre-colonial times and also during the colonial period, a warrior brought home the head of the foe he had killed as evidence of his deed. As an impure person he had to spend a number of days in seclusion until he was purified in a ritual and until the spirit of the killed person had been pacified by a sacrifice and sent away. Then he received an honorary name, *the moi-name*, as a sign of his bravery and new social status.

During the First and Second World Wars, Acholi soldiers in the King's African Rifles (KAR) brought home with them a memento, a piece of cloth, a button, or an insignia of the enemy they had killed and underwent the purification ritual. But in the confusion of the civil war, many soldiers were unable or unwilling to undergo the purification ritual, and thus, the *cen*, the spirits of those they had killed, were not pacified. The soldiers remained impure and the unpacified spirits of those killed were regarded as responsible for the misfortune that struck Acholi. The elders regarded the historical fall of Acholi, the loss of state power, AIDS, the growing internal conflicts, and the increasing use of witchcraft, as a punishment, a sign of condemnation resulting from a transgression against the moral order. Thus, the elders used the vocabulary of pure and impure to convey an idea of guilt that focused on the soldiers.

As with other forms of misfortune, death in war could and can be interpreted in the idiom of witchcraft. The enemy's bullet that killed an Acholi was not the true cause of his death. At the burial, if the relatives suspected someone, a spirit medium called up the spirit of the deceased and asked him to tell who had really killed him. Often it turned out that a relative or neighbour with whom the deceased had been in conflict had bewitched him to ensure that the enemy's bullets would hit him and no one else. The war against an external, alien enemy was thus turned inward, leading to an increase in tensions and conflicts in Acholi which might otherwise have remained latent. And since the idiom of witchcraft was used to interpret not only death in war but also death by AIDS, a disease which has spread at a terrifying rate in Acholi in recent years, Acholi was transformed into an impure country in which everyone was suspicious and attempted to inflict damage on everyone else. In addition, the two discourses on the moral crisis in Acholi were not only compatible with each other, they also strengthened each other.

The increasing number of witchcraft accusations led to a state of impurity and amorality in Acholi, leading – in the local perspective – to still more natural and social catastrophes such as AIDS, war, and drought as punishments for transgression against the moral order. The losses caused by these catastrophes were then interpreted again in part in the idiom of witchcraft, increasing the internal discord still further. And since neither the chiefs nor the elders were able to organize witch-hunts and break this cycle of terror, the preconditions were now given for what Edwin Ardener called a 'prophetic condition' (Ardener, 1989: 148).

While the NRA and the various resistance movements fighting against it, such as the UPDA and the UPA, all used a secularized political discourse, it was only the HSM that responded to the crisis with a religious and moral discourse trying to find a solution to these predicaments. Thus, it is no coincidence that Alice and the HSMF gained so much support.

At the very inception of the HSM, Alice (or rather Lakwena) invented a ritual of purification that cleansed her soldiers from witchcraft and the *cen*, the spirits of those who had been killed. Thus she did what the elders had not been able to do. By cleansing the soldiers, she not only reintegrated the former *internal strangers* but also rehabilitated them.

By issuing 20 Holy Spirit Safety Precautions, prohibitions against theft, plundering, lying, killing, sleeping with women, smoking cigarettes, etc., she tried to reconstitute the moral order and to control the soldiers. Lakwena promised that only those soldiers who were sinless would survive the battlefield, that is, those who abided by the Holy Spirit Safety Precautions. The battles became a sort of ordeal where the 'clean hearts' of the HS soldiers had to be proved. Thus, Alice again managed to do what the elders could not do: control the soldiers. However, the Holy Spirit Safety Precautions not only served to reconstitute the moral order, they also initiated a process I would like to call *culpabilization* (Delumeau, 1983; Kittsteiner, 1987).

Culpabilization refers to the creation of a consciousness of guilt that no longer attributes responsibility to another – as in the idiom of witchcraft – but which places the blame upon oneself. If an HS soldier broke or infringed one of the Holy Spirit Safety Precautions, this made him guilty. If a bullet hit him in battle, then his wound or his death would appear as a punishment for his own misdeed. No longer could another person be suspected or accused. In this way, the HSMF were able to keep the movement free from suspicion and accusations of witchcraft. Thus, the HSM's discourse on 'development' concentrated above all on a world without witchcraft. This does not mean that the HSM was able to eradicate belief in witchcraft. On the contrary, by fighting witchcraft its existence was once again confirmed.

The HSM was not only a military organization, an army that waged war, but also a new regional cult which spread its indigenized Christian messages as the army advanced. Not only the HS soldiers but also the civilians in the so-called 'liberated areas' became morally educated and rehabilitated. During the march towards Kampala, ritual centres, called *yards,* were established where people listened to Lakwena's teachings of love, unity and repentance. In addition, they were cleansed of evil spirits and witchcraft. They had to burn all their magic charms and were forbidden to go and see *ajwakas,* pagan spirit mediums, who worked as diviners and healers. In the HSM's discourse, these pagan spirit mediums were evil because they used witchcraft. Thus, the HSM adopted and transformed the Christian missionary's programme, fighting what the missionaries had defined as pagan.

The *yards* also became centres of healing. Since all the hospitals and health centres were closed or destroyed during the war and the time that followed, Lakwena decided to invent the so-called Holy Spirit Drug, a mixture of water, honey, and oil which had to be shaken 30 minutes beforehand in order to become effective. This drug and some other medicines were produced locally and given to the civilians who came to be treated in the *yards*. Thus, the HSM developed its own health programme.

However, health was not seen as a mere physical state of the body but also included a spiritual and moral condition. Lakwena taught that the Holy Spirit Drug would only be effective if people really believed and were without sin. While the HS soldiers had to follow strictly the aforementioned 20 Holy Spirit Safety Precautions, the civilians only had to obey four rules: They were not allowed to eat shibutter, a vegetable oil which was used to anoint the soldiers and make them bullet-proof, or honey, used to produce the afore-mentioned Holy Spirit Drug, and they were not allowed to kill bees and snakes because these animals were allies of the HSM. It seems that, especially in Kitgum, many people followed Lakwena. They left the established churches and went to pray and to be cleansed in the *yards*. Even today, so I have been told, one can find some *yards* in Kitgum still producing and adminis-tering the Holy Spirit Drug. In the *yards* established by the HSM, Lakwena would also try cases. Like a chief, Alice (or Lakwena) assumed responsibility for reconciling people in conflict (and bringing rain). Thus, the *yards* became the places where the New World of the HSM, their *instant millennium,* their ideas of development, were realized. These also included the equality not only of women and men but also of all creatures (of God) such as wild animals and even stones. However, while at the beginning of the HSM's war men and women would fight together against the enemy and men as well as women would look for firewood and water and prepare the meals, later, dur-ing the march on Kampala, the old structures of male domination were slowly re-established. Male soldiers would continue to fight while the women stayed behind performing the usual female tasks. Whereas the male soldiers were called *malaika,* angels, the women were named *agaba,* after a creeping plant associated with seduction and sexual inter-course. Thus, although equality of the sexes was promised, women nev-ertheless were identified with evil and made responsible for the sins that still prevailed in the world.

The HSM was also an army of some 7000 to 10,000 soldiers who had to have food and weapons. While the weapons were mainly taken from the NRA, the food supply had to be obtained from the local population. It does not seem appropriate to speak of the HSM as having a region-al cultic mode of production as, for example, Binsbergen suggested for other regional cults (see Binsbergen, 1981: 315). The HSM, like other guerrilla movements, was not able to produce the necessary food for its soldiers. Thus the HSM had a more or less predatory mode of pro-duction. While the UPDA, the UPA, and to some extent the NRA also used force to obtain food, the HSM succeeded at least in some regions in gaining the support of the rural population. It was the duty of the War Mobilizing Committee to organize supplies without using force, as Lakwena had ordered. Thus they founded committees in various sub-counties, established relationships with elders who agreed to sponsor them and organized rallies where Lakwena would first preach the mes-sage of love, unity and repentance, after which gifts and loans were col-lected. For every gift an acknowledgement receipt was issued detailing the date, the name of the giver, and the character of the gift. The loans were to be repaid without interest. But the generous givers were promised that after the victory they would receive not only what they had donated but also in addition some development projects. Thus, we find here a direct appropriation of the dominant Western discourse on development. In the HSM's discourse of development, development projects were promised as some sort of gift or reward for the support given to the HSM. Development as such, in its secularized form, so it seems, was not given much importance.

To conclude, I would like to reiterate that the HSM's discourse and practice attempted a holistic approach concentrating on the moral aspects of life. It was concerned more with salvation than with secularized 'development'. Thus, Western development projects were integrated only as future promises. The reconstruction which actually took place during the existence of the HSM, however, relied in no way on foreign aid but on local resources and local concepts, thus retaining its independence from the Western world. This corresponds, of course, to the modern trends in developmental policies of reducing dependence on the West, and making people use their own materials and capabilities.

The HSM was an anti-witchcraft movement and the New World, the instant millennium (Willis, 1970) it tried to establish in the *yards* was above all a world free of sin, that is, one free of witchcraft. Thus, the HSM's 'development' programme should be interpreted as a conscious counter-programme not only to the secularized NRA but also to the official dominant programmes of the developed countries which concentrate on material well-being and neglect the spiritual and moral aspects of life.

It is not by chance that the predatory post-colonial states are challenged by movements which invent a religious discourse. Since politics, not only in Uganda, is mainly the politics of eating or politics of the full belly, people do not trust it any more, if they ever did. Thus, politics which attempts to transcend selfishness and to create a new public space may have to rely on religious, other-worldly discourses that appear separated from all-too-human interests and desires.

Notes

---

1. My research was sponsored by the Special Research Programme of the University of Bayreuth for which I am very grateful. In addition, I would like to thank Claude Meillassoux for his critical and helpful remarks.
2. Attempts were made to unite forces with the other movements that were fighting among themselves, mainly for scarce resources, food supplies, weapons, etc.
3. Jean François Bayart has remarked that one of the paradoxes of modernity is that, despite the destruction caused by war, modernization and innovation take place. Without minimizing the effects of destruction caused by the war of the HSMF and the NRA, and bearing in mind the dialectics of destruction and construction, I shall concentrate on the positive side, on the innovations which were paradoxically made possible by the destruction caused by this war.

252

4. Kriger (1988, 1992) also describes a war within a war in the case of the Zimbabwean war of liberation.

5. Quotations without a reference are taken from the report some missionaries were given by three HS soldiers in June 1987.

6. For a more detailed analysis of this crisis see Behrend (1992).

7. In Acholi it is mainly women who conduct the discourse on witchcraft. However, their discourse is a more or less private and secret one. Because they are muted, i.e. excluded from the political and public sphere, they have to rely on the elders to take up their accusations and bring them to court. The elders,however, are not always interested; they are involved in their own power struggles and take up the accusations of women only when it suits them. Thus, very often the women are forced to protect themselves or to take revenge by going to a witchdoctor and using witchcraft in turn. In this way, the exclusion of women from the public sphere forces them to do themselves what they are fighting against: to use witchcraft. In addition, by using witchcraft, they prove what men always knew: that women are evil because they use witchcraft.

NINETEEN
Isolation and underdevelopment: periphery and centre

Aidan Southall

The periphery of a country can never hope to receive the same degree of attention as the centre, but democratic and fair-minded government must always endeavour to redress the geographical penalties imposed by historical accident. The 'centre', of course, is not to be understood dogmatically as the precise centre, but rather the area which combines the maximum economic, political and cultural activity with the best transport and communications. South Central Uganda, that is to say, Buganda, has always enjoyed this advantage, for historical reasons which are well known yet fiercely disputed. The problem in the African situation is that regional struggles for a fair distribution of resources are inevitably sucked into the structure of inter-ethnic conflict, which they greatly exacerbate. The British were beholden to the Baganda people and perhaps harboured hidden guilt feelings about it subsequently. In any case, their debt to the Baganda forced them to favour them above all other Ugandan peoples. When the first independent regime was led by a Northern politician, with majority support from outside Buganda, he tried to redress the balance in favour of the North and several important projects were undertaken to this end, but the balance remained extremely unequal. Every aspect of development activity was weaker in the North than elsewhere. (See map p. 260.)

The Alur people, with whom I have been closely associated for 45 years, live in the far Northwest and inevitably share in this imbalance. As they are very little known and poorly understood by other Ugandan peoples, it is worth setting down their major experiences as members of the Ugandan colonial state and independent nation, so that better knowledge of their plight may assist in winning them a fairer share of national attention and resources and enable them to make a more effective contribution to the progress of Uganda as a whole. The Alur are not the only people on the periphery, but their example may serve to illustrate the suffering of other peripheral peoples. The Alur were brought into Uganda, not because they were known or wanted, but simply because they were caught in the crossfire of the colonial struggle for control of the vast domains of the Sudan and Congo, between the British, French and Belgians.

What became for sixty years the West Nile District of Uganda was on the fringe of the Sudan reconquered from the Mahdi in 1898. The

254

southern part of the district was handed over to King Leopold as part of the Congo for a period of about ten years. In 1914 A.E.Weatherhead was sent from Entebbe to walk the 700 or so miles to Lado, on the River Nile beyond Juba, to arrange with the Sudanese authorities to establish an administration under the Uganda Protectorate. Weatherhead visited the Alur leaders, who gave him supplies, and after a few skirmishes established his authority also over the Lugbara further north. 'Among the Alur', he said, 'every clan head wants to be a chief; among the Lugbara every man wants to be a chief.'

The Alur or Jonam (the people of the Nile) had a prosperous economy based on fishing in the river and cultivating on both banks. In a succession dispute between two brothers, Owiny and Ongwech, for the throne of Ragem on the Nile, the British supported Owiny on the east bank while the Belgians supported Ongwech on the west, thus bringing international quarrels into local affairs. When the west bank returned to British rule, Ongwech inevitably lost but Weatherhead made him 'Town Chief' of Arua after he established it as the district capital, although it was in the middle of Lugbaraland. Tsetse fly took over the area east of the Nile devastated by the colonial war against Kabarega of Bunyoro, bringing sleeping sickness and the closing of the area. So the Jonam lost half their land resources, which they have never recovered. The northern and eastern groups of Alur were then cut off from those in the south and west by the demarcation of the boundary between Uganda and the Belgian Congo, which took no account of their existence but, by reducing them to less than half their full numbers, fatefully condemned them to negligibility in Ugandan affairs.

It is hard to imagine what benefit the Alur enjoyed from the first half century of British presence, apart from the privilege of paying taxes and serving and dying in two World Wars. However, I have to report that in the 1990s old men, looking back nostalgically at this time across the intervening years of turbulence and suffering brought by Idi Amin, perceived it as an era of peace and justice.

PHYSICAL AND MENTAL ISOLATION AND ITS CONSEQUENCES

The sheer travelling distance by car, truck or bus to the Alur from Kampala exhibited bizarre contrasts. Less than 300 miles as the crow flies from Kampala, it was often necessary to travel 600 miles to reach them, crossing the Nile twice by hand-propelled ferries. The steam boat from Butiaba to Pakwach cut this distance in half, but it went out of service and was superseded by the new railway and river bridge crossing at Pakwach. This tremendous leap forward did not last long for the railway was plundered and destroyed by the guerrillas who took possession of the Murchison Falls Park after Idi Amin's downfall and so cut off the Alur from the rest of Uganda more completely than ever before.

Almost fifty years ago the few roads through West Nile had a good, reliable gravel surface, well maintained by gangs of labourers stationed every ten miles or so. This maintenance is no more, and the traffic, despite the conditions, is heavier. In 1992 the main road to the Alur highlands was almost impassable, incomparably worse than forty or even fifty years before.

If the Alur have been subjected to extreme physical isolation, they have also been grossly misrepresented and consequently discriminated against. They are of course, Northerners, and share in the derogatory image which the South imposes upon the North generally, but besides that they were misrepresented in several insulting and often dangerous ways. Their true ethnic status as Lwo was rarely understood, because within West Nile they were joined with the Sudanic Lugbara and Madi as well as the Eastern Nilotic Kakwa (related linguistically to the Bari, Lotuko and Maasai). This melange was so hard to cope with, for southern Ugandans and foreigners alike, that they came to be carelessly regarded as a single ethnic group: 'West Nilers'. This was greatly resented by the Alur Lwo, who could not understand any of the other languages spoken in the District, but recognized their close links to the Acoli Lwo across the Nile to the east. As most of the northern groups were Nilotic speakers in the broad sense, the North as a whole came to be seen as Nilotic.

During the violence and impoverishment which proliferated after the accession to power of Idi Amin in 1971 until the successful takeover by Yoweri Museveni in 1986, the different ethnic groups regarded as the main culprits in each successive stage of upheaval had to endure the obloquy of the rest of the population. When Amin deposed Obote, the hatreds his regime had aroused were visited upon his fellow Lango and, as they were Nilotic, the Alur shared in this. Idi Amin was born in Kakwa and was therefore a West Niler, so the Alur shared in the growing hatred for West Nilers as Amin's unpopularity grew. During the brief prominence of the Acoli, their unpopularity was inevitably shared by the Alur as they were often not distinguished from them, and when the Lango returned to prominence with Obote's second regime, the Alur were again implicated. So they have faced unfair opprobrium as well as neglect.

The drafting of Alur for military service in the two World Wars brutally exposed them to the worst features of Western civilization. Until 1914 they had had very little knowledge of the outside world. With their lives disrupted by the war experience, many Alur could not readjust to their earlier existence and took to wage labour away from home. Many more followed their example as time went on, as there were virtually no cash-earning opportunities in their own district, either through wages or cash crops. Their homeland was very fertile, but their traditional agriculture remained unchanged and the lack of transport as well as the distances involved discouraged development. Great efforts were made to recruit labour in West Nile, especially by the Asian-owned sugar plantations in eastern Buganda and Busoga. The Lugbara went there to work in large numbers, but the Alur resisted

recruitment and, instead, made arrangements with Baganda landowners as share croppers and stayed there growing cotton and foodstuffs.
They referred to this as 'going across to Uganda'. Their main area of
concentration was in what later became the infamous 'killing fields' of
the Luwero Triangle in the early 1980s, whereupon the Alur had to
flee for their lives. Thus the tenuous string of Alur settlement which
had begun to link their homeland with the capital district of the country was broken and their isolation further accentuated.

In Uganda, as elsewhere, material events are reflected by their occult
and spiritual counterparts. When I began to study Alur culture in the
1940s, I was told that the worst thing the colonialists had done was to
prevent the trial and execution of witches. I tended to discount this at
the time, but when I returned to continue my study in 1992, I could no
longer ignore witchcraft as a major element in people's lives and a
dominant factor in the situation. I was reluctant to reach conclusions
without the widest possible evidence. I collected essays from hundreds
of secondary school girls and boys and interviewed people from many
walks of life after the subject had become ubiquitous in conversation.
The views expressed showed very little variation. Witchcraft fears and
accusations are ubiquitous. When I asked a sophisticated Alur woman
university student if she had really experienced witchcraft, she said that
when she was at Warr Girls School she saw witches every night.

Anyone who achieves success or distinction in entrepreneurship,
education or any other field is a target, to the extent that, with a few
exceptions, all who reach any significant level of education are expected to, and usually do, leave Alurland and go down country. Alur in
Kampala confirm this and say that they are afraid of going home
because their children and even they themselves would fall ill and possibly die. People in Alurland who become victims of witchcraft accusations are driven away from home. They try to stay elsewhere with relatives, but their ill fame often follows them and they have to settle in
remote parts of the country, thus extending the area of agricultural
production, but most often in north Bunyoro, which before the sleeping sickness epidemic was the home of the Nilotic Palwo, a privileged
group within the Bunyoro state. This has now become Nilotic again
with the settlement of the Alur, to the point that the Banyoro no longer
regard this country as part of Bunyoro.

The total area of Alur occupation has thus acquired the shape of an
hour glass. One sphere is the Alur homeland in the northwest with the
adjacent parts of Bunyoro across the River Nile, the other is the capital
district around Kampala in the southeast, where hundreds of the more
highly qualified Alur now work, mostly men but a significant number of
women also, with their spouses and their families. The two spheres are
tenuously linked by the few Alur now settled and working in between.
The net flow, as in an hour-glass, is downwards, from northwest to
southeast. Only an industrial revolution, as one Kampala Alur professional put it, could reverse the flow, turning the hour-glass on its head.

Development at the grass roots

The West Nile District no longer exists. The administrative map of Uganda was revolutionized by Idi Amin, who decided to reduce the size of districts and multiply their number by two or three times. This had the fortunate result for the Alur that they received a district of their own for the first time, as they had long demanded. It was wisely decided not to allow ethnic names, so the district is called Nebbi District. With this new-found basis of solidarity, including the construction of a new district headquarters at Nebbi, with a small town growing up around it, the Alur in Kampala organized the Nebbi Community, whose constitution declares its membership open to all, but which is clearly in practice the Alur Association. Alur would certainly regard the Nebbi District and the Nebbi Community as some of the few positive signs of development in many years.

DEVELOPMENT EPISODES

Losing one's freedom and becoming a colony is dramatic enough, but otherwise the Alur experienced very slow change between the two World Wars. Local notables were made chiefs and customary courts were established. Roads were created and bicycles introduced, markets started and money came into general use. Christian missions converted significant numbers, many went to school for two years and a very few reached secondary level. Dispensaries were started, compulsory famine reserves of cassava were created, which began the dietary change from millet to cassava with adverse effects on food intake. Hunting game without licence was prohibited, considerably reducing the dietary protein. There were few shops and only one was run by an Alur. All this can equally be called 'establishing basic infrastructure' or 'capitalist penetration'.

After World War II the colonial administration gradually recovered and began to initiate changes. An attempt was made to bring coffee cultivation to the Alur highlands which could grow the valuable Arabica; unfortunately the scheme was accompanied by such inept coercive and punitive measures that the people refused to have anything to do with it and Arabica had to wait another ten years for successful introduction. This was a dramatic change as the highland Alur gradually gave up keeping cattle, on which they had depended for bridewealth, funerals, milk, meat and cash, and turned to the cultivation of Arabica coffee instead. Unfortunately, by the late 1980s the price fell so low and transport conditions were so bad, that many people gave up. But a good deal of coffee is still produced. During the Obote I years of high crop prices and high investment in agricultural development, a promising tea scheme was also established in the Alur highlands. Unfortunately again, it was abandoned during the troubled years that followed Amin's takeover, when all agricultural services gradually broke down. The Alur midlands and lowlands also produced cotton after World War II. During Obote I the ginnery at Pakwach was acquired and operated by the Alur cotton co-operative. There have been many problems of man-

258

agement and embezzlement in the co-operative, as there have also been in the coffee co-operative which runs the processing factory in the highlands, but they are still in operation. The overall picture of Alur economic development therefore remains very depressing. The unavailability of paid employment, the infrastructural barriers to export from the district, on top of the loss of the traditional male roles of hunting, fighting and deliberating, cause an excess of male leisure time, which is often filled by drinking. The traditional, nutritious beer is still brewed and drunk, but excessive male leisure creates non-traditional demand for commoditized liquor, supplying which provides women with one of their few extra income advantages. The liquor is distilled from maize beer by home-made devices. Family members may be drinking it as it drips warm from their womenfolk's still by nine o'clock in the morning. To accuse the Alur of alcoholism would be absurd. The capitalist mode of production has destroyed their traditional way of life and its appropriate values, and provided little in its place.

Social development is dominated by the collapse of the health and education budgets of the central government. The big hospitals also planned during the Obote I expansion to help the North catch up, as in the case of Nebbi hospital, are only half staffed and therefore lie also half empty. Isolation and impoverishment also spelt staff shortage and lack of supervision as well as general disrepair and almost total lack of books and stationery at the primary school level. By 1992 the secondary schools at Nyapea in the highlands, and Goli in the midlands, both seemed to be running efficiently and enthusiastically, with encouraging plans for further improvement. There are many fine educational leaders, women as well as men, who, necessarily in the dearth of middle-class professionals, play a prominent part in political as well as social and educational life. They are proud of their attainments and achievements and many carry on with heroic energy, but they feel abandoned and are greatly distressed by the undeniable deterioration of staff, salaries and facilities as a whole. They speak bravely of development in public, but in private they say with profound sadness 'We have gone backwards'.

In the field of local government a major experiment in democracy was made in the last years of the colonial regime throughout Uganda, in which West Nile and the Alur participated. It brought elections for district councillors close to the people and gave considerable financial power and responsibility to councils. In addition, all councils demanded ceremonial heads in imitation of the Kabaka of Buganda, just triumphantly returned from exile. This was interesting as stimulating an embryonic bridging of ethnic differences, because the ceremonial head of West Nile was chosen from each of the District's major ethnic groups in turn. The whole experiment of ceremonial heads, local government elections, major financial responsibility and all, was abolished under the Obote I regime. Like the rest of Uganda, the Alur had to wait twenty years for local-level democracy to be brought to Nebbi District by the new Resistance Council system. In 1992 I witnessed the elections to these councils at the five levels in Nebbi District. There was no doubt about the depth of interest generated. As a first exercise this was a great step forward and constitutes the most important element of positive development in recent years, including the constitution of the district itself. The system clearly gave general satisfaction although, as elsewhere, there were calls for secret balloting and for direct elections to a national parliament together with the legalization of political parties.

In the conferences held in connection with this series of books we have considered several districts (Bunyole, Rakai, Bushenyi, Toro, Moyo) as well as reviewing particular problems in wider geographical terms. Problems of development may be treated nationally, statistically and synchronically, also aspirationally and futuristically. Here I have attempted to complement these approaches with an account which highlights the developmental problems of a neglected periphery.

Map 3 *Administrative Divisions of Uganda after 1976*

TWENTY

Theatre for development:
empowering Ugandans to transform their condition

Rose Mbowa

Two concepts of development are important in African societies today. One is a matter of figures and infrastructures, gross national product, the growth of industries, and suchlike. It is the concern of most African governments, Uganda's included. To be sure, it is of vital significance. However, it does not cater for the attitudes and potential of the great mass of Uganda's people, who remain to a very considerable extent illiterate and poor. Enlightening such people about their problems, and empowering them to transform their condition, are every bit as much 'development' as externally measured economic policies.

Indeed, we must go further. The thinking and cultural attitudes of illiterate and quasi-literate rural and peri-urban populations in Uganda may be out of step with structural changes taking place in the wider society but, unless people's consciousness is awakened to this realization, no meaningful change can take place, certainly no meaningful change which is beneficial to them. The first concept of development is therefore inadequate unless it interacts meaningfully with another analytical framework influenced by, and itself influencing, popular perceptions.

This is what makes a second concept of development so important – the 'mobilization and transformation of men and women – a nation's most important resource – to become the makers, the subjects and the objects of their own lives and history' (Kimani, 1983: 25). This focuses attention upon the marginalized people of Uganda and the importance of their attitudes, because a mind which is culturally enslaved will perpetuate its condition of servitude without realizing that there are better things in life. Culture is dynamic, not static, in character. That realization is the only really effective way to start to deal with the father-in-law in Toro, western Uganda, whose mindset persuaded him to have sex with his daughter-in-law 'to test where the cattle went that were paid as the brideprice' (Breitinger, 1994: 23). In this age of HIV/AIDs he will doubtless continue living a life of risks to all concerned, unless he participates in a truly critical examination of his past and present behaviour and then modifies it in consequence.

No one but he himself can do that. And it will only happen when he has liberated his mind along the lines of the Jamaican reggae redemption song: 'Emancipate yourself from mental slavery/None but our-

261

selves can free our minds'. It was to this end that yet another revolutionary, the Brazilian Paulo Freire advocated the need for 'problem-solving education, which breaks with the vertical patterns of education. [For] through dialogue ... teacher [and] student become jointly responsible for a process in which all grow' (Freire, 1990: 58–9, 67).

Theatre for Development discursive practice, which arose in Africa in the second half of the 1970s, was deeply influenced both by Freire's problem-solving educational ideas and by Augusto Boal's poetics of the oppressed: a 'rehearsal for a revolution' whereby power is no longer delegated by any more powerful person 'to characters either to think or to act in his place, [but] he thinks and acts for himself' (Boal, 1974: 155). In Uganda, Theatre for Development has been really significant only since the accession to power of the National Resistance Movement.

Under the dictatorial regimes of Obote I, Idi Amin, Obote II and Tito Okello between 1966 and 1985, attempts by conventional theatre to rouse popular consciousness in the country were paralysed. A pioneer and veteran of Luganda drama and theatre, Wycliffe Kiyingi, was arrested along with the cast of his radio play *Wokulira*, when it was banned a year after Milton Obote's usurpation of presidential power in 1966–7. Further advance in plays masking meaning in symbolic or allusive forms suffered a setback when the playwright Byron Kawaddwa was murdered in 1977 for his exposure of Idi Amin's excesses in *Wankoko*. A culture of silence descended upon Uganda, as intellectuals who remained in the country retreated into other activities and others went into exile. Falling into the former category were Noah Sentongo and Elvannia Zirimu, into the latter Robert Sserumaga and John Ruganda. Continuing theatre in the Luganda language in Uganda devoted itself principally to domestic entertainment and farce.

However, since the accession of the National Resistance Movement to power in 1986, artists have enjoyed freedoms not previously experienced in post-independence Uganda. Furthermore, the NRM's promotion of self-help drives in the work of reconstruction, rehabilitation and development of people's torn moral, cultural, social, political and economic fibres has proved catalytic for the creative encouragement of a wide range of developmental activity in the country.

Before commenting upon innovative examples from Uganda, a few comments are necessary. First, on Theatre for Development in neighbouring African countries. There popular criticisms of oppressive structures of power have been a prominent feature. This has not been the case in Uganda, where there has been nothing like the Kaririithu Theatre Experience in Kenya, which the authorities suppressed (Ngugi wa Thiongo, 1987: 42–62), or the Msoga Popular Theatre's enforcement of its village leadership's accountability for funds in Tanzania.

Second, a brief comment on continuing conventional theatre in Uganda's capital city. In popular commercial theatre in Kampala, ticket prices ranging from Shs4000 upwards effectively exclude peasants and other poor people from being its beneficiaries in any meaningful sense. Yet history testifies that peasants and poor people are the prime movers in national revolutions, whatever the country. Despite castigations of corruption in plays like *Wounds of Africa* (1992), *Liz* (1989) or *The Inspector* (1991) by the contemporary playwrights Mukulu, Mukiibi and Ebonita, the phenomenon has increased in scope and in scale. Audiences for such plays, however hard-hitting their criticisms, tend to remain passive. The principal value dictated by the power of the metropolitan audience's pocket is the audience's enjoyment, not its commitment to change. However, to ignore the poor and to assert that 'Theatre is not for peasants who don't appreciate classical music . . . but therapy for the rich who pay to release their emotions', as Mukulu writes in *New Vision* of 24 February 1994, is tantamount to denying peasants their role as agents of development.

Consequently, it is perhaps not surprising that Theatre for Developments projects in Uganda have been inspired by external agents or by staff at Makerere University, by personnel in NGOs or, to a smaller degree, by representatives of central government battling against epidemic diseases. This may suggest to some that the agendas for Theatre for Development are predetermined. To some extent, this is true. However, the extent to which ordinary Ugandans have been involved in formulating plans of action for their own benefit has had an important impact on the comparative success of Theatre for Development projects in the country. The particular examples I have selected for comment are the Muganga Natyole Popular Theatre Project and the Lubombo Participatory AIDS Theatre. I also refer briefly to the Kabarole/Bundibugyo Basic Health Theatre because, in my view, it also supports this view.

The Natyole Popular Theatre project started in 1986 as a result of concern about disease and increased deaths locally on the part of a professional agricultural officer and nutritionist, Vicencia Serwadda. Natyole parish lies in the Luwero Triangle. Many people there were displaced by strife and terror by troops from other parts of Uganda during the last years of the Obote II regime. Following the NRM's victory in January 1986, over 2,000 local people returned to their village. However, a majority of them suffered from scabies, dysentery, hookworm, kwashiorkor, malnutrition and various immunizable diseases inflicted by the extremely harsh conditions of life experienced in the early 1980s. Worst hit of all were the children, many of whom were dying in the later 1980s. By this time most adults' immediate concerns were clearing bush to plant food crops and erecting housing shelters to ensure longer-term survival for their families. Jonathan Muganga (1990: 1) reports that Vicencia Serwadda initially hoped to combat health problems in Natyole village by opening a primary health care centre funded by the Catholic Secretariat of Uganda. Her initial target group were the women of the village. She hoped to persuade them to attend discussions with her, at which health problems might be tackled and solutions suggested. But her efforts came to nothing; and this was despite advertising discussion meetings in advance at churches and mosques and through primary schools. The basic problem was that men in the area regarded such discussion meetings as sources of evil gossip. They therefore barred their women from attending them. In this community, too, deaths were routinely attributed to witchcraft by ill-intentioned neighbours. Suspicions and tensions multiplied as a result of Serwadda's various suggestions and activities, initially for other reasons as well. Fortunately Muganga, a Ministry of Health official then taking a music and drama course at Makerere University, knew Serwadda personally. He offered to mobilize the community to more effective action through a popular theatre project. Thereby local people might be persuaded to take on 'an active role and responsibility in shaping their own living and development' (Muganga, 1990: 4).

The suggestion worked. Muganga obtained the co-operation of community leaders for this project – the Resistance Council 1 chairman, church leaders and the local headmaster. With Vicencia Serwadda and several primary schoolchildren, local people were attracted to the grounds of the village's Catholic Church by drumming and dancing. The drum is a powerful emitter of messages in Uganda. It is also a great source of entertainment throughout the country. When a sufficiently large group of people had assembled, Muganga started a discussion. By the end of the first day six women had committed themselves to the project with the full support of their husbands. Soon the number rose to 14. Shortly after that, a club was established with the following interests:-

(i)   identification of health and other problems;
(ii) prioritization of problems;
(iii) the causes of problems;
(iv) possible remedies; and
(v)   community activities.

Subsequent meetings of the club identified and prioritized the Natyole village community's problems as: malnutrition and kwashiorkor, six immunizable diseases currently causing many village children's deaths, diarrhoeal diseases, alcoholism among men and, needless to say, poverty. Already the first stages of articulating more effective development strategies had been reached. At subsequent meetings in Natyole parish on Saturday afternoons – all meetings took place on Saturday afternoons – each problem was discussed in turn, and a start was made at composing songs relating to them. Then, with Muganga's assistance, these songs were elaborated further and incorporated with other creative material into plays. These plays dealt with local people's problems and possible solutions. When ready, the plays were performed in the local church grounds for the whole village; this was after forthcoming plays had been advertised through the resistance committee, at church services and via the mosque. Through plays, the community was enabled to debate its problems publicly and to arrive at collectively agreed solutions. Some performances revealed bad feelings arising as a result of husbands diverting too much cash to alcohol. Other performances exposed local ignorance. Village men criticized in these plays 'laughed and blamed each other in a funny tone; they admitted false behaviour [was widespread] but nobody admitted that it was him. Then Muganga asked what could be done to solve the presented problem. Lively discussion got going. Barriers between the sexes had been broken' (Paul, 1990: 46). A number of husbands assisted their wives on performance days by putting up papyrus screens to ensure their privacy when changing their costumes between performances and in other ways. This was not just a women's project, but one for the community as a whole.

The play *Endisa* (food) dealt with a proper diet for children and the negative impact of superstition on existing food policies. The play evolved into a development project which provided food not only for the village but for neighbouring ones as well. Central to the play's plot was a child whose food all day was posho (maize bread) while its mother spent most of her time clearing land and planting future food crops. The child grew sick, its hair turned brown, and it became very weak. Father and mother suspected a neighbour was bewitching them. They took the child to a traditional healer who prescribed drugs which had no positive effect on the child. A woman leader suggested that the mother should attend the Women's Club where she would learn how to feed her child properly. The husband refused to allow his wife to go. However, when a second visit to the traditional healer produced no positive result, he allowed her to go. The mother attended the club, where the woman leader was demonstrating various foods for a balanced diet. The mother went home with a gift of one of the foods demonstrated and fed her child with it. To her pleasure and that of her husband, the child's health improved.

During community discussion after the performance, the people agreed to plant demonstration gardens at the church for all parishioners to see and to copy them on their own farms. This was done and Vicencia's work effectively became that of follow-up. Eventually, everybody in Natyole village had the right balanced diet and enough food to eat. Other problems, such as water or immunization, were dealt with in a similar fashion. Poultry and animals were introduced into the project and, through the same process of popular theatre composition, performance and group discussion, agreement was reached to form a co-operative society to mobilize and market surpluses from family farms to neighbouring villages. The problem of poverty was thus dealt with at least partly in the short term. As a result, more 'men also joined in, so that the group had to be divided and four months later three other groups existed' (Paul, 1990: 46). The Natyole Project therefore raised critical consciousness among villagers and helped in developing a more dynamic culture cutting across earlier internal divisions. Villagers were awakened to their potential and persuaded to think for themselves and to solve problems by themselves. They gained confidence as a result, and started reaching out to other villages. In a society where many people have come to expect others to solve their problems, this Theatre for Development project is proof of what Ugandan local communities can do for themselves. Theatre of the people, by the people and for the people, must belong to the people. External control distorts it, at worst destroys it. The Natyole Catholic parish priest's eventual claim to own the project and his blocking of attempts by the villagers to get into contact with other villages, brought it to an end.

The next project, the Lubombo Participatory AIDS Theatre, was held in April 1994 in Lubombo parish, Mukono district, 57 kilometres east of Kampala. While this project shares a lot of features with the Natyole project, there are also considerable differences. The Natyole Popular Theatre, because of its continuous period of operation without external restriction until the priest's interference, had been able to draw the whole community gradually into its activities. That was not possible in Lubombo because of the initiator's prescriptive action in limiting its duration and deciding on several of its main features.

Action Aid, a Kampala-based NGO, had asked for a Theatre for Development workshop in order to impart community mobilization skills to its two AIDS counsellors, Ms Robina Kigozi and Mr Ssatawa. This agenda was not entirely appropriate for Lubombo. It was the rainy season and the community's priority was to plant crops, the cultivation of which occupied most of them all day. Time to get to know the villagers beforehand had not been built into the specification for the project. However, for popular theatre to empower people, facilitators need to be in full solidarity with them. 'There seems to be no other better way than associating fully with them, meeting them in villages, joining in their daily chores and sharing with them their life styles' (Eyoh, 1986: 28).

As a consequence, each of the facilitators, Baron Oron, Milton Bakebwa, Julius Gizamba and myself, lived in the village from 21 to 27 April 1994. An approach involving the whole community in the workshop was agreed. The people decided on the time of the meeting, and the venue, and carried out mobilization activities, information gathering, prioritization of issues, analysis, creation of artistic forms by improvization, while accommodating communal intervention and discussion during rehearsals and the final community presentation when collective solutions to problems were suggested.

To start with, a local animators' workshop was held on the morning of 22 April only. This involved the Resistance Council chairman Mr Sentamu, the women's leader, Ms Esther Mhagama, a youth leader, the two volunteer AIDS councillors, the assistant medical officer from the local clinic, and a teacher. These were selected 'not because they wield power but because they had credible potential and were willing to participate and could be good examples to their village mates' (Bakebwa, 1994: 79).

266

Subsequently, every day at 2 pm, the facilitators opened the workshop by drumming and dancing at a local school, as agreed collectively by the Lubombo community. This, together with a few games like 'Touching colours', broke down barriers and generated greater cohesion in the research effort. For academics especially, it is important to tickle the local community's sensibilities until differences between researchers become socially insignificant.

The day's main business then really got under way at 3.30 pm, by which time many local people had gathered together. Brainstorming on the causes of the spread of HIV/AIDS now commenced. Further information was gathered by the outreach flooding method, animators and interested residents spreading out in pairs in different directions in the parish, interviewing people wherever they met them – in gardens, at trading centres, along roads, at home. This helped to mobilize the whole community and to promote ownership of the workshop throughout Lubombo village.

Open discussion and prioritization of issues under the chairmanship of Councillor Sekatawa then ensued in the tradition of Resistance Council meetings established throughout Uganda since 1986. 'For Popular Theatre to work effectively as a tool of critical awareness and empowerment for oppressed peoples it must be rooted and begin with their cultural strengths' (Dwight, 1988: 181). Priority problems identified were:

(i) the growing number of orphans (150 quoted by Kigozi);
(ii) drunkenness leading to indiscriminate sex (this was treated alongside (i) in community dramas as requested by the local people);
(iii) increasing numbers of migrants to the village suspected of being infected with AIDS;
(iv) cultural practices and other kinds of activities at night encouraging the spread of AIDS.

People then divided into groups to discuss particular problems in detail. About 70 people in all were involved in these study groups.

The next day theatrical work started in earnest. The artistic riches of the people were celebrated through songs and the creative exploitation of proverbial names and sayings (Bakebwa, 1994: 91). Unlike the plays performed as part of the Natyole Project, the Lubombo Theatre employed continuous interventions by members of the audience posing and solving problems within the framework of more loosely structured dramatic sketches. As a new issue was raised by one of the characters in the sketch, the character would put a question to the audience and seek its opinion on a possible solution to the problem. Invariably, critical discussion ensued. In this way everybody who attended the three days of rehearsals participated. All got involved in discussing their lives as they addressed the dilemmas and contradictions highlighted in the sketches.

One such was 'The Orphan Problem'. This drama started with a drunk man meeting a drunk woman on a road.

It is late at night and the two drunks dragged each other into the bushes. One shocked man who witnessed what was happening, asks whether this is indeed what really happens in his village. Audiences at each rehearsal indicated that women ran much greater risks than men in such couplings; that they should therefore drink more frequently at home than away from their homes; that men should drink more frequently at home; and that too many homes were poor because some men drank all day instead of doing any work.

In the next episode the man is seen at home with his wife. He has many children but cannot pay school fees for them. He goes out of the house to escape their demands at the same time as his concubine arrives with yet more children, thereby further increasing the burdens imposed upon his poor wife. The concubine is sick with AIDS and is never seen again. When the husband returns and demands sex with his wife, she proposes that they use a condom. The husband declares that he cannot do this. It is like trying to suck a sweet in a wrapper. (This difficulty was repeatedly identified as a problem by men at the workshop.) In response to the woman's pleas for help, audience reactions revealed widespread ignorance about condoms and the risks of unprotected sex. The audience also knew very little about counselling – 'the assembly therefore decided that condoms [should] be sold at places of convenience like disco places. A weekly education session was [also] to be held at subcounty headquarters' (Bakebwa, 1994: 93).

Previously, counsellors had held advice sessions at which nobody turned up. Now the situation changed dramatically. Local people were empowered to review their personal situations and to make important decisions for change; as a result, meetings with counsellors were much better attended. 'For the issue is not just to plant a tree because the government has passed a decree but more importantly because you now have a clear understanding of the reasoning behind the planting of the tree' (Warritay, 1992: 92). This was further confirmed by the decision regarding orphans.

When the two parents eventually die, a crowd of orphans surround the surviving grandmother who bemoans her fate. Here theatre reflects life. Next to Mrs Kigozi's home in Lubombo village there was an elderly grandmother living with 13 orphans and no help. This community-wide situation, hitherto accepted as God-ordained and inevitable, now comes under a sharp spotlight. In the ensuing community discussion, the suggestion that the orphans should go for the monthly ration of one kilo of rice and beans which a certain Lugazi-based organization was offering to orphans, was rejected as insufficient – it would not even last for one week in a month, remarks one villager. The community therefore resolved that 'The village was to support the helpless orphans by identifying an income-generating project whose proceeds would go to support vulnerable groups like the children, the sick and the elderly' (Bakebwa, 1994: 94). The dependency mentality had met with a cure at local level – a critically awakened awareness shaping responsible action and behaviour.

The community had more effectively than hitherto become its own legislature. Bakebwa (1994: 96–9) lists the solutions proposed for all the problems raised in the dramatic sketches and the various solutions to them collectively agreed during the final theatrical performance at Lubombo village on 27 April 1994. What comes out clearly is that some solutions are concrete and action-orientated, like the orphans' project, the banning of traditional funeral-night shelters which promote sexual promiscuity, and the ending of evening discos and prayer meetings by 6.30 pm at the latest. This fulfilled popular theatre's objective of moving people gradually into taking action themselves for the positive transformation of their lives. Other objectives, such as parents behaving as better role models for their children, could not be achieved so quickly or so concretely. However, this too is 'development', mental development decided after collective reflection – without which Ugandans were, and are, unlikely to solve problems for themselves.

Gizamba's follow-up in August 1994 revealed an increased take-up of condoms in the village. Nightly prayer meetings had ended. Discos continued, however, because several villagers who made their living by organizing them refused to stop them. This underlines the importance of follow-up and evaluation in Theatre for Development projects. As actions are assessed and reassessed, bottlenecks and contradictions can be identified and dealt with. For the orphans' project a committee of five, chaired by the RC1 chairman, was set up to develop a carefully thought-out money-producing project; this stage had not been reached during the Popular Theatre week itself. Subsequently, the committee was to table specific proposals to the community RC meeting. In Uganda nowadays, Resistance Councils (now known as Local Councils) have the same objectives as Theatre for Development projects in encouraging local people to become participants in change.

Externally-conceived development projects are also increasingly recognizing the importance of ordinary people's participation in shaping decisions regarding their own lives. The German Technical Cooperation-funded Basic Health Project in Kabarole and Bundibugyo Districts inspired community groups in Remi, Katooke, Kamwenge, Kiyombya and Nyanjetera villages, each composed of elderly women, men and young people. These community groups were empowered to create Popular Theatre plays for their respective villages. Each play drew upon the local cultural heritage and values. Each led to collective analysis of social problems and to the proposal of culturally persuasive solutions.

Ugandan women in particular have been increasingly enabled to liberate themselves from the status of dependants and to promote themselves to more meaningful roles as planners of their own livelihoods in recent years. This is what Theatre for Development is also about. In the context of the vast socio-economic challenges facing Uganda today, it is

269

imperative that popular theatre expands nationwide. Transforming peasants into planners, it has within it the capability of enlarging the popular constituency for change. It can reduce the burdens on an overstretched, limited national budget by encouraging and empowering ordinary people to make many local but strategic decisions for themselves. In sum, it provides a powerful facility for the development of the country, attractive to the central government as well as to local people.

Bibliography

Abeywickrama, K., 1993, 'Privatization in Developing Countries', *New Vision*, 5 and 12 November

Abid, Syed (ed.), 1990, *Uganda Women in Development*, Kampala

ACFODE, 1989, *Survey on Women's Problems and Needs*, Kampala

Adam, C., 1992, 'On the Dynamic Specification of Money Demand', *Journal of African Economies* 1

Adam, C., Ndulu, B. and Sowa, N., 1993, 'Efficiency Gains v. Revenue Losses: Liberalization and Seigniorage Revenue in Kenya, Ghana and Tanzania', Centre for Study of African Economies, Oxford (mimeo)

Alnwick, D., 1981, 'Nutritional Status of Young Children in the Poorer Parts of Kampala', Kampala

Amis, P., 1992, *Urban Management in Uganda: Survival under Stress*, University of Birmingham

Antrobus, P., 1989, 'The Empowerment of Women', *Women and International Development* 1: 189–207

APC, 1990, *Agro-Economic Study of Cotton Production*, Lint Marketing Board

Appleton, Simon, 1994, 'Changes in Poverty in Uganda, 1989–92: Comparing Household Surveys over Time', Paper for Structural Adjustment Forum Conference on Poverty and Adjustment, University of Nottingham, 8–9 July

ApT Development and Design, 1992, *Review of Government Policy as it Affects Small-Scale Enterprises*, Ministry of Planning and Economic Development, Kampala, March

Apter, David E., 1977, *The Political Kingdom in Uganda*, 3rd edn, London

Ardener, Edwin, 1971, 'Witchcraft, Economics and the Continuity of Relief' in Mary Douglas (ed.), *Witchcraft Confessions and Accusations*, London

Ardener, Edwin, 1989, *The Voice of Prophecy*, Oxford

Austen, Ralph A., 1993, 'The Moral Economy of Witchcraft: an Essay in Comparative History' in Comaroff and Comaroff (eds)

Bakebwa, T.M., 1994, 'Theatre for Development in Uganda', MA thesis, Makerere University

Bakunzi, Didas, 1992, 'FAD Denies Allegations', *New Vision*, 28 August

Baliwa, Betty, 1986, 'NRM to Launch Women Politicisation', *New Vision*, 9 October

271

Bibliography

Bardhan, Pranab, 1993, 'The State and the Market' in Arve Ofstad and Arne Wiig (eds), *Development Theory: Recent Trends*, Proceedings of the NFU Annual Conference 1992, Bergen

Barnett, Tony, 1994, 'The Effects of HIV/AIDS on Farming Systems and Rural Livelihoods in Uganda, Tanzania and Zambia' (mimeo)

Barnett, T. and Blaikie, P., 1992, *AIDS in Africa: Its Present and Future Impact*, London

Basirika, E., 1992, 'Structural Adjustment and Women in the Informal Sector: A Study of Market Women', Kampala (mimeo)

Baster, Nancy, 1984, 'Development Indicators: An Introduction' in Nancy Baster (ed.), *Measuring Development: The Role and Inadequacy of Development Indicators*, London

Bayart, J.-F., 1993, *Religion et Modernité Politique*, Paris

Becker, G., 1981, *A Treatise on the Family*, Cambridge, MA

Behrend, H., 1992, 'Violence dans le nord de l'Ouganda. Le mouvement du Saint-Esprit (1986–1987), *Politique Africaine* 48

Behrend, H., 1993, *Alice und die Geister. Krieg im Norden Ugandas*, Munich

Bevan, D.L., Collier, P. and Gunning, J.W., 1989, *Peasants and Governments: An Economic Analysis*, Oxford

Bevan, D.L., Collier, P. and Gunning, J.W., 1992, 'Anatomy of a Temporary Trade Shock: The Kenyan Coffee Boom of 1976–79', *Journal of African Economies* 1

Bibangambah, J., 1992, 'Macro-Level Constraints and the Growth of the Informal Sector in Uganda' in R. Baker and J. Pedersen (eds), *The Rural-Urban Interface in Africa*, Uppsala

Bienen, Henry and Waterbury, John, 1989, 'The Political Economy of Privatization in Developing Countries', *World Development* 17 (5)

Bigsten, A. and Kayizzi-Mugerwa, S., 1992, 'Adaptation and Distress in the Urban Economy: A Study of Kampala Households', *World Development* 20: 1423–41

Bigsten, A. and Kayizzi-Mugerwa, S., 1994, 'Adaptation and Distress in the African Economy: A Study of Retrenchment and Reform in Uganda', Unit for Development Economics, University of Gothenberg

Binsbergen, W.M.J.van, 1981, *Religious Change in Zambia*, London

Boal, Augusto, 1974, *Theatre of the Oppressed*, London

Bok, Sissela, 1994, 'Population and Ethics: Expanding the Moral Space' in Sen et al. (eds)

Boyd, Rosalind, 1989, 'Empowerment of Women in Uganda: Real or Symbolic?', *Review of African Political Economy* 45/46

Brandt, J., 1987, 'Appraisal of Uganda' (mimeo)

Bratton, Michael, 1989, 'Beyond the State: Civil Society and Associational Life in Africa', *World Politics* 41 (3)

Bratton, Michael, 1990, 'Enabling the Voluntary Sector in Africa: The Policy Context' in *African Governance in the 1990s: Objectives, Resources and Constraints*. Working Papers from the 2nd Annual Seminar of the African Governance Program, Ebury University, Atlanta, GA, 23–5 March

Bibliography

Bratton, M. and van de Walle, N., 1992, 'Popular Unrest and Political Reform in Africa', *Comparative Politics*, 419–42

Breitinger, Eckhard, 1992, 'Popular Urban Theatre in Uganda: Between Self-help and Enrichment', *New Theatre Quarterly* 31, August

Breitinger, Eckhard (ed.), 1994, *Theatre and Political Mobilization: Case Studies from Uganda*, Harare

Brett, E.A., 1991, 'Rebuilding Survival Structures for the Ugandan Poor: Organisational Options for Reconstruction and Development in the 1990s' in Hansen and Twaddle (eds)

Brett, E.A., 1993a, 'Voluntary Agencies as Development Organizations: Theorizing the Problem of Efficiency and Accountability', *Development and Change* 24: 269–303

Brett, E.A., 1993b, *Providing for the Rural Poor: Institutional Decay and Transformation in Uganda*, IDS Research Report 23, Brighton, Sussex

Brett, E.A., 1994a, 'The Military and Democratic Transition in Uganda' in Hansen and Twaddle (eds)

Brett, E.A., 1994b, 'Rebuilding Organisational Capacity in Uganda under the National Resistance Movement', *Journal of Modern African Studies* 32 (1)

Brown, L.David and Korten, David C., 1991, 'Working Effectively with Nongovernmental Organizations' in Samuel Paul and Arturo Israel (eds), *Nongovernmental Organizations and the World Bank: Cooperation for Development*, Washington, DC

Burack, C., 1988/89, 'Bringing Women's Studies to Political Science: The Handmaid in the Classroom', *NWSA Journal* 1 (2)

Burger, K., Collier, P. and Gunning, J.W., 1993, 'Social Learning: an Application to Kenyan Agriculture', CSAE, Oxford (mimeo)

Burkey, I., 1991, 'People's Power in Theory and Practice: The Resistance Council System in Uganda' (mimeo)

Byanyima, K.W., 1992, 'Women in Political Struggle in Uganda' in Bystydzienski (ed.)

Bystydzienski, J. (ed.), 1992, *Women Transforming Politics: Worldwide Strategies for Empowerment*, Bloomington, IN

Chazan, Naomi, 1992, 'Africa's Democratic Challenge: Strengthening Civil Society', *World Political Journal* 9 (2)

Chew, D., 1990, 'Internal Adjustments to Falling Civil Service Salaries: Insights from Uganda', *International Labour Review* (Geneva) 18

Collier, P., 1994, 'Demobilisation and Insecurity: a Study in the Economics of the Transition from War to Peace', *Journal of International Development* 6: 343–51

Collier, P. and Gunning, J.W., 1995, 'War, Peace and Private Portfolios', *World Development* 23: 233–41

Comaroff, Jean and Comaroff, John (eds), 1993, *Modernity and its Malcontents: Ritual and Power in Postcolonial Africa*, Chicago

de Coninck, John (with additional material by Roger C. Riddell), 1992, *Evaluating the Impact of NGOs in Rural Poverty Alleviation: Uganda Country Study*, ODI Working Paper 51, London

Bibliography

Cornea, G., 1993, *The Invisible Epidemic: The Story of Women and AIDS*, New York

Cotton, D.J., 1994, *Pediatric AIDS: The Challenge of HIV Infection in Infants, Children and Adolescents*, Baltimore, MD.

Ddungu, Expedit, 1989, *Popular Forms and the Question of Democracy: The Case of Resistance Councils in Uganda*, Kampala

Ddungu, Expedit and Wabwire, Arnest, 1991, *Electoral Mechanisms and the Democratic Process: The 1989 RC-NRC Elections*, Kampala

Delumeau, J., 1983, *Le peche et la peur*, Paris

DENIVA, 1990, *A Directory of Non-Governmental Organisations in Uganda*, Kampala

Diamond, L., 1994, 'Rethinking Civil Society: Towards Democratic Consolidation', *Journal of Democracy* 5 (3)

Dicklich, Susan, 1993, 'The Feasibility of Multiparty Democracy in Uganda', Paper presented at 36th Annual African Studies Association Meeting, Boston, MA, 4–7 December

Dicklich, Susan, 1994, 'Indigenous NGOs and Political Transformation in Uganda: 1986–1994', Ph.D. dissertation, University of Toronto

Divestiture Secretariat, 1994, 'Review of the Divestiture Programme', Internal Memorandum, Ref. Mc/bm/WBA/DE MEMOIRE 3/94, 25 March

Dodge, Cole and Wiebe, Paul D. (eds), 1985, *Crisis in Uganda*, Oxford

Doornbos, M., 1978, *Not All the King's Men: Inequality as a Political Instrument in Ankole, Uganda*, The Hague

Dwight, C., 1988, 'Health Theatre . . . Performance, Communication and Culture', *Journal of Performance Studies*, Fall

Ecumenical Coalition for Economic Justice, 1990, *Recolonisation or Liberation: The Bonds of Structural Adjustment and Struggles for Emancipation*, Toronto

Edmonds, Keith, 1988, 'Crisis Management: the Lessons for Africa from Obote's Second Term' in Hansen and Twaddle (eds)

Efange, P.M. and Balogun, M.J., 1989, 'Economic Crisis, Organisation, Structure of Government for Recovery and Development: A Comparative Review of Experiences and New Perspectives' in G. Mutahaba and M.J. Balogun (eds), *Economic Restructuring and African Public Administration: Issues, Actions and Future Choices*, Hartford, CT

Elwert, G., 1984, ' Conflicts Inside and Outside the Household' in Joan Smith, Immanuel Wallerstein and Hans-Dieter Evers (eds), *Households and the World Economy*, London

Ensminger, J., 1992, *Making a Market: the Institutional Transformation of an African Society*, Cambridge

Evans, A., 1993, *Rural Labour Arrangements in Uganda*, Washington, DC

Eyoh, N., 1986, 'Hammocks to Bridges', Yaoundé (mimeo)

Fabian, Johannes, 1978, 'Popular Culture in Africa', *Africa* 48: 315–34

Fisiy, C.F. and Geschiere, P., 1990, 'Judges and Witches, or How is the State to Deal with Witchcraft?', *Cahiers d'Etudes Africaines* 18

Bibliography

Fortes, Meyer, 1969, *Kinship and the Social Order. The Legacy of Lewis Henry Morgan*, London

Freeman, D., 1991, *A City of Farmers: Informal Urban Agriculture in the Open Spaces of Nairobi, Kenya*, Toronto

Freire, Paulo, 1990, *Pedagogy of the Oppressed*

Fukuyama, F., 1994, 'The Mystery Deepens: The Persistence and Fragility of Civil Society', *Times Literary Supplement*, 28 October

Gartrell, Beverley, 1988, 'Prelude to Disaster: the Case of Karamoja' in Douglas Johnson and David Anderson (eds), *The Ecology of Survival*, Boulder, CO

Geist, J., 1994, 'Political Significance of the Constituent Assembly Elections' in Hansen and Twaddle (eds)

Gertzel, C., 1988, *The Politics of Uneven Development: The Case of Obote's Uganda*, Flinders University, Adelaide

Ghai, Y.P., 1993, 'Constitutions and Governance in Africa: A Prolegomenon' in S. Adelman and A. Paliwala (eds), *Law and Crisis in the Third World*, London

Ghai, Y.P., 1995, *Human Rights and Governance: The Asia Debate*, San Francisco

Ghai, Y.P. and Regan, A.J., 1992, *The Law, Politics and Administration of Decentralization in Papua New Guinea*. Port Moresby

GTZ/Dept. of Physical Planning, 1992, 'City of Kampala: Revision of Structure Plan', Kampala

Guwatudde, C., 1991, *The Role of the Ministry of Women in Development: Its Functions, Structure and On-going Programmes*, Kampala

Hansen, H.B., 1984, *Mission, Church and State in a Colonial Setting: Uganda 1890–1925*, London

Hansen, H.B. and Twaddle, M. (eds), 1988, *Uganda Now: Between Decay and Development*, London

Hansen, H.B. and Twaddle, M. (eds), 1991, *Changing Uganda: the Dilemmas of Structural Adjustment and Revolutionary Change*, London

Hansen, H.B. and Twaddle, M. (eds), 1994, *From Chaos to Order: the Politics of Constitution-making in Uganda*, London

Hansen, H.B. and Twaddle, M. (eds), 1995, *Religion and Politics in East Africa: the Period since Independence*, London

Hayward, Fred M., 1973, 'Political Participation and its Role in Development: Some Observations Drawn from the African Context', *Journal of Developing Areas* 7 (4)

Hazlewood, A., 1975, *Economic Integration, the East African Experience*, London

Herbst, J., 1990, 'War and the State in Africa', *International Security* 14 (4)

Hyden, Goran, 1994, 'Political Representation and the Future of Uganda' in Hansen and Twaddle (eds)

Hyden, Goran and Bratton, Michael (eds), 1992, *Governance and Politics in Africa*, Boulder, CO

Jackson, Michael, 1982, *Allegories of the Wilderness. Ethics and Ambiguity in Kuranko Narratives*, Bloomington, IN

Bibliography

Jackson, Robert H. and Rosberg, Carl G., 1982, *Personal Rule in Africa*, Berkeley, CA

Jaensen, Carol et al, 1984, *The Uganda Social and Institutional Profile (SIP) for USAID*, Kampala, August

Jamal, Vali, 1976a, 'Asians in Uganda, 1880–1072: Inequality and Expulsion', *Economic History Review* 19 (4)

Jamal, Vali, 1976b, 'The Role of Cotton and Coffee in Uganda's Economic Development', Ph.D. dissertation, Stanford University, CA

Jamal, Vali, 1978, 'Taxation and Inequality in Uganda, 1900–1964', *Journal of Economic History* 38 (2)

Jamal, Vali, 1985, *Structural Adjustment and Food Security in Uganda*, World Employment Programme research working paper, Geneva

Jamal, Vali, 1988, 'Coping under Crisis', *International Labour Review* (Geneva) 128 (6)

Jamal, Vali, 1991, 'The Agrarian Context of the Ugandan Crisis' in Hansen and Twaddle (eds)

Jamal, Vali and Weeks, John, 1993, *Africa Misunderstood, or Whatever Happened to the Rural-Urban Gap?*, London

Jeffries, R., 1993, 'The State, Structural Adjustment and Good Government in Africa', *Journal of Commonwealth and Comparative Politics* 31: 20–35

Joseph, Richard, 1989, *Democracy and Prebendalism in Nigeria*, Cambridge and New York

Kabeer, N., 1994, *Reversed Realities: Gender Hierarchies in Development Thought*, London

Kabukaire, Sarah Catherine, 1992, 'The Development of Women's Organisations in Kamuli District', MA thesis, Makerere University

Kadama, P.Y., 1994, 'A Healthy Peace? Post-conflict Rehabilitation in Uganda', Paper presented at health workshop, Child Health Development Centre, Kampala, 9 February

Kajubi, W. Senteza, 1991, 'Educational Reform during Socio-economic Crisis' in Hansen and Twaddle (eds)

Kasfir, N., 1991, 'The Uganda Elections of 1989: Power, Populism and Democratization' in Hansen and Twaddle (eds)

Kasfir, N., 1993, 'Strategies of Accumulation and Civil Society in Bushenyi, Uganda: How Dairy Farmers Responded to a Weakened State' in J. Harbeson et al., *Civil Society and the State in Africa*, Boulder, CO

Kasfir, N., 1994, 'Ugandan Politics and the Constituent Assembly Elections of March 1994' in Hansen and Twaddle (eds)

Kasozi, Abdu, 1986, *The Spread of Islam in Uganda*, Nairobi

Kimani, C., 1983, 'A Theatre for Development in Zimbabwe', *Africa Report* 25 (6)

King, Timothy (ed.), 1974, *Population Policies and Economic Development*, Baltimore, MD

Kingman, Sharon, 1991, 'Epidemic Threatens Food Supply in Africa', *Science and AIDS* (Daily conference bulletin of VIIth International Conference on AIDS), Florence

Bibliography

Kisamba-Mugerwa, W., 1991a, *Rangelands, Tenure and Resource Management: An Overview of Pastoralism in Uganda*, Kampala

Kisamba-Mugerwa, W., 1991b, 'Institutional Dimensions of Land Tenure Reform' in Hansen and Twaddle (eds)

Kittsteiner, H.D., 1987, 'Das Gewissen im Gewitter', *Jahrbuch für Volkskunde* 10

Korten, David C., 1990, *Getting to the Twenty-first Century: Voluntary Action and the Global Agenda*, Westford, CT

Korten, David C., 1991, 'The Role of Non-governmental Organisations in Development: Changing Patterns and Perspectives' in Samuel Paul and Arturo Israel (eds), *Nongovernmental Organizations and the World Bank: Cooperation for Development*, Washington, DC

Kriger, N., 1988, 'The Zimbabwean War of Liberation', *Journal of Southern African Studies* 14 (2)

Kriger, N., 1992, *Zimbabwe's Guerrilla War*, Cambridge

Kwesiga, J.B. and Ratter, A.J., 1993, *Realizing the Development Potential of NGOs and Community Groups in Uganda*, Kampala

Ladefoged, P., 1971, *Language in Uganda*, Nairobi

Laker-Ojok, R., 1992, 'The Rate of Return to Agricultural Research in Uganda: the Case of Oil Seeds and Maize', Dept. of Agricultural Economics, Michigan State University (mimeo)

Lan, D., 1987, *Guns and Rain*, London

Lateef, K. Sarwar, 1991, 'Structural Adjustment in Uganda: The Initial Experience' in Hansen and Twaddle (eds)

Leys, Colin, 1975, 'The Over-developed Post-colonial state: A Re-evaluation', *Review of African Political Economy* 5: 39-48

Livingstone, I., 1986, 'International Transport Costs and Industrial Development in the Least Developed African Countries', *Industry and Development* 19, October

Löffler, I., 1983, 'Hexen, Staat und Religion', *Peripherie* 12

Long, Norman, 1992, 'From Paradigm Lost to Paradigm Regained? The Case for an Actor-oriented Sociology of Development' in Norman Long and Ann Long (eds), *Battlefields of Knowledge. The Interlocking of Theory and Practice in Social Research and Development*, London

Low, D.A., 1971, *Buganda in Modern History*, London

Low, D.A., 1991, *Eclipse of Empire*, Cambridge

Lowith, K., 1953, *Weltgeschichte und Heilsgeschehen*, Stuttgart

Loxley, J., 1989, 'The IMF, the World Bank and Reconstruction in Uganda' in J. Campbell and B. Loxley (eds), *Structural Adjustment in Africa*, New York

Macrae, Joanne, Zwi, Anthony and Birungi, Harriet, 1993, 'A Healthy Peace? Rehabilitation and Development of the Health Sector in a Post-conflict Situation – the Case of Uganda', Report of a London School of Hygiene and Tropical Medicine pilot study, London

Mair, L.P., 1940, *Marriage in Buganda*, London

Bibliography

Makara, Sabiti, 1992, 'The Dynamics of Political and Administrative Change in Uganda: The Role of Resistance Councils and Committees in Promoting Democracy in Uganda', Makerere University.

Makerere Institute of Social Research and Land Tenure Center, 1989, 'Land Tenure and Agricultural Development in Uganda', Makerere University

Makerere Institute of Social Research and Land Tenure Center, 1993, 'Dynamics of the Land Market and the Issue of Compensation in Uganda', Makerere University

Mamdani, M., 1975, 'Class Struggles in Uganda', *Review of African Political Economy* 4

Mamdani, M., 1982, 'Karamoja: Colonial Roots of Famine in North East Uganda', *Review of African Political Economy* 25

Mamdani, M., 1988a, 'Democracy in Today's Uganda', *New Vision*, 16 March

Mamdani, M., 1988b, 'Uganda in Transition: Two Years of the NRA/NRM', *Third World Quarterly* 10 (3)

Mamdani, M., 1988c, 'State and Civil Society in Contemporary Africa: Reconceptualising the Birth of State Nationalism and the Defeat of Popular Movements', Paper presented to General Assembly of CODESRIA, Dakar, December (mimeo)

Mamdani, M., 1990, 'Uganda: Contradictions of the IMF Programme and Perspectives', *Development and Change* 21: 427–67

Mamdani, M., 1993a, 'Movement or Parties: Which Way Uganda?', *New Vision*, 16 February

Mamdani, M. 1993b, *Pluralism and the Right of Association*, Kampala

Mamdani, M., 1994a, 'NRM Attempts at Democratic Reform', *New Vision*, 17 February

Mamdani, M., 1994b, 'Africa was Highly Decentralised', Text of remarks made as discussant in response to President's Address on 'Political Systems and Separation of Powers' at Uganda Think Tank Foundation Seminar, 13 December, *New Vision*, 20 December

Mamdani, M., 1995, 'The Politics of Democratic Reform in Uganda' in J. Katorobo et al. (eds), *Uganda: Landmarks in Rebuilding a Nation*, Kampala

Matembe, Miria R.-K., 1993, 'NGO-Government Relationships in Africa' in Richard Sandbrook and Mohamed Halfani (eds), *Empowering People: Building Community, Civil Associations and Legality in Africa*, Toronto

Maxwell, Daniel, 1993, 'Land Access and Household Logic: Urban Farming in Kampala', Kampala

Maxwell, Daniel, 1994, 'Unplanned Responses to the Economic Crisis: Urban Farming in Kampala', Paper prepared for workshop on 'Developing Uganda', Denmark

Maxwell, D. and Zziwa, Samuel, 1992, *Urban Farming in Africa: The Case of Kampala, Uganda*, Nairobi

278

Bibliography

Mazrui, Ali, 1991, 'Privatization versus the Market: Cultural Contradictions in Structural Adjustment' in Hansen and Twaddle (eds)

Mbowa, Rose, 1994a, 'Artists under Siege: Theatre and Dictatorial Regimes in Uganda' in Breitinger (ed.)

Mbowa, Rose, 1994b, *Theatre and Performance in Africa*, Bayreuth Series 31

Meillassoux, C., 1993, 'A bas le développement!', *Cahiers des Sciences Humaines* (hors série)

Meir, M. Gerald, 1989, *Leading Issues in Economic Development*, 5th edn, New York

MFEP, 1992a, *Background to the Budget, 1992/93*, Kampala

MFEP, 1992b, *The Way Forward IV: Priorities for Social Services Sector Development in the 1990s*, Kampala, 5 June

MFEP, 1993, *National Household Budget Survey 1989/90*, Entebbe

Midgley, James, 1986, 'Community Participation: History, Concepts and Controversies' in James Midgley (ed.), *Community Participation, Social Development and the State*, London and New York

Miller, Norman N., 1971a, 'The Politics of Population', *American Universities Field Staff Reports*, East Africa Series 10

Miller, Norman N., 1971b, 'The Dynamics of Population in Uganda', *American Universities Field Staff Reports*, East Africa Series 10

Mingione, E., 1991, *Fragmented Societies: A Sociology of Economic Life Beyond the Market Paradigm*, Oxford

Ministry of Education, 1990, *Educational Census Results*, Kampala

Ministry of Health, 1989, *The Uganda Demographic and Health Survey 1988/1989*, Kampala

Morris, H.F. and Read, J.S., 1966, *Uganda: The Development of its Laws and Constitutions*, London

Mosley, Paul, Harrigan, Jane and Toye, John, 1995, *Aid and Power: The World Bank and Policy-based Lending*, 2nd edn, London

MPED, 1965, *The Patterns of Income, Expenditure and Consumption of African Unskilled Workers in Kampala*, Kampala, February

MPED, 1970, *Background to the Budget, 1970–71*, Kampala

MPED, 1982a, *Background to the Budget, 1982–83*, Kampala

MPED, 1982b, *Provisional Results of 1980 Population Census*, Entebbe

MPED, 1989, *Manpower and Employment in Uganda, National Manpower Survey*, MPED, Kampala

MPED, 1990, *The Household Budget Survey*, Kampala

MPED, 1991, *Report on the Uganda National Household Budget Survey 1989/90*, Kampala

MPED, 1992a, *Consumer Price Index, Kampala*, Kampala, March

MPED, 1992b, *Key Economic Indicators*, Kampala, April

MPED, 1992c, *Provisional Results, 1991 Population Census*, Entebbe

Mudimbe, V.Y., 1988, *The Invention of Africa*, Bloomington, IN and London

Mudoola, Dan M., 1991, 'Institution-building: the Case of the NRM and the Military in Uganda 1986–9' in Hansen and Twaddle (eds)

Bibliography

Muganga, Jonathan, 1990, 'Theatre for Development in Uganda: The Natyole Experience', Ministry of Health, Kampala (mimeo)

Mugira, James, 1991, 'The Non-governmental Organizations Registration Statute 1989: Realities Behind the Legal Facade', Makerere University

Mugisha, R., 1992, *Emergent Changes and Trends in Land Tenure and Land Use in Kabale and Kisoro Districts*, Kampala

Mukama, Ruth G., 1991, 'Recent Developments in the Language Situation and Prospects for the Future' in Hansen and Twaddle (eds)

Mukholi, D., 1995, *A Complete Guide to Uganda's Fourth Constitution*, Kampala

Mukulu, Alex, 1993, 'Does Theatre for Development Really Exist?', *New Vision*, 24 April

Mulyampiti, Tabitha, 1993, 'Political Empowerment of Women in Contemporary Uganda: Impact of Resistance Councils and Committees (A Summary Report)', MA thesis, Makerere University

Murphy, John D., 1972, *Luganda – English Dictionary*, Washington, DC

Museveni, Y., 1985, *Ten-Point Programme of the National Resistance Movement*, Kampala

Museveni, Y., 1992, 'What Is Africa's Problem?', Kampala

Mutibwa, Phares, 1992, *Uganda Since Independence*, London

Mvena, Z., Lupanga, I. and Mlozi, M., 1991, *Urban Agriculture in Tanzania: A Study of Six Towns*, Morogoro

Mwaka, V., 1993, 'The Relationship Between Personal Profiles of Women in Top Management in Uganda and their Access to Top Management Positions', Seminar paper, Kampala

National Council of Women, 1991, 'Directory of Women's Groups in Uganda: Results of a Survey Conducted under the UNDP/NCW/NGO Project "Partners in Development"', Kampala

Ndongko, A.W., 1991, 'Commercialization as an Alternative to Privatization: Problems and Prospects', *Africa Development* 3/4.

Nellis, J. and Kikeri, S., 1989, 'Public Enterprises Reform: Privatization and the World Bank', *World Development* 17 (5)

Nerfin, Marc, 1987, 'Neither Prince nor Merchant Citizen?', *Development Dialogue* 1: 170–95

Nkwenge, Lillian, 1992, 'Activists Urged to Foster Peace', *New Vision*, 5 May

North, D.C., 1990, *Institutions, Institutional Change and Economic Performance*, Cambridge

NRM, 1990, *Mission to Freedom. Uganda Resistance News 1981–86*, Kampala

NRM, 1991, *Uganda 1986–1991. An Illustrated Review*, Kampala

Nsibambi, A., 1993, 'Decentralization of Power in Uganda', Makerere University (mimeo)

Nyhart, D., 1959, 'The Uganda Development Corporation and Agriculture', *East African Economic Review*, December

Bibliography

Nyinya-Mijinya, 1989, 'The African Mind', *Journal of Religion and Philosophy in Africa* 1 (1)

Obbo, Christine, 1980, *African Women: Their Struggle for Economic Independence*, London

Obbo, Christine, 1988, 'Is AIDS a New Disease?' in R.R. Kuldstad (ed.), *AIDS*, Washington, DC

Obbo, Christine, 1991, 'Women, Children and a "Living Wage"' in Hansen and Twaddle (eds)

Obbo, Christine, 1992, *Kampala Health Needs, Demands and Resources*, Kampala

Obbo, Christine, 1993, 'HIV Transmission: Men Are the Solution', *Population and Environment* 4 (3), January

Ocaya-Lakidi, D., 1989, 'From Local Governments to Mere Local Administration, 1949–1972' in G.N. Uzoigwe (ed.), *Uganda: The Dilemma of Nationhood*, New York

Oehmke, J.F. and Crawford, E.W., 1993, 'The Impact of Agricultural Technology in Sub-Saharan Agriculture', Dept. of Agricultural Economics, Michigan State University (mimeo)

Okoth Ogendo, H.W.O., 1993, 'The African Convention on Human and Peoples' Rights: What Point is Africa Trying to Make?' in Ronald Cohen, Goran Hyden and Winston Nagan (eds), *Human Rights and Governance in Africa*, Gainsville, FL

Oloka-Onyango, J., 1989, 'Law, "Grassroots Democracy" and the National Resistance Movement in Uganda', *International Journal of the Sociology of Law* 17: 465–80

Onyach-Olaa, M., 1992, 'Privatization: Myths and Realities in the Uganda Context', Paper delivered at the Uganda Economics Association, September

Ottemoeller, Daniel J., 1996, 'Institutionalization and Democratization: The Case of Ugandan Resistance Councils', Ph.D. dissertation, University of Florida

Over, M. and Piot, P., 1992, 'HIV Infection and Sexually Transmitted Diseases' in D. Jamison and H.Mosely (eds), *Disease Control Priorities in Developing Countries*, New York

Panos dossier, 1990, *Triple Jeopardy: Women and AIDS*, London

Paul, Samuel, 1991, 'Nongovernmental Organizations and the World Bank: An Overview', in Samuel Paul and Arturo Israel (eds), *Nongovernmental Organizations and the World Bank: Cooperation for Development*, Washington,DC

Paul, T.A., 1990, *Tugende Kampala*, Berlin

Peel, J.D.Y., 1978, '*Olaju*: a Yoruba Concept of Development', *Journal of Development Studies* 14: 139–65

PERDS, 1993, *Public Enterprise Survey for Uganda*, Kampala

Pinstrup-Andersen, P., 1989, 'The Impact of Macroeconomic Adjustment: Food Security and Nutrition' in S. Commander (ed.), *Structural Adjustment and Agriculture: Theory and Practice in Africa and Latin America*, London

281

Bibliography

Rakodi, C., 1988, 'Urban Agriculture: Research Questions and the Zambian Evidence', *Journal of Modern African Studies* 26: 495- 515

Rakodi, C., 1991, 'Women's Work or Household Strategies?', *Environment and Urbanization* 3: 39–45

Ramchandani, R.R., 1976, *Uganda Asians*, Bombay.

Randall, V., 1987, *Women and Politics: An International Perspective*, Chicago

Ranger, T., 1992, 'War, Violence and Healing in Zimbabwe', *Journal of Southern African Studies* 18

Regan, A.J., 1995a, 'The Politics of the Provincial Government System' in R.J. May and A.J. Regan (eds), *Political Decentralization in a New State: The Experience of Papua New Guinea*, Bathurst

Regan, A.J., 1995b, 'Constitutional Reform and the Politics of the Constitution in Uganda: A New Path to Constitutionalism' in E. Brett et al. (eds), *Uganda: Landmarks in Rebuilding a Nation*, Kampala

Roesch, O., 1992, 'RENAMO and the Peasantry in Southern Mozambique', *Canadian Journal of Africa Studies* 16 (3)

Rondinelli, D.A., Nellis, J.R. and Cheema, G.S., 1983, *Decentralisation in Developing Countries: A Review of Recent Experience*, Washington,DC

Rugasira, A.M., 1995, 'Privatization: Must Everything Go?', *National Analyst*, 7 September

Rutaagi, R.K., 1993, 'Privatization, the Best Way Forward for Economic Recovery', Paper delivered at Workshop on Structural Adjustment Programmes: Causes, Purpose and Problems organized by the Foundation for African Development in Kampala, 29–30 September

Sandbrook, Richard, 1993, 'Introduction' in Richard Sandbrook and Mohamed Halfani (eds), *Empowering People: Building Community, Civil Associations and Legality in Africa*, Toronto

Sanyal, B., 1985, 'Urban Agriculture: Who Cultivates and Why?', *Food and Nutrition Bulletin* 8: 15–24

Saul, John, 1975, 'The Unsteady State: Uganda, Obote and General Amin', *Review of African Political Economy* 5: 12–36

Sawio, C., 1993, 'Feeding the Urban Masses? Towards an Understanding of the Dynamics of Urban Agriculture in Dar es Salaam, Tanzania', Ph.D. dissertation, Clark University, MA

Scheyer, Stanley and Dunlop, David, 1985, 'Health Services and Development in Uganda' in Dodge and Wiebe (eds)

Seers, Dudley, 1984, 'What Are We Trying to Measure?' in Nancy Baster (ed.), *Measuring Development: The Role and Adequacy of Development Indicators*, London

Sen, G., Germain, A. and Chen, L.C. (eds), 1994, *Population Policies Reconsidered: Health, Empowerment and Rights*, Boston, MA

Southall, Aidan, 1956, *Alur Society: A Study in Processes and Types of Domination*, Cambridge

Southall, Aidan, 1988, 'The Recent Political Economy of Uganda' in Hansen and Twaddle (eds)

Southall, A. and Gutkind, P., 1957, *Townsmen in the Making: Kampala and its Suburbs*, Kampala

Bibliography

Stamper, B. Maxwell, 1977, *Population and Planning in Developing Nations: A Review of Sixty Development Plans for the 1970s*, New York

Suruma, E., 1993, 'Privatization and Democracy', Paper delivered at a Public Lecture organized by the Uganda Economics Association, Kampala, 25 February

Tadria, Hilda, 1987, 'Changes and Continuities in the Position of Women in Uganda' in Dodge and Wiebe (eds)

Thiongo, Ngugi wa, 1987, *Decolonizing the Mind*, London

Topouzis, Daphne, 1994, *Uganda: The Socio-economic Impact of HIV/ AIDS on Rural Families with an Emphasis on Youth*, Rome

Tripp, Aili Mari, 1994, 'Gender, Political Participation and the Transformation of Associational Life in Uganda and Tanzania', *African Studies Review* 37 (1)

Tukahebwa, G.B., 1992, 'Canadian Foreign Aid Policy: The Case of Uganda Since Independence', unpublished MPA thesis, University of Manitoba

Tukahebwa, G.B., 1993, 'A Critical Appraisal of Privatization in Uganda: Policy Issues'. Paper delivered at International Conference on Institution Building and Reform, Makerere University, 11–12 December

Tumwebaze, H.K., 1992, 'Excess Capacity in the Ugandan Manufacturing Sector', MA Dissertation, Makerere University

Twaddle, M., 1983, 'Ethnic Politics and Support for Political Parties in Uganda' in Peter Lyon and James Manor (eds), *Transfer and Transformation: Political Institutions in the New Commonwealth*, Leicester

Twaddle, M., 1988a, 'Museveni's Uganda: Notes Towards an Analysis' in Hansen and Twaddle (eds)

Twaddle, M., 1988b, 'Decentralized Violence and Collaboration in Early Colonial Uganda' in Andrew Porter and Rob Holland (eds), *Theory and Practice in the History of European Expansion Overseas: Essays in Honour of R.E. Robinson*, London

Twaddle, M., 1993, *Kakungulu and the Creation of Uganda 1868-1928*, London and Athens, OH

Twinomujuni, G., 1992, 'Capital Goods Industry in Uganda: A Focus on Small-Scale Industry', MA Dissertation, Makerere University.

Udoji, J.O., 1975, 'Some Measures for Improving Performance and Management of the Public Enterprises' in A.H. Rweyamamu and G. Hyden (eds), *A Decade of Public Administration in Africa*, Nairobi

Uganda AIDS Commission Secretariat, 1993, 'Uganda National Operational Plan for HIV/AIDS/STD Prevention, Care and Support, 1994–1998', Kampala

Uganda Government, 1971, *Report on the 1969 Population Census*, Entebbe

Uganda Government, 1987, *Report of the Commission of Inquiry into the Local Government System*, Kampala

Uganda Government, 1989, Nongovernmental Organisations Registration Statute No. 5 of 1989, Entebbe

283

Bibliography

Uganda Government, 1990, 'Policy Framework Paper 1990/91-1991/92', prepared in collaboration with the IMF and World Bank

Uganda Government, 1992, *The 1991 Population and Housing Census*, Entebbe

Uganda Government, 1993a, Public Enterprises Reform and Divestiture Statute No. 9

Uganda Government, 1993b, *The Report of the Uganda Constitutional Commission. Analysis and Recommendations*, Kampala

Uganda Government, 1993c, *The Draft Constitution of the Republic of Uganda*, Kampala

UNICEF, 1898, *Children and Women in Uganda: A Situation Analysis*, Kampala

UNICEF, 1992, *New Phase of UNICEF Support for AIDS Control in Uganda*, Kampala

UNIDO, 1990, *Industry Sector Programming Mission Report, Uganda*, Vienna, March

UNIDO, 1993, *Private Sector Development and Privatization in Developing Countries: Trends, Policies and Prospects Report*, Vienna, December

US Bureau of the Census, 1993, *World Population Profile*, Washington, DC

Van de Walle, N., 1989, 'Privatization in Developing Countries: A Review of the Issues', *World Development* 17 (5)

Villadsen, S. and Lubanga, F. (eds), 1996, *Democratic Decentralisation in Uganda: A New Approach to Local Governance*, Kampala

Warritay, B., 1991, Lecture at Theatre Workshop, Nairobi, (author's notes)

Werbner, R.P., 1989, *Ritual Passage, Sacred Journey*, Manchester

Whyte, Michael A., 1988, 'Nyole Economic Transformation in Eastern Uganda' in Hansen and Twaddle (eds)

Whyte, Michael A., 1990, 'We Have No Cash Crops Anymore. Agriculture as a Cultural System in Uganda, 1969–1987' in Anita Jacobson-Widding and Walter van Beek (eds), *The Creative Communion: African Folk Models of Fertility and the Regeneration of Life*, Uppsala

Whyte, Michael A. and Whyte, Susan Reynolds, 1992, 'Boomtime in Busolwe: Culture, Trade and Transformation in a Rural Ugandan Town' in Hermine G. De Soto (ed.), *Culture and Contradictions: Dialectics of Wealth, Power and Symbols*, San Francisco

Willis, R.G., 1970, 'Instant Millennium' in M. Douglas (ed.), *Witchcraft, Confessions and Accusations*, London

Wilson, K.B., 1992, 'Cults of Violence and Counter-violence', *Journal of Southern African Studies* 18

Woods, D., 1992, 'Civil Society in Europe and Africa: Limiting State Power through a Public Sphere', *African Studies Review* 35 (2)

World Bank, 1988, *Uganda: Towards Stabilization and Economic Recovery*, Washington, DC

World Bank, 1989, *Sub-Saharan Africa: From Crisis to Sustainable Growth*, Washington, DC

Bibliography

World Bank, 1991a, *Public Choices for Private Initiatives: Prioritizing Public Expenditures for Sustainable and Equitable Growth in Uganda*, Washington, DC, 12 February

World Bank, 1991b, *Agriculture Sector Review Mission: Cotton Sub-sector Assessment*, Washington, DC

World Bank, 1991c, *Uganda: The Economic Impact of AIDS*, Washington, DC

World Bank, 1993a, *Growing Out of Poverty*, Washington, DC

World Bank, 1993b, *Uganda: Agriculture Sector Memorandum* (3 vols), Washington, DC

World Bank, 1993c, *AIDS and African Development*, Washington, DC

World Bank, 1993d, *World Development Report 1993; Investing in Health*, New York

World Bank, 1997, *World Development Report 1997: The State in a Changing World*, New York

World Bank/UNDP, 1991, *African Economic Indicators*, Washington, DC

Index

Abeywickrama, K. 60, 68
Abid, Syed 136
accountability 15, 69, 112, 121, 125, 146, 153–4, 167, 218, 222
accountancy/auditing 30
ACFODE 122, 140, 146, 153, 154
Acholi/Acholiland 5–6, 11, 12, 246–53 *passim*
Action Aid 266
Adam, C. 29, 30
adjustment, structural 2, 3, 9, 13–15 *passim*, 62, 69, 98, 100, 101, 113, 121, 142–4, 208, 215, 227; PAPSCA 134, 143
Agricultural Enterprises Ltd 64
agriculture 12, 14, 28, 53–5, 74–5, 88, 134, 136, 142, 178, 200, 216, 232, 234–6 *passim*; subsistence 8, 23–5, 73, 81; urban 98–108
aid 2, 8–10 *passim*, 14, 21, 22, 26, 31–2, 134, 148, 154, 188, 194, 195, 201; conditionality 9, 32
AIDS 13, 15, 143, 183, 188, 193–214, 249, 261, 266–8 *passim*; Commission 196–9 *passim*; Control Programme 196, 203–7; cost of 201–2; Save Children from 199
Ainsworth, Martha 194
Alma Ata Declaration 208
Alnwick, D. 100
Alur 11, 12, 254–60
Amin, Idi/regime 1–3 *passim*, 6, 11, 19–21, 38, 45, 59, 72–1, 100, 101, 130, 145, 147, 162, 176, 189, 255–8 *passim*, 262
Amis, Philip 15, 215–26
Amnesty International 2
Anderson, Roy 197
anti-clericalism/colonialism 12, 13
Antrobus, P. 134, 138
APC 54
APT Development & Design 56
Apter, David E. 12
Ardener, Edwin 237, 249
Asians, Ugandan 1–2, 19–21 *passim*, 23, 26, 45–7, 59, 75, 84, 216; Property Custodian Board 46, 226; return of 20, 26, 47
assets 20, 22–30 *passim*; foreign 29

associations 120, 121, 208, 238; women's 15, 120–32, 134, 144, 163, 238, 240
Auma/Lakwena, Alice 5, 246–7, 249–51 *passim*
Austen, Ralph A. 237

Bakebwa, Milton 266–9 *passim*
Bakusi, Didas 151
Balogun, M.J. 62
Banyole *see* Bunyole
Bardhan, Pranab 71
Barnett, T. 200
Basirika, E. 98, 101, 142, 143
Baster, Nancy 61
Bayart, J.-F. 246, 252–3
Behrend, Heike 5, 11, 12, 245–53
Belgium 255
Benin 246
Bevan, D.L. 32, 33
Bibangambah, J. 99
Bienen, Henry 60, 68
Bigsten, A. 27–9, 33–6 *passim*, 98
Binsbergen, W.M.J.van 251
Boal, Augusto 262
Bok, Sissela 189
Bond, George 13
bonuses 220–1
Boyd, Rosalind 130
Bratton, Michael 111, 146
Breitinger, Eckhard 261
Brett, E.A. 4, 153, 223
brideprice/wealth 140, 142, 181, 233, 261
Britain 8, 10–12 *passim*, 111, 254, 255
Buganda 1, 5, 10–12 *passim*, 169–70, 172, 177, 182, 187, 254, 257; Agreement 10, 184–1; Kabaka 1, 111, 259
Bunyole 11–12, 228–44
Burack, C. 138
Burkey, I. 164, 165, 167
business sector 24–6 *passim*, 35, 46, 59, 98, 243 *see also* entrepreneurs
Byanyima, K.W. 134, 140
Byekwaso, Gertrude 136
Bystydzienski, J. 138

Cameroon 237, 246
capacity utilization 38, 40, 43, 44, 52, 60

287

Index

Morris, H.F. 10
mortality 186, 189, 196–9 *passim*, 208;
 infant/child 136, 198, 208, 233–4
Mosley, Paul 3
Mozambique 246
MPED 55, 83
Mpologoma Bridge project 239–40
Msoga Popular Theatre 262
Mudimbe, V.Y. 245
Mudoola, Dan 4
Muganga, Jonathan 263, 264
Mugira, James 147
Mugisha, R. 137
Mugyenyi, Joshua 7
Mugyenyi, Mary 15, 133–44
Mukama, Ruth G. 11
Mukholi, D. 170, 182
Mukulu, Alex 263
Mulder, Dr Daan 196
Mulyampiti, Tabitha 122, 126, 127, 138
Munene, John 227–8
municipalities 222–6
Murphy, John D. 229
Museveni, Yoweri Kaguta/government 1,
 5, 7, 8, 10, 13–17 *passim*, 73, 110–13,
 116–19 *passim*, 125, 150, 163, 198, 203,
 246, 256
Mutesa II 1, 111
Mvena, Z. 99
Mwaka, V. 142

Nairobi 218
Nalweiso, Mrs 139–40
National Analysis 66
National Council for Civic Education and
 Election Monitoring 153
National Manpower Survey 51, 56
National Parks 65, 67
National Resistance Army 3–6, 20, 114,
 145, 187, 191, 246, 247, 249, 251, 252;
 women in 139–40
National Resistance Council 7, 65, 66,
 124, 125, 138
National Resistance Movement 2, 5, 7–8,
 13, 16, 39, 40, 60, 110–17
 passim, 121, 124, 127–34, 138–45,
 149–52 *passim*, 155, 159, 161–71, 262
National Water and Sewerage
 Corporation 15, 218–26
nationalization 59, 177
Natyole Popular Theatre 263–6
Ndongko, A.W. 60, 68
Nebbi District Association 258–60
Nellis, J. 60, 70
New Vision 64, 65, 67, 69, 70, 194, 203,
 263; Printing and Publishing
 Corporation 60
NGOs 9, 15, 122, 130, 145–59, 179, 184,
 192, 194, 201, 202, 242, 263; co-
 ordination 154–6 *passim*; Registration
 Board 149

Nigeria 66–7, 69
Nkengwe, Lillian 150
North, D.C. 22
Northern Uganda 4–6 *passim*, 11, 20, 33,
 75, 78, 84, 90, 112, 149, 161, 246–60
numeraires 26–7
Nyhart, D. 45
Nyinya-Mijinya 138

Obbo, Christine 13, 83, 98, 102, 142, 202,
 207–14
Obote, Milton/regime 1–3, 6–8 *passim*, 11,
 13, 38, 59–60, 111, 112, 130, 145, 162,
 187, 189, 191, 256, 258, 259, 262, 263
Odoki Commission *see* Constitution
Oehmke, J.F. 35
Okellos 5, 8, 128, 248; Gen. Tito 112, 262
Okoth Ogendo, H.W.O. 112
Olsen hypothesis 37
Ongwech 255
Onyach-Olaa, M. 65
Oron, Baron 266
orphans 198–9, 267–9 *passim*
Ottemoeller, Daniel J. 117
Over, Mead 194, 197
Owen Falls Dam 44, 215
ownership 46, 62, 65–7 *passim*, 69, 71,
 136–7, 141, 176, 178–80, 183
Owiny 255
Oxfam 202

Panos 207
parastatals/PEs 45, 56, 59–71 *passim*, 219
 see also divestiture
Parent Teacher Associations 15, 120, 191,
 223
Paris Club 7
participation, popular 114, 123–8, 135,
 138, 145, 146, 151–3, 238
patriarchy 136, 232, 233
patrimonialism 111, 112
patronage 113, 161, 162, 166, 170, 239,
 243
Paul, T.A. 265
'peace dividend' 26, 32
Peel, J.D.Y. 241
PERD 63; PERDS 60, 64–5, 71
Pinstrup-Andersen, P. 98
Pinto, Manuel 196
Piot, P. 197
polarization 36, 37, 114
politics 7–8, 17, 71, 109–20, 123–8, 135,
 138–41, 148, 161;
parties 13, 113, 114, 117, 125, 147, 151,
 163, 169, 187
polygyny 233
population 13, 16, 89, 185–93, 197–8,
 228–9; control 188 *see also* family
 planning; density 186; growth 14, 38,
 53, 74, 136, 185, 186, 188, 189, 193,
 197; National – Council 192

291

Index

Index